To Prof. Lawrence Solum

... it was very nice to meet you at the uni

COMPARATIVE LEGAL LINGUISTICS

Comparative Legal Linguistics

HEIKKI E.S. MATTILA
University of Lapland, Finland

Translated by
CHRISTOPHER GODDARD

ASHGATE

Published by
Ashgate Publishing Limited
Gower House
Croft Road
Aldershot
Hampshire GU11 3HR
England

Ashgate Publishing Company
Suite 420
101 Cherry Street
Burlington, VT 05401-4405
USA

Ashgate website: http://www.ashgate.com

British Library Cataloguing in Publication Data
Mattila, Heikki E. S.
    Comparative legal linguistics
    1.Law - Language 2.Comparative linguistics
    I.Title
    340.1'4

Library of Congress Cataloging-in-Publication Data
Mattila, Heikki E. S.
    Comparative legal linguistics / by Heikki E.S. Mattila.
        p. cm.
    Includes bibliographical references and index.
    ISBN 0-7546-4874-5
    1. Law--Language. 2. Law--Interpretation and construction. I. Title.

    K213.M385 2006
    340'.14--dc22

2006009707

ISBN-10: 0 7546 4874 5
ISBN-13: 978-0-7546-4874-1

Printed and bound in Great Britain by Antony Rowe Ltd, Chippenham, Wiltshire.

Contents

Foreword

The original of this work appeared in Finnish in 2002 (*Vertaileva oikeuslingvistiikka*. Helsinki: Kauppakaari), while a partly abridged French edition (*Linguistique juridique comparée*) will appear in the near future.

The fact that an English version of the book is now offered to readers is due to a happy coincidence. During a research symposium in 2004, the author made the acquaintance of *Christopher Goddard*, whose personal features include – in addition to the English sense of humour – two qualities essential in this context: he is an English lawyer, and a French-English translator. This meeting led to the idea of preparing an English version of the book as well, based on the French manuscript, to which the finishing touches were then being put. It turned out that Mr. Goddard works with extraordinary discipline and efficiency: the English translation that he produced, on top of his other commitments, was completed so quickly that the French and English versions will appear nearly at the same time. Naturally enough, the author checked the draft translation, especially from the standpoint of legal terms. During the final phase, the translator and the author worked together in Helsinki, at the same desk, revising the text of the main parts of the English version, in the delightful company of their wives, *Rasma* and *Virpi*. Apart from being pleasant, this cooperation has been highly instructive: work on the English version brought to light many weaknesses and errors in the French version that it was possible to correct before publication. Here, too, it became apparent just how useful the « co-drafting » approach is in preparing two language versions of the same text at the same time.

The background and birth of the Finnish original are described in the foreword to that version, of which a translation appears below. In addition, credit is due to those who contributed to the preparation and publication of the French and English versions. Here, four individuals feature pre-eminently, for having commented on the manuscript of the French version: *Reiner Arntz*, professor at the Institute of Applied Linguistics at the University of Hildesheim (Germany), *Jean-Claude Gémar*, professor at the School of Translation and Interpretation at the University of Geneva (today, a professor in Canada), *Christopher Goddard*, already referred to above, and *Kari Liiri*, head of the Finnish division of the Translation Directorate of the Court of Justice of the European Communities. Professor Arntz read the entire manuscript, Professor Gémar the chapter on legal French, Mr. Goddard the chapter on legal English, and Mr. Liiri – both in French and English – the passages on the legal languages of the European Union. Later, the German lawyer, *Mathias Siems*, associate professor at the Riga Graduate School of Law read the English version of the chapter on legal German, and *Naveed Ahmad*, assistant professor at the Department of English at the Bahauddin Zakariya University (Pakistan), the passages on legal English in the Indian sub-continent. At the pre-publication stage, the author asked

Dennis Kurzon, professor at the Department of English Language and Literature at the University of Haifa (Israel), to consider whether he might endorse the book. For this purpose, Professor Kurzon read the whole manuscript and made many important remarks. The comments of all these persons have fundamentally improved the quality of the text. Naturally, the author alone accepts responsibility for any errors and omissions in the final version.

At the same time, warm thanks are due to *Ashgate Publishing Ltd*, who kindly agreed to publish this book, and their staff, in particular (the names in alphabetical order) *Nikki Dines*, Assistant Editorial Manager, *Donna Hamer*, Assistant Editor, *Alison Kirk*, Senior Commissioning Editor, and *Gemma Lowle*, Desk Editor.

Finally, thanks from the author go to *Terttu Utriainen* and *Ahti Saarenpää*, former deans of the Faculty of Law at Rovaniemi, for their continuing support. The author also recalls with pleasure the assistance provided by the *Library of the Faculty of Law at Helsinki*, the *Library of the Finnish Parliament* and the *Library of the University of Lapland*, in particular the indispensable support provided by their directors.

Heikki E.S. Mattila
Rovaniemi and Helsinki, February 2006

Foreword to the Finnish Original

Over thirty years ago, I was a novice researcher, under the guidance of my university Tutor, *Aulis Aarnio*. With his vast learning in the field of philosophy and theory of law, and with pursuits in all general legal matters, Professor Aarnio awoke in me an interest in foreign legal orders, and the background factors influencing their development. At his encouragement, in the 1970s I undertook studies in comparative law in France and research on socialist law in Poland. These in turn drew my attention to foreign legal languages: comparative law includes analysis of differences between legal concepts among different legal systems; these concepts are expressed through the terms of the legal languages that those systems employ.

At the beginning of the 1980s, in my capacity as an official of the Helsinki Child Welfare Bureau (*Helsingin lastensuojeluvirasto*), I became aware of the practical importance of familiarity with foreign legal languages. The Bureau was responsible for hundreds of international cases involving family law. Virtually every file contained translations into a foreign language of judicial decisions or other legal documents from Finland, and translations into Finnish of foreign judicial or other legal documents. While involved in these cases, I saw the seriousness of problems of legal translation. Later, my own translation activities and involvement as an expert on the Finnish Translator Examination Board (*Kääntäjien tutkintolautakunta*), increased my awareness of the difficulty of this kind of translation.

In the 1990s, I worked as editor-in-chief of the *Encyclopædia Iuridica Fennica* (EIF). This lexicographical work led me still further towards the field of legal language, owing to the general focus of the EIF and linguistic cooperation in compiling it. His Honour Judge *Juhani Wirilander,* president of the editorial committee of the EIF, strongly stressed the importance of including in it articles on general legal matters. One of these concerned legal languages, both the national ones, Finnish and Swedish, as well as foreign languages. At the same time, the project to compile the EIF was carried out in cooperation with the Research Institute for the Languages of Finland (*Kotimaisten kielten tutkimuskeskus*), represented on the editorial comittee by Professor *Tuomo Tuomi*, director of the Institute, *Esko Koivusalo,* head of section responsible for language quality, and *Risto Haarala*, editor-in-chief of the General Dictionary of the Finnish Language (*Suomen kielen perussanakirja*). Furthermore, editing of the EIF was physically located on the premises of the Research Institute for the Languages of Finland. This allowed daily cooperation with specialists in the Finnish and Swedish languages.

All these experiences are reflected in the content of *Comparative Legal Linguistics*. The aim is to provide a panorama of the subject, a mix of linguistic, legal, and cultural information. The book examines the functions and characteristics of legal language, the specific features of legal concepts and terms, the heritage of legal Latin, the major modern legal languages, and problems of legal translation. In the main, the chapters of the book were originally written as rough notes for courses and conferences, given in various teaching establishments. Noteworthy here are the University of Helsinki (Faculty of Law and the MonAKO study programme in issues of multilingual professional communication), the University of Lapland (Faculty of Law) and the Kouvola Institute for Translation Studies. Comments received from students were valuable in developing the outline of the book.

The final push to write *Comparative Legal Linguistics* (in Finnish) was provided by the needs of legal-linguistic teaching at the Faculty of Law at the University of Lapland – which began at the initiative of the University's Centre for Languages. In that context, I am bound to mention the name of Professor *Terttu Utriainen*, whose contribution was also decisive in setting up scientific research in this field in Finland. The Academy of Finland (*Suomen Akatemia*) offered practical working possibilities by appointing me to the post of researcher and financing the legal linguistic project led by me from 1999 to 2001. I was thus enabled to carry out basic research in the field of legal linguistics, involving the international understandability of legal Latin in particular.

This book is mainly intended for teaching and reference. For that reason, it contains many repetitions: different parts of the book deal with the same matters but from different angles. To ensure that the reader can find individual passages, a detailed index at the end of the book is supplemented by internal references in footnotes.

The book aims to be of use both to translators of legal texts and lawyers in need of legal linguistic information. It deals not only with the major legal languages but also with the legal orders behind those languages. In this way, several disciplines are combined: history of law, comparative law, classical and modern philology, research into languages for special purposes, terminological research, theory of translation, as well as - to some extent - communication theory, and legal semiotics. Such a multiplicity of aspects increases the risk of author-induced mistakes and misunderstandings, inaccuracies and errors. For this reason it is fortunate that a number of linguists and lawyers were willing to read and comment on the manuscript. Some of these read the whole text or particular chapters from the standpoint of their own discipline, while others checked the author's spelling of foreign expressions or translations of those expressions. And so the author himself stands solely responsible for any faults or omissions in the final printed text.

It is my pleasant task to thank the following university researchers (professors and other teachers of law and linguistics) and practising lawyers (judges, administrators, and advocates): *Ellen Eftestøl-Wilhelmsson, Richard Foley, Minna Heikkilä, Hagen Henrÿ, Risto Hiltunen, Jean-Michel Kalmbach, Jorma Koivulehto, Arja Laakso, Pertti Laakso, Aila Laamanen, Martti Leiwo, Pia Letto-Vanamo, Lauri Lindgren, Sten Palmgren, Aino Piehl, Heikki Pihlajamäki, Jarna Piippo, Reijo Pitkäranta, Anu Sajavaara, Sami Sarvilinna, Iris Tukiainen, Caroline Westerling, Thomas Wilhelmsson* and *Juhani Wirilander*.

The author also wishes to thank the firm of *Kauppakaari / Talentum Media Oy* for enabling publication of the book through themselves, as well as *Arja Lappeteläinen,* head of publishing, for a pleasant climate of discussion and a prompt decision on the question of publication. Besides, *Maria Kangasluoma*, publishing editor, performed an important task in the final phase by reading the whole manuscript from the standpoint of language quality. She then presented a large array of improvements, which the author was delighted to take on board. As to correction of proofs, technical checking and compiling the index, the author should mention his wife *Virpi Korell* as well as arts students *Maria Basdekis, Outi Kaltio* and *Liisa Metsola*. Particularly, it has to be said that it was Mrs. *Metsola* who followed the author's instructions in painstakingly compiling the book's table of foreign terms and the index. The manuscript was made up by *Anne Hotti* and printed by *Gummerus Oy* printers. The elegant cover was designed by *Lauri Karmila.*

The Institute of International Economic Law (*Kansainvälisen talousoikeuden instituutti, KATTI*) of the University of Helsinki made available to the author a comfortable office and (indispensable today) access to computer networks. In addition to thanking Doctor *Pia Letto-Vanamo*, director of KATTI, I would also like to include *Gunilla Häkli*, director of the KATTI library, and *Anna-Maija Ekström*, secretary of KATTI.

The author collected the greater part of the linguistic and legal literature used as sources for the book during study trips in France, Germany, Greece, Italy, Luxembourg, the Nordic countries, Poland, Portugal, Russia, Spain, and Tunisia. These trips, which also enabled discussion of questions of legal language with numerous specialists, were in the main financed by the Academy of Finland. The Academy also subsidised the various symposiums organised by the legal linguistics project; the knowledge obtained and the contacts created during these symposiums proved of great value in compiling this book. The materials from the symposium on the history of legal languages, which was organised in cooperation with the University of Lapland (Rovaniemi, Finland) in 2000, appear almost simultaneously with this book (*The Development of Legal Language*. Helsinki: Kauppakaari 2002).

Long ago, the author dedicated his doctoral thesis to the memory of his mother *Vieno Mattila*. This work is dedicated to the memory of *Lauri Mattila*, the author's father, and to the memory of his goddaughter *Tiina*, who died before her time.

Heikki E.S. Mattila
Helsinki, 23 April 2002

PART 1
General Introduction

Chapter 1

Legal Language and Legal Linguistics

1 The Concept of Legal Language

Legal language does not qualify as a language in the same way as French, Finnish, or Arabic, for example. According to Carles Duarte, the Catalan linguist, it operates as a functional variant of natural language, with its own domain of use and particular linguistic norms (phraseology, vocabulary, hierarchy of terms and meanings). Legal language possesses a number of specific features. These are morphosyntactic, semantic, and pragmatic. This language is used in particular social roles: pleading, claiming, and so on.[1]

It is clear to see that legal language is based on ordinary language. For that reason, the grammar and – in general – the vocabulary of legal language are the same as in the case of ordinary language. However, legal language is a language for special purposes. This means, first of all, that a large number of legal terms exist whose properties vary according to the branches of the law. In addition, the legal languages of different countries and of different periods possess, to a varying degree, characteristics that distinguish them from ordinary written language (e.g., sentence structure). One may speak of a specific legal style. For those reasons, it often occurs that legal language may be incomprehensible from the standpoint of the general public.

Legal language is often characterised as a technical language or "technolect", which is to say a language used by a specialist profession. That is accurate, but only with certain reservations. True, legal language is, first and foremost, used by lawyers. Nevertheless, in the courts and still more in the government are professionals who are not lawyers properly so-called (jury-members, lay judges, and administrators). At the same time, it seems natural to say that a citizen who, for example, writes his own will following a model form (as often occurs in the Nordic countries) is using legal language. Still more important, by contrast with most other languages for special purposes, the target of messages transmitted in legal language often consists of the whole population, certain layers of the population, or a number of particular citizens. For example, a law normally requires compliance of all the people, while a court judgment relates, first and foremost, to the parties involved in the case. Thus, legal language is not an instrument aimed solely at internal communication within the legal profession.

---

1   Prieto de Pedro 1991: 131–132.

Use of legal language is notable for the fact that it is very widespread: it governs all areas of social life, and it can, through intertextuality, be combined with language from any and every domain. Furthermore, legal language is very old, which is not necessarily the case with most other languages for special purposes. This is why, historically, it has shaped the ordinary language of various countries, and in a significant way. Illustrations might include documents from royal chancelleries in France at the close of the Middle Ages and the beginning of modern times, as well as *Las Siete Partidas* in medieval Spain. However, this is not a matter of a unique historical phenomenon. Even today, legal language still influences ordinary language.

It is not clear that the domain of usage of ordinary language and that of language used in legal matters are geographically identical. The population can make use of another language than that forming the basis of a country's legal language. In the Middle Ages and, in part, at the beginning of modern times, Latin was the language of legal proceedings, and notably of written judgments. Another example: Swedish constituted the sole language of legal life in Finland until the second half of the 19th century. Today, the official language – as well as the language of legal affairs – of many African countries is French or English, in spite of the fact that the population speaks one or several African languages.

2 Genres of Legal Language

2.1 Division into Sub-genres

Legal language can be divided into sub-genres, particularly according to the various sub-groups of lawyers. This is explained by the fact that the language of each sub-group of lawyers to some degree possesses particular characteristics (vocabulary, style). This is notably so as to the language of *legal authors*, *legislators* (laws and regulations), *judges*, and *administrators*, as well as *advocates*.

The division of legal language into sub-genres is a relative matter.[2] Here, the traditions of the country concerned play an important part. For example, in continental Europe one can refer to *notarial language*. The reason is simple. In these countries – notably Latin countries – private-law documents have been drawn up, for a thousand years, by a separate body: the notarial profession. A notary is a lawyer who can be styled part official, part advocate. The long traditions of the notarial college explain the specific characteristics of their language.

The language of legal authors is characterised by greater freedom than the other sub-genres of legal language. At the same time, legal authors employ a good deal of scholarly vocabulary, notably Latin terms and sayings. Courtroom language is especially formal, often archaic. It often has a categorical character, in that judges use unreserved declarations and peremptory orders. In certain countries, such as

---

2   Kurzon 1997: 119–123 and Arntz 2001: 282–291, where a number of divisions are presented.

France, courtroom language is also laconic when it comes to reasoning of judges. By contrast, detailed argumentation, along with an abundance of rhetoric, typifies the language of counsel. In certain domains of legal language, notably in judgments, highly complex sentence construction was formerly used – in some countries, that still remains the case today. Finally, texts of whatever genre of legal language understandably include many legal terms.

Besides, legal language can be divided into sub-genres on the basis of branches of law. The main distinguishing criterion then becomes the specialist terminology of each branch. It goes without saying that a large part of the legal terminology of the various branches of the law is universal. However, that is not true of terminology overall. Criminal law, for example, contains scores of terms that are almost never used in texts on the law of property or constitutional law. Equally, in some branches of the law legal terminology is mixed with non-legal technical terminology: for example, criminal law involves psychiatric terminology, while land law involves surveys, and tax law involves accountancy.

2.2 Related Linguistic Phenomena

2.2.1 Legal Jargon The style of legal language forms a spectrum that extends from the solemn cast of the Constitution to everyday legal texts, with their more laid-back style. This spectrum becomes complete with legal jargon. All professions develop their own jargon, which significantly strengthens internal relationships as well as the coherence of the group in question. Part of legal jargon is common to all sub-groups of lawyers (e.g., judges, advocates, civil servants). Nevertheless, other expressions also exist that are only used within the ranks of a single sub-group of lawyers, or even within a particular court or department (e.g., ministry, supreme court).

As to the origin of legal jargon expressions, this varies. For example, in the Nordic countries these expressions are often deformations of legal Latin terms, which illustrates the strength of Roman law traditions in the periphery of Europe. At the same time, it can be said that no clear borderline exists between lawyer-to-lawyer jargon and layman's slang relating to legal phenomena. Certain expressions referring to legal circles, perhaps somewhat facetious in nature, are also used by the general public. To give a Polish example, an *advocate* in Poland is an "apostle" (*apostoł*), a "missionary" (*misjonarz*), a "parrot" (*papuga*) or – after the shape and colours of the advocate's gown – a "green penguin" (*zielony pingwin*).[3]

Legal jargon often takes the form of abbreviations, notably in internal court documents. Replacing explanations as to legal institutions by the numbers of articles constitutes a particular genre of abbreviation. This involves a phenomenon known in all legal cultures. In the Soviet Union, this form of replacement was particularly common. Thanks to Russian memoirs and literature about the prison camps, the numbers of certain articles of Soviet penal and procedural legislation became notorious even abroad. To illustrate, in a recent work a Russian legal linguist

---

3   Hałas 1995: 43–44.

mentions *vypolnit' 201-iu* (выполнить 201-ю, 'doing a two-oh-one', which means 'disclosing case documents to the accused in line with Article 201').[4]

2.2.2 The Counter-language of the Criminal Fraternity Linguists often characterise the language of offenders (the criminal fraternity) as a counter-language of legal language, notably that of criminal law.[5] The heart of this counter-language is formed by *prison slang*.

Counter-language satisfies several needs. It strengthens relationships of groups of prisoners in relation to the "enemy", that is, prison officers and the justice system in general. Thus, it forms part of the mental resistance, by virtue of which prison society maintains itself against "repression", through linguistic means. It is symptomatic that, in the slang of Finnish prison officers, the word "rat" (in Finnish *rotta*) means "prisoner", whereas in prisoners' slang this word has the sense of "grass" (informer). At the same time, prisoners' counter-language operates as a secret code, rapidly-changing, and largely unknown to the prison officers. It is also very much about linguistic "fireworks" that lightens the overwhelming burden of the prison atmosphere. As with slang in general, the frequency of synonyms is typical of prisoners' slang. For example, in Finland empirical research found that prisoners have around 70 expressions to describe a police officer, and about 30 expressions to describe imprisonment.[6]

In the major languages, dictionaries exist of the counter-language of offenders – even some bilingual dictionaries on the subject are available. One illustration is Jean-Paul Brunet's *Dictionnaire de la police et de la pègre: américain–français français–américain / A Dictionary of Police and Underworld Language French–American American–French]* (2nd ed. 2000). Today, one useful information tool on offenders' – and police officers' – argot is the Internet. There you can find, searching under *police slang,* a large number of Anglo-American, as well as French, lexicons of this kind (some of them bilingual).

3 Legal Linguistics as a Discipline

3.1 The Beginnings of Interest in Legal Language

In the modern sense, legal linguistics is a discipline that has only recently become established. However, legal language has aroused interest for thousands of years, from various angles. Law is necessarily bound to language (notably in matters of legal interpretation), and in that sense legal language has existed as long as the law. In certain contexts, the language aspect of law dominates: legal translation, legal lexicography, and legal rhetoric. In ancient times, the goals of interest in legal language were mainly practical.

---

4   Vlasenko 1997: 98.
5   Schmidt-Wiegand 1990: 346.
6   Lipsonen 1990: 15, 18.

Indeed, legal translation has left a particularly long trail behind it. The first legal text translated from one language to another, and which has survived until today, is the peace treaty in two languages between the Egyptians and the Hittites, dating from 1271 B.C. There followed innumerable legal translations, as much in the international sphere as for domestic needs of various States. A famous example is the *Corpus juris civilis*, first translated into Greek and later into many other languages.[7] In medieval times, legal translation focussed around Latin: texts were translated from different vernaculars into Latin and from Latin into the various vernaculars.

Legal research science goes back to Rome and, as to research methods, to ancient Greece. This involved creating a conceptual system of law,[8] which presupposes clarifying connections between specific legal concepts. That meant having to define the terms expressing the concepts. This task led to compiling legal lexicons. The first legal lexicon still known today is that of Gaius Aelius Gallus. This lexicon, *De verborum quae ad jus pertinent significatione* ['On the meaning of words referring to the law'], dates back to the 1st century B.C.[9] The tradition of legal lexicography was carried on in Byzantium and in Western Europe. In the countries of Western Europe, medieval legal dictionaries were first published in Latin, but later in the new national languages.

The first bilingual lexicons of legal language were compiled in Byzantium (certain lists of translated legal words existed even earlier). This involved Latin-Greek lexicons. These lexicons became necessary during the period when the Greek language was beginning to replace Latin in legal affairs and when, as a result, Byzantine jurists' grasp of Latin was on the wane. In character, these lexicons were partly encyclopaedic dictionaries, partly dictionaries of definitions. Later, an analogous need arose in Western Europe as to links between Latin and the new national languages. As West European lawyers' grasp of Latin weakened, dictionaries of legal Latin assumed growing importance. When Latin was replaced by modern languages in international legal communication, the need also arose to compile legal dictionaries between the various European national languages.

Rhetoric had already become a science in Antiquity. In Ancient Greece, this science was closely connected with the activities of advocates before the courts. The first treatise on rhetoric was written by Corax of Syracuse in the 5th century B.C. Its focus was the theory of legal rhetoric. Even today, Corax and his pupil Tisias are considered the fathers of the science of rhetoric. Until the 19th century, rhetoric occupied a place of prime importance in the education of the young Western man. In the Middle Ages, it was one of the three subjects of the teaching *trivium*. This background explains why rhetoric has always occupied an important place in the training and work of European lawyers.

---

7 Šarčević 1997: 23–28.
8 See pp. 125–126.
9 Fiorelli 1947: 293.

3.2 Legal Linguistics Today

Phenomena concerning human speech have long aroused the interest of scholars, but modern linguistics only developed at the beginning of the 20th century. This has opened up opportunities to examine legal language from the viewpoint of linguistics proper. At the same time, the enormous strides of science and technology in the 20th century gave birth to the need to study the various languages for special purposes (*Fachsprachen, langues de spécialité*) both comparatively and in relation to ordinary language. We should also bear in mind the flowering of the philosophy of language in the 20th century.

Contemporary research into legal language is accounted for by this background. It should be stressed that this research does not always go by the name of *legal linguistics* and that its content is variable.[10] In his work *Science et technique en droit privé positif*, ['Science and Technics in Positive Private Law'], volume III (1921), the well-known French jurist, François Gény, offers a chapter entitled *Observations générales, tendant à préparer l'élaboration de la linguistique juridique* ['General Observations with a View to Elaborating Legal Linguistics']. The term *linguistique juridique* constitutes a French invention. In the francophone world, this term is today established as designating research into legal language based on modern linguistics (often, and above all in Canada, expressed as *jurilinguistique*). A corresponding term, *Rechtslinguistik*, is also found in Germany, but there it is not as common as in the francophone countries. Moreover, *Rechtslinguistik* is sometimes associated rather with research involving philosophy of language[11] than involving linguistics proper. In Poland, legal linguistics is known as *juryslingwistyka* and in Russia as *pravovaia lingvistika* (правовая лингвистика). By contrast, in the Anglo-Saxon countries the term *legal linguistics* or *jurilinguistics* appears to be unknown, at least up until now. It is also not in use in the Spanish-speaking world; at any rate, the author has not come across it in recent treatises on legal language.[12]

> In the English-speaking countries can be found the term *forensic linguistics*, which refers to one of the areas of legal linguistics (see below). When speaking generally of research into legal language, Anglo-Saxon authors often use the expression *law and language* (as also occurs in German-speaking countries: *Recht und Sprache*). Several years ago, in Finland, an association was set up to promote research into legal language. The English variant of its name, used by the association itself, is *Legal Linguistics Association of Finland*. The term *legal linguistics* similarly appears in the English summary annexed to a recent Russian work.[13] It remains to be seen if this English designation becomes widespread among genuine Anglo-American authors. Some signs of this exist. In 2005, a bilingual compilation of articles with the title *Jurilinguistique – Jurilinguistics* was published in Canada (see Gémar & Kasirer 2005).

---

10 Nussbaumer 1997: 10.
11 For example, Müller 1989.
12 Martín *& al.* 1996, Duarte & Martínez 1995 and Prieto de Pedro 1991.
13 Vlasenko 1997.

Research into legal linguistics accentuates different aspects country by country. It is natural that francophone authors in this discipline are linked to the tradition based on the observations made by Ferdinand de Saussure. Thus, Gérard Cornu writes in his treatise that "[la] linguistique juridique telle qu'elle est ici envisagée se réfère à l'œuvre de Ferdinand de Saussure" ['(l)egal linguistics as here envisaged refers to the work of Ferdinand de Saussure'].[14] At the same time, American works on textual linguistics have much inspired researchers into legal language, both in the United States and Europe. Russia stands as an exception: Russian legal linguistics is essentially based – at least up until now – on linguistic science expressed in Russian.[15]

Frequently, research into legal language is synchronic, that is, it focuses on contemporary language. Notably in Canada, this research takes the form of contrastive analysis of the two legal languages (French and English), which is why Canadian legal linguistics is closely bound up with the science of translation.[16] This type of legal linguistics has spread from Canada to other countries, such as Poland, for example.[17]

Research comparing the characteristics and use of various types of languages for special purposes (medical, technological, legal) is particularly developed in the German linguistic area (*Fachsprachenforschung*). Today, the scientific community in this discipline is fairly international, and it publishes, notably in English, many studies under the heading *LSP research*. In the Nordic countries, it is above all Denmark and Sweden that can be counted amongst the pioneers in this subject. Amongst other things, the Danes promote international cooperation among researchers in languages for special purposes, by publishing two important journals (*LSP and Professional Communication, Hermes – Journal of Linguistics*). As for Finland, special mention can be made of an international symposium (*Porta Scientiae*) organised in Vaasa (Vasa) in 2001.

Interaction between the various schools undertaking research into legal language is not always particularly close. It should also be borne in mind that the major linguistic areas are somewhat self-contained. Notably, for understandable reasons Soviet and Russian legal linguistics was until recent years isolated from the West European schools. The sources for the work of N. A. Vlasenko, *Iazyk prava* (Язык права, 'Language of the Law', 1997), are symptomatic in this regard. This work is based almost solely on linguistic and legal studies published in Russia during the Soviet period and in Russia in the 1990s. In the introduction to the work, Vlasenko mentions that he was strongly influencd by M. M. Bakhtin, I. R. Gal'perin, M. N. Kozhina and D. E Rozental.[18] The one chapter (I.2) where this author cites foreign researchers is the one concerning – in a somewhat detached manner – the Historical

---

14 Cornu 2005: 32.
15 Vlasenko 1997: 7.
16 Especially Gémar 1995.
17 Pieńkos 1999.
18 Vlasenko 1997: 7.

School of Law having played an important part in 19th century Germany. The main source for this chapter is Georg Friedrich Puchta, the classic author on German legal science. In a note, can also be found the name of Jean Carbonnier, the French civilian and sociologist, whose main work on legal sociology is available in a Russian version. It should be stressed that, in spite of this isolation, Vlasenko's work is of very high quality.

The above description does not cover all research on legal language. Notably, some important studies exist on the history of various legal languages. One example, already a classic, is David Mellinkoff's work, *The Language of the Law* (1963), relating to legal English. Similar studies have been published even in some smaller countries, such as Finland: Paavo Pajula, *Suomalaisen lakikielen historia pääpiirteittäin* ['The History of Finnish Legal Language in Broad Outline', 1960]. In this context, too, should be mentioned research into legal Latin.

The different training of researchers into legal language results in differences in the focus of studies – a positive advantage. In all schools undertaking research into legal language, lawyers as well as linguists are to be found. Researchers often possess dual training, or a study is carried out in close cooperation between lawyers and linguists. An illustration of this is *Le langage du droit* ['The Language of Law'] by Sourioux and Lerat (1975): Pierre Lerat is a linguist and Jean-Louis Sourioux a lawyer. It is natural that a linguist should regard legal language from a greater distance than a lawyer – but, thanks to that, he is also more objective.

Today, researchers with linguistic training often apply quantitative methods in their studies, with the aid of a computer. A typical research subject consists of occurrences of terms, other words, or other linguistic elements (e.g., prefixes, suffixes) in legal texts. The interest of linguists may equally focus on legal documents from the textual standpoint, without laying emphasis on vocabulary.[19] A research topic of another kind is, for example, understandability and readability of these texts, from the standpoint of non-lawyers.

Lawyers, by contrast, see the language of their profession from the inside. Their studies are often diachronic in character and are closely connected with the history of law. It is rare that lawyers researching legal language quantitatively measure the occurrence of words or other language elements. Their aim is, rather, to ensure that the characteristics and vocabulary of legal language are comprehensible to non-members of the profession. That may involve, as a result, an exaggerated justification of traditional language of the law, but also constructive criticism. One typical context where lawyers consider the characteristics of legal language is legislative drafting. Works of legislative drafting often contain a section concerning the terminology of the proposed legislation. These matters are discussed during seminars and symposiums. One illustration is the round table on Russian legal language (2000), organised in connexion with a seminar on legislative technique.[20]

---

19   For example, Engberg 1997.
20   Morozova 2000: 108.

3.3 Research Topics and Disciplines Connected with Legal Linguistics

3.3.1 Overview: Defining Legal Linguistics Legal linguistics examines the development, characteristics, and usage of legal language. Studies in this discipline may equally concern vocabulary (notably terminology), syntax (relationships between words), or semantics (the meaning of words) of the language.

It cannot be said to be a branch of linguistics. It would be better to say that the language of the law is examined, in the frame of legal linguistics, in the light of observations made by linguistics. That is why one author characterises legal linguistics as being a synthesis between legal science and linguistics, notably applied linguistics. The topic of legal linguistics contains problems that, strictly speaking, do not fall within the domain of linguistics. However, this first discipline is broadly based on the theory of linguistics, notably sociolinguistics.[21]

It is useful to examine the position of legal linguistics in relation to the different branches of linguistics. Firstly, the connection of this discipline with semantics is very close. Indeed, lexicology – which forms part of semantics – occupies a central position in legal linguistics. This is accounted for by the fact that it is essentially through terminology that legal language differs from ordinary language. One important application of lexicology is legal lexicography, that is, compiling legal lexicons and dictionaries.

At the level of syntax, legal linguistics examines, e.g., sentence length, and frequency of subordinate clauses. On the other hand, morphology, phonology, and phonetics are further away from legal linguistics: their importance in legal contexts is reduced by comparison with semantics and syntax. However, as to morphology, some phenomena can provide important research topics. Amongst other things, this concerns the construction of compound words, from the standpoint of their clarity and modifications then taking place in the original words forming part of the construction. In certain languages (e.g., German, Swedish, Finnish), studies of this type are particularly important, because the structure of these languages favours construction of compound words. And finally we come to *forensic linguistics*, which is especially developed in English-speaking countries and which examines production and perception of utterances from the legal standpoint, notably in the courts. This discipline has several applications, e.g.: phonetic analysis of the human voice (for example, in the case of threatening telephone calls), verifying the authenticity of documents.[22]

A very different aspect exists: research into legal style. This research has a particular application in the field of rhetoric.[23] As mentioned, the traditions of legal rhetoric go back to Antiquity. In the frame of legal rhetoric, questions include how advocates convince judges of the worth of their messages.

---

21 Pieńkos 1999: 18–29.
22 Solan & Tiersma 117–178.
23 See pp. 38–39.

Historical and sociological angles are often fruitful – even indispensable – in legal linguistics research. Areas of study include how the vocabulary of legal language has changed over time (there have also been complete language changes); what are the countries and epochs of origin of borrowed legal words; how is legal language used in the various legal sub-cultures (e.g., researchers, judges, advocates); to what extent is legal terminology known by the general public? Throughout Europe, legal Latin enjoyed privileged status. That is why it is important to examine how and when lawyers in various countries began to use modern languages instead of Latin and what is the current importance of Latin in the vocabulary of today's legal languages.

In German-speaking countries, the term "geography of legal languages" (*Rechtssprachgeographie*) was once used. Such research was closely linked to the history and sociology of law. One classic study examines the differences in terminology of customary law within the German linguistic zone.[24] Today, linguistic studies of this kind could clarify – for example – the relationship between the geographical domains of various languages used by the population in daily life and those used by courts and government offices. Africa, notably, can provide an example to illustrate the important differences on this topic: in sub-Saharan Africa, French, English, Portuguese, and Spanish, depending on the region, enjoy official status as legal languages, in spite of the fact that the populations speak African languages.[25]

Some phenomena connected with legal language are difficult to place, unequivocally, in the frame of established linguistics areas. An illustration is the problem of pronunciation of legal Latin in the English linguistic zone.[26] Common-law lawyers normally pronounce Latin expressions and sayings following English language rules of pronunciation (though it is true that some tendencies exist among younger lawyers towards Italianate pronunciation of Latin). This phenomenon is phonetic but can also be seen from the perspective of sociology of language. From a more general point of view, this involves forming a phonetic system in a hybrid language.

3.3.2 Legal Semiotics and Legal Symbolism Spoken language is only one means of communication. Animals transmit messages effectively without human language. Human beings themselves also communicate in different ways. Semiotics examines all kinds of communication together. In legal contexts, one may speak of legal semiotics.

Much legal-semiotic research is theoretical.[27] Dedicated research is promoted by the *International Round Tables for the Semiotics of Law*, a merger of two earlier institutions in the field, closely associated with the names of Bernard Jackson and Roberta Kevelson (*Law and Semiotics* 1987–1989). Many studies published in the

---

24 Künssberg 1926.

25 As for French, see pp. 215–216.

26 See pp. 239–240.

27 For example, Dubouchet 1990 and Jackson 1997.

International Journal for the Semiotics of Law are good examples of legal-semiotic research. Theoretical legal semiotics stimulates deeper analysis of legal language. One of its practical applications is research into the symbols of power and judicial rituals. This involves messages that are not legal, properly speaking, but that express the authority and prestige of judicial bodies. The solemnity of court-houses, the judges' dress, the positioning of the judges and parties in the courtroom, and the rituals of legal procedure are all wordless messages.[28]

Legal semiotics is closely linked to legal linguistics. Some phenomena are placed half-way between linguistics and semiotics. As for oral presentations, illustrations might include, for example, the tone of the judge, the prosecutor, and the advocate, rhetorical pauses in their speech, and the requirement that the public maintain absolute silence. As for written presentations, one illustration would be the material, colour, and decoration of documents. The Finnish linguist Ulla Tiililä finds as follows: "the material bears and creates meanings of its own accord, and so we should take these into consideration in interpreting a text, besides choices made as to language and appearance of the text". This is why a judicial or government decision is written on white paper with black text. These means lend an impression of substance and objectivity. A decision of this kind is normally adorned with an emblem, which lends it a dignified, official air.[29]

At the same time, legal circles employ non-verbal signals that transmit legal messages as such. These can be considered from the standpoint of semiotic theory: how effective is legal communication by non-verbal means? Indeed, it is not uncommon that a legal rule or clause be partially expressed by a non-verbal message. For example, drawings or charts may be annexed to a contract or a law. These drawings or charts then assume legal meaning: the text of the document refers to them.

Such contexts are referred to, in Russia,[30] as legal symbolism (*pravovaia simvolika,* правовая символика). This goes for both legal messages as such, expressed by means of non-language symbols, as well as symbols expressing the authority of who or what is sending the message. Besides mathematical formulas, maps and charts, legal messages can be expressed by body language (for example, traffic police hand signals), by a variety of visual signs (for example, road signs, landmarks) as well as by sound signals (for example, river traffic communications). As for symbols expressing authority and esteem, one Russian author mentions heraldry, flags, diplomas, and medals.

In spite of what has just been said, it can be stated that legal texts differ considerably from technological (or medical) texts as to the importance of visual presentation.[31] In technological matters, images often make communication far more economical. It is almost impossible to explain the workings of a complex motor by purely language means,

---

28 See pp. 49–51.
29 Heikkinen & *al.* 2000: 229.
30 Vlasenko 1997: 28–32.
31 Arntz 2001: 78.

while a detailed drawing, with a key or caption, works perfectly from the communicative standpoint. By contrast, opportunities to use images for legal phenomena are far more limited. Here, only certain conceptual schemata (e.g., presenting links between main and subordinate concepts) are feasible, although this does not detract from the usefulness of schemata in terminological tasks and in legal didactics.

3.3.3 Legal Informatics Legal informatics "examines and teaches the various forms of relationship between the law and information and between law and informatics, as well as related problems of legal regulation and interpretation".[32] Issues forming part of this subject might include legal style, structure of laws, and intertextual references. For example, in the *Encyclopædia Iuridica Fennica* the section on legal informatics includes several items on legal communication, including the style of judicial and administrative decisions.[33] The encyclopedia also contains items on the structure of laws and other legal texts (e.g., compilations), on internal references in these texts, and on footnotes in scholarly works, to give further examples.

This demonstrates that the line between legal linguistics and legal informatics is unclear. Later, we shall be looking at, amongst other things, the systemic nature of law.[34] Issues relative to systematisation of legal texts can often be considered as much from the standpoint of legal linguistics as from that of legal informatics. Blurring of the line between the two is especially noticeable in the area of legal linguistics that Russian legal linguists call "legal graphics" (*iuridicheskaia grafika,* юридическая графика, *normativnaia pravovaia grafika,* нормативная правовая графика). In Russia, researchers perceive this area very broadly: it covers issues relating to structure of legal texts, use of notes and appendices, methods of emphasizing passages in the text and of showing links between different parts of the text (e.g., chapter and paragraph numbering, bold or italic script for headings and key words). On that basis, one study was carried out on the matter of whether the size and font of characters used in appendices of certain Russian laws were in proper proportion with the size and font of characters used in the text of the laws themselves. Also noted by Russian researchers is the high profile of artistic symbolism in banknotes and valuable securities, such as shares.[35]

3.4 The Link with Legal Science

3.4.1 Legal Science in General Legal linguistics differs from legal science as to the topic of research. Legal science is mainly interested in abstract entities – concepts – that are to be found in the background of terms, that is, in the meanings of terms. This science systematises the legal order through legal concepts. Terms are designations of concepts, necessary to legal science. However, the primary interest of this science does not have bearing on legal terms but on the concepts themselves.

---

32 Saarenpää 1999a: 713.
33 Saarenpää 1999b: 940.
34 See pp. 77–80.
35 Vlasenko 1997: 128–140.

By contrast, in legal linguistics it is the terms as such that constitute the primary object of research.

Because of the link between the two disciplines, legal linguistics requires support from legal science: it is the latter that shows the meaning of legal terms. At the same time, legal theory, legal informatics, legal sociology, and history of law assume fundamental importance from the standpoint of legal linguistics. In the development of legal language, the history of language and history of law are fused, and it is impossible to understand the circumstances in which legal language is used without knowing any sociological data. By the same token, comparative law studies produce information that helps the legal linguist to understand the interactive links between the various languages used for legal purposes.

Actually, the advantages are reciprocal. Scholarly authors and practising lawyers have to interpret laws, which entails giving meaning to expressions from laws and other sources of law.[36] Legal interpretation is a complex phenomenon in which semantic and syntactic arguments play an important part.[37] Even if problems of legal interpretation cannot be resolved on the sole basis of these semantic and syntactic arguments (there are several other types of argument), they form an important element of legal interpretation. Thus, linguistic methods, notably those of textual linguistics, are very useful to legal scholars and practical lawyers in the task of interpreting.

Legal linguistics can even be useful to legal science at a more general level. It uses statistical methods that complete the picture of legal language – and of the law itself – obtained through other sources of information. Regularities that can be observed in usage of legal language are of great interest from the standpoint of theory and sociology of law. By the same token, foreign influences on national legal science can be brought into the open. With that aim, a sufficient sample of legal works is examined, assembling all citations in foreign languages found in the text or index of these works. By dividing the citations into groups according to the various languages, it is possible to identify which foreign legal cultures have influenced national legal thinking and, indirectly, the legal system of the country in question.

In a modest way, this idea is put into practice in relation to an empirical research into legal Latin.[38] The author's research assistant collected all foreign language citations from the indices of law theses and textbooks published in Finland in the 1950s and the 1990s. As for the 1950s, results were as follows (the first figure gives the absolute number of citations, while the second gives the percentage relative to all citations): Latin 824 (73%), English 142 (13%), French 86 (8%), German 48 (4%), Italian 4 (0.4%), Greek 2 (0.2%), Danish 2 (0.2%), and Spanish 1 (0.1%). Corresponding figures for the 1990s are: English 790 (48%), Latin 627 (38%), French 94 (6%), German 73 (4%), Norwegian 10 (0.6%), Italian 7 (0.4%), Danish 7 (0.4%), Dutch 2 (0.1%), and Greek 1 (0.05%).

---

36 Aarnio 1984: 393–401.
37 Aarnio 1999: 17–24.
38 Mattila 2000 and 2002.

Given that the number of Finnish law theses and textbooks today is markedly higher than in the 1950s, the absolute figures are not comparable. By contrast, the percentages are. We can thus conclude that the traditional *lingua franca* of lawyers – Latin – has somewhat given way. It has passed from first to second place. In spite of that, Latin remains an important source of citations: almost 40% of foreign language citations used by Finnish legal authors today are in Latin. Among modern languages, English has clearly improved its position: today, almost a half of foreign language citations are in English. French and German are placed far behind in relation to English but their importance stays basically unchanged from the 1950s to the 1990s.

Thus, it can be concluded that Finnish legal science is nowadays mainly influenced by English and American legal circles but that the traditional Latin culture continues to be of great importance. This demonstrates the power of the old Romano-Germanic legal culture in Finland, because, historically, legal Latin arrived in Finland via Germany in the form developed by German legal science on the basis of *jus commune*.

3.4.2 Comparative Law Research in legal linguistics often focuses on a single legal language. However, some major studies also compare the development, structure, and vocabulary of two or more languages. Studies of this kind examine, amongst other things, the interaction of legal languages (e.g., how words pass from one language to others). A good example is presented by the comparison of variants of legal Latin, as used in various countries. As the title of the present work shows, this type of research can be called "comparative legal linguistics".

All those legal linguists that have studied various legal languages in relation to others, emphasise the importance of comparative law in this context.[39] Comparitivists aim, on the one hand, to develop methods for comparing legal cultures and, on the other, to draw conclusions on the basis of differences and similarities found. A typical example of these conclusions is the division of legal systems into major families and sub-families of law.[40]

Comparative law can promote research in legal linguistics in a number of ways. Firstly, comparative lawyers contribute to shedding light on the factors that influence the development of the systems of concepts standing in the background of legal terms. This enables a better understanding of the characteristics of legal terminology. Secondly, legal translation and compilation of dictionaries of legal translation presuppose that the correspondence of concepts belonging to the legal systems in question would have been carefully analysed. Knowledge is required of the various institutions in these systems, notably of institutions of procedural law. This is the research that forms the core of comparative law. One watchword is micro-comparison. Peter Sandrini, the Austrian terminologist, states: *"Die funktionale Mikrovergleichung stellt für jede terminologische Arbeit den Ausgangspunkt und zugleich die thematische Eingrenzung dar"* ['Functional micro-comparison forms

---

39 For example, Pieńkos 1999: 101–110.
40 See pp. 106–107.

the point of departure of all terminological work and at the same time defines the theme of this work'].[41]

Conversely, research in legal linguistics is suitable for clarifying analyses of comparative law. For example, linguistic theory draws a clear distinction between "concept" (a mental abstraction) and "term" (the appearance of a concept[42]). This is why it is surprising that there should be treatises on theory and methodology of comparative law where the problem of legal language is hardly considered.[43] Naturally, it is not always so. For example, Léontin-Jean Constantinesco analyses problems of legal terminology in his *Rechtsvergleichung / Traité de droit comparé* ['Treatise on Comparative Law']. He discusses in detail the distinction between concept and term, legal and language features of legal translation, dangers caused by the misleading appearance of words, and the value of multilingual dictionaries.[44] Michael Bogdan's work *Comparative Law* also succinctly deals with issues of legal translation.[45]

3.4.3 Language Law Legal linguistics is closely connected with language law. This term may be understood in two different ways. According to Gérard Cornu, for example, language law covers, on the one hand, legal effects of and, on the other hand, legal rules on the use of language.[46]

When considering this question from a more general standpoint, under the focus of semiotics, it is possible to speak of the "law of signs". This then involves, for example, regulation of symbols used before and by the courts. In France, advocates are obliged to wear a robe before the court. Failure to observe this requirement may lead to punishment.[47]

The most important question, on the subject of laws concerning use of language, is that of the right of an individual or a group of the population to be taught in their own language, and of the public use of that language. This may also involve protecting the language of a region or a Member State of a Federation (the province of Quebec, the province of Åland in Finland). The Constitutions of bilingual or multilingual countries often contain articles on this matter. As an example, let us take Finland:

Right to one's language and culture.
The national languages of Finland are Finnish and Swedish.
The right of everyone to use his or her own language, either Finnish or Swedish, before courts of law and other authorities, and to receive official documents in that language,

---

41 Sandrini 1996: 169.
42 See pp. 108–109.
43 Arntz 1999: 190–192.
44 Constantinesco 1972: 80–81, 164–172.
45 Bogdan 1994: 50–51.
46 Cornu 2005: 43–45.
47 Gridel 1979: 142.

shall be guaranteed by an Act. The public authorities shall provide for the cultural and societal needs of the Finnish-speaking and Swedish-speaking populations of the country on an equal basis (Sec. 17, subs. 1 and 2). – Translation published on the Internet by the Finnish Ministry of Justice.

Unfortunately, the content of laws on the use of language may also be repressive: throughout the world there have existed – and still exist - a number of States where the language law aims to stifle use of languages other than the one that dominates as the language of instruction and of public life. For this reason, it is no surprise that the right of individuals or groups to use their own language should also be a matter of regulation under public international law.[48] The language regime of the European Union is equally weighty on this matter: the languages of Member States enjoy equal status (even if the major languages dominate as working languages).

Language law can also aim to safeguard the purity of the national or regional language, under pressure from another language or several other languages. Even in France, the home of one of the international languages, legislation of this kind was considered necessary, because of the invasion of English. This legislation (inspired by Quebec's Law 101) presupposes the use of French, notably in advertising, and also protects the vocabulary of the language.[49]

In recent years, a new problem has entered into the discussion on language law. This involves the right of citizens to require courts and authorities to use a language that they clearly understand. Traditionally, the language of courts and public authorities is hard to understand and self-contained; the ordinary citizen has trouble in understanding it. The struggle against this phenomenon has been going on for a long time – it was already thus in the Byzantine period.[50] Today, the right to clear, comprehensible language is also asserting itself from the standpoint of basic citizens' rights. This is manifest by, amongst other things, the fact that the parliamentary ombudsman in Finland considers, according to a recent opinion, the understandability of laws and regulations to be a matter of statutory protection.

In the present work, language law presents itself, in certain contexts, as a background factor that partially explains the characteristics and use of the legal languages examined. Indeed, the current position of legal languages is often the result of old regulations to achieve some linguistic policy. This also concerns borrowed words: the status of Latin as sole official language of courts and governments has strongly shaped the terminology of modern legal languages.

3.4.4 Linguistic Risk The issue of linguistic risk is most discussed in the German linguistic area.[51] Who bears the risk that a party to a contract – above all, in the case of a standard contract – may misunderstand the content of the contract for linguistic reasons? Standard contracts (such as contracts of assurance) include, as is well

---

48 Dunbar 2001.
49 See p. 211.
50 See pp. 96–97.
51 Jayme 2001: 28–30.

known, a large number of standardised conditions that are often highly complex. These conditions are hard to understand from the standpoint of the ordinary citizen. This led to adoption of the rule in the field of contract law according to which standard clauses vaguely formulated are interpreted to the disadvantage of their author (*in dubio contra stipulatorem*). Thus, in the case of standard contracts, it is the specialist that drew up the contract who bears the risk.

Cases with international features, notably those involving immigrants, cause particular problems: the contract in itself is clear but, in spite of that, one party does not understand it. In Germany, allocation of linguistic risk has provided a topic of lively discussion in the case of employment contracts of immigrant workers. The same problem arises, for example, in relation to maintenance agreements in favour of a child, where the debtor (normally the father) is a foreigner and translation or interpretation is poor or absent altogether.

4 The Importance of Legal-linguistic Knowledge

4.1 The Viewpoint of Related Sciences

We have established that legal linguistics promotes legal research. Equally, it can be useful in general linguistic theory. Fred Karlsson, the Finnish linguist, sets out several questions that linguistics aims to answer in his work *Yleinen kielitiede* ['General Linguistics'].[52] One of these questions concerns the limits of variation of natural languages and languages for special purposes. As for legal language, it is legal linguists that can answer this question. Legal linguistics can also be useful in other matters. A good example is the following question, presented by Karlsson: What are the principles of language change? Legal linguists can shed new light on this question. At the same time, they can examine how the language of judges and officials influences the development of ordinary language or the domain of use of different languages in society. This last question is closely linked to the position of languages under threat throughout the world – a question much debated by linguists.

4.2 Practical Lawyering

Legal language is the lawyer's basic tool. Thus, familiarity with this language is a matter of great importance for them. Traditionally, this familiarity has been obtained indirectly: in studying the content of the legal order, the young lawyer simultaneously adopts legal terminology and style. However, a practical process of this kind only provides familiarity of a certain type. Above all, the historical aspect remains in the dark. Under these conditions, the lawyer is in no position to understand all

---

52 Karlsson 1994: 31.

the important characteristics of legal language. Some of these are accounted for historically, through the development of this language.

More serious still, indirect adoption is often less critical. Only a purposive study of the characteristics of legal language will clearly reveal the shortcomings of that language. Such studies enable improvements in the quality of legal language. When this language provides the focus of explicit attention, lawyers are better placed to see the related problems. Experience shows that complex documents poorly drafted often allow several interpretations: an outsider may understand them quite differently from what the author intended.

Today, it is often not enough for lawyers to be familiar only with their own language. They need to cooperate with foreign colleagues. If they come from one of the smaller linguistic zones, they have to use a foreign language for legal purposes. This requires a long training process. General familiarity with foreign legal languages can accelerate and promote this process. Lawyers with an overall picture of the history, structure, and basic vocabulary of a foreign legal language are better placed to learn more easily and rapidly the particular terminology and style of this language in the field of their specialism (e.g., royalties, consumer law).

Another point of view exists. In the case of foreign languages, lawyers cooperate not only with lawyers from other countries. They very often work with language specialists (linguists, terminologists, translators). Under these conditions, familiarity with the history and features of legal languages operates as an aid to better understanding of the linguistic factors bearing on, e.g., creation of neologisms, and translation between two languages.

4.3 Translation

Not only lawyers can benefit from familiarity with legal-linguistic matters. Europe, in a state of ongoing unification, increasingly needs translations of legal texts (e.g., laws, judgments, administrative decisions, private documents). The majority of these translations are very often done by linguist-translators, not by lawyers.

Technical tools as aids to legal translation have been considerably developed over recent years. European Union translators regularly use automated translation tools and computer-aided methods of human translation. However, in the final analysis, automated translation and use of terminological databanks presupposes human control. It has not been possible to completely automate translating in the Union, even in cases involving translation of simple text between two very similar Romance languages. Legal translation will remain an essentially human activity, at least in the near future.

At the end of the day, human control of automated translation or with the aid of computers is based on the culture and general knowledge of the translator. That is why the translator needs information on the characteristics of legal language from a universal standpoint, as well as on the history and features of the legal languages concerned. Given that translation tools and instruments are inevitably imperfect, this general knowledge is the key to eliminating mistakes and misunderstandings.

4.4 Lexicography and Terminological Work

Legal linguistics is closely connected with legal lexicography.[53] Legal linguists study legal vocabulary and its characteristics and in doing so pave the way for the practical work of compiling dictionaries and lexicons. A substantial lexicographical work is based on legal-linguistic studies.

Nowadays, a large number of monolingual, bilingual, and multilingual law dictionaries have been compiled in various countries. To this lexicographical work is added work on legal terminology.[54] The standpoint of terminologists, compared with that of lexicographers, is quite the opposite: the point of departure for terminological work is *concept*, while that for lexicographical work is *term*. A terminological study is based on careful analysis of systems of concepts, and the glossaries resulting from that are highly accurate. By contrast, the strength of classic dictionaries lies in the fact that they take into account the caprices of legal terminology. As we shall see later,[55] legal terms often have multiple meanings (polysemy). So it can be said that, in legal matters, terminological studies operate as an essential support for traditional lexicography. Terminological work involves analysing terms corresponding to the systems of concepts that form the focus of interest. The results of this work can be used as a basis for legal dictionaries, completed by studies as to meanings appearing in the actual use of legal terms

5 Structure and Content of this Book

5.1 Outline

In various countries, works are found under the heading "legal linguistics". Comparison of these works shows that the standpoints of the authors differ considerably. As we have seen, the term "legal linguistics" currently has no set content. For this reason, the outline of the present study does not follow models provided by previously published works. Its content is informed by the author's experience as a (comparative) lawyer, and as a legal linguist, as well as by the author's own research over recent years, notably into legal Latin. Since the study contains information from several countries, juxtaposed and analysed in relation to one another, the title includes the adjective "comparative".

As the table of contents shows, the study is divided into three main sections: general introduction; legal language as a language for special purposes; and the main legal languages. In the following section (relative to legal language as a language for special purposes), the functions, features, and terminology of legal language are examined in a general way. In the section on the main legal languages, the first

---

53 See, generally, Groffier & Reed 1990.

54 Arntz 2001: 236–273.

55 See pp. 109–111.

chapter concerns legal Latin. After that, a general picture of the *linguae francae* of today's lawyers is given.

> The Finnish version of this study also contains a fourth section: on legal translation. This section has been eliminated from the English version for one important reason: the text focuses on translation problems between Finnish and certain other languages, which is not interesting from the standpoint of the foreign reader. Moreover, the Finnish examples used in that section are not translatable into other languages. One might also point out that a body of high quality literature exists on the basic problems of legal translation.[56]

The table of contents of this study reflects the author's understanding of the kinds of information that are important from the reader's standpoint: the need for theoretical and general knowledge of legal language as well as familiarity with the background and use of specific legal languages, notably of the *linguae francae* used by lawyers at the international level. This explains why the author's approach can be characterised as historico-cultural. This approach is completed by a presentation style that can be described as through use of examples: throughout the book, linguistic phenomena are illustrated by concrete examples taken from various languages. Some of these examples come from minor languages, notably the Nordic languages or from otherwise less well known languages (e.g., Polish, Modern Greek). In the author's view, this is not a disadvantage: sometimes, less well known languages bring out linguistic phenomena more clearly than the major international languages. To facilitate access to these examples, an English translation is given.

In the Finnish version of this book, the presentation of each major legal language is preceded by a separate chapter on the history and characteristics of the legal system in the background of that language. The reason for this solution is straightforward: the features of a legal language can largely be accounted for by the legal system on which the language is based. To save space, in this English version the description of the legal systems has been reduced only to those aspects that are crucial for an understanding of the legal language concerned, and these descriptions form an integral part of the presentations of the legal languages themselves.

5.2 Choice of Legal Languages Examined

The third section of this book begins by dealing with the heritage of legal Latin. This is followed by presentation of legal German, legal French, and legal English. This choice requires an explanation.

5.2.1 The Reason for Including Legal Latin   The fact that the third section of this book begins by dealing with legal Latin is accounted for by the importance of the legal and language heritage of Rome. At the end of the Middle Ages and the beginning of modern times, lawyers had already been using Latin for fifteen centuries, in national and international contexts. In the Europe of the Middle Ages,

---

56   e.g., Arntz 1995, Gémar 1995, and Šarčević 1997.

this great cultural language was used in various countries as an administrative and judicial tool. Judgments, in particular, were written in Latin. This was so even for the periphery of Europe, as in the kingdom of Sweden (to which Finland also belonged) from the end of the 13th century to the mid 14th century. At the international level, Latin was still the language of inter-State relations at the beginning of modern times. International treaties were among the documents drawn up in Latin. Academic legal science operated in Latin for an even longer period, throughout Europe, up until the 19th century.

This means that the Latin language enables us to clarify and understand the history of laws and legal languages going right back to Antiquity, both at international level and within various countries. Latin is the main common denominator of almost all European legal languages: it explains a good deal of the features that these languages still have today. Besides, Latin is still used, in various countries, in the form of direct citations, although there may be differences of usage between these countries. As a result, familiarity with legal Latin (and the differences in its usage) is essential for lawyers in our time.

5.2.2 The Choice of Modern Legal Languages As for modern legal languages, the choice of these for this book was informed by their historical and current position as *linguae francae*, that is, as tools of communication between lawyers of different mother-tongues. This is why the author has left aside certain major linguistic zones which, it is true, are of global importance but which are less in common use in communication going beyond linguistic borders. At the same time, emphasis is placed on the use of legal languages of European origin, notably on their use in Europe. This gives rise to study of the major legal languages, first of all on a global scale and afterwards in the frame of the European Union.

Global rivalry of the major legal languages. The importance of global languages is a complex question. The number of persons speaking a language fails to provide an accurate picture of the importance of that language. As a result, authors dealing with this question have sought to develop parameters that take account of several factors: these include, e.g., number of individuals speaking the language, the economic importance of the countries using the language, the number of those countries, use of the language in international organizations, use of the language as a *lingua franca* in other contexts. The number of people speaking the language highlights Chinese or Hindi, the economic importance of the countries using the language highlights German and Japanese for example, the number of countries using the same language highlights Spanish, French, Arabic, and so on. The importance of French is emphasized by the international use of that language. As for English, several factors come into play.[57]

---

57 Examples of books on the importance of the major languages that the author has examined include Barrat 1997, Crystal 1997, and Marqués de Tamarón (ed.) 1995 (notably the article by Otero 1995 : 235–282).

Besides world languages, there are some languages whose usage goes beyond one or several State borders. This then involves languages that have a certain supranational importance – even though limited. Examples include Dutch (the Netherlands, Belgium) or Swedish (Sweden, Finland). Naturally, a precise distinction between world languages and those of the latter type is impossible. The number of lusophone (Portuguese-speaking) countries is not very large but they can be found on four continents (Angola, Brazil, Guinea-Bissau, Cap Verde, Mozambique, Portugal, São Tomé and Principe as well as, from 2002, East Timor once again), while one of those countries (Brazil) is of world importance. In a parallel way, German is only spoken in Central Europe, but legal scholars from various European countries, notably in the Nordic countries and those of Central and Eastern Europe, often have a good command of it (if only passively). For this reason, German can be classed as a major legal language (not global, it is true).

The relative importance of languages has never been stable – and this is no different today. One of the reasons for this fact is active States policy to gain international linguistic dominance: such dominance assures considerable power to dominant language countries. Through linguistic means, they can exercise great political, economic, and cultural influence in the international arena. At the same time, citizens of these countries enjoy a considerable advantage in various negotiations: the rhetoric of someone pleading in their mother tongue is always more convincing than rhetoric in a language of which one has less than full command. This last problem can also be seen within the frame of the European Union. The search for remedies has even included a suggestion to adopt Latin as the sole language of the organs of the Union.[58]

The most notable current trend is the strengthening of the position of English worldwide, including in legal circles. Up to a point, this is also true of Spanish: the number of Spanish speakers worldwide is not far from that of English speakers. It is typical of hispanophones that they are highly aware of the importance of their language and use it regularly in the frame of international organisations. By contrast, an opposite trend is perceptible in the international use of Russian, partially, too, in the case of French and German. However, the position of French remains quite strong, notably in Europe (where German is also of considerable importance).

The rivalry between French, the classic language of international relations since the 17th century, and English, newly arrived on the scene, is visible in various contexts. The use of the major languages in the frame of the United Nations Organization well illustrates this viewpoint.

At the 1997 General Assembly, 185 States members in all were represented. Of those States, 99 communicated in English, 27 in French, 20 in Spanish, 17 in Arabic, 7 in Russian, 1 in Chinese, and 12 in some other language. As for Russian, it was noticeable that the representatives of certain former Soviet republics, today independent countries separate from Russia, listened to the debates of the General Assembly in Russian but delivered their own addresses in English. As for the representatives from Latin American countries, these only spoke English in the

---

58   Sturm 2002: 318–320.

various organs of the United Nations Organization in cases where Spanish was not one of the working languages of the organ in question.

In sum, it can be said that the Americas (if Spanish is excluded), the countries of the British Commonwealth, many Asiatic countries, and former Soviet (Russian) republics generally use English in the frame of the United Nations Organization, while a great many African countries and certain European countries use French. The position of the latter language remains relatively strong: the Francophone Group at the UNO in New York consists of 56 States.[59]

However, a sharp decrease in the use of French was visible during the 1990s: the number of speeches in that language in the General Assembly fell from 19% in 1992 to 13.8% in 1999.[60] Encouraged by this trend, the United States has proposed, in recent years, limiting the amount of translations into languages other than English, "for economic reasons". By contrast, representatives of the other major languages have sought to strengthen the position of their languages in the frame of the UNO.[61] They obtained support from the Secretary-General, who presented several reports to that effect. In a report from 1997, amongst other things, he "encourages his staff to use both working languages equally in their official communications", that is, also to use French as the second working language of UNO structures.[62]

Rivalry of the major legal languages in the European Union. According to the principle of linguistic equality adopted by the European Union, all Member State languages, declared official in those States, enjoy the status of an official language of the Union. This principle is wholly in force as regards publication of official documents. As to oral communication, the principle of linguistic equality is also respected as far as possible. Nevertheless, in practice this is impossible in the case of internal working languages of Union institutions (the difference between working language and official language is not always clear). The languages of Member States are equal – but, in reality, some are more equal than others. Union officials normally work in English and French, so that documents drawn up in those languages are, *de facto*, the original versions, even though all versions are formally equal. The inevitable language inequality is reflected in translation work undertaken within the Union: in the majority of cases, English and French are the source or target language for translations. As for the Court of Justice, the Court of First Instance of the European Communities, and the European Union Civil Service Tribunal, the principles relating to the language of procedure contribute to this state of affairs.[63]

According to established practice, passive and active interpreting is guaranteed for all official languages during sessions of the Council of the European Union, whereas in the Committee of Permanent Representatives (COREPER) only English, French, or German are used. As for the Commission of the European Communities,

---

59 Bar 1999: 309–313.
60 Calvet 2003: 103.
61 Bar 1999: 313.
62 Calvet 2003: 102.
63 Berteloot 1998.

this has three working languages: English, French, and German. This is prescribed by an internal Commission ruling according to which documents necessary to deal with business at these sessions should be available in these languages. In practice, the situation is different: the real working languages are only English and French; the position of German is clearly weaker. This results from the fact that it is not always possible to ensure interpreting between the three languages and that not all the participants understand German.[64]

In 1994, a survey carried out on the practical use of languages by European Union officials revealed that 59% of them were then using French, 33% were using English and 6% were relying on German. However, only 3% of officials (normally amongst those whose mother tongue was Dutch or Danish) were then using German as a foreign language. In internal Union communications, the dominance of French was clearer still: French was then being used by 69% of officials as compared with 30% for English. In clear contrast, in the field of cooperation outside the Union, the relationship between the two languages was the other way round; 30% of officials using French as against 69% for English – the share of German then made up no more than 1%.[65] It should be noted that the last but one Union enlargement in 1994 (including, besides Austria, two Nordic countries) sharply reinforced the position of English. According to recent information, at the beginning of the third millennium English is the language most used in informal discussions in the various offices of the Union.[66]

The Court of Justice of the European Communities. The Court of Justice of the European Communities is a judicial organ that supervises respect for the constituent treaties and derivative law (regulations, directives, decisions) of the Communities. The Court is composed of 25 judges, which is to say one judge for each Member State, and eight advocates-general. Proceedings there may be commenced – depending on circumstances – by a Union institution, by a Member State, or by an individual.

As to use of languages in the frame of the Court of Justice (and, by analogy, in the frame of the Court of First Instance and the Civil Service Tribunal), the following rules are respected:[67]

a. The internal working language of the Court of Justice is French. This means that the judges use that language when deliberating and formulating judgments. The help of an interpreter is never asked for. Quite exceptionally, German-speaking or English-speaking judges may have recourse to their mother tongue, in order to clarify the position they have taken, thus avoiding misunderstandings. The judge-rapporteurs also give their reports in French. Nevertheless, the advocates-general form an exception to the principle of exclusive use of the French language: they draw up their conclusions in their

---

64   Martiny 1998: 234–238 and Ammon 2002: 27.
65   von Polenz 1999: 225.
66   As for the position of French in the European Union, see also pp. 216–218.
67   Martiny 1998: 238–239 and Sevón 1998: 933–950.

own language. These conclusions are always translated into all the Union official languages.

b. In each case, the procedural language is chosen separately from among Member State languages, following detailed rules. As for direct actions, for example, the procedural language is chosen by the applicant (except in cases where the defendant is a Member State or a legal or natural person having the nationality of a Member State). In principle, Member States' languages are equal as procedural languages. In practice, this is not the case. If the applicant chooses, as procedural language, a minor language that the judges do not personally understand, then the risk arises of legal messages becoming distorted through translation errors. For that reason, an applicant representing a smaller country, with its own language, often chooses a major language as the procedural language. This has led, amongst other things, to an increase in the number of hearings in English. Yet, French remains the most important language in the frame of the Court of Justice of the European Communities, with German occupying second place. The strong position of German is accounted for by the fact that Germany and Austria together form a particularly important Community macro-region, and that these countries are aiming to strengthen the position of German in the European Union. In general, as we have seen, German is used far less than French and English in the various Union institutions, but in the case of the Court of Justice the linguistic policy of the German-speaking countries has been crowned with greater success. This success has been facilitated by the fact that German is the classic *lingua franca* of lawyers from Central Europe and that the judges of the Court of Justice normally have a command of it. As a result, the choice of German does not include communication risks from the applicant's standpoint.

c. The Reports of Cases before the Court of Justice and the Court of First Instance are published in the languages of all Member States. In principle, the version in the procedural language is officially considered as the only authentic version. In practice, however, the version in the working language (that is, the French version) is the most important as a source of interpretation.

Conclusion. On the basis of the above study, it goes without saying that English legal language, as the language most used on a global scale, and also particularly important in the frame of the European Union, should be separately presented in this book. Equally, the use of French is also widespread from the global standpoint, and it remains, in spite of some weakening in its position over recent years, one of the two dominant legal languages in the European Union, notably in the frame of the Court of Justice. As a result, it is equally clear that a chapter relating to French should be included in this book.

The international position of legal German sharply diverges from that of legal English and French: German is not a world language for lawyers. Nevertheless, the situation is different on a European scale: German is the traditional *lingua franca* of lawyers in Northern, and in Central and Eastern, Europe. In spite of the fact that the importance of this language decreased during the second half of the 20ᵗʰ century, a large section of lawyers in these regions have some command of it, at least passively, as is partly true of lawyers in some Southern European countries. As we have seen, German is also used in the European Union and in the Court of Justice in particular. Moreover, as we shall see below, the influence of legal German also explains a great many characteristics of legal languages in countries that have traditionally been under German cultural ascendancy. For all these reasons, this book also examines legal German, although that study will be somewhat more concise than is the case with English and French.

As for other major Indo-European languages, a question arises, especially for Spanish and Russian. According to the above description, Spanish is one of the major global languages. However, it is less used as a *lingua franca,* that is, in communication with non-hispanophones. Moreover, this language is mainly used in Latin America; in Europe, Spanish is little used outside the Iberian peninsular. As for Russian, its use as a *lingua franca* was formerly manifest (non-Russian Soviet republics, people's democracies) but – as information relating to the United Nations Organization shows – some weakening is perceptible here following the collapse of the Soviet Union. Besides, Russian is naturally not in use in the frame of the European Union. For these reasons, this work does not include separate presentations on legal Spanish and legal Russian – at the same time, fully recognizing the great value and importance of these languages. However, examples taken from, amongst other languages, Spanish and Russian will be used while dealing in a general way with the functions, characteristics, and terminology of legal language. Non-European legal languages (e.g., Arabic, Chinese) have been entirely left aside, due to the author's lack of competence (other than a few examples taken from Indonesian, with which the author has some familiarity).

PART 2
Legal Language as a Language for Special Purposes

Chapter 2

Functions of Legal Language

1 Importance of the Theory of Communication

On the basis of the theory of communication, it is possible to distinguish several functions of legal language. The most spectacular of these functions is achieving Justice by means of language, that is, producing legal effects by speech acts. On the other hand, it is clear that legal language transmits legal messages. At a more general level, this language reinforces the authority of the Law, which contributes to maintaining order in society. In the next place, legal language, as a differentiated and endogenous language, is apt to reinforce the team spirit of the legal profession. Lastly, this language has often had linguistic policy goals. Those goals are closely linked to the cultural task of this language.

In the present chapter, we examine these functions of legal language. It goes without saying that the classification adopted is relative. Clearly, the functions of this language could also be grouped in different ways. For example, the exercise of power, almost an intrinsic element in all use of legal language and which we shall deal with in connection with the functions mentioned, could be separately presented. To illustrate, the exercise of power in connection with speech acts (2.1), with classifying and interpreting citizens' messages by the authorities (3.2.4), and with the choice of official State language (6.2).

2 Achieving Justice

2.1 Speech Acts and the Legal Order

According to the theory of speech acts, originally developed by John L. Austin and John Searle, human language is used not only to transmit messages or influence people's behaviour but acts are also realized through this language. This is notably so for religion and law.

Speech acts are of fundamental importance from the standpoint of the legal order. Given that the law is a metaphysical phenomenon that is only "alive" in language, it is only by language means that it is possible to change legal relationships. The langage of the law is thus an instrument of speech acts: it has a performative function. This is hardly a coincidence if, in the Latin language, the word *instrumentum* signifies, besides "instrument" or "means", "document" as well. This double meaning also appears in modern languages, notably in English and in the romance languages (*instrument, strumento, instrumento*).

It is the legal order that gives the meaning of a speech act to words expressed orally or to a signed document: in this way, it links rights and obligations to those words or to that document. When we say that "B has made a rental agreement", this sentence expresses an institutional fact, that is, a fact that can be perceived by interpreting the behaviour of B in the light of a constitutive rule concerning the entry into force of a rental agreement.[1] In the final analysis, it is the supernatural power of the Word that stands in the background of the effects of a speech act. That is clearly visible in the fact that ritual expressions were once of great importance in realizing speech acts: if, in Ancient Rome or in medieval England, the claimant made even a small mistake in reciting the required form of action, then he lost the case. Equally, without the word *spondeo* ['I promise'] being pronounced, a contract of *stipulatio* character did not arise under Roman law.[2]

By a speech act,[3] the legislator can sanction a legal rule, a judge can take a judicial decision, or an individual can enter into a contract, to give just a few examples. A parliamentary law comes to life when Parliament passes a bill and the head of State promulgates it. In the same way, a valid judgment (though perhaps subject to appeal) is produced by the competent judge declaring: "On these grounds, the Court (...) awards the mother / father custody of the minor child (...)".

2.2 Form as Affirmation of Speech Acts

Legal certainty presupposes that the existence of a speech act – a legal act – can be verified in a trustworthy way. This is why legislation often requires a specific form for such acts. This requirement of form is, in certain cases, very strict, and is normally achieved through language: e.g., written form, signatures of the parties or a notary, signature and countersignature of the authorities.

> The functions of formal requirements are not only linked to the question of proof. Thanks to these requirements, it is also possible to identify the type of legal act in question. At the same time, formal requirements can guarantee the publicity of the act, and enable conservation of the information concerning that act. Besides, these requirements promote mature reflection by the parties. As we shall see below, they also lend dignity to the act, and contribute to the personal involvement of the parties to it.[4]

Even if it is rare that use of strictly-defined linguistic expressions is required for a legal act to be valid, such an act is often realized by ritual words. In English legal language, for example, three formulas are in use.[5] The performative character

---

1   Helin 1983: 77.
2   Kaser 1968: 40 and Wacke 1990: 879.
3   Kurzon 1986: 5 & *seq.*
4   Cf. pp. 83–84.
5   Tiersma 1999: 104.

of a document is expressed 1) by adding the word *hereby* (*I hereby promise...*), 2) by adding the auxiliairy verb *do* (*I do promise*), or 3) by adding the words *by these presents* ['by this document'].

2.3 Semiotic Acts

In societies of the distant past, a speech act was often reinforced by a semiotic act. To take an example from the oldest Roman law: the *mancipatio*, an important type of transfer. Such transfer consisted of a symbolic exchange, in the presence of five witnesses, where the acquirer placed his hand on the person (slave), animal, or good comprising the object of the act (the term *mancipatio* comes from this gesture: *manus* = 'hand', *capere* = 'take', 'take hold of'). After pronouncing the ritual words, the acquirer placed a coin on the plate of the scales of the weightman (*libripens*), to symbolise the selling price.[6]

Semiotic acts are not only a historical phenomenon. Modern examples are illustrated by the gavel struck by the chairman of a meeting, to confirm a decision taken, and the handshaking of negotiators on concluding an agreement. Indeed, speech acts are today increasingly being replaced by semiotic acts, in matters of routine contracts. At the till in a food shop, a customer in a hurry may simply hand over the items picked up and money enough or a credit card, without a word (or, at most, acknowledging the assistant). On concluding such a routine contract, no words are used at all; language is replaced, on the one hand, by the fact of the customer handing over the food items along with the money or a credit card, and on the other hand, by the fact of the assistant handing over a receipt. An Italian researcher aptly calls this phenomenon "silent law" (*diritto muto*). The same researcher also says that, in the case of routine contracts, sighted man, *homo videns,* has nowadays been substituted for speaking man, *homo loquens.*[7] It goes without saying that a semiotic act (shaking the head, for example) can replace a speech act in certain other cases, as with those who are sick or handicapped. Lastly, we should stress that it is not always easy to classify acts: signing a document is rather a semiotic act than a speech act, given that it does not include a language statement as such.

3 Transmission of Legal Messages

3.1 Communication Theory and Law

Legal language transmits messages relative to the law, and facts of legal importance. Through this language, we can become familiar with the content of laws and regulations, judgments and administrative decisions, briefs and pleadings of advocates, indictments of prosecutors, and so on.

---

6   Kaser 1989: 42–45.
7   Benedetti 1999: 138–139.

Legal communication comes up against the same kind of problems as those appearing in all human communication. In communication theory, this is known as "interference": obstacles, loss, distortion, and noise.[8] Obstacles to communication would include: mistaken address, disappearance of the message during transmission, failure to perceive the message, absence of communicative competence on the part of the sender, and delay of the message. Under the category of information loss, diminution or impairment of information and negative attitude (repression) on the part of the recipient can be distinguished. As to distortion, this can result from faulty understanding or interpretation of the message, due to its ambiguity or to the fact that an intermediary has changed the content. Noise means impeding elements mixed up with the message.[9]

All these types of interference appear in legal communication. For example, a message may sometimes be lost due to technical difficulties or mistaken address: an application is sent to an authority lacking competence. A message may also be delayed too long in transmission, preventing delivery of a summons to the defendant before the deadline. In the same way, it may be that the recipient represses the message: for example, he resents the content of a law, and as a result does not want to know anything about it. Finally, the correct understanding of a message often presupposes that the recipient has sufficient prior knowledge of the matter in question. In the case of legal communication, this last problem appears above all in relations between lawyers and lay individuals but also in international communication between lawyers from two or several countries.

3.2 Interference in Legal Communication

Legal linguistics has an interest in interference in communication linked, in one way or another, with language. This involves the incomplete, unintelligible, or equivocal nature of the message, change of information during transmission, signals that impede the message, and the recipient's negative attitude.

3.2.1 Message Incomplete Examples of incomplete messages might include witness statements imperfectly recorded in case files or court minutes. This problem is particularly acute in countries where the trial is essentially based on documents prepared during different phases of the proceedings (including pre-trial investigation and preparation of the case). For this reason, the Finnish legislator recently, for example, broadened the possibilities for higher courts to hear complementary evidence from witnesses, or to rehear their evidence entirely. Nevertheless, that could also lead to loss of information, although in a different way, given that the hearing of witnesses before a superior court only takes place after a markedly long

---

8   Wiio 2000: 81–82.
9   Wiio 1989: 220–235.

time-gap has passed since the events in question. In which case, witness recall also lacks clarity and completeness.

3.2.2 Message Closed In legal language, it often occurs that communication fails because the message is hermetic, or closed. A legal message is sometimes formulated in such a complex way that a lay individual can hardly understand it. For example, this is often the case with laws and regulations, and with judicial decisions. Above all, it is in the domain of *justitia distributiva* that regulation is especially hard to understand. The problem is that this area, which deals with the correct distribution of a benefit or an obligation, presupposes highly detailed regulation.

Equally, archaic or foreign vocabulary can also impede understanding of the message. Examples include foreign words in legal texts: e.g., *causa, ordre public*. Communication theory refers to "the contagious effect" linked to unintelligible words: the text as a whole becomes unintelligible. At the same time, from the standpoint of citizens, legal terminology is abstract, and therefore obscure. This is notably the case with legislative language, whose abstract character is accounted for by the fact that legal rules have to be applied to a series of specific cases that are incapable of precise advance definition.

> Paradoxically, foreign terminology can also improve the understandability of a legal text. This is so where a language becomes involved in legal dealings for the very first time, which presupposes the creation of new terminology. In these cases, a method often employed is to duplicate those legal words that are still vague in the language recently introduced in legal dealings: they are followed – in parentheses – by corresponding words from another, established legal language, notably Latin. The same method is sometimes used in international conventions. In this way, it is possible to ensure that technical legal terms are understandable in cases involving a legal language that is less established, or of which one of the parties at the convention has insufficient command.

The influence of administrative efficiency and that of democracy are often contradictory when it comes to understandability of legal language. The European Union is a good example of this. A centralized legislative system, based essentially on regulations and directives, is required to ensure the smooth functioning of the European Communities. Community legislation is translated into all the national languages of the Union, of which Finnish is an example. However, the mechanics of this legislation reflect the traditions of the larger countries of the Union. For the lawyers – not to mention the citizens – of the smaller countries on the periphery with their different traditions, it is often difficult to understand this legislation, in spite of the fact that it is translated into the national language in question. It is not easy to reconcile the requirements of the exercise of centralized power and the principle of legal communication close to the citizens.

A question of prime importance is that of knowing who constitutes the target of legal language.[10] Where a legal text is intended for use only between lawyers,

---

10 See p. 99.

the requirement of understandability is less emphasized than would be the case for texts intended for reading by the general public. Nevertheless, the borderline is not always clear: the same texts are often important as much from the standpoint of legal professionals as from that of the plain citizen. In these cases, the guarantee of legal protection requires that texts intended in the first place for use by lawyers should be easily understandable to every citizen.

3.2.3 Message Ambiguous Natural language often allows two or more interpretations of the same text. This may arise from multiple meanings of words (polysemy), or for syntactic reasons. The interpreter of the text is then obliged to establish the meaning of the crucial words and, at the same time, to identify the words to which relative pronouns refer, for example.[11]

Interpreting a legal text is a highly complex matter, notably because distilling meaning does not depend solely on linguistic arguments. Here, these last mingle with arguments of other types, such as natural justice. It is not enough for the interpreter to succeed in clarifying unambiguously the goal sought by the legislator or other author of the text. Nor is it enough to establish that that goal is in harmony with the legal system overall. It still remains to be resolved whether the text should properly be interpreted in that way when taking into account the circumstances of the case in question.

Legal science and the legislator aim to facilitate the task of interpretation. For cases of contradiction between legal texts, legal science has constructed hierarchies of sources of law. Likewise, general points of departure exist for legal interpretation. For example, in the common law countries, legislation should be narrowly interpreted. However, at the end of the day legal interpretation is often guided by the intuition of the interpreter.

That said, the major codes sometimes include norms as to interpretation of their rules. One example is the Swiss Civil Code: *Kann dem Gesetz keine Vorschrift entnommen werden, so soll das Gericht nach Gewohnheitsrecht und, wo auch ein solches fehlt, nach der Regel entscheiden, die es als Gesetzgeber aufstellen würde. / À défaut d'une disposition légale applicable, le juge prononce selon le droit coutumier et, à défaut d'une coutume, selon les règles qu'il établirait s'il avait à faire acte de législateur. / Nei casi non previsti dalla legge il giudice decide secondo la consuetudine e, in difetto di questa, secondo la regola che egli adotterebbe come legislatore* ['Absent an applicable legal disposition, the court may decide in accordance with customary law and, where that is absent, in accordance with the rules that it would have established if acting as legislator'].

Likewise, the Civil Code of Louisiana (Art 4, in the text from 1987) declares: *When no rule for a particular situation can be derived from legislation or custom, the court is bound to proceed according to equity. To decide equitably, resort is made to justice, reason, and prevailing usages.* It is important to note that the word *equity*

---

11   Aarnio 1999: 17–24.

here means 'fairness' or 'natural justice': the system of concepts and terminology of Louisiana civil law are, in spite of their expression in English, of French origin.[12]

3.2.4 Mutation of Message Content in Transit The problem of message mutation also appears in legal communication. A witness statement can be recorded not only incompletely but also erroneously. By analogy, renewal of testimony before a higher court, long after the incident to which it relates, often changes the content of testimony.

Apart from the clearest cases of message mutation, it should be remembered that handling judicial and administrative matters always requires interpretation and classification of the facts of the case at hand. In consequence, the court or authority here exercises linguistic power, as is appropriate to influence the content of the message. Empirical research has shown that documents drawn up by the administrative authorities rarely conform to the manner of expression of citizens themselves. An authority interprets the message from the standpoint of its activities, and the process follows its course by means of administrative language, which makes the original message far more abstract. Self-evidently, this strengthens the institutional hegemony of the authority.

> Once, the power of classification, interpretation, and abstraction was far more important than nowadays. Extreme examples are found in the colonial era. One such is in Latin America, where the Spanish power aimed to wipe out "superstition", "sorcery", and "magic" among the populations of Indian and African origin. Criminal trials were common in this respect. Legal historians have noted that statements by those accused and testimony by *mestizos*, afro-americans, and poor whites were recorded in administrative and judicial minutes in a "purified" form. These minutes employ only Spanish with a legal-theological polish that would have been incomprehensible to anyone lacking a higher education. Worse still: one section of those accused and witnesses possessed no knowledge of Spanish. Under these conditions, it is not hard to fancy how an accused was able to defend himself, and how justice was meted out.[13]

It is in the sphere of international cooperation where the risks attaching to transmission of legal messages are the greatest. Legal documents originating from a foreign State very commonly have to be translated, for example to be executed in the country where a debtor habitually resides. This task is highly difficult and errors often occur in legal translations. Problems linked to these translations are aggravated in cases where there is a need to operate through an intermediary language, before the final translation. A text is translated, let us say, from Greek into English, then from English into Finnish.

3.2.5 Signals Impeding the Message In the terms of communication theory, irrelevant signals that impede the main message are "noise". From the standpoint

---

12   *Cf.* p. 223 and p. 251.
13   Ceballos Gómez 2001: 9–12.

of legal language, this noise may appear in various contexts. In the proper meaning of the term, this might involve the hubbub of the public present in the courtroom, hampering communication between the parties to the proceedings. In the Middle Ages, such interference amounted to a real problem: with significant variations as to the authority between different courts, the public could often go out of control and start noisy demonstrations of discontent.

Another type of "noise" is caused by over-long documents (e.g., witness statements, written pleadings), containing, apart from important information, irrelevant information that tires the reader and makes it difficult to follow the author's reasoning. Often, such information appears in the form of clumsy subordinates. Indeed, we might also mention certain countries with over-detailed grounds of judgments: with a view to greater certainty, these contain information of doubtful legal value.

Likewise, language rituals – both oral and in written form – constitute a kind of "noise". It is primarily in matters of international law that documents (e.g., charters, conventions) contain ritual expressions such as the parties' mutual assurances of goodwill, in line with diplomatic tradition. The volume of "noise" resulting from language rituals is largely dictated by the stylistic ideal fashionable in the society in question. For example, the style of legal Latin of Antiquity was clear and concise. By contrast, that of medieval legal Latin is highly complex. According to one theory, this difference originates from the divergence between the Romans' concept of style and that of the ancient Germans: a descriptive and repetitive language was especially typical of the ancient Germans. Correspondingly, the legal language of the baroque period was characterised by complexity and decorative extremes. Legal texts were peppered with quotations taken from classic humanist writers and the Bible.[14] This expressed the general baroque concept of aestheticism, dominated by the overwhelming desire to decorate everything. During the baroque period, it was hard work indeed to find the real legal message in documents, beneath a wealth of decoration.

3.2.6 Negative Attitude of Recipient It may be that the message does not achieve its goal due to the recipient's negative attitude. This explains the high importance of presenting message content in such a way as not to leave the recipient cold. The problem is that of rhetoric, developed as far back as Antiquity.[15] This involves the important art of persuasion. A convincing presentation is well constructed, and includes all necessary arguments in an appealing form.

In the Nordic countries, advocates develop their oratory in somewhat dull fashion: they present their arguments rather neutrally and simply. In Central and Western Europe, where rhetoric occupies a more important place, advocates employ the classic methods of rhetoric: hyperbole, metonymy, litotes, archaisms, neologisms,

---

14 Bader 1963: 114–116, 127–128.
15 See p. 7.

foreign words, paradoxes, paraphrases, deliberate stylistic faults, plays on words, antithesis, surprise arguments, apostrophes, deliberate howlers, and metaphors.[16]

In a rhetorical discourse, the power of the word is reinforced by changes in tone and by gestures. According to the code of conduct of certain legal cultures, the prosecutor should become carried away as his address proceeds, and his voice should rise in pitch. The impression is completed by body language, notably by using the eyes and the hands. This is emphasized in Latin countries, amongst others. For example, the Brazilian legal linguists Regina Toledo Damião and Antonio Henriques speak of the "dance of the eyes" (*dança dos olhos*) and present in detail how to make effective use of the eyes. According to them, raising the eyes helps in forming images, but if used at the wrong moment could easily be taken for ostentation or off-handedness. In glancing downwards, to the left, the prosecutor or advocate emphasizes his state of mind; in looking downwards, to the right, he "moves on in his manuscript". The hands speak, too. Open, palm upwards, they signify a speaker presenting a trustworthy case.[17]

4 Strengthening the Authority of the Law

4.1 Overview: Aims and Methods of Legal Authority

A law is intended to be respected by all citizens. A penal judgment endeavours to put the offender back on the right path and, at the same time, to deter individuals with a tendency to commit crimes. In these contexts, legal language is an instrument of social management and control. One of its important tasks is to consolidate social structures, the legal order, and the taking of decisions on the basis of laws. The aim is by means of this language to influence the behaviour of an individual, a section of the population, or the people as a whole.

When the authority of the law is strengthened by legal language, psychological means are used. It is important to guarantee, on the one hand, that citizens understand and remember legal rules and on the other that they be committed to observing them through fear of sanctions. We examine these questions in the following paragraphs.

4.2 Understanding and Memorising Legal Rules

Under simple social conditions, understanding the content of legal rules posed little problem. On the other hand, it was often difficult to know what rules were in force in society: at one time, written law did not exist. This explains why in ancient societies and communities specific individuals were charged with commiting the laws to memory. Even so, the importance remained of all members of the society in question remembering the content of laws. To ensure this, two mnemonics were used. The first of these was based on the concrete character of the law: old laws would describe

---

16 See pp. 75–77 and Haft 1999: 124–129.

17 Damião & Henriques 2000: 243.

specific cases, often highly colourful, that would become engraved in the mind of those that heard them. To illustrate this, there follows an extract from a law called "pagan law" from Sweden of the 11th century (author's translation):

> One man insults another man: "You are not a true man, and you have no manly courage". Now, they have to meet at the crossing of four ways. There comes he who spake those words but not he to whom those words were directed; then, so be he who was thus called. He is not worthy of taking an oath or bearing witness, either in matters concerning a man, or in matters concerning a woman. There comes he to whom the words were directed but not he who spoke the words; then, let the first thrice proclaim: "No-one", and let him place a sign on the ground towards him who is absent. Then, let him be deemed a lesser man who said that the other man should not be held to be a true man. Now, armed to the teeth they meet. Falls he to whom the words were directed; be paid amends at half of full for his death. Falls he who spake the words; let him remain without compensation, for insulting words are the worst of things, and the tongue is the slayer of the head.

We can be sure that the dramatic character of the presentation ensured that the content of the pagan law was engraved in the mind of the Swedes of old (the values expressed by the law, interesting as they are, are left aside in this context).

A second very frequent mnemonic is based on the concise, often rhythmic, character of legal language. In the Middle Ages, some laws were drawn up in poetic, or at least rhythmic, form. This was likewise the case for legal maxims. As is well known, a medieval student of law had to undergo seven tests, to demonstrate his scholarship. One of these tests was the formulation of propositions (*loci generales, generalia, brocarda, notabilia*) relating to passages from the *Corpus juris civilis*. To help memorise these propositions, they were expressed in the form of rhythmic maxims, in line with the style of Latin poetry. For that reason, these maxims were often elliptical: the verb or the main clause in the strict sense were missing. Examples include: *in dúbió pro réo* (an iamb with three feet with feminine ending), *lócus régit áctum* (a trochee with three feet), *audjátur et áltera párs* (an anapaest with three feet). Maxims of this type, which are easy to remember, do not go back to ancient Rome but to the amphitheatres of the medieval universities – although their content was formulated on the basis of Roman legal texts of the imperial era. Nor, technically, does the rhythm of the maxims in question go back to Antiquity: it is not based on the quantity of syllables (the distinction between long and short syllables had already disappeared from Medieval Latin) but on the stress (explicitly marked in the above examples). It is hard to overstate the importance of these rhythmic maxims in times past when the training of lawyers was essentially based on oral communication of legal information, in spite of the art of writing and the existence of manuscripts of legal works.[18]

A recent example of the concise character of the law (though of course lacking rhythm) is the French Civil Code. The writer Stendhal considered the articles of the code so well contrived that he read them regularly, to improve his style as a

---

18 Liebs 1981: 160–164.

novelist.[19] To illustrate, Article 2 of the Civil Code declares: "The law provides only for the future; it has no retroactive effect" (*La loi ne dispose que pour l'avenir; elle n'a point d'effet rétroactif*).

In our times, a legislative text may only rarely be drawn up concisely. Complex modern society presupposes rules that are precise and detailed. Laws and regulations intended only for expert use are on the increase. In fiscal and social matters, it is not unusual for an article of a law to express the content of some mathematical formula, in a highly complex language form. Needless to say, such a regulation is totally incomprehensible from the citizens' standpoint.

That explains why another method is increasingly used to inform the general public about legislation. This involves short-form bulletins that summarise the content of laws and regulations in simple language, using clarifying typographical means (e.g., character style). The same principle is applied in electronic media, which often use graphics to inform citizens about laws. Today, simplified bulletins have largely replaced authentic laws and regulations as a source of information, from the standpoint of the general public. One recent proposal recommends that directives from the European Communities be provided with an easy-to-read summary.[20] As to the needs of citizens concerning detailed information on legislation, these are satisfied by modern computerised means. In various countries, citizens can have free access to legislative databanks.

4.3 Citizens' Commitment to the Law

State power broadly speaking takes the form of word power. In society, the most important category of power in written form is the law, which under democratic conditions calls on the understanding and loyalty of citizens as members of a legal community. On that basis, Josef Isensee declares that in a democracy the law possesses a function comparable to that possessed, under a despotic government, by physical violence and its counterpart, fear.[21] The democratic State aims to achieve a situation in which citizens genuinely feel about law and justice as their own. It matters that they respect the law and judicial and administrative decisions of their own full accord. The legal community is essentially a community of persuasion (*Überzeugungsgemeinschaft*), not a community of constraint.[22] In the final analysis, respect for the law is doubtless a question that relates to the content of the legal order: an unjust law is not observed by citizens. However, the appearance of laws is likewise important: successful choice of words and appropriate style stimulate citizens to commit themselves with regard to laws and to justice.

---

19 Zweigert & Kötz 1996: 90.
20 Cutts 2001: 4.
21 Müller-Dietz 1997: 25.
22 Großfeld 1996: 89.

4.3.1 Declarations of Fundamental Values Constitutions, often like other legislative texts, also contain declarations that relate to the fundamental values of society. Examples include the right of citizens to obtain work and enough to live on. One classic value of particular importance declared by Constitutions is equality of citizens. A modern novelty in this respect consists of declarations concerning protection of the environment.[23] The status of these declarations is vague: do they amount to legal rules in the strict sense, in spite of not being immediately enforceable?

The values of society can likewise be underlined indirectly, to induce citizens to become committed to the law. One classic method consists of the names assigned to legal institutions. This process is traditionally employed during revolutions and independence struggles. The central institutions of state structures – often the State itself – are renamed. It is especially common to emphasize the popular character of institutions. The former socialist countries provide good examples: *people's democracy, people's court, people's commissar*. In the German Democratic Republic, for example, existed companies whose names showed they were owned by the people (*volkseigener Betrieb*), and *people's property* (*Volkseigentum*) was in general parlance.[24] State authority has always given consideration to the importance of use of language in creating a new impression of legal institutions – although in reality the substance of these institutions has scarcely changed. The French Revolution and Nazi Germany are likewise rich in examples.

This phenomenon also appears during periods of stability. Here, the legislator lays emphasis on equality among citizens with the help of legal language. It strives to eliminate words and expressions that certain groups of the population might feel insulting. For this reason, it adopts neologisms and euphemisms. To illustrate: designations relating to children in France born outside marriage. The word "bastard" (*bâtard*) was long ago abandoned. More recently, the term "illegitimate child" (*enfant illégitime*) was replaced by the term "natural child" (*enfant naturel*), which does not provoke the impression of contravening the law. By analogy, the term "incestuous child" (*enfant incestueux*) was replaced by a long paraphrase:[25] "If between the mother and the father of the natural child exists one of the impediments provided for under Articles 161 and 162 above by reason of consanguinity…" (*S'il existe entre les père et mère de l'enfant naturel un des empêchements à mariage prévus par les articles 161 et 162 ci-dessus pour cause de parenté* ... (French Civil Code, Article 334-10). The reason is simple: inventing a neutral term is very difficult in this last case.

In recent times, and in certain countries, individuals are referred to in legal texts in neutral terms as to masculinity and femininity. As a result, legislative texts have been rewritten in this way – in Switzerland, for example, from the mid-1990s. In the German linguistic zone, the aim today is as a matter of course to create the feminine form of various job descriptions and titles, by using the *–in* ending. This requires

---

23 Nussbaumer 2002: 185–201.
24 As to Soviet terms, see pp. 94–96.
25 Leveneur 1999: 20.

considerable creativity to avoid clumsiness in legislative text because of frequent repetition of the masculine and feminine forms of job descriptions and titles, for example, *der Richter* ['male judge'] – *die Richterin* ['female judge']. Thus, during the recent (1999) reform of the Swiss Civil Code (1907), the legislator systematically replaced all occurrences of the word "judge" (*der Richter*) with the word "court" (*das Gericht*) in the German version of the Code. This solution also aroused criticism: instead of a flesh-and-blood judge, judicial decisions today are taken by an "abstract entity".[26] – It is worth mentioning that the French and Italian versions of the Code speak always of "the judge".

4.3.2 Textual Style The style of text is a matter as important as terminology from the psychological standpoint. It speaks for itself that the language of a law or judicial decision should not come across as comedy or irony. At the same time, it should not be over-solemn or archaic. Clearly, it should not be so complex as to overawe.

If these conditions are not fulfilled, legal language can become the target of biting wit. In France, legal language had become petrified by the 16th century. This language had its own archaic terminology and style. Further, the grounds of judgments were highly complicated and almost beyond comprehension from the standpoint of the people. That is clearly evident in François Rabelais' classic of world literature, Pantagruel (1533). In this satire, the giant Pantagruel pronounces an impressive judgment at the end of legal proceedings between two lords:

> Having seen, heard, calculated, and well considered of the difference between the lords of Kissbreech and Suckfist, the court saith unto them:
> That in regard of the sudden quaking, shivering, and hoariness of the flickermouse, bravely declining from the estival solstice, to attempt by private means the surprisal of toyish trifles in those who are a little unwell for having taken a draught too much, through the lewd demeanour and vexation of the beetles that inhabit the diarodal (diarhomal) climate of an hypocritical ape on horseback, bending a crossbow backwards, the plaintiff truly had just cause to calfet, or with oakum to stop the chinks of the galleon which the good woman blew up with wind, having one foot shod and the other bare, reimbursing and restoring to him, low and stiff in his conscience, as many bladder-nuts and wild pistaches as there is of hair in eighteen cows, with as much for the embroiderer. (...)
> But, on the other part, the defendant shall be bound to furnish him with hay and stubble for stopping the caltrops of his throat, troubled and impulregafized, with gabardines garbled shufflingly,
> And friends as before, without costs and for cause.[27]

---

26 Nussbaumer 2002: 205–206.

27 Rabelais 1533: Translated into English by Sir Thomas Urquhart of Cromarty and Peter Antony Motteux. – The text of the first Two Books of Rabelais has been reprinted from the first edition (1653) of Urquhart's translation. Footnotes initialled 'M.' are drawn from the Maitland Club edition (1838); other footnotes are by the translator. Urquhart's translation of Book III. appeared posthumously in 1693, with a new edition of Books I. and II., under Motteux's editorship. Motteux's rendering of Books IV. and V. followed in 1708. Occasionally

As a counterbalance, it has to be stressed that the legislator should also avoid an over-relaxed style. In the same way, it should employ everyday words in legal language only with the utmost caution. Legal language always evolves some way behind normal language, without being allowed to lag too far. Laws should create a serious, but not over-solemn, ambience (this matter is dealt with in more detail in Chapter 3, 8.1, pp. 92–93).

4.3.3 Personal Commitment by the Citizen Notably, the oath has always been the instrument through which it was sought to ensure that the citizen makes his own the orders of the authorities and the provisions of the law by commiting himself to the truth in his declarations. The importance of an oath is heightened by its religious background, and its ritual and solemn character. At the same time, it involves a strictly personal commitment, based on the understanding of the individual taking the oath. This explains why the authorities have often required that the oath be taken in the mother tongue of the individual in question although the language of the proceedings to which the oath relates may have been different. That way, it was possible better to ensure the existence of the element of personal commitment. To illustrate this, a very old example: the bilingual oath of Strasbourg (842), taken simultaneously in Teuton and Old French. In the same way, soldiers of the imperial Austrian army took their oath in their mother tongue in spite of the fact that German was that army's common language. In Hamburg, in the 19th century, oaths were still being taken in Low German (*Plattdeutsch*) although High German (*Hochdeutsch*) had long been the language of the city's courts and public offices.[28]

4.4 Authority of the Law and Fear of Sanctions

4.4.1 Peremptory Character of the Law Unfortunately, there are some citizens who do not respect the law by making their own the values expressed by legal rules. For this reason, the public authorities need mechanisms reinforcing the authority of the law, notably sanctions. This involves penalties (prison, fine), damages, and so on. Fear can also reduce the workload of the authorities and promote understanding between citizens. This was well understood by K'ang Hsi, the great Chinese emperor of the 17th century:

> Law suits would tend to increase to a frightful amount, if people were not afraid of the tribunals, and if they felt confident of always finding in them ready and perfect justice. As man is apt to delude himself concerning his own interests, contests would then be interminable, and the half of the Empire would not suffice to settle the law suits of the other half. I desire, therefore, that those who have recourse to the tribunals should be

---

(as the footnotes indicate) passages omitted by Motteux have been restored from the 1738 copy edited by Ozell. http://etext.library.adelaide.edu.au/r/r11g/index.html.

28 Künnsberg 1926: 13–14, note 26.

treated without any pity, and in such a manner that they shall be disgusted with law, and tremble to appear before a magistrate.[29]

Since legal language has the character of a language of power, it is often categorical. Normally, laws do not contain justifications, in themselves, and they do not aim to edify. The style of legislative acts expresses the State's perception of its peremptory power. At the language level, this character is most plainly evident in verbs that give positive orders (e.g., *must, is required/obliged to*) or negative orders (e.g., *is forbidden*). In the matter of criminal law, the legislator's orders are expressed implicitly, through the medium of the sanction involved: "Those guilty of wilful murder, parricide and poisoning will be punished by death" *(Tout coupable d'assassinat, de parricide et d'empoisonnement sera puni de mort)* (French Penal Code of 1810, Art. 302).

However, the peremptory character of the law is often invisible at the language level: the present indicative is used. This gives the impression of a simple description of facts, though in reality it involves an order: "During marriage, the father and mother exercise their parental authority jointly*" (Pendant le mariage, les père et mère exercent l'autorité parentale en commun)* [Swiss Civil Code, Art 297, p. 1]), which means that parents *must* exercise that authority jointly. In the final analysis, an order is involved even in cases where a new institution is created by legislation. In French legal literature, the expression used is "text of principle" *(texte de principe)*. Orders in the proper meaning are then included in other legal dispositions, with which the text of principle forms a whole. In these cases, the appearance of the text also resembles a description: "Majority is set on attaining 18 years, the age of capacity for all acts of civil life" *(La majorité est fixée à 18 ans accomplis; à cet âge on est capable de tous les actes de la vie civile,* French Civil Code, Art. 488, p. 1). Finally, it is thus for definitions given in legislation.[30] As for judicial and administrative decisions, the exercise of power is expressed by words like *order, sentence,* and so on.

It has to be stressed that peremptoriness is not a feature of all use of legal language. In particular, the langage of legal scholars and of advocates is of a different character: it aims to convince the reader or listener. An abundance of argument is typical of this latter language, and coherence of the text is ensured by words expressing a conclusion, such as *thus, therefore.* The language of legal scholars and of advocates contains many quotations (laws, judgments, legal works) on which the author of the text comments. This is largely a matter of metalanguage.

4.4.2 Sacred Character of the Law Earthly sanctions against transgressors are traditionally reinforced by the belief according to which the law is sacred in character. The priest-kings of far-off times exercised a power at once temporal and eternal. We recall that Moses received the Commandments straight from the hand of God. In this

---

29 David & Brierly 1978: 480, note 22, according to S. Van der Sprenkel.
30 Bocquet 1997: 21–28.

set of beliefs, the administration of justice lay under the protection of the Most High. In consequence, contempt for the law and justice were considered as contempt for God himself. Earthly sanctions were complemented by celestial ones.

The sacred character of the law has always been heightened by means of language and ritual. This relies on legal language and semiotics. For example, preambles to laws have often indicated – and still do so today – in the most solemn language, or at least implicitly, that the legislator has been empowered by the Supreme Being. This holds true as much for Europe as for the Muslim world. As an example, let us take the the the opening of the implementing provision of laws and decrees in Tunisia.

During the protectorate (from the end of the 19th century to the middle of the 20th century), the real holders of power in Tunisia were the French, and French was, along with Arabic, the official language of the country.[31] The former sovereign, with the titles *pasha* and *bey* of Turkish origin, had been authorized to preserve the solemn forms of his former power. This was also true of the short transition period when Tunisia was a monarchy (from March 1956 to July 1957). During this period, the *pasha* promulgated the *decree of 13 August 1956 / 6 moharem 1376 bringing into force the Code of Personal Status*. The opening of the preliminary disposition of this decree was as follows (*Code of Personal Status* 2000):

Praise be to God !
We, Mohamed Lamine Pasha Bey, Holder of the Kingdom of Tunisia;
Having regard to the decree dated the 25 May 1876 (30 rabia II 1293) ...

Many countries have abandoned the tradition underlining the sacred character of the law. This is also evident in Tunisia. The opening provision that we have just referred to was already replaced by a simpler, secular formula in the 1960s. In recent years, with the spread of democracy, the royal 'we' and the Islamic calendar have also disappeared from this provision. Only the expression *in the name of the people* expresses the solemnity of the act of promulgation:

In the name of the people,
The Chamber of Deputies having adopted,
The President of the Republic promulgates the law as follows:

Still today, in the preambles to Constitutions of various countries the connection between law and religion often remains visible. One example is the 1949 Basic Law of the Federal Republic of Germany: *Im Bewußtsein seiner Verantwortung vor Gott und den Menschen... hat sich das deutsche Volk... dieses Grundgesetz... gegeben* ['Aware of its responsibility before God and man... the German people have assumed this Basic Law...']. In the same way, the preamble of the Federal Constitution of the Swiss Confederation begins: "In the name of Almighty God!" (*Au nom de Dieu Tout-Puissant*).

---

31 See p. 214.

By analogy, certain formulas employed by the courts express the concept according to which the Supreme Being is present in legal proceedings. This especially concerns formulas for taking the oath, where personal commitment (as we have seen) is strengthened by Eternity – even in countries considered to be lay-leaning. In Finland, for example, witnesses, experts or insolvent debtors who are members of the Church swear to tell the truth – according to the case – "by God Almighty and All-knowing" or "by God and His Holy Gospel". The oath is not the only way of underlining the sacred character of justice. Until 1970, court sessions of the first instance in Finland had to begin with a religious service.

In former times, the sacred character of the law was evident, not only in various acts and instruments of the authorities, but also in private documents, notably wills. As to these, their substance was largely inspired by ancient handbooks on the art of dying, *ars moriendi*. One recent Polish study analyses the language of some 200 wills, from the 16th century to the beginning of the 20th century. It shows that old Polish wills were not furnished with any title. The function of title was fulfilled by a religious declaration. This was the norm until the 18th century and still common enough at the beginning of the 20th century. For example, one highly popular opening was *W Imię Ojca, Syna i Ducha Świętego amen* ['In the name of the Father and of the Son and of the Holy Spirit, amen'] or the same in Latin *In nomine Patris et Filii et Spiritus Sancti. Amen.* Thus, the testator removed his act into the Holy domain and professed his faith and confidence in salvation. In this way, the will itself gained a celestial authority which, in turn, ensured its observance.[32]

4.4.3 Magical Character of Legal Language In former times, much of the power of legal language was based on its hypnotic rhythm and on magical elements, other than those of religion strictly speaking. Indeed, rituals always have an impact on the human mind, especially in the case of rhythm comparable to an incantation. This strengthens the authority of the law and inspires fear in those with a disposition to delinquency. This psychological truth was already known to the ancient Germans: their law often took a highly rhythmical form.[33] Archaic German law was expressed through magical formulas, whose melodious character affirmed in listeners a depth of feeling that ensured respect for legal rules. Thus, listeners were linked to the rhythmic movement of speech that led them to the magical space of archaic law.[34]

To that effect, binary formulas were especially frequent in old legal German. These expressed an obligation simultaneously rejecting its opposite:[35] *das Recht stärken und das Unrecht kränken; die Wahrheit sagen und die Lüge lassen* ['to strengthen the law and weaken injustice; to tell the truth and forgo falsehood']. The rhythmical effect of utterance was often heightened by alliteration (e.g. *nutzen und nießen,* 'employ and exploit'). In the Middle Ages, legal language might contain repetitions formulated up to seven times, by using a chain of synonyms or quasi-synonyms. As we know, the number seven possesses a special magical property.

32 Żmigrodzka 1997: 8–9 and 73–75.
33 Bader 1963: 108–112.
34 Schmidt-Wiegand 1990: 346, 351–352.
35 Wacke 1990: 884.

Nearer to our own times, we could mention Polish wills of the 17th and 18th century, where the crucial verb might still be repeated four times: *leguję, daję, daruję i zapisuję* ['I leave, present, give and enjoin', Żmigrodzka 1997: 56]. Traces of this tradition are still in evidence today. We can cite as an example the binary formula *Treu und Glauben* ['faith and trust', that is to say 'good faith'] in the German Civil Code. The phenomenon is especially clear in the English language.[36]

> The power of language might also be strengthened by magical gestures. According to Bavarian law at the end of the Middle Ages, the claimant was supposed, while reciting the formula of the claim, to touch the defendant with a walnut branch, a traditional magical object.[37]

In repetitions, the magic of numbers only appears indirectly. However, numbers are often present as such in laws. It may be that an element of magic lies behind their choice. They also perform a semiotic function. As we have seen, the number seven has always had an especially sacred character: God created the world in seven days. It is no coincidence that the number of nomophylaces in Ancient Greece was seven and that the *Présidial* (a certain appellate court) of old France comprised seven judges. Still today, the number seven often appears in rules of competence and term (time limits). In France, the *Cour d'assises spécial* (special criminal court) is composed of seven professional judges; until very recently, the mandate of the president of the Republic lasted seven years; a limited company requires seven members; and a seven-day term has importance in connection with conclusion of contracts.[38] In Finland, correspondingly, the disciplinary commission for advocates consists of seven members, apart from the president, while notification of appeal has to be given by the seventh day after delivery of judgment. Likewise, the number seven appears in international legal contexts, such as the Charter of the United Nations (Art. 109 s. 3).

In the human mind, all that is strange and incomprehensible easily obtains magical dimensions, at the very least arousing respect. For this reason Adolf Hitler, otherwise a chauvinist, was fond of words of foreign origin. They impressed those who listened to them: *"Das Fremdwort imponiert, es imponiert um so mehr, je weniger es verstanden wird"* ['A word of foreign origin impresses, it impresses all the more, the less it is understood', Klemperer 1969: 255]. Through the ages, legal language has benefited from this.

The basis of Western law is Roman law, with Latin its classical instrument.[39] Latin has been used to express technical legal concepts, as well as underlining the authority of justice. In the Middle Ages, court proceedings could take place in Latin, despite the fact that the parties themselves did not understand the language. Judgments were still being given in Latin at the beginning of modern times. Because of that, the

---

36 See pp. 233–234.
37 Kauffmann 1984: 72.
38 Gautier 1994: 170–174.
39 See pp. 128–131.

administration of justice was an event beyond comprehension from the standpoint of the people – and consequently impressive and awesome. Even today, Latin is often used during judicial ceremonies (e.g., opening of sittings). The doorways and walls of courts of law are decorated with Latin adages. Likewise, legal documents are often peppered with Latin maxims. Apart from Latin, listeners can be impressed by the use of another language, incomprehensible but high-status. For example, in medieval England the courts used an old form of French (*law French*). Still, today, in the United States the usher may announce the arrival of judges in the courtroom in French: *Oyez! Oyez! Oyez!*

4.4.4 Requirement of Humility before the Court Phrases expressing the humility of those seeking justice and respectful body language also reinforce the authority of the law and the authorities. By tradition, this is evident in ritual compliments when an individual addresses a judge or an authority or on sending a formal document to a court or public office.

The classic formulas of these compliments underline religious values and the inferiority of those seeking justice in relation to the public powers. In Spain, for example, the ending of a correctly-worded application took the following form: *Es gracia que espera alcanzar de V.I. (= Usía Ilustrísima), cuya vida guarde Dios muchos años*. ['(The undersigned) hopes to find favour with Your Excellency; may God grant Your Excellency long life']. These compliments also contained such adjectives as *Magnífico y Excelentísimo*.[40] By analogy, in England the parties are traditionally required to address judges in a precisely defined manner that depends on the type of court in question and its position in the hierarchy: *My Lord, Your Lordship, Your Honour, Your Worship*.

4.4.5 The Solemn Forms of Justice Apart from language means, the public authorities have always reinforced the authority of justice and upheld the exercise of judicial power by semiotic means of a more general character. In medieval Germany, the audience chamber of a court always contained a painting of the last judgement.[41] Symbols of justice include the scales, the sword, the lictor's fasces, the axe, and the blindfold. The last of these dates from the era of humanism, the other symbols from Antiquity. The sword and the axe go back to Ancient Greece and the lictor's fasces to Rome. The origins of the scales as a symbol go back even further. In ancient Egypt, Osiris used scales to weigh the souls of the dead. Still today, these emblems of justice are used throughout the Western world. For example, the courthouse of Vaasa (western Finland) is decorated by the emblems in question.[42] Solemn legal language forms only part of the means that aim to arouse respect for the law among citizens.

As for rituals and external frameworks underlining the authority of the court and lending a solemnity to justice, the following will illustrate: tokens and signs that

---

40 Martínez Bargueño 1992: 20–21, Duarte & *al*. 1998: 29, Martín & *al*. 1996: 55–56.
41 Harju 2000: 37.
42 Harju 2001a: 19–24 and Harju 2001b: 35–37.

indicate the beginning and end of sittings (e.g., ringing of church bells, fanfares); allocation of space to participants in the audience chamber (judges on a rostrum, prosecution and defence benches on opposite sides of the room); movements and gestures of participants (who should stand while speaking and when); special clothing of judges and counsel (e.g., wig, gown); the solemnity of the building where the court sits (in many countries termed "palace"). These features are worth a brief examination.

Traditionally, a courthouse in southern, western, and central Europe is built in imitation of the form of a Graeco-Roman temple. The façade of the building is furnished with columns and the main doorway, situated quite high up, is reached by often wide and impressive steps. It speaks for itself that this symbolism imitates a religious ascension. The building often contains a statue of the goddess of Justice. The internal architecture of the audience chamber follows a strict plan. This is especially so of the judges' rostrum: placed, like an altar, on a platform, above the parties and the public. Thus, the latter have to look upwards when listening to the judges. All of this underlines the sacred origins and the authority of the law.[43]

Semiotics is also in evidence in the dress of the actors in the legal drama: they communicate through their clothing. In many countries, judges wear a special outfit for the proceedings. English judges wear a wig, French judges a robe with a band and a cap. A French judge's robe is very full, with particularly wide sleeves. This symbolism goes back to times long past: wide sleeves, of little practical use in physical work, were even in Antiquity a sign of belonging to the governing social classes who merely gave orders.[44]

> An interesting phenomenon is Anglo-Saxon symbols of justice and their diffusion into countries whose legal tradition is other than common law. The reason for this phenomenon is simple: imported television series about court proceedings. In countries such as Finland where these series are popular, the press often uses the wig as a symbol of justice, even in purely national legal affairs, despite the fact that Finnish judges do not wear a wig.

An important aspect of legal semiotics consists of judicial rituals. The judges enter the audience chamber in a particular order. Then others present in the room have to stand. Leave to speak is given by the main judge according to a set procedure; the parties stand while speaking; the main judge silences the room by raising a hand. As the statues of Roman emperors show, a raised hand has always meant authority and command. Moreover, the wide sleeve, symbol of power, is clearly visible when the hand is raised.[45]

Rituals reinforcing the authority of justice have been particularly dignified in England. There, the higher courts of the land also hold sittings in provincial towns. Until not long ago, judges arriving in a town where they were to administer justice

---

43   Garapon 1997: 23–49, Modéer 2000: 1067–1069.
44   Garapon 1997: 72–91.
45   Garapon 1997: 53, 73–74.

were greeted by a trumpet blast. They also reviewed a guard of honour.[46] Solemn processions and escorts have also formed an essential part of English judicial rituals. For instance, the legal year was traditionally inaugurated in London by a walk of two miles from Temple Bar to Westminster Abbey. However, a tendency away from rituals is also discernible in England: the way from Temple Bar to Westminster is nowadays taken by car.

Some phenomena are placed mid-way between the semiotic and the linguistic. Examples include tone of voice, pauses in discourse, the silence of the public. In a written text, this might involve page layout of documents addressed to the authorities, reflecting the respect of sender to recipient. In Finland, for example, it was once required that the first page of a document intended for the highest representatives of the executive power or judiciary (the presidency of the republic, the cabinet, the supreme court, the administrative supreme court) should contain only three lines. As for courts of appeal and comparable institutions, the corresponding number of lines was five and, in the case of courts and authorities of lower rank, it was seven.[47] This custom has gradually disappeared.

4.5 Overcoming Judicial Uncertainty

The exercise of power weighs heavily. This also applies to the judge's task. We should remember that legal language is an instrument of dramatic deeds that can completely change the course of a life or – in some countries – even bring an end to a life (the death penalty). The possibility of a mistake, issuing from a flawed judgment, is often real. For their part, the means dealt with above through which the authority of Justice is reinforced, lighten the judge's mental load.

In times past, this load was relieved by the belief according to which the Most High was present during the proceedings. By language means, the judge was freed from responsibility regarding flawed judgments. In medieval England, for example, the claimant had to present his case by reciting a long and complicated formula. If there was one mistake, even minuscule, in the recitation, he lost his case: a language error was considered to be no accident, but a sign from God that the claimant was pleading an unjust cause. Responsibility for the judgment was therefore taken by the Celestial Father.

Still today, legal language lightens the load of the judge (or government official) – even if in more secular form. Legal language is perhaps the most important of the means by which a judge (or official) "dresses up" in their role. In many countries, such as France and Finland for example, judges speak in the name of their institution and by their authority: "On these grounds the court [...] declares [...]". The official role and the solemn, ritual language for their part create a feeling of certainty, leaving aside the subjective element of the decision. All this helps the judge or official better

---

46   Petersen & Soukka 1965: 224–225, photograph.
47   Caselius & Muukkonen 1966: 6 and Kemppinen 1999: 1291–1292.

to overcome uncertainty when faced with difficult matters, and better to tolerate the pressures of their profession.

5 Strengthening Lawyers' Team Spirit

5.1 Legal Language and Group Cohesion

Different professions develop forms of speech that suit them and that satisfy their needs. Each of these forms of speech is intended for communication within the profession. At the same time, it operates as an esoteric language that monopolises information. The special language of a restricted group is incomprehensible to outsiders. Theo Rasehorn declares bluntly: use of a precision language amounts to a distancing strategy (*Distanzierungsstrategie*).[48] The other side of the coin is that a specialist language strengthens group cohesion. This holds true, too, for the legal profession: an in-house language encourages among lawyers a feeling of solidarity towards their colleagues; it consolidates professional identity in legal circles, and expresses the commitment of lawyers to the values and traditions of their profession. From this standpoint, Latin and legal jargon possess a special value.

5.2 Latin as a Cohesive Factor in the Legal Profession

At one time, European lawyers could easily consolidate their professional identity through a particular language. Latin being the language of the legal profession from medieval times, it remained comprehensible only to social elites. In the Middle Ages and at the beginning of modern times, court judgments were generally drawn up in Latin. The same language was also otherwise used in legal dealings. This consolidated lawyers' team spirit and, at the same time, their power – the *vulgus* was excluded from legal communication.[49] Even after Latin was abandoned in its capacity of legal language in the strict sense, legal documents were long peppered with a large number of Latin maxims. To cite an example from the periphery of Europe, the votes of the judges in the Swedish courts of appeal were, in the 17th century, drawn up in a mixed language in which Swedish and Latin intermingled, so that at times Latin clearly dominated.

In our times, legal documents are required to be understandable to the general public. For this reason, it is no longer as easy as it once was to consolidate the coherence of groups of lawyers through Latin maxims. Nevertheless, such a possibility still exists in some sectors and in some countries. On the one hand, legal scholars in the West still cultivate Latin in their publications, even in northern Europe: in Finland, it is possible to find some 600 different Latin maxims in current legal literature.[50] On the other hand, in some countries Latin is still in evidence in

---

48   Rasehorn 1984: 270.
49   Waquet 1998: 280–281.
50   See p. 139.

judgments and other legal documents. Even in countries where Latin is *de jure* or *de facto* forbidden in official documents of courts and the authorities, Latin quotations are often found in the internal working documents of these organs.

It is therefore with good reason that one author declares that Latin maxims constitute the "much-loved folklore" of lawyers – folklore that a law student rapidly takes on board, even though Latin is not reappearing in the curriculum. Almost everywhere throughout the Western world, learning to use Latin maxims, in imitation of more experienced colleagues, forms part of the process of socialisation for future lawyers.[51]

5.3 Legal Jargon: the Lawyer's Secret Language

Lawyers' need to use an esoteric language also appears in a different way. In the introductory chapter, legal jargon was already mentioned.[52] Given that this involves strengthening professional solidarity and affinity, jargon differs from legal language in general in that it expresses emotions. Subjectivity, fantasy, and comedy are typical features of legal jargon, as with all professional jargon.[53] This naturally strengthens group ties between lawyers. Some areas of legal jargon are so hermetic that they are mastered only by a specially-initiated sub-group of lawyers. This above all concerns jargon from institutions rich in tradition, where a career as a lawyer can move forward without the need to leave the institution itself. The jargon of Finnish court of appeal judges and referendaries, for example, is largely incomprehensible to other Finnish lawyers.

6 Linguistic Policy

6.1 Minority Protection vs. Language Unification

Linguistic policy aims to preserve or to change either the relationship between two or more languages, or the properties (vocabulary, grammar, style) of a single language. Such policy is sometimes protective, but may also be dictated by the needs of the exercise of power. Very often, a contradiction occurs: it may be desirable, from the standpoint of equality, to strengthen the status of regional or minority languages; however, the effectiveness of the exercise of power requires consolidation of the position of the dominant language. In the latter case, linguistic policy is based on the idea that the functioning of government presupposes linguistic unification of the country. The idea is that only linguistic unity can ensure that authorities throughout the country understand a legal message, immediately, and in precisely the same way, without translation. At the same time, the central power often aims to change linguistic conditions in a country, so as thus to strengthen its cohesion.

---

51 Kramer 1995: 141–142.
52 See pp. 5–6.
53 Hałas 1995: 44.

For these reasons, centralised states endeavour to impose a single legal language for the whole country. France offers a particularly clear example of this.[54] With the strengthening of the French State and the territorial extension of France, the Latin dialect of the Île-de-France, French, was adopted as the sole administrative and judicial language throughout the entire realm. In the same way, once the Great Powers had partitioned Poland in the 18th century they imposed their national languages as judicial and administrative languages of the Polish territories that they occupied. As for medieval England, this is an example of the fact that a language used only by an elite minority can also become the judicial language of the country. At that time, the language of the English royal courts was French (*law French*), incomprehensible to the Anglo-Saxon people.[55] This, in turn, facilitated the exercise of power and prevented anyone calling it into question. Even today, examples of policy dictated by the needs of the exercise of power are many. Illustrations include some Latin American countries where Spanish (or Portuguese) is the sole legal and administrative language, including in regions where the populations speak native or aboriginal languages. In countries of sub-Saharan Africa, French, English, Portuguese, and Spanish occupy a corresponding place.

Unifying the judicial and administrative language, dictated by the needs of the exercise of power, has often radically influenced the linguistic conditions of a country: it has led to the total abandonment of languages previously spoken. Indeed, the central power has often intended such a change: a single national language is appropriate for strengthening national identity and preventing the dissolution of the State. Administrative and judicial language hastens that change through its status as a model. The population seeks to imitate the language spoken by the authorities, and social advancement is only possible by adopting that language. Simultaneously, individuals who have stood by the original language of the population find themselves cut off from communication. Gradually, the language of the authorities ousts the original language of the population. This occurred in France from the end of the Middle Ages to the beginning of modern times, and elsewhere. Today, a corresponding process is taking place in the countries of Latin America, where Spanish and Portuguese are in course of ousting the Indian languages, because of the privileged status of the former (administration, justice, education, the media).

In contrast to a linguistic policy satisfying the needs of the exercise of power stands a linguistic policy that aims to protect threatened languages. Here, the legal language may also be of considerable importance. In recent years, the languages of aboriginal peoples in particular have obtained an increasing importance in legal activities, thanks to national and international measures. For example, since 1991 the Lapps in Finland have had the right to use the Lapp language (Sami) before the courts and administrative authorities of the regions they inhabit and even before some of the country's central authorities.

54　See pp. 187–190.
55　See pp. 226–227.

It is not only in the smaller countries where a protective linguistic policy is exercised. In recent decades, the once-expansive French language is finding itself on the defensive in relation to English, whose influence is rapidly growing worldwide. In consequence, new French legislation, inspired by Quebec's Law No. 101, aims to limit the use and influence of English in France. At the same time, administrative orders presuppose that France's representatives always use French in the international arena. In Quebec, legislation protecting the position of French as an administrative and judicial language is particularly strict, because of linguistic pressure from English-speaking America and the Anglo-Saxon culture that surrounds it.[56]

The relationship between legal language and linguistic policy is complex. For example, equality of legal languages fulfils divergent functions in different conditions, from the standpoint of linguistic policy. Regulation as to the status of Finnish and Swedish in Finland provides a good example of this.

6.2 An Example: Finnish and Swedish in Finland

6.2.1 General Finland has two official languages: Finnish and Swedish. Finnish is the language of the majority. Today, the percentage of Finnish speakers is 92.5% and that of Swedish speakers 5.7%.[57] Finnish is a non-indoeuropean language, a distant relative of Hungarian. By contrast, Swedish is a Scandinavian (Northern Germanic) language, very close to Danish and Norwegian – all three mutually comprehensible, particularly in the written form. The relationship between them can be compared to that between the languages of the Iberian peninsular: Castilian, Portuguese, and Catalan.

Finnish and Swedish are thus completely different as languages. However, this does not mean that Finnish speakers and Swedish speakers live apart. These populations live, in large measure, intermingled in the coastal regions of the country. Their habits, customs, and way of life are much the same. In addition, many Finns are bilingual. Swedish is an obligatory language in Finnish schools, which means that Finns with a university degree – such as lawyers – know Swedish, at least passively.

At a time when Finnish did not enjoy the status it merited in the country (*vide infra*), tensions existed in relations between Finnish speakers and Swedish speakers. Today, these relations are excellent. Mixed marriages, crossing the linguistic border, are very common and well illustrate the good state of these relations. Paradoxicallly, close relations between the two linguistic groups creates a problem from the standpoint of maintaining the Swedish language in Finland. Because of the clear domination of Finnish, mixed marriages often mean that the second generation of the family is Finnish-speaking. At the same time, Finnish strongly influences the local Swedes, as much regarding vocabulary as regarding style. For this reason, Swedish in Finland is at risk of being deformed in comparison with the Swedish of Sweden.

---

56 See p. 194.
57 *Uusi kielilaki* 2001: 47.

Nevertheless, Finnish specialists in the Swedish language are still struggling against these phenomena. They stress the importance of bringing up children of mixed couples with good Swedish, and carefully follow the linguistic evolution of the language in Sweden, including the evolution of legal Swedish.

6.2.2 Evolution of the Status of National Languages Finland formed part of the Kingdom of Sweden from the 12th century to the early 19th century. During this long period, the inhabitants of the country fully adopted Swedish legal culture; the same laws came into force in Finland as well as Sweden. The Swedish language was also continually gaining ground in Finland. Even a thousand years ago, Swedish immigrants settled in the coastal regions of Finland, while later the main language of the realm spread geographically as well as from the standpoint of social classes. Finnish speakers who gained entry to the higher social classes adopted the Swedish language. This was most marked in the course of modern times (early 16th century to late 19th century). At the end of the Swedish period, and into the early 20th century, the percentage of Swedish speakers in Finland was 13%.[58] The Swedish-speaking population lived – and still lives – in the coastal regions (both southern and western coasts) of the country, normally more or less intermingled with the Finnish-speaking population.

Finland formed an equal part of the Kingdom of Sweden. For example, the inhabitants of the former took part in the activities of the Diet with the same right as the inhabitants of Sweden proper. However, in one important aspect this equality did not exist. The sole official language of the realm was Swedish. Thus, administrative and judicial decisions in Finland were always written in Swedish. Senior officials posted to Finland only rarely mastered Finnish.[59]

Sweden ceded Finland to Russia in 1809. Fortunately, the Tsar of Russia at that time, Alexander I, was an enlightened monarch. He thus gave autonomous status to Finland. The Nordic legal order and the country's general way of life were fully safeguarded. Nor did linguistic conditions in the country change immediately after the separation between Sweden and Finland. On the contrary, the representatives of the peasantry, mainly Finnish-speaking, proposed during a session of the Finnish Diet in 1809 that the official language of Finland should continue to be Swedish. As a backdop to this proposition lay the fear that the Tsar might introduce Russian as the official language of Finland, despite the fact of the almost total absence of Russian speakers in the country.[60]

From the 1820s, the situation began to change, partly because of pan-European currents of thought. Documents (e.g., contracts of sale, wills) relating to the rights and interests of the inhabitants of the country were required to be drawn up in their own language, so that they could understand them. For this reason, legal manuals were rapidly translated from Swedish into Finnish, with formulas for various

---

58 *Uusi kielilaki* 2001: 26 and 32.
59 Pajula1960: 123–124.
60 Pajula 1960: 129.

documents. This same activity led to creation of judicial Finnish language. The year 1856 marked the first time that a judge used Finnish in order to preside over a Finnish court of first instance.[61]

The pace of change quickened after the mid-19th century, largely thanks to the tsar, who was keen to weaken ties between the Finns and Sweden, the former ruling power and a Swedish-speaking country. The position of Finnish gradually improved and its equal status was definitively recognized by the statute of 1902 on the use of the Finnish and Swedish languages in Finland. This change was sealed by the radical modernisation of the parliamentary regime (1906), indirectly strengthening the position of the workers in political power.[62] The workers in general were Finnish-speaking.[63]

6.2.3 Current Situation The fact that Finnish attained official status in Finland does not mean that Swedish was abandoned. The first Constitution of independent Finland (entitled "Form of Government") of 1919 and the new Constitution of 1999 have both prescribed that the two languages possess equal status. According to Article 17 of the new Constitution "[the] national languages of Finland are Finnish and Swedish" and continuing "[the] right of everyone to use his or her own language, either Finnish or Swedish, before courts of law and other authorities, and to receive official documents in that language, shall be guaranteed by an Act" (semi-official translation published by the Finnish Ministry of Justice).

One of the consequences of this equality is the fact that Finnish and Swedish legislative texts have the same value.[64] The Constitution requires that these should always be published in both languages (sec. 79, subs. 4). This is also the case for the great semi-official compilation of the country's laws and regulations comprising almost all parliamentary laws and the most important regulations. It appears both in Finnish (*Suomen Laki*) and in Swedish (*Finlands Lag*).

The equality of the two legal languages is of considerable importance from the standpoint of the Swedish minority, above all in the country's bilingual coastal areas and in the province of Åland, which is entirely Swedish-speaking. The value of this is as much symbolic as practical. In particular, a portion of legal proceedings takes place in Swedish (the procedural language is chosen according to a particular regulation). This is also true of various administrative procedures and of legal circles in general. Notably, the status of legal Swedish in Finland is vital from the standpoint of legal scholarship. Swedish-speaking authors write important monographs, while basic legal works are often published in both languages, especially if the author's mother tongue is Swedish. There also exists a highly authoritative Finnish legal review in Swedish (*Tidskrift utgiven av Juridiska föreningen i Finland*).

---

61 Pajula 1960: 143–144.
62 *Uusi kielilaki* 2001: 30.
63 See for more detail Mattila 2002: 151–159.
64 *Uusi kielilaki* 2001: 73.

6.2.4 Conclusion As we have seen, Swedish language laws, in force in Finland until the end of the 19th century, reflected a power policy aimed at ensuring the cohesion of the Kingdom of Sweden: the sole official language of the country was Swedish, as was also the case in Finland despite the fact that the great majority of the population were Finnish-speaking. Linguistic equality was gradually achieved following claims by Finnish speakers, including before the courts and the public authorities.

Today, the focus has changed: linguistic equality operates in favour of Swedish speakers, who constitute a small minority in independent Finland. From the standpoint of Swedish speakers today, this amounts to a protective language policy. Under these conditions, the fact that Swedish enjoys the status of second official language in Finland protects and supports the minority Swedish culture in the country. One important element of that protection is the use in Finland of Swedish legal language in court proceedings and government. The pressure from Finnish is heavy and it is crucial for Swedish speakers to be able to call for legal services in their own language, in spite of the difficulties that may at times arise therefrom in the country's courts and government offices. At the same time, the status of legal Swedish maintains the country's Swedish-speaking culture at a more general level: academic legal writing in Swedish forms an important part of Swedish-language literature in Finland. That also shows that this literature is still very much alive and well there.

7 The Cultural Task of Legal Language

Justice forms part of human culture. It follows that the language of the law forms part of general linguistic culture. Nor is this an insignificant part: the history of various countries bears witness to it. Given that legal language is used in important contexts and that by nature it is dignified, even solemn, this language strongly influences ordinary language – sometimes negatively, sometimes positively.

7.1 Preserving the Linguistic Heritage

Every social institution has a tendency to ossify. Human beings have a need for security. For this reason, they are determined to hold on to familiar things, to traditions. Legal language is no exception. It is often archaic. One important reason for this fact is stability of legislation: laws, notably civil laws, often remain in force for decades, sometimes centuries. It is natural that the terms of these laws remain in use, in spite of being old-fashioned. The fact that lawyers have long formed a separate profession has generally contributed to ossification of legal language. The traditional language of Latin notaries is a good example. In England, the legal profession, formed by judges and advocates, has been especially hermetic, as remains evident in the archaic terminology of legal English.

Ossification of legal language is a negative phenomenon from the standpoint of understanding it. By contrast, the phenomenon is positive from the standpoint of preserving the cultural heritage. The conservative nature of legal language allows a clearer view of linguistic evolution than ordinary language. Ossified legal language is a kind of linguistic museum that enables archaeology of language. The grammar, vocabulary, and style of former epochs live on particularly tenaciously in legal language. A major part of this linguistic heritage consists of foreign influences. This is why legal language shows the factors forming a country's linguistic culture over different epochs.

Legal language in particular demonstrates which languages were previously used in official contexts in a given country. As already indicated, language changes, notably those in written language, have been frequent enough phenomena over the centuries. In different countries, Latin was abandoned in favour of a modern language, passing sometimes from one modern language to another (in Finland, for example, from Swedish to Finnish). Because of the conservative nature of the legal profession, the legal language of today contains elements – often important – of one or more former languages. This is especially evident in legal terminology and in stock phrases. The clearest example of these linguistic traces is Latin in modern legal languages.[65] Another example, geographically more restricted, is the French heritage in legal English. French was the legal language of England in the Middle Ages, notably in the 13th and 14th centuries, which to this day remains in evidence in English legal terminology.[66]

Interest in the use of an archaic legal language is not confined to linguists trying to discover the various stages of development of the language in question and foreign influences upon it. The archaic character of legal language may also be of strong display value: it symbolises the uninterrupted continuity of a country's culture, and links the present to the wonderful, model ancestral past. This language, then, is given the function of strengthening national feelings of dignity, consolidating identity, as in the case of Greece (see below 7.3).

7.2 Developing the Language

Historically, legal language has been of great importance from the standpoint of ordinary language. Sometimes, "development" of language has impelled that of the power centre to oust entirely the original language or the dialect of the people. As just indicated, public offices and the courts have often played a leading role in this process.

However, the influence of legal language has also been considerable in cases where a language has been developed on its own foundations. In the Middle Ages and at the beginning of modern times, the rules and orthography of the written language were often set by the language of public offices and courts of law, which represented the country's central power. Once again, France offers an example. The royal chancellery and the *parlements* greatly contributed to establishing the

---

65 See pp. 136–139.
66 See pp. 231–232.

grammar and vocabulary of the French language.[67] In the same way, legislative style has managed to influence the style of ordinary language.

The cultural function of legal language is still manifest today. This is especially true of the vocabulary of a language. Legislative language, for example, spreads neologisms into ordinary language. After a new term is adopted into a law, all public offices and all courts of law use the term (in some cases, such use is a duty imposed by office). In consequence, the new term rapidly appears in thousands of documents read by citizens. If the term is impressive, it may later acquire, through semantic derivation, a meaning going beyond the borders of legal usage. In the same way, the style of official documents influences that of normal language.

It is therefore understandable that efforts should be made in different countries to improve the quality of legal language, by keeping in mind the value of this language from the standpoint of linguistic culture generally. For example, this is in evidence on the Iberian peninsular following the end of dictatorships. The old cultural languages of the peninsular, left in the shade for centuries by Spanish (*español* or *castellano*), began spreading, both in general life and in legal dealings. Above all it is the Catalan linguists who are highly aware of the effects of administrative and judicial language on linguistic culture generally. Castilian linguists also underline these effects.

The Spanish Constitution prescribes that the languages of Spain form a cultural patrimony (*patrimonio cultural*) which should be respected and protected (sec. 3 para. 3). Jesús Prieto de Pedro interprets this prescription in such a way that it forbids deterioration of the patrimony through poor administrative and judicial language.[68] A civilized State cannot allow the authorities to degenerate the linguistic capital created by ancestors. Furthermore: administrative and judicial language should influence ordinary language in such a way as to strengthen democracy. In consequence, terms of address expressing humility (e.g., *Usía Ilustrísima*) in communications with the authorities are considered to be contrary to the principles of civil society.[69] Another important aspect of this linguistic democracy is the principle according to which the language of official documents should be easy to understand from the citizens' standpoint. It therefore follows that the language of the courts and public offices should be developed towards the ideal of simplicity and unambiguity.

7.3 Tension between Cultural Heritage and Democracy: Legal Greek

Preserving the linguistic heritage and the goal of democratic development of language often stand in contradiction. Sometimes, this contradiction can be aggravated. By way of example, Modern Greek well illustrates this proposition.

7.3.1 Evolution of the Greek Language Greek is a language of great antiquity: its written use goes back to times as distant as Chinese (15th century B.C.) if taking into

---

67 See p. 188.

68 Prieto de Pedro 1991: 148.

69 Duarte & *al.* 1998: 29–30.

account Cretan syllabic writing (Linear B). Greek literature reached its first zenith some two and a half millenia ago. Clearly, spoken language changes considerably over such a long period. However, in Greece a variant based on the classical language was used as the written language until the early 19th century. With the strengthening of Greek national sentiment, and after the war of liberation against Turkey in the 1820s, the need to create a modern national language was born.

A variant of Greek called Katharevusa (καθαρεύουσα, lit. 'pure language'), based on a "purified" form of the spoken language, was then created.[70] Elements of foreign origin were eliminated from this spoken language, and these were replaced by classical words or neologisms. Diacritic signs were retained, in spite of their no longer being of importance as rules of pronunciation. This variant of Greek was accepted with time, even by conservatives who had upheld use of the classical language.

In spite of its basis on the spoken language, Katharevusa differed considerably and its system of writing was complicated. For this reason, some writers began to use a variant based directly on the spoken language, Demotic Greek (*dimotikí*, δημοτική, lit. 'popular language'). However, it should be noted that even this latter variant also did not abandon certain fundamental approaches to orthography from classical Greek: the same phoneme is expressed in writing in different ways when it appears in different positions. Moreover, the orthography of Demotic Greek has been variable until now. Unsurprisingly, a subject specialist, Argýrios Stavrákis, was obliged to define "true" Demotic Greek in his recent work on legal language.[71]

Until the 1970s, supporters of Katharevusa and those of Demotic Greek were involved in a fierce struggle. It was the latter who finally won. In spite of the intensity of this struggle, the two variants are not so very different as a novice might suppose. True, Katharevusa as used in official contexts might to some extent be described as a "wooden" language, and this variant includes words unknown in everyday language. Even so, difficulties arose above all in the active use of Katharevusa. According to its orthography, word endings in the written language included letters that have not corresponded to any sounds in the spoken language since far-off times and – as already mentioned – ancient diacritic signs. Equally, however, it is fair to say that Demotic script is itself not always easy, because – as mentioned above – certain orthographic approaches from the classical language have been preserved.

The difference between Katharevusa and Demotic Greek can be demonstrated by the name of the country's Civil Code (as an illustration, the Greek diacritic signs are conserved in the following transliteration). This name reads in Katharevusa: Ἀstikòs Kôdix (Ἀστικὸς Κῶδιξ), and in Demotic: Astikós Kódikas (Αστικός Κώδικας). The two variants show that the divergence is usually not great. As stated above, Katharevusa and Demotic Greek mostly differ in word endings, along with signs expressing breathing and tonic accent, sometimes in changes of accent (and in

---

70 Politís 1973: 80–81.
71 Stavrákis 1995: 61–68.

vocabulary). These differences cause not so much difficulties of comprehension as difficulties of active usage of language and orthography.

7.3.2 Transition to Demotic in Practical Lawyering Katharevusa became the legal language of Greece after independence. In connection with reform of the Constitution in 1911, a provision was added guaranteeing the status of Katharevusa. A corresponding provision was also included in the 1952 Constitution.[72]

In spite of that, throughout the entire 20th century some legal circles made efforts to introduce Demotic into legal activities. The confrontation could be serious. For example, documents drawn up in Demotic were considered void by courts of law.[73] Nevertheless, some enthusiasts worked ceaselessly in favour of Demotic. This was especially the case with the advocate Hristóforos Hristídis, who over the decades translated into Demotic – the "language of the Greek people", as he himself put it – the Constitutions of 1952 and 1975 along with the country's essential codes: the Civil Code, the Civil Procedure Code, the Criminal Code and the Criminal Procedure Code.[74]

After 1967, Katharevusa reached its final peak. The military government took on the responsibility of backing up the position of this variant of Greek.[75] With the fall of the military government, the position of Katharevusa began to falter. The change was not easy. In legal dealings, the transition lasted nearly a decade. This period is worth looking at in more detail.

The 1975 Constitution played a decisive role in the process of switching over to Demotic Greek. In contrast to the Constitutions of 1911 and 1952, it contained no special provision on the official language of the Greek State. This lacuna was a deliberate choice: the intention was to create the conditions necessary for Demotic Greek to be taken into use as the official language. The supporters of Demotic considered that it was not only a matter of the new Constitution permitting a change in the variant of Greek. According to them, this Constitution explicitly required that Demotic be taken into use. The Greek legislator had to communicate to the people the real goal of all Greek laws and regulations and to convince them that these were just. To arrive at that end, a language was needed that the people really understood. At the same time, the supporters of Demotic linked the use of Demotic to the principles of equality and promotion of the free development of citizens' personality, as expressed in the new Constitution.[76]

After the 1975 Constitution, a number of laws and regulations strengthened the position of Demotic Greek in courts of law and public offices. In consequence, the use of Demotic in legal dealings spread like lightning. Judges began drawing up judicial documents (e.g., summonses, judgments) in Demotic. New laws and

---

72 Stavrákis 1995: 55.
73 Stavrákis 1995: 56–57.
74 Stavrákis 1995: 57–58.
75 Giannópoulos 1982: 35.
76 Stavrákis 25–28, especially note 12.

regulations, as well as administrative documents, were also drawn up in this variant of Greek. It followed that legal scholars passed into Demotic.[77]

Nevertheless, lawyers who supported Katharevusa mounted a late but energetic struggle. They started by relying on the fact that the 1975 Constitution was itself drawn up in Katharevusa. They maintained that this fact presupposed that other Greek laws and regulations should also be drawn up in Katharevusa. This argument later lost its validity after translation of the Constitution into Demotic in the mid-1980s, and its entry into force in that variant of Greek. At the beginning of the 1980s, supporters of Katharevusa were still troubled at the "danger that judges who have started to use Demotic are covering themselves with ridicule".[78]

These supporters also employed legal means in the struggle. A case was laid before the Greek Supreme Administrative Court (Συμβούλιο της Επικρατείας / *Symvoúlio tis Epikrateías*) with a view to its declaring null and void the decree eliminating diacritic signs. The Court was asked to forbid the authorities to use "artificial" writing stripped of the spiritus signs. However, in 1987 the Court declared that the decree was in line with the Constitution. According to the Court, Demotic was the result of natural and organic evolution of the Greek language, and not an artificial or imaginary language.[79] Supporters of Katharevusa also claimed that judicial independence called for linguistic independence. The opposition party rebutted this view by detailed arguments.[80]

The defenders of Demotic relied on several arguments, often ideological. They sought to show that Demotic was an instrument wholly capable of expressing a developed legal thought. At the same time, these defenders also criticised the conservatism of the linguistic culture of the Greek State in the 19th and 20th centuries. A. K. Papachrístos wrote in 1982 that the law was applied in Greece in a manner "isolated from the values and expectations of the people". According to him, "the usage of Katharevusa not only in large measure served the conceptualisation and formalism of legal thinking, but also at the same time has decisively contributed to the fact that the people had become distanced from the law and its application".[81] For that reason, this author found the introduction of Demotic highly important from the standpoint of democracy and social life. He also believed in the immediate effects of such a change from the standpoint of good usage of legal language: when Demotic is used, ambiguities and inaccuracies are eliminated from legal texts and verbiage is discarded.[82]

As already indicated, the language of all legal dealings is currently Demotic. Nevertheless, a reminder of the language struggle is evident in the fact that the proponents of Demotic still underline today the usefulness of this variant of Greek:

---

77 Giannópoulos 1982: 36.
78 Papachrístos 1982: 195.
79 Stavrákis 1995: 46–47.
80 Stavrákis 1995: 18–29 and 41.
81 Papachrístos 1982: 196.
82 Papachrístos 1982: 197.

Demotic "is absolutely perfect and sufficient for all scientific use and thus for legal use, which is to say that through this language it is possible to express completely and without ambiguity (...) all legal and scientific ideas".[83]

7.3.3 Conclusion Examination of the Greek language shows that the objective according to which the written language should be developed towards the spoken language, in order to advance democracy and ensure ease of its comprehension and usage, can lead to strong emotions under certain conditions. Possibly, this objective comes into collision with values underlining the importance of a country's linguistic heritage: this heritage should be preserved, above all when it involves one of the great languages of civilization, bearer of a nation's identity. If such a tension is intense enough, two variants of the same language, each with its own particular linguistic norm (grammar, orthography, vocabulary), can coexist, at least for a while, in legal circles. Language struggles are not the sole preserve of countries with different ethnic groups, or totally different languages.

A second European example of rivalry between two variants of the same legal language is Norwegian. Danish and Norwegian are both Scandinavian (North Germanic) languages closely related to one another. Since Norway for several centuries was united with Denmark, its written language developed on the immediate basis of Danish. As a reaction against this "linguistic dependence", a rival written language was created in the 19th century, on the basis of western Norwegian dialects, to express the country's "true" cultural heritage. All Norwegians understand both variants without difficulty, but for ideological reasons a fierce struggle between them has been going on for more than a hundred years – including in legal circles. The variant based directly on Danish (*bokmål*, lit. 'written language') has a clearly dominant position.[84] This is also true of legal dealings, but the variant based on west Norwegian dialects (*nynorsk*, lit. 'new Norwegian') is also in usage among lawyers. In the Parliament, the president of the parliamentary commission examining a draft bill decides which variant is chosen for reading the bill in the *Odelstinget* (assembly for legislative affairs). Most legislation is promulgated in *bokmål*. As for courts of law, judges may also choose the variant used in their judgments. Among judges, as elsewhere, *bokmål* dominates but some judges do use *nynorsk*, especially in western Norway. In the Norwegian Supreme Court, one judge uses (2002) *nynorsk*. As for legal scholars, some of them write in *nynorsk* but the majority use *bokmål*.[85] In sum, the rivalry between both variants of legal language is still in progress.

---

83   Stavrákis 1995: 77–78.

84   Brækhus 1956: 8–1 and Myklebust 1996: 44–47.

85   The author owes this last information on today's practice to Professor Kåre Lilleholt.

Chapter 3

Characteristics of Legal Language

The functions examined in the last chapter largely impose the specifics of legal language. This possesses a number of special characteristics in comparison with ordinary language. These characteristics are to some extent in evidence in the same way in all legal languages (e.g., French, Finnish, Polish). The following paragraphs aim to illustrate this by examples taken from various legal orders and from various linguistic zones. The specific properties of legal language only show themselves when under examination at textual level. It is the concept of text that unites the elements of the language: semantic, lexical, syntactic, and stylistic, as Jean-Claude Gémar puts it.[1]

1 Precision

1.1 Importance of Political Factors and Use of Written Form

Accuracy and precision are considered fundamental characteristics of legal language. This essentially results from the requirement for legal protection and legal certainty. To avoid the possibility of arbitrariness, legal rules should be formulated without ambiguity. In a democratic State, linguistic clarity is an absolute norm of legislation. In a less democratic State, the situation is more complicated. In some cases, a dictatorship also prefers clear legal language. This concerns situations where those in power want to ensure performance of their orders. However, dictatorships can easily move over to a form of language that is intentionally unclear, if that movement serves their interests. In international relations, linguistic ambiguity may also be a conscious choice in certain negotiating situations. For example, negotiators can leave equivocal an article of an international treaty on which they have not reached agreement. This also occurs within the frame of the European Union. Such a process allows the parties later to make a "corridor compromise", without endangering the entry into force of the treaty.

Written form is a necessary condition for accuracy of legal language. Oral legal knowledge is always uncertain and changeable. It was for this reason that archaic law had a summary character: at the language level, this law was composed of adages concerning concrete situations, presented in rhythmical form for mnemonic reasons.[2] By contrast, the complexity of modern society necessarily requires use

---

1 Gémar 1995: 103 note 23.
2 See pp. 39–40.

of written legal language. This requirement is heightened by legal positivism and the idea of the rule of law (*État de droit, Rechtsstaat*). Parliamentary laws are of vital importance as sources of law. True, legal language often appears initially in oral form: advocates' courtroom speeches are oral, not to mention consultations in lawyers' offices. However, these are later recorded in written form.

1.2 Tautology

The accuracy of legal language presupposes that legal terms are employed logically and consistently. Changing terms easily gives rise to doubt as to the possibility that the meaning has also changed. This is why tautology is not discarded in legal language – as opposed to ordinary language. The basic goal of legal language is to transmit legal messages with absolute clarity and without ambiguity. In consequence, stylistic considerations should always give way to the accuracy of legal messages.

In reality, even legislative language is not always entirely logical and consistent as to terminology. One of several reasons for this is that the laws and regulations forming the whole of the legal order come from different epochs. Directives from the European Communities cause particular problems: they sometimes contain terms that differ from those used in Member States' national legislation. This often involves a deliberate choice on the part of the national legislator: if a term that differs from one ingrained in previous national legislation is adopted in a Community directive, then the national legislation implementing the directive may stay with the ingrained term. This is especially the case where the meaning of the term adopted in a directive only approximately covers the meaning of the established national term.

The accuracy of legal language also presupposes that a noun in a sentence is not replaced by a pronoun if that can cause ambiguity as to the subject or the object of the sentence. In the past, lawyers have been highly cautious in this respect: they not only always repeated key substantives but added a precision-word, above all *(the) said*, in front of substantives. This tradition goes back to medieval times and is still partly to be seen in what is called chancellery style in various countries.[3]

1.3 Definitions

1.3.1 Rationale, Significance, Use, Classification In common with words from natural language in general, terms from legal language have multiple meanings (polysemy). For this reason, legal terms are often defined within a particular context, to avoid mistakes and misunderstandings. This implies that legal language contains many definitions.

Definitions of terms are especially typical of a developed legal system. Justinian, the Byzantine emperor, had Roman law collected in three compilations (the Code, the Digest, and the Institutes), published between 529 and 534, and completed by a series of new laws, Novellae (the whole formed by these compilations was later

---

3   See pp. 149–150.

entitled *Corpus juris civilis*). The Digest contained 246 legal definitions (D.50.16 *De verborum significatione*).

Analogically, current legal literature and legislation contain many definitions. However, the attitude of lawyers towards definitions is ambiguous. On the one hand, their utility is considered obvious but on the other hand a certain scepticism exists. To justify this scepticism, it is enough to open the Digest, mentioned a moment ago: *Omnis definitio in jure civili periculosa est* ['In positive law, all definitions are dangerous', D. 50. 17. 202].[4] Besides, the overly abstract character of legal definitions has long been criticized, as in Italy for example. Thanks to these criticisms, the definitions included in the Italian Civil Code in force (1942) are less theoretical and more rarely cross-referenced than those in the Civil Code of 1865.[5]

Legal definitions can be classified in several ways. Let us take two examples. First, the distinction drawn between "real definitions" and "terminological definitions".[6] The first concern entities that exist in reality in the physical world (e.g., real property). To quote Article 527 of the French Civil Code: "Goods are movable by their nature, or if the law so determines" (*Les biens sont meubles par leur nature, ou par la détermination de la loi*). As to the second, these concern entities that only exist in legal reality (e.g., an obligation). In practice, the borderline between real definitions and terminological definitions is often vague.

Next, the dichotomy of "extension" (the class of entities to which a term refers) and "intension" (common characteristics of all the meanings of the term) is fundamental in the field of logic. This forms the basis to speak of extensional definitions and intensional definitions. Extensional definitions are formulated by enumerating the sub-classes that form the class to be defined. This is possible where the sub-classes are well-known and their number is limited, or when it is difficult to formulate an intensional definition. As to intensional definitions, here the *definitio per genus et differentiam* stands first and foremost in importance. The starting point, then, is to indicate the class (*genus*) to which the sub-class to be defined (*species*) belongs. The next step is to show the elements by virtue of which the sub-class to be defined differs from the other sub-classes included in the class. The popularity of this type of definition in legal language is largely explained by the fact that the legal system is based on classifications. It follows that it is important to show classes and sub-classes in definitions. Indeed, the use of *definitio per genus et differentiam* is very common in the Italian Civil Code, for example.[7]

Additionally, codes and other major pieces of legislation contain definitions of terms that can be characterised as "implied": the content of a term used in a code can, at least in part, be determined from the position of the term in the systemic structure of the code. The

---

4   Mori 1997: 323. – As for the term *jus civile*, see p. 110.
5   Belvedere 1994: 424–427.
6   Pieńkos 1999: 88.
7   Belvedere 1994: 429–437.

headings of the code (books, titles, chapters, sections, subsections, paragraphs) function as parts of the definition.[8]

1.3.2 Legislation The legislation of various countries combines the characteristics of real and terminological definitions as well as those of extensive and intensive definitions. These definitions can be extremely detailed, notably in the common law countries. For example, sections (articles) 2 to 4 of the English law entitled *Leasehold Reform Act* (1967) read as follows: (2) *Meaning of "house" and "house and premises", and adjustment of boundary,* (3) *Meaning of "long tenancy"* and (4) *Meaning of "low rent".* In printed form, these comprise almost five pages. To quote from the beginning of Section (article) 2:

> 2. MEANING OF *"HOUSE"* AND *"HOUSE AND PREMISES"*, AND ADJUSTMENT OF BOUNDARY. *– (1) For purposes of this Part of this Act, "house" includes any building designed or adapted for living in and reasonably so called, notwithstanding that the building is not structurally detached, or was or is not solely designed or adapted for living in, or is divided horizontally into flats or maisonettes; and –*
>
>> *(a) where a building is divided horizontally, the flats or other units into which it is so divided are not separate "houses", though the building as a whole may be; and*
>> *(b) where a building is divided vertically the building as a whole is not a "house" though any of the units into which it is divided may be.*
>
> *(2) References in this Part of this Act to a house do not apply to a house which is not structurally detached and of which a material part lies above or below a part of the structure not comprised in the house.*
> *(3) Subject to the following provisions of this section, where in relation to a house let to and occupied by a tenant reference is made in this Part of this Act to the house and premises, the reference to premises is to be taken as referring to any garage, outhouse, garden, yard and appurtenances which at the relevant time are let to him with the house and are occupied with and used for the purposes of the house or any part of it by him or by another occupant.*
> *(4) In relation to the exercise by a tenant of any right conferred by this Part of this Act there shall be treated as included in the house and premises any other premises let with the house and premises but not (...)*

This is no mere exception: the Canadian Penal Code includes nine pages of definitions. Today, the problem is clearly evident in the legislation of the European Communities. Excessive use of definitions has also aroused criticism. For example, in Russia some authors have stated that new Russian legislation contains definitions of terms that were not even used in the law in question. At the same time, the size of articles (sections) made up of definitions has increased disproportionately.[9]

In the same way, the principal terms used in international treaties are often defined in the treaties themselves. This is partly because legal institutions differ from one country to another. Further, the interpreters of a treaty form a heterogeneous audience

---

8   Belvedere 1994: 434.
9   Vlasenko 1997: 156–157.

characterised by linguistic pluralism. A definition helps resolve these problems. To quote the (Hague) Convention on the Law Applicable to Agency (*Convention de la Haye sur la loi applicable aux contrats d'intermédiaires et à la représentation*): "For the purposes of this Convention (...) (b) a trustee shall not be regarded as an agent of the trust, of the person who has created the trust, or of the beneficiaries" (*Aux fins de la présente Convention (...) (b) le trustee n'est pas considéré comme un intermédiaire agissant pour le compte du trust, du constituant ou du bénéficiaire*). Because the institution of trust is traditionally unknown in continental Europe (using a quotation in the French version of the text to designate this institution is a symptom), it was necessary to define the connection between this institution and the Convention.

1.3.3 Court Decisions and Private Documents It is not only statute law that contains a large number of legal definitions. These also appear in judicial and administrative decisions. A good example is the judgment of the Imperial German Supreme Court (*Reichsgerichtshof*), which includes the definition of *railway* (1879):

(Eisenbahn ist) "ein Unternehmen, gerichtet auf wiederholte Fortbewegung von Personen oder Sachen über nicht ganz unbedeutende Raumstrecken auf metallener Grundlage, welche durch ihre Konsistenz, Konstruktion und Glätte den Transport großer Gewichtsmassen beziehungsweise die Erzielung einer verhältnismäßig bedeutenden Schnelligkeit der Transportbewegung zu ermöglichen bestimmt ist, und durch diese Eigenart in Verbindung mit den außerdem zur Erzeugung der Transportbewegung benutzten Naturkräften (Dampf, Elektrizität, tierischer oder menschlicher Muskeltätigkeit, bei geneigter Ebene der Bahn auch schon der eigenen Schwere der Transportgefäße und deren Ladung, usw.) bei dem Betrieb des Unternehmens auf derselben eine verhältnismäßig gewaltige (je nach den Umständen nur in bezweckter Weise nützliche oder auch Menschenleben vernichtende und die menschliche Gesundheit verletzende) Wirkung zu erzeugen fähig ist." (RGZ = Reichsgericht in Zivilsachen I, 247.)

(A railway is) "an undertaking arranged for the repetitive locomotion of persons or things over not wholly insignificant courses on a metal base which through its consistency, construction and smoothness is aimed at enabling operation of the transport of large weight masses or at reaching a proportionate significant speed of transport movement, and which, through this peculiarity in combination with the natural forces used to produce the transport movement (steam, electricity, animal or human muscular activity, and also, on inclined surface of the way, the transport vessel' s own weight and its load, etc.), is capable of taking on itself, in the running of the undertaking, a relatively important effect (according to the circumstances, only useful in the intended manner, or also destructive of human life and dangerous to human health)." (Author's translation.[10])

Foreign authors have sometimes presented this definition as an example of the German mindset and linguistic tradition, of an extremely fastidious character. Nevertheless, this definition appears in a different light if its goals are taken into

---

10   With assistance of Associate Professor Mathias Siems, Riga Graduate School of Law.

account. In the background of this judgment stands a law (the *Reichshaftpflicht-gesetz,* adopted in 1871), which imposed strict liability on railway companies for risk created. With the coming into force of this law, lawyers for the railway companies attempted by all means to limit the notion of railway in order to avoid strict liability, which from their standpoint was uncomfortable. The judgment from which the citation was taken prevented these attempts by formulating a watertight definition.[11]

Private documents may also contain legal definitions. This is widespread in common law countries. For example, commercial contracts and wills drawn up by common-law lawyers often include definitions. Even if English and American guides on legal drafting lay stress on problems caused by over-use of definitions, it is difficult to break with tradition. To quote from the definitions section of a typical Anglo-American will:[12]

ARTICLE ONE
DEFINITIONS

"Beneficiary" means the recipient of a bequest made by this Will.

"Bequest" means a gift made by this Will.

"My children" means my daughter REBECCA SUSAN WEISS ("REBECCA"), born January 24, 1987; my son CHRISTOPHER MICHAEL WEISS, JR. ("CHRIS"), born June 5, 1990; my stepson WILLIAM PAUL WEISS, whether or not later adopted by me, and any other children born to or adopted by me after I execute this Will.

"Per stirpes" means "by stocks," referring to a method of dividing shares of a bequest, according to which if a beneficiary does not survive the testator, that beneficiary's children share equally the bequest to that beneficiary.

"Testator" means a person who makes a Will.

ARTICLE TWO
BEQUESTS

A. Real Property

(...)

B. Primary Bequest of Personal Property

"Personal property" includes all of my clothing, jewelry, household goods and furnishings, automobiles, and all other similar property. "Personal property" does not include my paintings or my books. (...)

1.3.4 Problems of Legal Definitions Detailed definitions give the impression that legal language is entirely accurate and without ambiguity. This is not the case. Legal vocabulary is full of words with multiple meanings, while no amount of detailed definition can avoid all cases of ambiguity. Indeed, the likelihood of ambiguity increases with more detailed definition: it is necessarily complicated as to its structure and it is attractive to consider it complete, in spite of the possibility of gaps. In

---

11 Marburger 1984: 279.

12 Child 1992: 246–247.

consequence, the result may be quite the opposite of what was intended. Moreover, legislative definitions possess particular features that cause additional problems. This partly involves knowing to what extent a legislative definition is conditional on the law in question still remaining in force in unchanged form. Further, it often occurs that the concept expressed by the definition may have been essentially broadened or narrowed by case law or by legal science. In these cases, the genuine full definition is not evident from the law in question.[13]

1.4 Enumerations

Apart from definitions in the strict sense, enumerative lists are typical of legal language. Here is the beginning of Article R551-2 of the French Woodlands Code (*Code forestier*):[14]

> *Au sens du présent titre, on entend par: Matériels de base, générateurs des matériels forestiers de reproduction; - les peuplements, notamment les vergers à graines, pour les matériels de reproduction générative; - les clones et les mélanges de clones en proportions spécifiées pour les matériels de multiplication végétative; Matériels forestiers de reproduction: - les semences: cônes, infrutescences, fruits et graines, destinés à la production de plantes par voie générative; - les parties de plantes: boutures, marcottes, racines et greffons destinés à la production de plantes par voie végétative, à l'exclusion des plançons; - les plants: plantes élevées au moyen de semences ou de parties de plantes, plançons et semis naturels. Matériels de reproduction sélectionnés dénommés ci-après matériels sélectionnés: les matériels issus de matériels de base admis conformément à l'article R. 552-1, ou pour les matériels admis dans les autres pays membres, aux exigences définies à l'annexe I de la directive susmentionnée du conseil des communautés européennes; (...).[15]*

Within the meaning of this title, the following definitions apply:
Basic materials generating woodland reproduction materials:
- stocking, in particular seed orchards for generative reproduction materials ;
- clones, and mixtures of clones in proportions specified for vegetative reproduction materials ;
Woodland reproduction materials:
- seeds: cones, infrutescences, fruits and seeds intended for the production of plants by generative means ;
- plant parts: cuttings, roots and grafts seeds intended for the production of plants by vegetative means, other than shoots and saplings ;
- seedlings: plants raised by means of seeds or plant parts, natural shoots saplings and seedlings.
Selected reproduction materials (hereinafter called "selected materials"): materials resulting from permitted basic materials in accordance with Article R. 552-1, or (for

---

13 Sandrini 1996: 54.
14 Decree no. 79-812 of 19 September 1979, Art. 9, *Journal Officiel* of 22 September 1979.
15 Source: Légifrance.

materials permitted in other Member States) with the requirements set out in Appendix I
of the above-mentioned directive of the Council of the European Communities: (…)

Enumerative lists often raise the problem of knowing if they are exhaustive or
merely explanatory, that is, if only examples are involved. At times, this problem
is difficult to resolve. For that reason, English and American lawyers in particular
make themselves explicitly clear on the subject when drawing up contracts.[16]

2 Information (Over)load

In a modern, highly complex society, the number of legal rules is enormous. To
speak of a flood of legal rules aptly sums up the situation. To help stem the tide, legal
language should be as concise as possible, to avoid laws and regulations that would
otherwise be over-long and unclear. At the same time, legal language should avoid
over-abstraction, in that way enabling decoding with minimum effort.

Harmonising these goals is not easy. The key is to know for whom laws are
written: experts or citizens? Even laws concerning fundamental questions of
citizens' lives are often written for experts because it is experts who are charged
with their technical application. Examples include matters of social and fiscal law. In
these matters, laws are necessarily highly complex: this is a question of distributive
justice, which presupposes highly detailed rules. These rules might even express in
language form a mathematical formula relating to the calculation of some welfare
allowance or a tax to be paid. This means that social and fiscal laws should be written
very compactly, with as high a density of information as possible, to prevent their
becoming over-long.

The legislator does not suppose that laws of a technical character are understandable
from the standpoint of the general public. As we have seen, the principles of these
laws are communicated to citizens by means of short-form bulletins, leaving out the
details.

It is easy to understand that the problem caused by the great density of information of legal language concerns not only legislative language. In many civil-law
countries, like France or Finland, the language of judgments is traditionally loaded
with messages: it is compact and full of expressions that have the appearance of
abridged codes. Today, following criticisms from linguists, judgments in some
countries, e.g. Finland, are written in a language closer to ordinary language.
However, some Finnish lawyers have commented that this means, on the one hand,
that judgments have become too long, and on the other hand, that their internal logic
is weakened: a judgment formulated in ordinary language contains more secondary
– even meaningless – elements, impeding transmission of the legal message, than a
traditional compact judgment.

---

16 See pp. 237–238.

3 Universality and Aloofness

3.1 Abstraction and Hypothetical Character

Modern law regulates ordinary features of complex and highly varied facts and events. For this reason, judicial language often contains semantically open expressions, in spite of the problems that result from the standpoint of the accuracy of such language. This above all concerns general clauses (e.g., good faith, good practice). Likewise, modern law has an abstract character. In the final analysis, it regulates entities that are mere mental creations: rights and duties. That is clearly visible at the level of legal language: only 5–8% of verbal substantives in Swedish legislation refer to entities that exist in time and space.[17]

It also has to be stressed that the law is based on experience drawn from the real world but that it regulates hypothetical future cases. In consequence, the timespan linked to legal rules is often characterised by a certain universality, impossible to see from the chronological standpoint. The expression used by one French author is "timelessness of law" (*intemporalité de la loi*).[18] This is evident, for example, in the use of verbs in legislative language. The conditional is common, while the present tense dominates. The word *if* is also especially frequent in legal language. In Norway, for example, it was established that the conjunction *hvis* ['if', 'when'] was placed 27 on the list of frequency of legislative language; as to ordinary language, the corresponding placing was 123.[19]

Law becomes reality in decisions by the authorities and in private documents. Given that this is about making the law real, the language of these decisions and documents has less of an abstract character than that of legislation. However, the language of private documents possesses certain features similar to those of laws. This is explained by the fact that the parties have to prepare for possible change of circumstances, that is, to some extent the clauses have to allow for hypothetical situations.

3.2 Impersonality and Objectivisation

The frequent use of the passive is characteristic of legal language. This brings the object of the action into the foreground, giving the actor only a secondary role. This feature is clear to see in all specialist languages, but is a particular highlight in legal matters.[20] In this way, authors of legal texts underline the objectivity of their findings and conclusions.

Even in cases where actors are in the foreground, individuals are, especially in civil-law countries, pushed into the background by personification of authorities

---

17 Nordman 1984: 960.
18 Gémar 1990: 724.
19 Bing 1980: 48–49.
20 Nordman 1984: 961.

and corporations: *the ministry orders* (...), *the court finds* (...). Further, the actors do not often appear, in Continental legal documents, under their private names but are called by their titles or functions in the activities concerned: *director, president, referendary*... It is notable that, apart from the authorities, private persons are named according to their roles: *applicant, appellant, defendant*... For this reason, the language of the authorities is often felt to be formal, distant, even abrupt.

> The same features are visible in the language of legal scholars, although less obviously so. Here too, differences exist between the various legal cultures. French and German authors do not address the reader in discussion. By contrast, the works of English lawyers often contain rhetorical questions presented to the reader: *How will you find ...?, How will you discover ...?*.[21]

Objectivisation appears particularly clearly in the language of advocates. These seek to lend their arguments an appearance of objectivity, to make them credible and convincing. For example, an advocate writes: "It appears that Article 27 of the law on judicial records should be interpreted so that (...)." but not "It seems to me that Article 27 (...)." Here, objectivising the assertion operates as a rhetorical tool.

3.3 Neutrality

In the chapter on functions of legal language, we saw that at one time the intention was to impress readers or listeners by a legal text, notably by stressing the sacred character of the law and by using magical rhythm. Some features still exist: the language of oaths or the Constitution, the rituals of justice...

However, *grosso modo*, legal language today tends to be official and formal. The style of this language is as neutral as possible because the main intention is to have an effect on the understanding, rather than the feelings, of the reader or listener. This is why one author says that the style of legal language is "cold": it rejects all that is affective and does not include emotional elements. This is why legal texts contain practically no exclamation or question marks. Nor should legal language give rise to irrelevant associations that distract the attention of the reader of the document or discourse in question. The neutrality of legal language is largely guaranteed by the fact that many legal texts (e.g., laws, administrative instructions, on the Continent also judgments) pass through the offices of several commentators and stylists before receiving their final form: they are not from a single hand. N. A. Vlasenko says pertinently that legal language is characterised by its "zero style", *nulevoi stil'* (нулевой стиль).[22] However, this is not the case in all contexts where legal language is used. For example, advocates' closing speeches are often affective.

The sobriety of legal language is clearly visible in legislative texts. Neverthless, exceptions can be found in the preambles to laws, whose style at times is full of pathos and emotion. To take a Russian example: the draft bill on outlawing fascist

---

21 Ballansat-Aebi 2001: 6–7.
22 Vlasenko 1997: 19.

propaganda in the Russian Federation (1996). The preamble to this law declares that "the peoples of our country played a crucial role in wiping out fascism and saving humanity, under threat from fascist slavery and genocide." One Russian author concludes that a text of this type belongs more to the journalistic genre than the legislative.[23]

As already shown in the chapter on functions of legal language,[24] the neutrality of this language has a particularly important aspect: the designations of legal institutions and phenomena. The legislator discards expressions that might be felt to be insulting. Though some issues are undoubtedly volatile, legal language still strives to deal with these neutrally. A word that in ordinary language has clear affective weight, sometimes in legal language has an absolutely neutral technical meaning – which can appear almost grotesque to the layman's eye. A good example is the German term *erfolgreicher Mord*,[25] which literally means "successful murder / killing". This term is certainly bizarre, given that the word *erfolgreich* (successful) normally refers to something highly positive.

The rigorousness of the requirement for linguistic neutrality varies according to the general culture and traditions of the country in question. In Finland, for example, it is self-evident that a judge should express himself in an absolutely calm and composed way. On this topic, it appears that Anglo-American judges enjoy a far greater freedom. An illustration of this is the dissenting opinion of judge Musmanno, of the Pennsylvania Supreme Court, in the case relating to Henry Miller's work, "Tropic of Cancer":[26]

> *"Cancer" is not a book. It is a cesspool, an open sewer, a pit of putrification, a slimy gathering of all that is rotten in the debris of human depravity. And in the center of all this waste and stench, besmearing himself with its foulest defilement, splashes, leaps, cavorts and wallows a bifurcated specimen that responds to the name of Henry Miller.... From Pittsburgh to Philadelphia, from Dan to Beersheba, and from the Ramparts of the Bible to Samuel Eliot Morison's Oxford History of the American People, I dissent.*

3.4 Metaphors

Modern legal language is neutral. In contrast to medieval times, it is no longer figurative. Only a few modest traces remain of the colourful legal language of yesteryear, mostly in the form of legal maxims. In modern legal language, metaphors in particular are rare.

Nevertheless, some exceptions exist to this absence of imagery. First of all, metaphors are common enough in solemn speeches on the notion of law, its fundamental principles, and so on. Metaphors such as "landscape of legal culture"

---

23 Vlasenko 1997: 20.
24 See pp. 42–43.
25 Oksaar 1989: 223–224.
26 Tiersma 1999: 140–141.

recur.[27] This is also true of polemic legal debate. For example, at the end of the 19th century, Rudolf von Jhering (1818–1892), a strong critic of the school of *Begriffsjurisprudenz*,[28] wrote a satire entitled *Im juristischen Begriffshimmel. Ein Phantasiebild* (1884). As the title of the satire shows, he speaks of the "heaven of concepts".[29]

Secondly, some legal terms in the strict sense, even fundamental, originate from metaphors. The reason is simple: a metaphor is a highly useful linguistic means in cases involving something brand new that has yet to be named. It brings out features analogical to the new and the old. Thanks to a metaphor, it is possible to describe the functions and structure of a phenomenon, without defining it in detail.[30] This, then, enables expression of a process or state of affairs without inventing a new term, which always requires a 'running in' period. Take the term *virus* in the world of computers. This word pertinently expresses the essential features of a harmful programme: contagion without capability of immediate detection, dangerous for the host computer, and so on.

As examples of metaphors in legal language, take *burden of proof*, which designates the "requirement that the claimant establish (if these are contested) the facts on which the success of his claim depends".[31] This image comes from Roman lawyers (*onus probandi* – *onus* meaning literally 'burden') and it appears as direct calques all over Europe, e.g.: βάρος της απόδειξης (*város tis apódeixis*, Greek), *onere della prova* (Italian), *carga de la prueba* (Spanish), *charge de (la) preuve* (French), *Beweislast* (German), бремя доказывания (*bremia dokazyvaniia*, Russian), *ciężar dowodu* (Polish), *bevisbörda* (Swedish), *todistustaakka* (Finnish). The list of metaphorical terms could with great ease be lengthened, e.g.: *source of Law*,[32] *ruling estate* (Lat. *praedium dominans*). As to legal argumentation, metaphors are also common. For example, Italian authors often use images that express combat (e.g., *difesa, combattimento*) or the process of thought (e.g., *il percorso argomentativo seguito, itinerario di recostruzione*).[33]

Metaphors appealing to the sentiments of readers or listeners are especially popular amongst advocates. Throughout Europe, the terms *lion's (leonine) partnership* (Lat. *societas leonina*) and *lion's share* (Lat. *pars leonina*) are classic examples that go back to Aesop's fables. Advocates in the Romance countries use these images fairly often. At one time, this was also true of the Nordic countries. Take Matthias Calonius, the classical author of Finno-Swedish legal science at the turn of the 19th century, who was still writing in Latin: *Neque jure naturali subsistit conventio sic inita, ut alter omne lucrum alter omne damnum ferat, aut ut quis majorem quam*

27　Hallberg 2001: 17.
28　See pp. 170–171.
29　Jhering 1904: 245–333.
30　Oksaar 1989: 221.
31　Cornu 2004.
32　See p. 148.
33　Veronesi 2000: 374 and 376.

pro modo bonorum collatorum vel lucri vel damni partem percipiat. Dicitur talis societas leonina, ex notissima fabula Aesopica apud Phaedrum Lib. 1 fab. 5.[34] This translates as: 'Natural law does not accept a contract according to which one party obtains all profit and the other party bears all loss, or according to which there accrues to one party a greater part of the profit or loss than that corresponding to their input into the company. Such a company is termed a lion's partnership after the famous fable by Aesop reproduced by Phaedrus (book 1, fable 5).' Today, Finnish lawyers no longer employ the image of a lion's partnership: they speak, without fantasy, of the "inequitable share".

4 Systemic Character

4.1 Interrelationship of Different Elements of the Law

The legal order has a systemic character: each element of the order forms part of a greater whole. An article (section) forms part of a law, and a law forms part of legislation. In civil-law countries, precedents complement legislation; in common-law countries they are of fundamental importance. Legal science should not be forgotten either. The result of this should be that each element is in harmony with the entirety of the legal order.

The systemic character of the legal order is highlighted when a new law is adopted or an old one is reformed. This is normally reflected in a great number of laws and regulations that include articles (sections) in direct contradiction or otherwise in discord with a new or reformed law. The dispositions of those other laws and regulations need to be modified. Let us take as an example the Swiss federal law on aid to victims of offences, of 4 October 1991. The appendix relating to amendment of federal laws reads as follows (in French and English; in the original publication, the articles are printed one below the other):

1. Le code pénal suisse est modifié comme suit : Art. 37, ch. 1, 1er al., Art. 60

2. La loi fédérale sur la procédure pénale est modifiée comme suit:

Titre précédant l'article 74, Art. 88bis, Art. 106, al. 1bis, Art. 115, 1er al., Art. 120, Art. 137, 1er al., troisième phrase, et 175, 3e al. abrogés, Art. 210, Art. 221 al. 1 et 1bis, Art. 228, 2e, 3e al., Art. 228, 4e al. abrogé, Art 231, 1er al., Art. 238, 2e al., Art. 270, 1er al., Art 270, 3e et 4e al., Art. 278, 3e al.,

3. Le Code pénal militaire est modifié comme suit: Art. 42a

4. La procédure pénale militaire est modifiée comme suit: Titre précédant l'article 74, Art. 84a, Art. 112, Art. 113, Art. 114, 1er al., Art. 118, Art. 119, 2e al., let. D, Art. 122, 1er al., Art. 154, 2e al., Art. 163, Art. 164, 1er, 4e et 5e al., Art. 173 al. 1bis, Art. 174, 2e al., Art. 175,

---

34 Calonius 1908: 514.

2ᵉ al., Art. 179, titre médian et 1ᵉʳ al., Art. 181, 2ᵉ al., Art. 183 al. 2 et 2ᵇⁱˢ, Art. 186, al. 1ᵇⁱˢ, Art. 193, Art. 196, Art. 199, Art. 202, let. d.

Translation (by the translator of the present work):

1. The Swiss Criminal Code is amended as follows: Art. 37, Ch. 1, 1ˢᵗ paragraph, Art. 60

2. The Federal Criminal Procedure Law is amended as follows: Title preceding Article 74, Art. 88ᵃ, Art. 106, paragraph 1ᵃ, Art. 115, 1ˢᵗ paragraph, Art. 120, Art. 137, 1ˢᵗ paragraph, third sentence, and 175, 3ʳᵈ paragraph repealed, Art. 210, Art. 221 paragraph 1 and 1ᵃ, Art. 228, 2ⁿᵈ, 3ʳᵈ paragraph, Art. 228, 4ᵗʰ paragraph repealed, Art 231, 1ˢᵗ paragraph, Art. 238, 2ⁿᵈ paragraph, Art. 270, 1ˢᵗ paragraph, Art 270, 3ʳᵈ and 4ᵗʰ paragraph, Art. 278, 3ʳᵈ paragraph,

3. The Military Criminal Code is amended as follows: Art. 42a

4. The Military Criminal Procedure is amended as follows: Title preceding Article 74, Art. 84a, Art. 112, Art. 113, Art. 114, 1ˢᵗ paragraph, Art. 118, Art. 119, 2ⁿᵈ paragraph, note D, Art. 122, 1ˢᵗ paragraph, Art. 154, 2ⁿᵈ paragraph, Art. 163, Art. 164, 1ˢᵗ, 4ᵗʰ and 5ᵗʰ paragraph, Art. 173 paragraph 1ᵃ, Art. 174, 2ⁿᵈ paragraph, Art. 175, 2ⁿᵈ paragraph, Art. 179, subtitle and 1ˢᵗ paragraph, Art. 181, 2ⁿᵈ paragraph, Art. 183 paragraph 2 and 2ᵃ, Art. 186, paragraph 1ᵃ, Art. 193, Art. 196, Art. 199, Art. 202, note d.

At the technical level, the systemic character of the legal order appears more clearly by the fact that the components of the order are linked to one another by references. Even the fundamental notion of references presupposes a dependent relationship; this involves intertextuality. Given that law relies on authorities (e.g., the legislator, the courts), a legal text always has a dependent relationship with other texts. According to the traditions of the legal culture in question, an article (section) of the law refers to other articles of the same law or to other legislative texts, a judicial decision refers to laws and – in civil-law countries – to *travaux préparatoires* (and, as in Germany, to academic legal writing), a legal textbook or treatise refers to laws, *travaux préparatoires* and other textbooks and treatises, and so on. These references can thus be characterised as horizontal (between two laws, for example) or as vertical (from a decree to a law, from a judicial decision to a decree, for example).

The frequency of references is largely influenced by ideological factors and by the traditions of the legal culture involved. For example, in the German-speaking linguistic zone the Swiss and German Civil Codes differ considerably from one another. The German Code is a codification intended for use by professional judges, aiming to give the answer to every legal problem that might appear. For that reason, it contains a very large number of references. By contrast, the Swiss Civil Code is intended for all citizens. In consequence, it includes somewhat few references. As to common law countries, typically their judges as well as their university authors refer above all to precedents and less to other sources of law. This is explained by the original doctrine of sources of law in these countries.

In the same way, the frequency of references varies in all countries according to branches of the law. When a highly technical branch is involved, many references are used. This is notably the case for, e.g., land law, water rights, finance, and welfare.

4.2 Functions of Referencing

According to analysis by Nicolas Molfessis, references perform several functions:[35]

1. In reinforcing the systemic idea of the legal order, references are appropriate for eliminating internal contradictions in that order. If the content of a legal rule is repeated in several articles (sections), the risk increases of changing the content: the rule is often repeated with some small change in external form, which can cause differing interpretations.
2. References show the wider contexts to which the different elements of the legal order belong. Therefore, references have an informative and mnemotechnical function. A reference shows that another legal text exists that links to the issue involved. At one time, this was particularly important, given the absence of regular bulletins of laws (and decrees) and legislative compilations. However, the modern reader should also be able to identify the relevant legislative texts in each case since the number of laws and regulations is immense. Sometimes, a reference also shows the priority of the text in question in relation to other texts.
3. Since references eliminate repetitions, the text becomes lighter and more economical as to space required. A text of general character may refer to often complex rules of exception or to rules that are more precise. For example, a parliamentary law refers to certain rules that are included in a decree.

4.3 Problems of Referencing

Use of references causes serious problems.[36] First of all, references can lead, even initially, to several interpretations. They can also become ambiguous following changes to the texts to which they refer. Does the legislator presuppose that the reference will still be valid in relation to the amended text? Occasionally, one can come up against the problem of void references: the reference indicates a repealed legislative text or one still at the preparatory stage (for example, to a later decree relative to the entry into force of the law in question) that is never promulgated.

Secondly, too many references make a text difficult to understand, thus potentially causing mistakes and misunderstandings. A legal text becomes a non-linear "hypertext", weighed down with a large number of references and making the reader lose the thread of the document. Such a text saves space but is heavy from the

---

35 Molfessis 1999: 55–68.
36 Molfessis 1999: 69–72.

reader's standpoint. To take an example, also earlier cited, from German legislation on firearms:

(Ordnungswidrig handelt) wer entgegen § 4 Abs. 2, § 26 Abs. 1, § 27, § 28 Abs. 1 o. 2, § 28a Abs. 1 o. 2, § 34 Abs. 2, § 38 Abs. 1 o. 2 oder § 42 Abs 2, 3 o. 4 eine Anzeige nicht, nicht richtig, nicht vollständig oder nicht rechtzeitig erstattet oder entgegen § 26 Abs. 2, § 34 Abs. 2, § 38 Abs. 2 oder § 42 Abs. 3 o. 4 die vorgeschriebenen Unterlagen nicht beifügt." (§ 43 Ziffer 5 der VO zum Waffengesetz von 1976).

A person who fails to make a declaration, or who does not make it in a correct or complete manner, or in due time, contrary to paragraph 2 of Art. 4, paragraph 1 of Art. 26, Art. 27, paragraph 1 or 2 of Art. 28, paragraph 1 or 2 of Art. 28a, paragraph 2 of Art. 34, paragraph 1 or 2 of Art. 38 or paragraph 2, 3 or 4 of Art. 42, or who fails to attach the items prescribed by law to the declaration, contrary to paragraph 2 of Art. 26, paragraph 2 of Art. 34, paragraph 2 of Art. 38 or paragraph 3 or 4 of Art. 42, contravenes the law (decree implementing law on firearms, Art. 43, p. 4). (Author's translation).

It should also be recalled that the text to which the particular reference refers may not be easily available. For example, the text may not have been included in the same legislative compilation since this involves special legislation. In the same way, a reference to a rare treatise or textbook, to provide grounds for an interpretation, requires considerable effort on the part of the reader who wants to ascertain the value of the reference. In the matter of criminal law, a particular problem exists: if penal legislation refers to texts beyond the scope of criminal laws as to description of elements constituting the offences in question, some specialists consider that the principle of legality is under threat.

So, it is not surprising that lawyer-linguists underline the problems caused by over-use of references. These should not be used where the legal order risks becoming less transparent as a result. Conditional references should also be avoided. When used at all, their object and content should be specified with enough accuracy.[37]

4.4 Logical and Consistent Use of Terms

Apart from references, the systemic character of the legal order appears in terms: lawyers aim to use these as logically and consistently as possible in all legal contexts. Naturally, this is not always possible, but linguistic cohesion is the aim of the exercise. In different laws, the same terms obtain the same content as far as possible.

---

37 Molfessis 1999: 72.

5 Structure and Formalism in Legal Texts

5.1 Logical Disposition of Legal Texts

The structure of legal texts is carefully elaborated. Amongst other things, logical disposition of these texts helps to place legal information in a hierarchy. A legal text moves from the abstract to the concrete, from the substantive to the procedural. The structure of the text should be consistent: the principal items are presented before secondary items, and general rules before special conditions and exceptions. Often, the formal disposition of a text imitates the logical progression of legal discourse. The structured character of legal texts forms part of their formalism. However, it should be noted that this formalism goes beyond the organisation of the structure of the text: it involves fixed formulas at the level of sentences and phrases. Legal texts contain many ready-made sentences and petrified phrases.

In the following paragraphs, we start by very briefly examining the structure of legislative texts. We then go on to examine in greater detail the formalistic character of judgments and private documents. The reason for so doing is that problems relating to the structure of legal text are manifest more clearly in laws (and in regulations). Because of the size of legislative texts, a code may include thousands of articles. By contrast, formalism extending down to details appears above all in judgments (notably in civil-law countries), in administrative decisions, and in private documents, in which practically the same text is repeated, sometimes almost interminably. However, we should highlight that judgments, administrative decisions, and private documents are also structured, and that laws contain largely formalistic sections (e.g., declarations of promulgation, entry into force).

5.2 Structure of Legislative Texts

Laws and regulations are divided into smaller wholes, in a logical order (e.g., abstract – concrete, substantive – procedural). It speaks for itself that details vary according to legal cultures and according to content. When it comes to particularly comprehensive laws (i.e., codes), the division of the text can be fairly complicated. Take the Brazilian Civil Code (*Código civil*). This code contains a division into eight or even nine gradations: part, book, title, chapter, section, article, paragraph, sub-paragraph, and/or indent (*parte, livro, título, capítulo, seção, artigo, parágrafo, inciso*, and/or *alínea*).[38] Beyond the titles of different gradations, the detailed division of a legislative text presupposes consistent numbering, in order to cite a particular element of the text (e.g., chapter, article, indent). The logic of numeration is not always the same. Each sub-unit of a legislative text can start with article number 1. The numbering can also run without interruption throughout the entire law. To overcome the problem of frequent reforms, the numbering of important laws, such as codes, may be

---

38 Xavier 2001: 139.

decimal: a series of numbers, separated from one another by decimal points, shows the systematic position of the particular article in the overall code. This system of numbering was also adopted in France during recent work on codification.[39]

Codification of the law has advantages from the standpoint of legal language. The logical structure of a code informs the reader about hierarchies of legal concepts as well as about the terms expressing those concepts. Thanks to such a structure, it is easy for a lawyer or translator to find in a code the terms they are looking for and to establish the contexts in which these terms are used. Further, the structure of a code is reflected in the interpretation of its terms: the position of an article influences the content of terms employed within it.

In countries lacking major codifications, laws and regulations are often systematised in semi-official or private compilations, to facilitate the application of legislation. One example is Finland, where a large, two-volume compilation of legislation is regularly published in two languages, Finnish and Swedish.[40] The structure of these compilations may vary within the same country and may easily change over time. One should therefore be cautious in drawing any conclusions on the field of usage of terms, by virtue of the construction of these compilations.

5.3 Model Forms of Judgments and Private Documents

5.3.1 Factors Contributing to Formalism in Legal Language It is characteristic of the language used in institutional contexts that it is adapted to formulas defined in advance more often than in ordinary language. This is illustrated by a recent Finnish survey, where over half of civil servants stated that they follow models of texts drafted in advance in their written work – "somewhat freely" it is true.[41] In extreme cases, a model form provides an absolute paragon for an oral or written text. Notably in civil-law countries, such cases are to be found in judicial language, but also in private documents. This is a striking analogy with the language of religious cults.

In archaic law, formalism was heightened by the magical functions of the law.[42] With the help of language rituals, the Most High was invited to the judicial process and His will could be interpreted. The idea of magical repetition is still reflected today in the formulas of the oath. On the other hand, repetition underlines the authority of judges or civil servants. In consequence, this technique is used in formulas of judgments and administrative decisions, as in Spain for example:[43] *debemos condenar y condenamos* ['we should and do condemn'], *pronunciamos, mandamos y firmamos* ['we declare, order and sign'], *vengo en proponer y propongo*

---

39 Rémy 1994: 178–179.
40 Mattila 2002c: 160.
41 Heikkinen & *al.* 2000: 276.
42 See pp. 47–49.
43 Martín 1996: 49.

['I undertake to propose and do propose'], *visto y examinado* ['seen and examined'].
In Anglo-American documents, the rituals of repetition are especially frequent.[44]

> Clearly, the use of binary formulas also has other functions in legal language. These
> formulas highlight hierarchies and conceptual opposites, and they guarantee the
> understandability of synonyms.

After the archaic period of the law, other factors promoted and maintained the
formal character of legal language. Above all, the development of written law should
be taken into account. The written form guaranteed the stability of the law to a far
greater extent than the oral form. At the same time, this first form was suited to
petrifying the law and making legal language more formalistic. One factor heightened
formalism still further: printing enabled, amongst other things, efficient distribution
of collections of model texts.

5.3.2 Functions of Model Forms in Legal Language As we have just noted, the
formalism of legal language had its roots in a magical function but it also stabilised
the content of the law. In part, it is the natural need of human beings to maintain
rituals that explains the formalism of legal language. This concerns one means of
struggling against the inevitable passage of time and of safeguarding the familiar
and certain. This is why model legal forms bear with them many already antiquated
elements. This especially applies to the heavy structure of the text and archaic
expressions that only specialists can decode.

Today, model legal forms are no longer rhythmic, or even laconic. Under
these conditions, formalism often means a stereotypical and monotonous kind of
language. For example, in administrative language the same words and expressions
appear over and over again. One might thus be led to imagine that the formalism of
legal and administrative language is no more than a negative fact. Nevertheless, the
formalistic character of this language is understandable for quite rational reasons.
The standardisation of structuring of legal texts and expressions in the language of
the law has several important advantages.

Firstly, as we concluded when dealing with the functions of legal language,
legal protection and certainty of procedures require repetitive models of action
in the application of the law. In general, standardised words and phrases have an
established interpretation. This avoids disputes as to the content of a particular
document. The importance of this conclusion is heightened by the intertextual
character of legal language and by the fact that legal reasoning is largely based on
the authority value of sources used.[45] Often, legislative texts are cited as such, in
judgments, in administrative decisions, and in private documents. An exact citation
allows the draftsman of the text to avoid assertions that he is incorrectly interpreting
the law. In the same way, the draftsman avoids the fatigue resulting from elaborating
an original text. This explains why important articles from laws can appear literally,

---

44 See pp. 233–234.
45 Aarnio 1987.

word for word, in the grounds of judgments. By analogy, a lawyer copies *mutatis mutandis* a ready-to-use form from a collection of model documents at his disposal or from a contract that he has himself previously drafted.[46]

Secondly, an established model ensures that the legal act in question is performed in the form required by law. This is particularly important in countries such as Finland, where important documents can be signed without any contribution from a notary or a lawyer. For example, when a Finnish testator uses a printed form of will from a collection, the formal requirements of Finnish law will automatically be fulfilled: e.g., written form, testator's signature, signature of two witnesses.

Thirdly, use of a model form signifies that the document is structured and arranged at both paragraph and sentence level. A model form arranges and composes the text of a document clearly and systematically. The importance of this goes beyond mere construction of the text: it operates as a model down to the fine detail of the text and influences the use of particular words. A model form standardises the use of words and prevents the document from becoming over-long. It also serves the goal of economy of legal language. That, in turn, is linked to saving time: self-drafting a judgment or a contract would take a great amount of time and would require vast knowledge. Nor should we forget the advantages from the standpoint of data management. When documents are drawn up on the basis of detailed models, it is easier to archive them and retrieve them by computerised means.

5.3.3 Domain of Use of Legal Forms Legal forms may be more or less fixed or flexible. Often, they are used in performative language acts, but they also appear in other contexts. Characteristically, a form only appears as an invariable unit within the genre of the text in question. Model forms are linguistic petrifications, whether used as a whole or subject to minor variations. The syntax of legal forms often has archaic features. For example, the operative part of some Danish judgments still includes the following sentence: *sagsøgte bør for sagsøgers påstand fri at være* ['the defendant is acquitted of the plaintiff's claim']. According to the normal word order, the end of this sentence would be: *bør være fri*.[47]

At times, a document is almost wholly dictated by formula. In other cases, formalism only concerns certain expressions. This notably involves opening and closing phrases in documents, as well as expressions that signal that a new section of the text begins from that point. Examples from France include the expressions *considérant que* ['whereas'], *attendu que* ['whereas'], *par ces motifs* ['on these grounds'], amongst others. These also serve as signs of transition marking the start of a new section of the text. This technique is also used elsewhere – for example, in Denmark all judgments contain the archaic expression *thi kendes for ret* ['it is therefore considered just']. This expression solemnly informs the reader that the text continues as the operative part of the judgment.

---

46 Charrow & *al*. 1982: 187.
47 Kjær 1997: 159–160.

5.3.4 Forms of Judgment Traditionally, significant differences exist between the great legal cultures as to style of judgments.[48] Above all, this appears in the judgments of higher courts, which *de jure* or *de facto* are of value as precedent.

In judgments of common law courts, the judges as individuals are clearly visible: their grounds are full and detailed, their language often colourful. This is also true of dissenting opinions that form part of these judgments. The position taken by the court is expressed by the "we" form, and that of the judges as individuals by the "I" form. A judge may even openly admit to having made an error. This is well illustrated by the opening to the speech of Lord Steyn in a recent case (*Morgans v Director of Public Prosecutions*):[49]

> *My Lords, in giving the judgment of the Court of Appeal (Criminal Division) in R v Effik (1992) 95 Cr App R 427 I gave a restrictive interpretation to s 9 of the Interception of Communications Act 1985, by holding that it contains no provision making clear that any evidence obtained as a result of an interception will be inadmissible. Eight years later, aided by the incisive arguments of counsel in the present case, I have had the opportunity to re-examine the point. I am now fully persuaded that my earlier interpretation was wrong. And I agree with the speech of Lord Hope of Craighead. But it is appropriate, if only for the historical record, that I explain shortly the reasons for my conversion.(...).*

In Germany, grounds of a judgment are widely based on positions taken by legal science; these grounds regularly cite books and articles by academic lawyers. German judges write their grounds as scientific essays, which allows a dialogue with legal science. The scientific essay quality of judgments appears in the form of frequent references to legal scholars. For example, the grounds of a recent judgment concerning the barring of a debt included – according to my calculations – 24 references to academic legal writing.[50]

In France, on the other hand, judgments are condensed into a fixed formula in which the grounds are somewhat succinct and formal. They contain no dissenting opinions. A French judgment consists of a single sentence (*jugement à phrase unique*) structured by "key-words". They vary somewhat between courts. To express grounds, these key-words are *attendu que* in the Court of Cassation (*Cour de cassation*), i.e. the Supreme Court, and general courts of first instance (*tribunaux de grande instance*), while administrative courts and certain courts of appeal use the expression *considérant que*. Legal provisions referred to are preceded by the word *vu,* and the operative part of the judgment always begins with the words PAR CES MOTIFS (written in block capitals).

In 1977, a new style of drawing judgments was put into practice. With this style, the facts, the development of the proceedings, and the claims of the parties are presented in discursive form. Only the grounds and the operative part of the

---

48 Goutal 1976: 43–72, Lashöfer 1992: 109–110, 127–129, and Ballansat-Aebi 2000, s. 713–736.

49 *The All England Law Reports* 2000/2: 526–527.

50 *Entscheidungen des Bundesgerichtshofes in Zivilsachen* 142/2000, no. 4.

judgments are drawn up in a single sentence. Nevertheless, the new style has not found favour in all judicial circles. The courts of appeal are divided: some of them always formulate their judgments in a single sentence with the words *considérant* and *attendu*. Others draw up the whole text of the judgment in discursive form. Nor is the practice of the general courts of first instance more consistent.[51]

This comparison shows that judgments in France are drawn up much more formally than in Germany or the common law countries. Notably, the votes of judges of English and American higher courts are written individually, often highly personally. In spite of that, some classification exists as to the style of these votes.[52] Recent times have seen reductions in differences of style of judgments, at least up to a point. On this topic, we should not overlook the courts of the European Communities, where the different legal traditions of the countries of the Union mingle.[53] Further, divergences are smaller in routine cases decided by the lower courts: decisions delivered in these cases are everywhere formal. For example, in the common law countries – as elsewhere – decrees of divorce between consenting spouses are often written to a very simple formula. However, differences between the major legal cultures are still visible in the drawing up of judgments.

5.3.5 Model Forms in Private Documents   A thousand years ago, the notarial profession as an institution developed in Northern Italy, later spreading elsewhere in Europe. One of the main tasks of the notarial profession lay in drawing up private documents. For repeat cases, model forms were developed and established, partly in Latin, partly in the vernacular languages. This tradition is still in evidence in the Romance countries in the form of highly voluminous collections of legal forms, such as the *Juris-Classeur Notarial* in France. Analogically, heavy form books constitute part of the necessary equipment of a law firm in the United States. In recent times, electronic forms have replaced paper collections.

The language of these model forms of private documents is traditionally as complicated and embellished as that of judgments and other official documents. Some established expressions go back to very old times, while the solemnity of the forms is still clearly visible today. At one time, it was also typical of legal forms that their text would be composed and laid out in a manner that was far from clear. As for sentences, these were long: in extreme cases, they might cover several pages.

Certain characteristics of old forms of private documents are still present in English legal language. The particular features of common law have notably contributed to their survival.[54] For example, forms for wills are complicated, often running to several printed pages in length.[55] As to the ritual character of English legal language, the following declaration will illustrate:

---

51   Ballansat-Aebi 2000: 716–718.
52   Gémar 1995: 124.
53   Pescatore 2004: 255–256.
54   See pp. 232–236.
55   Child 1992: 246–247 and 271–272.

SIGNED, SEALED, PUBLISHED AND DECLARED by the above-named person as and for a Last Will and Testament, and we did, in his presence, hereunto subscribe our names as witnesses thereto.

In this declaration, it is above all the quadruple repetition (*sign, seal, publish and declare*) that attracts the reader's attention. It is therefore unsurprising that in the common law countries increasing attention has been paid to clarifying the forms of private documents. Traditional wills have notably been characterised as "warehouses of clutter", packed with babble such as synonyms and useless detail.[56] Indeed, an American lawyer, Thomas S. Word Jr., has proposed forms for drawing up a will in understandable language – the *plain-language will*. To illustrate this concept, let us compare the beginning of a traditional will with one drawn clearly and unequivocally:[57]

Original Will

I, John Quincy Doe, now residing in the city of Richmond, State of Virginia, being of sound mind and memory, do hereby make, publish and declare this to be my last will and testament, hereby revoking, annulling and canceling any and all wills and codicils heretofore made by me.

Revised Will

I, John Quincy Doe, of Richmond, Virginia, make this will, and revoke all earlier wills and codicils.

According to the author of the revised will, it would also be possible to eliminate the word *codicil* from this last form, given that revocation of previous wills logically means revocation of codicils (an analogous example can be found in Chapter 8, 3.2.2, p. 234).

By way of comparison, it is interesting to note that in Germany can be found forms for wills that are drawn up in simple, clear language, without over-solemn or archaic declarations. To take an example from an authoritative collection:[58]

Unser Testament

1. *Ich, ... (Name, Vorname, Anschrift) setze meine Ehefrau ... (Name, Vorname, Geburtsname, Anschrift) zur Hälfte*
   und unsere Kinder auf die andere Hälfte des Nachlasses ein.
2. *Ich, ... (Name, Vorname, Geburtsname, Anschrift) setze meinen Ehemann ... (Name, Vorname, Anschrift) zur Hälfte*
   und unsere Kinder auf die andere Hälfte des Nachlasses ein.

---

56 Child 1992: 260.
57 Child 1992: 261.
58 Wurm & al.1989: 1149.

Sämtliche zu unserem Haushalt gehörenden Gegenstände und die Hochzeitsgeschenke soll der überlebende Ehegatte als Vorausvermächtnis erhalten.

..... *den* ....

                                                                    (Unterschriften)

Translation:

Our Will

1. I, ... (surname, first name(s), address) appoint my wife ... (surname, first name(s), maiden name, address) as heir of half my heritable property, and our children as heirs of the other half of that property.
2. I, ... (surname, first name(s), maiden name, address) appoint my husband ... (surname, first name(s), address) as heir of half my heritable property, and our children as heirs of the other half of that property.

All our household objects and wedding presents shall devolve as a specific legacy to the survivor of us both.

..... date ....

                                                                    (signatures)

(Author's translation).

6 Frequency of Initialisations and Acronyms

Legal language uses many initialisations and other abbreviations. This results from the fact that lawyers rely ceaselessly on authoritative texts in their activities: for example, a court order or an assertion of an advocate is grounded by referring to a law or regulation, to a judicial decision, to a legal treatise, and so on. At the same time, legal language is rich in argumentation: assertions are grounded in detail. This means that the same sources (e.g., laws, judgments) are continually repeated in texts. It should also be borne in mind that the official title of a law, a publication, or an office can be long and complicated (for example: *Recueil de jurisprudence du droit administratif et du Conseil d'État*). In consequence, the use of initialisation (in the example: *RJDA*) as a solution considerably facilitates references to various texts. For these reasons, it is often opportune, even necessary, to use initialisations: they shorten sentences. This is space-saving, while sentence structure appears more easily to the reader.

However, the other side of the coin is clear: initialisations that are unfamiliar to the reader make the text more difficult to understand. At times, the message remains totally hidden. In spite of that, initialisation is widespread in academic legal writing in various countries. Documents – administrative, judicial, and private – also often contain initialisations. This is criticised by language and communication specialists.

In Russia in the 1990s, some specialists noted that frequent use of initialisations was typical of legal texts of the Soviet era. However, more recently the enthusiasm for using initialisations remains notably undiminished since Soviet times. These still abound in legal documents of different kinds.[59]

Use of legal initialisations is problematic for several reasons:

1. Often enough, use of initialisations is an end in itself in legal circles: a title is abridged even though it appears once, perhaps twice in a particular text.
2. Use of initialisations is unstable because they are only rarely ratified officially. Most often, they become established solely through practice.
3. Initialisations often have multiple meanings, in that the same initialisation may be used in several meanings. For example, in France the initialisation *AP* has seven meanings: *administration pénitentiaire, agent de probation, annales parlementaires, arrêté préfectoral, assemblée plénière, assistance publique, autorisation de programme* (prison administration, probation officer, parliamentary annals, prefectorial order, plenary assembly, social assistance, budget grant covering a number of years).[60]
4. It is not always easy to know what language lies behind an initialisation. Especially in the smaller linguistic zones, the initials of international institutions (NATO, WTO) can result from their titles in English, despite the fact that the complete (decoded) forms of these titles are normally expressed in national languages.
5. The manner of constructing initialisations is not uniform. Sometimes, the first letter of each word that appears in the title or in the designation is included in the initialisation, but often several words are omitted. In recent times, acronyms – initialisations pronounced as ordinary words – have become common in various countries. To enable pronunciation of acronyms, these include not only the first letters of the words concerned but often additional letters (vowels) within those words. This makes decoding of acronyms still more difficult.
6. It also has to be borne in mind that the culture of initialisations is not necessarily uniform amongst lawyers even from the same country. Many initialisations are only known by lawyers of a particular branch of the law, even from a particular court or government office. Often, in the old higher courts of different countries, each has its own culture of initialisations and abbreviations.
7. As for dictionaries of initialisations and abbreviations, the situation varies considerably from country to country. In some cases, voluminous dictionaries exist,[61] while in others (notably in smaller countries), there are only modest lists – or nothing at all. In addition to national dictionaries, the *World Dictionary of*

---

59 Vlasenko 1997: 126–127.
60 Gendrel 1980: 12.
61 e.g., Kirchner 1993.

Legal Abbreviations covers legal cultures speaking English, French, Italian, Portuguese, and Spanish.[62] Even so, some sections of this work remain somewhat incomplete, while German culture is notably excluded.

Recently, a dictionary of legal abbreviations has been compiled in Finland on the basis of a comprehensive frequency study. Since all the meanings of initialisations and other abbreviations given in this dictionary are followed by a frequency figure, it may contribute to the stabilisation of use of abbreviations in the country.[63]

Apart from initialisations, lawyers also use abbreviations of a different kind. Notably, and regularly, they shorten Latin words, e.g.: *ib.* or *ibid.* [= *ibidem*, 'in the same work', 'in the same passage']. A special type of abbreviation is formed by symbols. For example, in Finland the courts have traditionally expressed *versus* (in the caption of judgments) by the sign >. In the case of a counterclaim, the sign was ><.[64] In German-speaking countries and some others such as the Nordic countries, the most important legal symbol is § meaning 'article'. For example: *nach § 775 BGB* ['under article 775 of the Civil Code'].

7 Sentence Complexity and Diversity of Language Elements

In various sections of this book, we have touched on the fact that sentences in legal language are traditionally very long and complicated. This is largely due to force of tradition: legal language involves a language for special purposes of great antiquity whose stylistic elements often stem from Medieval Latin.[65] In the background stands, amongst other things, the old language of royal chancelleries and of the Latin notarial profession. As we shall see below, in recent years language specialists have been seeking to improve the quality of legal language, notably by proposing the shortening of over-long sentences. There are also some results. We have already noted the reform of the form of French judgments.[66] In Finland, the change has been even more spectacular. A traditional Finnish judgment was made up of a few gigantic sentences, sometimes as long as a printed page, without indents in the margin or without words typically indicating the beginning of a new element of the text. The description of facts and earlier stages of the case, as well as the grounds and the operative part of the judgment, were all presented in these enormous sentences, broken up by numerous subordinate clauses. This style was supported by the requirements of legal logic. Today, Finnish judges draw up their judgments using sentences of fairly normal size. To make the construction of the judgment clearer, they use sub-titles.

---

62 Kavassa & Prince 1991, looseleaf.
63 Mattila 2006 (in press).
64 Gadd 1935: 33–34.
65 See pp. 148–150.
66 See pp. 85–86.

Even in our times, complicated and useless expressions are added to legal texts, making them more difficult to understand. For example, in the United States there is a fondness for using expressions considered "polished" and "energetic":[67] *at slow speed* instead of *slowly, in the event that* instead of *if, prior to* instead of *before, subsequent to* instead of *after*. This habit is international. In Norway, it is often written: *i tilfelle av morens sykdom forårsaket av svangerskapet* ['in the case of an illness caused by the pregnancy of the mother'], which could be replaced by a simpler formulation: *hvis moren er blitt syk på grunn av svangerskapet* ['when the mother has become ill due to pregnancy'].[68]

Difficulties of understanding also occur because legal and administrative language places less emphasis on verbs than ordinary language. This is partly explained by the notion according to which a noun gives a more objective impression than a verb, notably in cases involving findings of fact. For example, recent linguistic research reveals that half the words in Finnish administrative texts are nouns. In ordinary language texts, nouns make up only one-third of words.[69] Sometimes, the use of nouns by legal authors is carried *ad absurdum*. In such cases, Nordic linguists speak of "noun sickness".

The wealth of nouns in legal and administrative texts is accentuated by the fact that these nouns often form phrases (groups of words forming a lexical unit) or – notably in some languages, such as German, the Scandinavian languages, or Finnish – compound words. This is because a term created to express a new legal concept should also be as transparent as possible, that is, it immediately shows, *grosso modo*, the uninitiated what it is about. If the particular words forming part of the phrase or compound word in question each express an essential feature of the new concept, then such transparency is ensured. The following examples will illustrate: in French, *contrat de transfert de processus technologique, Cour de justice des Communautés européennes* or – in German – *Aussageverweigerungsrecht, Klageerzwingungsverfahren*. These examples show the price of transparency: expressions in legal language are often very heavy.

Further, different language elements mingle in legal language. Firstly, this language contains words from ordinary language used in their ordinary meaning. Secondly, it contains words from ordinary language used in a technical sense. Thirdly, it presents words that are only technical terms. These last may be legal terms, or terms from other specialisms. Linguistic research affirms that in legal texts the number of such legal terms that have only a legal meaning is relatively limited in comparison with other specialist languages. The majority of legal terms are words from ordinary language that possess a particular meaning in legal contexts. This is sometimes dangerous: the uninitiated reader imagines having understood the meaning of the term, but in reality the term means something else in legal language.[70]

---

67 Tiersma 1999: 59–60.

68 Vinje 1990: 62–63.

69 Heikkinen & *al*. 2000: 44.

70 See p. 100.

On the other hand, legal texts almost always contain terms from other specialisms (e.g., commerce, technology, land surveys). One illustration is texts produced by organs of the European Union. A directive of the European Communities on agriculture may include terms from law, agronomy, commerce, and technology. A full understanding of such a directive requires knowledge of all these sciences, which deepens the hermetic character of the text.[71] Indeed, some linguists speak of the "accumulation" of factors contributing to this feature.

8 Archaism and Solemnity

8.1 Requirement of Gravity

In the chapter on functions of legal language, we found that the legislator seeks to ensure respect for legal rules, notably by linguistic means. Gravity, often solemnity, of expression is one of those means. Some State Constitutions and comparable documents breathe a particular solemnity. The entry into force of a Constitution is often performed by a formula full of dignity, while the articles are preceded by a preamble of declaratory character. To illustrate – the Spanish Constitution of 1978:

La Nación española, deseando establecer la justicia, la libertad y la seguridad y promover el bien de cuantos la integran, en uso de su soberanía, proclama su voluntad de:

Garantizar la convivencia democrática dentro de la Constitución y de las leyes conforme a un orden económico y social justo.

Consolidar un Estado de Derecho que asegure el imperio de la ley como expresión de la voluntad popular.

Proteger a todos los españoles y pueblos de España en el ejercicio de los derechos humanos, sus culturas y tradiciones, lenguas e instituciones.

Promover el progreso de la cultura y de la economía para asegurar a todos una digna calidad de vida.

Establecer una sociedad democrática avanzada, y

Colaborar en el fortalecimiento de unas relaciones pacíficas y de eficaz cooperación entre todos los pueblos de la Tierra.

En consecuencia, las Cortes aprueban y el pueblo español ratifica la siguiente Constitución

The Spanish Nation, desiring to establish justice, liberty, and security, and to promote the well-being of all its members, in the exercise of its sovereignty, proclaims its will to:

Guarantee democratic coexistence within the Constitution and the laws, in accordance with a fair economic and social order.

Consolidate a State of Law which ensures the rule of law as the expression of the popular will.

---

71 Strouhal 1986: 143.

Protect all Spaniards and peoples of Spain in the exercise of human rights, of their culture and traditions, languages and institutions.

Promote the progress of culture and of the economy to ensure a dignified quality of life for all.

Establish an advanced democratic society, and

Cooperate in the strengthening of peaceful relations and effective cooperation among all the peoples of the earth.

Therefore, the Cortes pass and the Spanish people ratifies the following (...).[72]

8.2 Causes and Results of the Phenomenon

A close connection exists between the gravity of a text and its archaic character. Exaggerated archaisms can make a text comical but, lightly used, this feature has the opposite effect: the text becomes more dignified and serious. This is why laws written in an overly popular manner have sometimes been criticised, on the basis that the gravity of the legislative text is endangered.

However, legal language has recently been modernised in various countries. In spite of these modernising tendencies, lawyers (e.g., judges, notaries) still use archaisms. Forms of judgment and of private documents contain many repetitions and obsolete words of command (imperatives). Equally, inversion (i.e., reversal of the usual or natural order of words) is typical of legal and administrative language. We have already pointed to a Danish example.[73]

The archaic character of legal language can be explained in several ways. First and foremost, the mentality of lawyers tends to the conservative: they stick to traditional expressions even long after these have disappeared from ordinary language. Sometimes, these expressions move from one language to another through translation. Next, it has to be remembered that expressions in legal language are often immured in a law that has been in force for decades, even centuries. For example, Russian legal terminology remained in a state of petrification in the 18th century because no new codification was put into effect at the time; the legislator had simply put together old laws for republication as larger units.[74]

Russian lawyer-linguists have recently revealed that the Soviet legislative style was still alive in Russian laws and decrees of the 1990s. Some formulations of new draft bills resembled slogans from the Soviet era. Take the word "mass" and its derivatives to designate the population of the country or a region. A regional draft regulation from Irkutsk *oblast'* on family protection, motherhood, fatherhood, and childhood, was drawn up in 1996. The bill aimed to "strengthen family values in the consciousness of the masses" (*utverdit' v massovom soznanii naseleniia semeinye tsennosti*, утвердить в массовом сознании населения семейные ценности).[75]

---

72 Translation published on the Internet (http://www.congreso.es/ingles/funciones/constitucion/preamb.htm).

73 See p. 84.

74 Pigolkin 1990: 48–49.

75 Vlasenko 1997: 24.

Nevertheless, it should not be ruled out that the legislator itself may explicitly want to adopt an archaic style. In Norway, texts revising the Constitution are still written in obsolete language, to ensure homogeneity of style in the basic law, dating from the early 19th century. Similarly, in the 19th century Netherlands a draft Criminal Code was drafted in a (then) obsolete orthography. This was, truth to tell, modernised in the final draft.

The use of archaic language may also be dictated by political reasons. Under authoritarian political conditions, language is often solemn and conservative. A good example (as already indicated in the chapter on the functions of legal language) by way of illustration comes from Greece.[76] At the beginning of the 1970s, during the military dictatorship, the official language of the country was still the scholarly variety of Greek, Katharevusa (καθαρεύουσα), also used by courts and government offices. After the fall of the military junta, the country fairly quickly moved to the Demotic variant of the Hellenic language (δημοτική).

However, caution is needed in drawing conclusions on this subject: it is possible that archaisms in legal language are no reflection at all of an authoritarian society. The reasons may be quite different. Apart from the Norwegian example already cited, we can mention Finland, the author's own country. There, it is strictly forbidden to modernise the orthography of texts of parliamentary laws in force, without submitting the smallest corrections on the topic to the Parliament, thus respecting the normal legislative procedure required to amend a law. Old laws still in force are continually printed in their original form. The explanation for this tradition lies in the Finns' fears at the time when Finland formed an autonomous Grand Duchy attached to Russia. Finland's autonomy signified that the country had its own legal order, very different from that of Russia. To prevent the central power in St. Petersburg from russifying Finnish legislation, under the pretext of modernising the appearance of legislative texts, the Finns took a highly formal position as to the orthography of laws. Today, in independent Finland, this fear no longer exists, but a solidly established tradition still has great continuity.

8.3 Abandoning Conservatism: Revolutionary Legal Language in Soviet Russia

During periods of upheaval and revolution, the typical conservatism of legal language has sometimes given way temporarily to a radicalism requiring its total reform. This was the case during the French Revolution, when legal terminology dating from the feudal era was replaced by a terminology expressing bourgeois values. Another example that illustrates this notion particularly well, is the October Revolution in Russia.

The first years of Soviet power constituted a generally radical period. That was also evident in legal language. The former style of Russian chancelleries was abandoned and legal terminology was reconstituted. Terms considered to be expressions from autocratic structures of the tsarist regime (for example *gubernator*, губернатор,

---

76 See p. 62.

'governor') or as symbols of injustice and oppression (for example, *politseiskii,* полицейский, 'police –' or *ekzekutor,* экзекутор, 'executor of a punishment') were abandoned. The same applied to expressions considered abasing to human dignity (for example, *poddannyi,* подданный, 'subordinate'; also 'subject', or *proshenie,* прошение, 'entreaty'), or as deriving from the archaic and solemn language of the Church. Naturally, other terms eliminated also included those expressing rejected social relationships (for example, *aktsionernaia kompaniia,* акционерная компания, 'limited liability company', or *torgovyi kapital,* торговый капитал, 'business capital'). As a counterweight, terms were created reflecting the socialist character of the new law (for example, *sovet,* совет, '[revolutionary] council' or *prodrazverstka,* продразвёрстка, 'obligation to hand over foodstuffs').[77]

The most radical reformers considered that the former terminology was entirely unsuited to the needs of the new society. It did not correspond at all to the revolutionary spirit of the times.[78] In consequence, the term "offence" (*prestuplenie,* преступление), for example, was replaced by the expression "anti-social behaviour" ("socially dangerous act)" (*sotsial'no opasnoe deistvie,* социально опасное действие) and the term "punishment" (*nakazanie,* наказание) by the expression "measure of social protection" (*mera sotsial'noi zashchity,* мера социальной защиты). As to the Civil Code of Soviet Russia (1922), the traditional terms "property" (*sobstvennost',* собственность), "rent" or "lease" (*arenda,* аренда) and "sale" (*kuplia-prodazha,* купля-продажа) were severely criticised. The latter term is a literal translation of the term *emptio-venditio,* deriving from classical Roman law.

The radical change of legal terminology was accentuated by the fact that the first decrees of Soviet power were not drawn up by professional lawyers but by ordinary citizens elected to decide common affairs. Account should also be taken of the revolutionaries' general mistrust of lawyers – a typical phenomenon of societies undergoing drastic transformation. All of this contributed to the fact that the first decrees of Soviet power contained very few legal terms in the strict sense.[79]

Later, from the 1930s, the thought occurred in the Soviet Union that terminological radicalism had gone too far; it was a case of "childhood illness". Indeed, the Soviet legislator abandoned the terms introduced during the revolutionary fervour and returned to the terms of former times. Illustrations of terms re-introduced include: "minister" (*ministr,* министр), "embassy" (*posol'stvo,* посольство), "prison" (*tiur'ma,* тюрьма) and – a term already mentioned above – "offence". The admission was made that the language of socialist law and that of bourgeois law were broadly the same, despite the fact that – according to socialist beliefs – both types of law were essentially different.[80] This is why it was thought that the language traditions of the feudal and bourgeois periods could usefully benefit socialist society. In consequence, legal language once again became conservative under conditions

---

77   Pigolkin 1990: 49–50.
78   Pigolkin 1990: 10.
79   Pigolkin 1990: 10 and 50.
80   Pigolkin 1990: 9.

of "established socialism". In the 1980s, Soviet lawyer-linguists underlined that legal language ought to have a stable character: in legislative texts, especially, it was impossible to allow language experiments.[81]

9 Proper Use of Legal Language

9.1 Historical Survey

It can generally be said that almost all the characteristics examined in the present chapter deepen the obscurity of legal language. It is evident that the wealth of initialisations and other abbreviations of this language, along with its archaisms, have such an influence and that this is equally true of "noun sickness", the aspiration for accuracy, and so on.

It is therefore unsurprising that proper use of legal language has already long attracted the attention of the public authorities. The first attempts to enhance the quality of legal language were made in Antiquity. When the Byzantine Emperor Julian had Roman legal texts codified in the 6th century, he decreed that the language of the new codification should be laconic and understandable. The draftsmen were to "put together [the texts of] accurate laws drawn up in concise language" (*certas et brevi sermone conscriptas ... leges componere*).[82]

The discussion on proper usage of legal language was very lively in the Prussia of the Age of Enlightenment, at the end of the 18th century, as is clearly evident from the legislation of the time. The celebrated Prussian codification, the *Allgemeines Landrecht für die preußischen Staaten* (1794), is one of the principal monuments of the history of the German language in general. This codification is characterised by the clarity of the language and by the fact that it avoids loan words. For example, in the provisions on divorce of the *Allgemeines Landrecht,* terms of foreign origin are far fewer than previously.[83] It also appears that Ernst Klein, one of the architects of the codification, especially counselled the lawyers not to add too many subordinate clauses within sentences: they are a sign of "deficient thinking".[84] – The *Allgemeines Landrecht* provided a model for later codifications in Austria, Germany, and Switzerland.

In the Age of Enlightenment, the trouble taken to ensure proper usage of legal language was practical and concrete – but doubtless initiated by the upper strata of society. When it was deplored, in the Austria of Empress Maria-Theresa, that the language of bureaucrats was incomprehensible to Hungarians, even in the Hungarian version, those charged with preparing laws introduced a comprehension test.[85] Law texts were given for test reading to an amenable ordinary Hungarian, "the man in

---

81 Pigolkin 1990: 51.
82 Hattenhauer 1987: 39.
83 See pp. 168–169.
84 Hattenhauer 1987: 50.
85 Strouhal 1986: 130.

the street", or – as it was put more bluntly – "the stupid man" (in Hungarian *buta ember*).

Care over proper usage of legal language radiated from German-speaking countries to other corners of Europe. This included Russia, where German influence was always considerable (not forgetting the German origin of certain Russian sovereigns). Instructions given during the reign of Catherine II to the commission charged with preparing laws, aimed to ensure the quality of legislative language. According to these instructions, new laws were to be drawn up in simple language, using words that everyone could understand, and concisely. At the same time, the paternalism of the instructions was apparent. These anticipated that laws would be written "as much for those of mediocre intelligence as for the mentally gifted". These laws were not to be based "on scientific knowledge that defines rules corresponding to human reason but on the judgement of a father taking care of his children and his family".[86]

One aspect of the understandability of language is the tension between what is native and what is foreign. During certain periods, this involved nationalist purification of language. For example, in Germany at the end of the 19th century, the aim was to eliminate from German legal language – to all intents and purposes completely – elements considered foreign (*Eindeutschung*).[87] Driven from this language were foreign loan words that did not express "the genius of the German people, its figurative and poetic character". In Germany, this trend was called "aesthetic criticism of legal language".

9.2 Factors Contributing to Obscurity of Legal Language

In spite of efforts by language specialists, legal language tends to remain complicated and hermetic.[88] The presentation of functions and characteristics of this language has already shown, explicitly or implicitly, the reasons for that fact. However, we believe that a general summary (based essentially on von Polenz 1999) is useful.

9.2.1 Force of Tradition Generally, comparative studies show that the greater the density of terms in a language for special purposes, the simpler is the sentence structure. This is true of the language of technology and natural sciences, for example. These languages contain many terms that express difficult concepts but the sentences are short and their structure simple. By contrast, this finding is not valid for legal language, despite the fact that the latter is equally rich in technical terms.

---

86 Iurtaeva 2000: 150.
87 See pp. 167–169.
88 von Polenz 1999: 485.

Sentences in legal language are longer than those of other languages for special purposes and they contain more subordinate clauses.[89]

To explain this difference, the fact has to be taken into account that legal language is a language of great age – perhaps the oldest of all languages for special purposes. Legal language has been formed over two millenia. By contrast, most other languages for special purposes go back no further than the beginning of modern times. Some of them developed only in the 19th or 20th centuries. Therefore, a large difference exists between these languages, from the standpoint of their traditions. At the same time, we should bring to mind the specifics of the notion of style in the Middle Ages, and the fact that notions of style are deeply ingrained. In consequence, the great age of the traditions of legal language is certainly one important explanation for the complexity of its sentences.

9.2.2 Ensuring the Authority of Justice A second cause of the obscurity of legal language lies in ensuring the authority of Justice – sometimes, too, lawyers' desire to impress the layman. In the chapter on functions of legal language, we saw the importance of this aspect. Legal language is an instrument of the exercise of power reinforcing the authority of judges and government officials.

It is especially interesting to note that sometimes citizens themselves want legal language to underline the authority of the law and the importance of legal acts. This applies as much to speech acts of a public character as to those of a private character. Let us take an example from the United States. The language of a traditional common-law will is – as we have seen (pp. 86–87) – archaic and ritual. According to one author, a section of American testators explicitly want their will drawn up in line with a ritual and complicated formula, so that this important document should "really be a will". In these cases, the lawyer includes in the will all the archaic phrases and expressions, despite the fact that simpler forms exist.[90]

9.2.3 Requirement of Legal Protection In the application of the law by courts and public offices, legal protection and legal certainty require established forms of procedure, clearly defined party roles, accurate text citations, and models for guidance based on unambiguous formulas. This necessitates detailed regulation of procedures, which in turn implies complicated language.

In the same way, a private document deals with important matters and is final after it has been signed. If such a document is ambiguous or incomplete, these defects cannot normally be put right afterwards. That is why lawyers who draft contracts add as a matter of routine and for absolute certainty every type of clause they can think of. This means that legal documents are tending to become longer – even if today their individual sentences are shorter, thanks to the efforts of language specialists. So the main message risks disappearing in the abundance of text. Further, a long

---

89 Laurén 1993: 64, 74.
90 Child 1992: 259.

document tires the reader: he no longer follows the text. A long document is an obscure document.

One important cause for the proliferation of standard clauses is the development of computers: adding clauses no longer presupposes the effort of writing. The text is created in an instant on the basis of prior recording. According to American experience, it appears that standard provisions are still growing in contract.[91] New clauses are added as lawyers invent them but the old clauses are rarely eliminated. Indeed, a long document is more impressive – and also means a bigger fee.

9.2.4 Complexity of Society Society is becoming increasingly complex. In conse- quence, it needs highly specialised systems of legal rules, which in turn requires stocks of new legal terms. Only a portion of these legal rules of modern society are aimed to be applied to every citizen. In the main, these rules are written for lawyers. At the same time, a citizen who wants to read them is always less well-placed than a lawyer. This is as true for the substantive content of texts as for the terms expressing that content.

In some way, this development means a return to the past. In the days when legal Latin was the dominant legal language, legal texts were only intended for social elites. In the Middle Ages, the notion that the immediate addressees of legal texts would be the common people would have been totally foreign (with some exceptions, such as penal rules). Once upon a time, the people only indirectly obtained informa- tion on the content of the law, for example in connection with religious services. This classic way of transmitting legal information to the people is certainly comparable to the treatment nowadays of new laws, on television and in the newspapers, in the form of simplified communications.

9.3 The Utopia of Easily Understandable Law

For all the reasons cited above, the ideal of the Age of Enlightenment, according to which legal language should be understood by every citizen, has been shown to be largely utopian. The same also applies for the modern, democratic, rule-of-law State. Often, criticisms from citizens about the obscurity of legal language are in reality due to difficulty with the matter itself. A text under criticism is intended for use among lawyers, who alone have the competence to understand it. The problem becomes complicated by the fact that the legislator or other authority often regulates technical matters from other specialisms through legal language. This leads to an accumulation of obscurity: the language of the law, that of technology, that of commerce, and others, intermingle in the script. This makes the text doubly difficult from the standpoint of the uninitiated. Today, this applies especially to texts from the European Union.

Language specialists can only help to correct some faults of legal language: heavy sentence structures, useless repetitions and abbreviations, archaisms, over-learned

---

91   Tiersma 1999: 59.

words, and so on. Nevertheless, the basic difficulty resides in the fact that in legal language the words of ordinary language often have a technical meaning hidden behind an apparently clear expression. This gives rise to the problem of illusory comprehension: the reader imagines having understood the text, although the reality is that this understanding amounts to misunderstanding. Illusory understanding is often far more dangerous than the situation where the reader notices at once that he does not understand the text.

Finding a universal solution to this problem is difficult. Ensuring good quality legal language requires a constant struggle against several powerful factors that are apt to deepen the obscurity still further. The struggle is difficult: eliminating one factor often means aggravating another. Rejecting a noun-heavy style may lead to using complicated sentences. Rejecting archaisms implies introducing unknown neologisms. Rejecting special terms means resorting to circumlocution.[92] The same applies to eliminating loanwords. Replacing a loanword with a word from ordinary language of national origin can easily result in the technical meaning hidden behind the word leading to illusory comprehension.

This problem is well illustrated by a collection of legal forms published recently in the United States. The author of the collection recommends that in their will testators should present apologies to their heirs for having used formal legal language in the document: *I trust that the formal terminology in this Will and absence of personal messages will not cause you to doubt my affection for you (...).*[93]

Litany-like insistence on the importance of the quality of legal language is often a sign of powerlessness. Nevertheless, quality can be – and should be – improved. We will deal briefly with this topic.

9.4 Improving the Quality of Legal Language in Our Time

9.4.1 Establishing the Need for Improvement In recent decades, the obscurity of legal language has come under far more severe criticism than previously. The intention is to prevent lawyers from becoming isolated behind their hermetic language. This demand has been heard notably from language specialists, as well as some popular movements. An example is the *Plain English Movement*, especially powerful in the United States. In various countries, these activities have led to instructions and recommendations from the authorities concerning legal language. For example, in England in 1996 a report on access to justice was drawn up by Lord Woolf (*Report on Access to Justice*), that is, citizens' right to bring their cases before the courts. In the report, the author pays attention, amongst other things, to the understandability of judicial language. In consequence, the legislation on civil procedure (Civil Procedures

---

92   von Polenz 1999: 486.
93   Tiersma 1999: 103.

Act 1997) was reformed in 1999 in such a way that most of the recommendations presented in the report were achieved.

In modern society, legal rules are constantly proliferating. Recent times have seen an awareness of the problems caused by this flood of norms. Legislators and governments have eliminated many useless provisions, which has shortened laws. These measures are also important from the standpoint of the quality of legal language: the shortened texts are easier to understand. In the same way, those charged with preparing laws are trying to construct legal texts more intelligibly than previously. Indeed, today we know that the structure of text is of great importance from the standpoint of its clarity. Beyond brevity, logical construction facilitates comprehension of a text and makes it easier to remember.[94]

Apart from the length of text and its poor construction, complicated sentences also impede comprehension. In Spain, emphasis is placed on maximum sentence length of 20 words in a quality newspaper. If a slow reader is involved, the length should not exceed 16 words. This explains the attempt to eliminate useless repetitions, double negatives, and so on. The aim is also to reduce the number of nouns in sentences.[95] For example, the expression *estar en posesión* ['to be in possession'] was simplified to the form *poseer* ['to possess'].[96] As a counterbalance, it has to be said that "telegram style" is also harmful from the standpoint of understandability of the text: links between sentences become unclear and the text is no longer coherent.

Good construction of the text as well as short, simple sentences make legal language clearer. Nevertheless, that is not enough. Account also needs to be taken of the difficulties linked to terminology. We have already noticed the problem of illusory comprehension of legal terms. Often, a correct understanding of these terms is impossible without substantive knowledge of the subject involved. However, the obscurity of terms can be partly remedied. Legal terms sometimes lack transparency, that is, they give away little of their content to the uninitiated. They can even be severely misleading. Therefore, creating new legal terms requires ensuring their transparency so that they give every citizen at least a summary idea of their content. In spite of that, it is true that the difference between a lawyer and a layman as readers of a legal text persists even after such terminological labour: an expert knows in detail the socio-cultural conditions in which technical terms are used, while a laymen only roughly.[97]

Improving the quality of legal text should start with laws and regulations: the language used by the legislator is passed on to the courts and government offices. A Brasilian author, Ronaldo Caldeira Xavier, sums up the properties required of legislative language as follows: (1) When a law is drafted, it should be strictly limited to what is necessary (conciseness). (2) Legislative language should faithfully respect established rules of grammar (correctness). (3) It should use terminology consistently

---

94 Gutman 1999: 82.
95 Prieto de Pedro 1991: 180–192.
96 Duarte & Martínez 1995: 115.
97 Oksaar 1989: 221–222.

according to the nature of the case (precision). (4) So far as possible, the legislator should use expressions that are not open to several interpretations and that are not otherwise ambiguous (clarity). (5) Laws and regulations should be formulated in a strictly logical way, and the reasoning should be coherent.[98]

Apart from improving legislative language, only recommendations and training can influence the language of courts, given the independence of the judicial authority. Efforts should be directed towards the higher courts, since inferior courts follow the language model that the former create. An example of recommendations given to courts is provided by the French circular of 31 January 1977 on presentation of judgments.[99] Naturally, higher government offices should not be overlooked as training subjects.

In fact, considerable results have been achieved. In many countries legal language has become clearer and, consequently, more intelligible for ordinary citizens. This concerns, for instance, legal English.[100] Nevertheless, much remains to be done: in English pension-assurance contracts, sentence length can still reach from 160 to 220 words.[101] Improving the quality of legal language presupposes continuous training of judges and government officials. Further, it is necessary that ministries, the courts, and government offices should possess enough staff to draw up laws and draft documents of a legal nature. Practical experience shows that pressure of work is one of the main threats to high-quality legal language. For example, a draft parliamentary bill may be radically changed at the very last moment due to political compromise. The rapid formulation of amendments in good legal language presupposes competent lawyers immediately available to focus on the task.

9.4.2 Quality Assurance of Legal Language in the European Union The European Union is characterised by linguistic pluralism, which lends special importance to ensuring the good quality of legal language in the frame of Union institutions. This importance is largely due to the fact that in reality Union documents (e.g., regulations and directives, judicial decisions) are always or often prepared as translations from the standpoint of most Member States. It is known that a text resulting from translation easily becomes very heavy, even artificial.

On that account, attention has already long been paid to the linguistic quality of texts of the European Communities. The first steps in developing the language of Community institutions date from the mid-1980s. More recently, new steps have been taken. A particular illustration is the Inter-institutional Agreement of 22 December 1998 on common guidelines for the quality of drafting of Community legislation.[102]

---

98 Xavier 2001: 142.
99 See p. 209.
100 Kurzon 1997: 131–132 and Hiltunen 2001: 63–65.
101 Cutts 2001: 3.
102 Official Journal of the European Communities, 1999/C 73/01.

On the basis of this accord, a guide called the Joint Practical Guide of the European Parliament, the Council, and the Commission for persons involved in the drafting of legislation within the Community institutions was published in 2003. This guide exists in all the Union languages and contains detailed instructions for formulating normative acts of the European Communities. According to the guide, those charged with drawing up Community texts should, in particular, avoid using over-long sentences and articles, uselessly complicated expressions, and unecessary abbreviations. The same applies to "jargon expressions, vogue words, and certain Latin words diverted from their current legal meaning" (for example, *a contrario*). Further, technical terms should always be used logically and consistently. The guide also contains detailed instructions on, e.g., titles, textual construction and signs, as well as on references between various normative acts and various legal provisions.

Chapter 4

Legal Terminology

1 Legal Concepts

1.1 Distinguishing Features of Legal Language

Legal language differs from most other languages for special purposes in that it describes a metaphysical phenomenon. Law does not exist in the physical world. Since it is entirely created by humans, law is always linked to the culture of any particular society: it therefore constitutes a social phenomenon. Because of this interconnection, legal rules differ in different legal orders. Legal concepts also differ, because in the final analysis they are crystallisations of legal rules.

> On this theme, legal science clearly differs from the natural sciences: the laws of nature are the same everywhere. The difference is evident in the relationship between language and its object. The language of a natural science cannot change reality: if a plant is described wrongly or inaccurately, it remains as it was none the less. But if the legislator, in a new law, describes a legal phenomenon otherwise than in an earlier law, then the legal reality changes: law only exists in human language.[1]
>
> However, the difference between the natural sciences and legal science is not as radical as might be imagined. The conceptual systems of the natural sciences, and the languages that reflect them, are also partly linked to the culture of society. For example, the conceptual system of medicine is influenced by the cultural distinction between what is psychic and what is physical. Likewise, wetlands can be classified from different viewpoints: on the basis of vegetation, on the basis of soil, and so on. These differences of classification are evident in the terminologies of that science that are in use in various countries.

Where the concepts of two legal systems differ, the semantic domains of legal terms do not correspond with one another. How serious this problem is depends on the historical interaction between the societies in question. The legal concepts of Sweden and Finland are very close, since Finland formed part of the Kingdom of Sweden for over six centuries. In the same way, the legal concepts of England and the United States share much in common: English law was applied in the former British colonies where the US was founded.

---

1   Brækhus 1956: 14.

1.2 Legal Families and Conceptual Kinship

1.2.1 Overview: Avoiding Conceptual Misunderstandings   The legal systems of the world can be divided into major legal families, in line with certain criteria, notably conceptual relationship. The main justification for this division lies in the fact that a knowledge of the similarities and differences between legal concepts of various countries helps avoid misunderstandings in international cooperation.[2] Such knowledge will enable a lawyer or legal translator to detect cases of mistake or misunderstanding. This, in turn, will lead to checking the matter in a trustworthy source. Risks of mistake and misunderstanding especially concern the relationship between civil law and common law. Importantly, we should remember that general classifications always involve "soft" facts: a particular term may form an exception to the general rule. Caution is continually necessary.

1.2.2 Common Law and Civil Law   Today, comparative lawyers distinguish two major legal systems of worldwide significance that correspond to the regulatory needs of modern society: common law[3] and civil law (also called the Romano-Germanic or Continental family of law).

The first system is applied as such in the English-speaking countries, notably in England and the United States. The second system chiefly covers the countries of continental Europe and Latin America. As a matter of note, the countries of Eastern Central Europe and Eastern Europe, representing the socialist law family during the (first and) second half of the 20th century, today belong to the civil-law family. The traditions of these countries are continental. Since the fall of socialism, they have returned to their former legal systems. The laws of the Nordic countries also form part of the civil-law family, even if they possess certain particular features.

Beyond the zone of European culture, the conceptual systems of legal orders largely correspond either to common law or to civil law. This is explained partly through the colonial era, partly through the general westernization of other continents. Nevertheless, legal concepts of major traditional cultures are of importance in Asia, and notably in the Islamic countries. As for Africa, we should distinguish between State law on the one hand and – on a local scale – customary law, where legal concepts of European origin are unknown.

The conceptual differences between the system of civil law and that of common law are explained by their history. Originally, the civil-law system developed in medieval universities on the basis of Roman law. This is why its divisions and its concepts were formulated first of all on the basis of substantive law, which was founded on a number of abstract principles, often theological or philosophical. By contrast, the common law was formed in the courts of England following the Norman Conquest. In consequence, the system-building and conceptual apparatus of the common law were defined by the requirements of medieval judicial procedure.

---

2   David & Brierley 1978: 6–17.
3   See pp. 221–224.

This background explains why these two legal families still differ today as to fundamental divisions and concepts of law, as to the degree of generality of legal rules, and as to doctrine on sources of law. Further, the centre of gravity of common law is placed more clearly on judicial procedure than is the case with the civil-law family. As a result, judges on the bench in England are still more respected than in the countries of continental Europe. However, we should note that in our times common law and civil law are in process of converging. The reason is twofold. On the one hand, the law of the United States has assumed increasing importance in continental Europe since the Second World War. On the other hand, the legislation of the European Communities is continually unifying the legal orders of the Member States, England included.

1.2.3 The Legal System of the European Communities The European Union consists of three "pillars". The most important of these pillars is formed by the European Communities. Previously, these communities were three in number: the European Community (in the singular), the European Atomic Energy Community, and the European Coal and Steel Community. From 2002, this last community no longer exists.

The law of the European Communities, "European law" or "Community law", today forms a legal system of its own, partly superimposed on those of Member States.[4] Given that the founding States of the early Communities form part of the civil-law legal family, the legal system of the European Communities is also built on civil-law foundations, from a legal-technical standpoint. In particular, French law has considerably influenced the principles and basic concepts of Community law. The methods for ensuring legal protection before the Court of Justice of the European Communities are essentially based on those of the French *Conseil d'État*. The institution of *commissaire du gouvernement* served as a model for that of Advocate-General.

At the same time, German law has also been of importance in developing Community law. Illustrations of legal principles received from Germany include, e.g., the principle of proportionality (in administrative matters) and that of reciprocal loyalty and trust (in performing contracts). Furthermore, the role of academic legal writing when the Court of Justice of the European Communities takes its decisions is worth mentioning – again, a feature from the German legal tradition.

Following accession of the United Kingdom to the European Communities in 1972, common law also began to influence Community law. Of particular importance is that a technically refined doctrine concerning the importance of precedents, a form of *stare decisis*,[5] is under development, in harmony with common law traditions, in the Court of Justice of the European Communities. This court's judicial procedure also possesses some common law features. The same applies to the style of judgments: in the 1950s and 1960s, judgments of the Court of Justice of the EC were

---

4   De Cruz 1995: 157–158.

5   See p. 224.

direct stylistic copies of French judgments, especially as to their construction and disposition (e.g., the signal words *attendu que*). Over time, the style of the Court became more independent: the construction of its judgments does not come directly from any legal order of Member States.[6]

Thus, the legal system of the European Communities has received significant inputs from various directions. It can rightly be described as a sort of hybrid, mixed law, in which the legal traditions of Europe increasingly intertwine.[7] The methods of interpretation used by the Court of Justice of the EC are a specific mix of traditions typical of the various legal cultures of Europe. At the same time, the legal system of the European Communities is developing by interaction between Community organs and national legal orders, in a way not directly borrowed from any legal order of the Member States. Many Community institutions and basic principles have been constructed in line with the needs of the European Communities. A good example is the principle of subsidiarity.

In short, we can point to an entirely new type of legal system, the law of the European Communities, with its own characteristics, gradually developing in Europe, side by side with civil law and common law. This applies as much to legal systematization and to doctrine relating to sources of law as to individual institutions and principles. These new elements are partly evident in the form of new terminology. Partly, too, they lie hidden behind established terms coming chiefly from France. These old terms possess a new conceptual content in Community law.[8]

2 Characteristics of Legal Terminology

2.1 Legal Concepts and Legal Terms

A *"concept"* is the mental representation of an object. It involves an abstract image created by the human mind on the basis of the features peculiar to a thing or matter. A *"term"*, as such, is the technical designation of a concept; the appearance of that concept. In consequence, a "term" defines as the verbal expression of a concept belonging to the conceptual system of a language for special purposes.[9] Such an expression may be a single word or a compound word, but often involves a phrase (e.g., "good faith", "free movement of persons"). Normally, terms are nouns. Verbs and adjectives can also be classed as terms. As to the word "referent", this designates entities that exist physically or metaphysically and that fulfil the conditions imposed by a given concept. In France, the number of referents of the concept of "general court of first instance" (*juridiction de droit commun du premier degré de l'ordre judiciaire*), expressed by the term *"tribunal de grande instance"*, is 175 (overseas

---

6   Ballansat-Aebi 2000: 720 and Berteloot 2000: 529.
7   de Cruz 1995: 158–163 and 180.
8   See pp. 118–119.
9   Laurén 1993: 96–97.

territories excluded). By contrast, only one referent in France is connected with the concept expressed by the term "*Cour de cassation*".

The difference between legal terms and other words in a language is vague. According to a classic German dictionary, the *Deutsches Rechtswörterbuch* (1914), words of a legal character (*Rechtswörter*) are chiefly met with in the form of expressions that are not imaginable without a legal relationship, or for which the necessary condition is a legal relationship. Further, expressions that can be used in other contexts, but that have a particular content in certain legal relationships, are also legal in the broad sense. In contemporary France, Gérard Cornu defines "legal term" in greater detail. According to him, it is possible to "recognise a native legal-ness (*juridicité*) in all that owes its existence to the Law, that is, on the one hand, all that the Law establishes (legal institutions), on the other hand all that can only be constituted in line with the Law (on this basis all legal acts the constitutive elements of which are defined by the law can be included without any doubts)". It is also possible to include, amongst legal terms, words expressing legal facts in cases where the features "to which the Law attaches effects answer to the conditions that the Law imposes and thus to a legal notion that confers on them a meaning with regard to the Law". A good example is the word "error".[10]

It should be stressed that a legal term can just as well be a word or phrase that only appears in legal language ("abuse of process", "criminal responsibility") as a word or phrase that also forms part of ordinary language but that has a special meaning in legal language.

Some researchers of languages for special purposes distinguish between "nomothetic" sciences (rule-forming) and "ideographic" sciences (describing specific cases). The natural sciences chiefly rank among the first category, whereas historical research belongs to the second. It is natural that nomothetic sciences, which formulate generalisations, have a greater need for terminology than ideographic sciences, which focus on individual phenomena. Legal science falls among the nomothetic sciences. This is why legal texts are so rich in terms. For example, in Swedish legal texts researchers noted that every fifth word is a term.[11]

2.2 Polysemy

2.2.1 Diachronic Polysemy We have already concluded that a term is the verbal expression of a concept. According to one particularly important observation, legal terms are characterised by polysemy: depending on context, a single term can express several concepts.[12] Although polysemy causes difficulties, as R. A. Budagov puts it, "it allows the vocabulary of the language to transmit the infinitely varied ideas and feelings that arise in social life".[13] The phenomenon of polysemy is rather the rule

---

10 Cornu 2004: ix.
11 Laurén 1993: 99.
12 Cornu 2005: 93.
13 Vlasenko 1997: 48.

than the exception in legal language. This is basically explained by the fact that legal orders are continually changing over time. To take an example – the Latin term "*jus civile*" and its variants in modern languages.

The term *jus civile* has had several meanings which have overlapped each other over two millenia. In Ancient Rome, the term referred to classical Roman law (as opposed to *jus honorarium*) on the one hand and, on the other, to the law applied to Roman citizens (as opposed to *jus gentium*). In Byzantium, in medieval Europe, and still at the beginning of modern times, *jus civile* generally referred to Roman law and – still more broadly – to temporal State law, as opposed to the divine law imposed by God (*jus divinum*) or natural law (*jus naturae, jus naturale*). For example, Samuel Pufendorf uses the term *jus civile* in the meaning of "positive law", in his work *De officio hominis et civis juxta legem naturalem libri duo* ['The Two Books on the Duty of Man and Citizen According to the Natural Law', 1673].[14]

Later, the modern meaning of civil law developed. In medieval Europe – a mosaic of kingdoms and principalities – legal rules concerning the organisation of State power were not in common currency in the same way as in Ancient Rome or Byzantium. This is why medieval legal science focused on the study of those parts of the *Corpus juris civilis* dealing with legal relationships between private individuals. This gradually affected the language, and the term "civil law" obtained its current meaning as a branch of law: it refers to a whole formed by legal rules relative to relations between private individuals.[15] This historical background explains the fact that the term *civil law* possesses three meanings in legal English. Sometimes, the term still refers to Roman law. In comparative law, it denotes continental laws (strongly influenced by Roman law) – in relation to classification of legal orders. Finally, the term refers to private law (a Civil Code exists in some states of the United States).

It should be emphasised that the frontiers of "civil law" are not necessarily quite the same from country to country. In Germany, *Zivilrecht* generally designates the law applied in relations between private individuals. It is synonymous with the term *Privatrecht*. In other countries, civil law is understood more narrowly. For example, commercial law in France is not included in civil law.

2.2.2 Orderly and Disorderly Polysemy   As to orderly (consistent) polysemy, a legal term has two or three closely connected meanings.[16] Often, the concepts expressed by a particular term are hierarchical or partly imbricated (overlapping). The phenomenon of orderly polysemy is very common, even as to terms of prime importance in legal systems. A good example is the term *common law*, which has three hierarchical meanings as far as the legal systems of English origin are concerned.[17] Further, the term is misleading from the international standpoint. The English common law is something quite different from the pan-European *jus*

---

14   Bergh 2001: 10.
15   Roland & Boyer 1998: 240–241.
16   Cornu 2005: 95–99.
17   See pp. 221–222.

commune (which literally means "common law"). The first term refers to the law developed by the English courts over the centuries. The second term refers to the law developed in European universities in the Middle Ages and in early modern times. As for disorderly (inconsistent) polysemy, the meanings of the term diverge to such an extent that they no longer have anything in common.[18]

> In homonymy, two words (at least) exist that are externally identical (homographs) but whose origins are totally different. These words only look the same by chance. One illustration is the word *police* in French, in the sense of the law enforcement agency, which comes from the Greek word politeía (πολιτεία – other meanings of the word include 'governmental measures', 'political regime'), and the word *police*, in the sense of 'contract' (e.g., *police d'assurance*), which comes from the Greek word apódeixis (ἀπόδειξις – 'proof', 'receipt'). Sometimes, disorderly polysemy is not far from homonymy.

Examples of disorderly polysemy include the French terms *"prescription"* and *"disposition"*. The meanings of the first term can be split into two groups: on the one hand, it involves different modes of acquisition or extinction and, on the other, a judicial order or a legal rule. As for the term *disposition*, this refers on the one hand to action to dispose of a good (chattel), and on the other hand to a legal rule, to a contract clause, or to a head in the operative part of a judgment.[19] These two terms therefore have one common meaning – "legal rule" – but also meanings that totally diverge.

2.2.3 Consequences of Polysemy Where polysemy occurs, interpreters of the text should be able to assign to the term the meaning appropriate to the context. They should be aware of the fact that the term may also have meanings other than the one first perceived. Given that the phenomenon of polysemy is very common, the interpreter has good reason for always being on guard. Often, it is easy to distinguish between the different meanings of the term. Sometimes, however, the reader feels ill at ease: it is impossible to tell what is the correct interpretation of the text. Such ambiguity is chiefly possible in the case of orderly polysemy.

2.3 Synonymy

Synonymy as a phenomenon stands opposite to polysemy: two or several terms express the same concept. For example, where magistrates arrange an inspection on the scene, legal French uses synonymous terms. These are *"visite des lieux"*, *"transport sur les lieux"*, *"descente sur les lieux"* or *"vue des lieux"*. Linguists find that synonymy is a common enough feature of legal terms. In legal languages with several layers of language, such as English, this phenomenon is especially frequent.

---

18 Cornu 2005: 99–102.
19 Cornu 2004.

For example, legal English often expresses the same concept by an Anglo-Saxon term, a French term, and a Latin term.

The counterpart of synonymy is antonymy. In that event, meanings of words are opposite to one another (e.g., "hot" and "cold"). One Russian author concludes that practically no legal texts exist that do not benefit from the phenomenon of antonymy.[20] Legal regulation rests largely on this phenomenon. For example, an antonymic connection exists between the words "right" and "duty". Nevertheless, it should be noted that antonymy is a highly complex phenomenon and difficult to analyse. In legal texts, terms such as "judicial decision" and "contract" may appear in the nature of antonyms.

Partial synonyms are especially misleading. In general, mistakes and misunderstandings are possible where the semantic fields of two terms stand side by side. Good examples are the terms "*juge*" ['judge'] and "*magistrat*" ['magistrate'] in legal French. At the same time, partial synonymy is a very useful phenomenon in legal language.[21] Thanks to quasi-synonyms, it is possible to draft a legal provision or a clause in a contract without leaving gaps: listing a number of quasi-synonyms leads to blanket coverage of the semantic field intended. This is especially in evidence in contract practice in common law countries.[22] It is also true for other legal languages. For example, Russian enables reference to a contractual relationship through several terms which are wholly or partly synonyms: *dogovor* (договор), *kontrakt* (контракт), *soglashenie* (соглашение), *pakt* (пакт), *konventsiia* (конвенция), *konsensus* (консенсус), *angazhement* (ангажемент).[23]

Sometimes, the choice between quasi-synonyms is a question of political utility. Reforms in Russia in the 1990s provide a good example. Compare the terms *natsionalizatsiia* (национализация, 'nationalisation') and *sotsializatsiia* (социализация, 'socialisation') or the terms *narodnyi* (народный, 'national', 'people's') and *gosudarstvennyi* (государствен-ный, 'State –').[24]

3 Formation of Legal Terminology

3.1 Birth and Death of Legal Terms

In matters of legal language, the birth of a term can often be pinpointed fairly accurately. Sometimes, a term is coined in legal language through the will of the legislator. This also applies to the disappearance of words: a term is deleted from legislation and replaced by another. It is even possible for the legislator to banish a term formerly in use, notably in connection with revolutions. When a term is deleted

---

20   Vlasenko 1997: 73–74.
21   Vlasenko 1997: 60–61.
22   See p. 237.
23   Vlasenko 1997: 65.
24   Vlasenko 1997: 67.

from legislation, the language of citizens changes only gradually but that of the authorities is immediately or at least rapidly revised.

The vocabulary of legal language – like that of other languages for special purposes – can be formed in three ways: (a) a word already in existence in ordinary language, or in the language of another specialism, obtains a specialised or broader meaning; (b) a neologism of national origin is created; (3) a word is borrowed from a foreign language (or from another national language).

3.1.1 Legal Usage of Words in Everyday Use More than other languages for special purposes, legal language contains words from ordinary language whose meaning is precisely defined or even diverging from that of ordinary language. Linguists speak of semantic derivation.[25] The explanation is simple: legal messages are normally aimed at all members of society. Often, these messages, transmitted through legal language, deal with matters connected with the daily life of citizens (e.g., marriage, birth, work). In branches of law *in statu nascendi*, introducing words from ordinary language into legal usage is especially frequent. A good example would be new terms in environmental law.

Generally, it is true to say that legal language is conservative and, as a result, includes words that have long since disappeared from ordinary language. However, the legislator, judges, and civil servants can also be the forerunners. We shall see later how the royal chancelleries contributed to the development of written French. In the same way, the major codifications have often influenced usage in ordinary language and have produced many new words. Perhaps the best example is the French *Code civil* and, as to new words, the German *Bürgerliches Gesetzbuch*. An example going back to Antiquity is the word "emancipation", used today in the context of equality between the sexes. Originally, *emancipatio* was a strictly formal legal act in Roman law, releasing a minor from paternal guardianship.[26]

3.1.2 Neologisms of National Origin In the vocabulary of languages for special purposes, the evolution of language is particularly clearly in evidence. Neologisms are typical of these languages.[27] Notably, neologisms are created in legislative reception, that is, in situations where a State puts into effect legislation coming more or less directly from another State belonging to a different linguistic zone.[28] Lexical neologisms are formed in several ways: by creating entirely new words; by deriving new words on the basis of words already in existence (normally, by raising the level of abstraction of the original word); by forming compound words and phrases. In our times, it is rare to create elementary legal words that are entirely new and of national

---

25   Hałas 1995: 54–57.

26   Kaser 1968: 261–262.

27   Pieńkos 1999: 74.

28   Sacco 1992: 488.

origin (i.e., not borrowed). However, it is common enough to form acronyms, that is, initialisations pronounced like ordinary words.

One interesting phenomenon is the reintroduction of former terms into legal language. These terms had once been in use but were later deleted. After an interval, they come back into use in legal language. In recent times, this phenomenon has been observed in Russia and other former socialist countries. The legal terminology of the Russian Empire has experienced a renaissance in the Russia of the 1990s. Let us take two examples from the fields of administrative law and company law: *gubernator* (губернатор, 'governor'), *tovarishchestvo na vere* (товарищество на вере, 'limited partnership company'. Legislation on Federal State emblems and their different constituent parts (especially heraldry) presents a particularly large number of historical words revived in Russia. Sometimes, the exact meaning of recently reintroduced terms goes back to the days of the Empire. For example, the Constitution of the Russian Federation (1993) designates persons elected to the Upper Chamber (*Sovet Federatsii*, Совет Федерации) as "members" (*chlen*, член) and persons elected to the Lower Chamber (*Gosudarstvennaia Duma*, Государственная Дума) as "deputies" (*deputat*, депутат). This terminological distinction comes from the *ukaz* ['edict'] of Nicholas II of 20 February 1906.[29]

The derivation of new words on the basis of words already in existence is often linked to the fact that law and legal science are complex, abstract phenomena that one seeks to manage by fine distinctions. Such distinctions have notably been drawn on the basis of the fundamental words "law" and "right". This is evident in all legal languages. For example, in French the Latin word "*jus*" forms the basis for several derivatives: "*juste*", "*justice*", "*justiciable*", "*justificatif*", "*justification*". In legal German, the number of abstract derivatives is particularly high.

Everywhere, the most popular method of producing legal neologisms lies in forming compound words and phrases. The number of elemental words not belonging to legal language is not large. However, that number is multiplied manifold with the addition of epithets to elemental words. Compound words are typical of some languages, such as the Scandinavian languages, Finnish, or German. To take a few German examples: *Gesetzgebungsermächtigung* ['qualification with a view to legislating'], *Kollektivvertragsgesetz* ['law on collective agreements'], *Stimmrechtsabtretung* ['transfer of the right to vote']. Other languages, such as English or French, favour phrases (as translations of German terms indicate). The number of typically legal compound words or phrases is immense in no matter what legal language. Often, these words and phrases are combinations of nouns, but different classes of words can also be combined.

In forming compound words and phrases, two purposes are opposed. On the one hand, a compound word or a phrase should be "transparent" and without ambiguity, that is, it should give the uninitiated a proper picture of the particular concept, by expressing all its essential characteristics, while avoiding confusion with other concepts. On the other hand, the compound word and phrase should not be over-

---

29   Vlasenko 1997: 83.

complicated as a language expression: otherwise it would be difficult to understand, to write, and to remember.

3.1.3 Loanwords

Technical and ideological aspects. Adopting new foreign words into a language is a complex phenomenon. Beyond the technical aspect (formation of loanwords), the phenomenon can also be considered from the ideological standpoint. For example, the history of German legal language shows that at certain times it has received loanwords in considerable volume, while at other times it has radically purged itself of these borrowings. One argument justifying this purging maintained that a legal language, freed of words of foreign origin, was far more understandable and closer to citizens. However, this argument is open to challenge: established loanwords are often more intelligible than their rarely-used "national" equivalents.[30] It should also be remembered that many laws are aimed not at citizens but at experts.

Ideological problems with borrowings have been particularly evident in countries once dominated by others with a different language. Early 20th century Finland saw a desire to purge Finnish legal language of borrowings from Swedish. Beyond Europe, these problems are linked to colonialism in the proper sense. We will take a South-East Asian example: Indonesia.

Indonesian and loanwords. The official language of Indonesia is Indonesian (*Bahasa Indonesia*). In practice, Indonesian is the same language as Malaysian (*Bahasa Malesia*). This involves a standardisation of Malay (*Bahasa Melaju* or *Bahasa Malaju*), which belongs to the Indonesian language group. In the various regions of Indonesia and Malaysia, hundreds of other languages are spoken. Amongst these, the most important is Javanese, the classical language of culture in the region. For its part, Malay has for centuries been the *lingua franca* of commerce throughout the East Indies. The Dutch also used Malay as a language of colonial government. After Indonesian independence, Malay was given the name of "Indonesian language", to consolidate national unity. In all official contexts, only the Indonesian language is used.

Thanks to Indian cultural influence over thousands of years in the South-East Asian archipelago, Arabic – having arrived in the region through India as the language of the Muslim religion – is clearly in evidence in the Malay vocabulary.[31] Arabic is the language of the Koran and enjoys a special status in all Muslim countries, including those that are not Arabic-speaking. With the general spread of Islam throughout the East Indian archipelago, Malay obtained a good deal of vocabulary from the Arabic language. Given that Islam is a religion based on Divine Law, it brought Muslim law in its wake. This is why Malay's loanwords from Arabic especially cover the legal and administrative domains. Typical examples include: *hukum* ['objective law'], *hak* ['subjective right'], *hakim* ['judge'].

---

30 von Polenz 1999: 487.

31 The same can be said about ancient Sanskrit.

The Dutch colonial power imposed European law in the region. The former customary laws of the various ethnic (*adat*) laws were retained but systematised in the European way. Further, they were complemented by law of European origin, to satisfy the regulatory needs of modern life. In order to express law of European origin in Malay (Indonesian), all kinds of devices were employed to formulate new legal terms. A number of terms coming from Muslim law were first given a new meaning within the frame of secular law of Western origin. An example is the term *hukum*, which is linked in some Islamic countries with the Holy Law of the Koran. A large number of calques (close copies) were also used to express technical-legal concepts from Western law. For example, the Dutch term *rechtskracht* ['finality of a judgment', 'res judicata'; 'binding effect of a judgment'] was directly translated by the expression *kekuatan hukum*. Words of European origin likewise were introduced, in slightly modified form: e.g., *kasasi* ['cassation'], *eksekusi* ['execution']. In some cases, legal authors began to use direct quotations, especially Dutch terms.[32]

Following independence, the attitude of Indonesian lawyers to terminology of Dutch origin has been ambivalent. Researchers underlining the country's Islamic heritage endeavour to dispense as fully as possible with use of words that can be recognized as being of Dutch origin. As a counterbalance, the work of some legal authors is swarming with legal Dutch phrases and maxims.

> To demonstrate this fact, my research group carried out a detailed examination of a relatively recent work on the conflict of laws of a domestic nature. This is Sunarjati Hartono's book *Dari hukum antar golongan ke hukum antar adat* ['From the law regulating relations between ethnic groups to the law regulating relations between customs', 1991]. While the work is fairly concise (119 pages), it contains – according to our calculations – some 180 legal Dutch phrases, maxims or terms. Some of these are fairly long quotations, sometimes as long as a paragraph. The work further contains some 70 English quotations, 20 Latin quotations, 3 German quotations, and 2 French quotations.

Works by Indonesian authors that cite Dutch expressions and maxims show that the legal language of the former colonial power still exercises a considerable influence in Indonesia. Given that the modern legal system of the country is of civil-law origin, the importance of legal Dutch in certain branches of the law remains greater than that of legal English, based on common law. We should also note the use of Latin quotations in Indonesia, which explains publication there of a legal Latin dictionary of considerable size.[33]

In this regard, in their work *Bahasa Indonesia Hukum* ['Indonesian Legal Language', 1998], the Indonesian legal linguists Bahder J. Nasution and Sri Warjiyati find that legal words of Western origin and direct Western quotations are still needed today because a large part of Indonesian legislation in force comes from the colonial era. However, Nasution and Warjiyati consider that these could be abandoned later, with the growth of purely Indonesian legislation. In the same

---

32   Nasution & Warjiyati 1998: 91–97.
33   See p. 139.

way, Western calques that have no basis should be eliminated from Indonesian legal language. For example, "subjective right" is often expressed mechanically by the calque *hukum subjektiv*, despite the fact that the Arab tradition has given Indonesian (Malay) a special word designating "subjective right" (as already mentioned above): *hak*.[34] The authors' final goal is thus an Indonesian legal language without words that are perceptibly Western, also otherwise purged of excessive impact from Europeans. These demands are exactly comparable to those of Finnish authors in the 1920s and 1930s, with their protest against the subjection of legal Finnish by Swedish language culture.

3.2 The European Union

3.2.1 Organisation of Terminological Work In developing legal terminology of the European Union, difficulties abound. First and foremost, the number of official languages is considerable (21).[35] It should also be borne in mind that the administration of the Union forms an enormous office complex. Each institution (the Council, the Commission, the Parliament, the Court of Justice) enjoys autonomous responsibility for the language of its texts, and for their translation. New terms are often born during the course of practical translation. Time pressures often rule out terminological work properly so-called, along with coordinating solutions for the various institutions, despite the existence of terminological databanks. Further, the Union institutions can sometimes consciously end up with diverging terminological solutions.

> The Commission occupies centre stage as to creating the Union's legal language. Many Community legislative texts are ultimately drawn up on the basis of projects and proposals coming from the Commission. Often, these texts have to be formulated and translated under conditions in which the vocabulary has yet to be established. This is why the Commission maintains a Terminology Unit, which takes part in planning vocabulary, helps translators, and gathers terms in the Commission's terminological databank.

On the other hand, it has to be said that it is not possible to take into account all the linguistic zones in the early stages of drawing up the Union's legislative, judicial, and administrative texts. From the outset, these texts are normally drawn up in French or English, sometimes in another language. It may even occur that the working language changes during the process of text preparation. Further, the original choice of terms may be unimpressive because drafters of a text often have to use a language other than their mother tongue. Different versions can only be compared later. Translations into cognate languages can then be placed side by side. In practice, only the most important problems form the focus of detailed discussions.

---

34 Nasution & Warjiyati 1998: 91–92.

35 Council Regulation (EC) No 920/2005, 13 June 2005, OJ L 156, 18.6.2005, p.3. As for the position of other Member States languages, see Council conclusion of 13 June 2005, OJ C 148, 18.6.2005, p. 1.

The lawyer-linguists from each linguistic zone are entirely responsible for ensuring that the original text and their own language version correspond.

In organisational frameworks, it is vital to find terms that are pertinent, transparent, and distinctive, to express the Union's new legal concepts in all official languages. On the one hand, terminological unity between the various languages has to be ensured. Yet again, terms created have to be adapted to the peculiarities of each language. This is the front line between the goal of harmonising Community terminology and the language traditions of the various Member States, along with their particular needs.

This is already evident in the case of French, the pivotal language of terminological work in the Union. As a language, French is less flexible when it comes to forming new derivatives by adding endings to existing words, and producing new meanings for old derivatives. However, practical needs provoke the creation of neologisms of a kind that, in light of French linguistic tradition, can be termed "*barbarismes*" (abusive use of foreign words). Two concrete examples will illustrate: *proratisation*, derived from the term *calcul au prorata*, and *affectation du commerce entre États membres*, formed on the basis of the expression *affecter le commerce entre États membres*.[36]

3.2.2 Terms Expressing New Concepts To express original concepts of Community law, the attempt has been made to create entirely new legal terms. Good examples are the *acquis communautaire* (see below) and the *principle of subsidiarity*. In creating new Community terms, the aim is to avoid expressions closely associated with the content of the legal order of any one Member State. This goal of neutrality sometimes results in creation of somewhat complicated terms, or use of circumlocution. However, in legal contexts a complicated or banal term is better than a misleading term. It should also be borne in mind that Union civil servants often read texts in languages other than their mother tongue. It is therefore important to use terms that are easy for a foreigner to understand.

In some cases, one might wonder whether the fear of terminological confusion is genuine enough to justify a complicated term. To illustrate, the term "*personne chargée du contrôle légal des documents comptables*" ['person responsible for carrying out the statutory audits of accounting documents']. This term was chosen because legal French has two "national" terms to express the concept hidden behind it: "*commissaire aux comptes*" [lit. 'accounts commissioner', in France] and "*réviseur d'entreprises*" [lit. 'company auditor', in Belgium]. To avoid an over-close association with one or other of these countries, the end result was the complicated term quoted above.[37] Nevertheless, it is hardly possible that the difference in detailed regulations on verifying accounts in France and Belgium could cause mistakes and misunderstandings. Independently of the chosen term, it is clear that verifying

---

36 Berteloot 2002: 95.
37 Woodland 1991: 103.

accounts in the frame of the European Union is carried out in line with the Union's own regulations.

Further, in the European Union generic terms are often used in a specialised sense. The Union institutions are notably designated by words whose semantic field is very broad indeed (e.g., "Union", "Community", "Council", "Commission", "Court of Justice"). In official texts, these words are supplemented by epithets (e.g., "Commission of the European Communities", "Council of the European Union"). Normally, however, they are used alone. This can cause confusion if the context is unclear.

An example that well illustrates this fact is the basic term "community", which – depending on the context – designates different entities. This is explained by the structure of the European Union. As already mentioned, the first pillar of the Union consists of "the European Communities" (in the plural) which currently number two; previously, there were three. The most important of these communities was – and still is – the "European Community" (in the singular), originally called the "European Economic Community". The two other communities were the "European Atomic Energy Community" and the "European Coal and Steel Community". As we have seen, as of 2002 the last of these (Coal and Steel) no longer exists.

Construction of the Union's first pillar is therefore complicated, as is reflected at the terminological level. In works on European law, the word "community" may refer to (a) the European Community (the former European Economic Community); (b) one of the two (formerly, three) communities (the European Community, the European Atomic Energy Community or – before 2002 – the European Coal and Steel Community); (c) to the whole formed by the two (three) communities.

3.2.3 Formulating Terminological Equivalents The majority of terms in use in European law correspond to the common tradition of the legal languages of Europe. This involves terms expressing general legal concepts (e.g., "burden of proof", "author's rights"). These concepts are already expressed by established terms in the Community legal languages. In some cases, a particular concept is only known in the legal order of a single country or in those of certain Union countries, notably in French law. Finally, as indicated, many concepts are brand new: they were created within the frame of the Union itself, often at first in the French language. In these latter cases, the concepts in question have to be expressed in the various Member State languages.

When transferring new concepts into Union languages, different methods are used to produce terms after a foreign model (quotations, words of foreign origin, calques, borrowed meaning). Sometimes, the equivalent of the original term is formed in the same way in all or almost all languages, but normally the various versions of terms are not formulated by identical means. Often, the new national term is a modification of the original term (word of foreign origin), sometimes a direct quotation from the latter, but there are also calques and borrowed meanings. Further, neologisms are formed expressing the particular concept freely. The attitude of language specialists towards what is of national origin and what of foreign origin is complex everywhere.

To illustrate, we present a number of examples concerning the translation of basic Union concepts into Member State languages. (Upper and lower case letters are written according to their orthography in the Eurodicautom).

We find first and foremost that calques are easily accepted everywhere: the foreign element of the word is not in evidence. For example, the national versions of the French term *"marché intérieur"*: *mercato interno* (Italian), *mercado interior* (Spanish), *Mercado Interno* (Portuguese), *Internal Market* (English), *Binnenmarkt* (German), *interne markt* (Dutch), *indre marked* (Danish), *inre marknad* (Swedish), *esoterikí agorá* (εσωτερική αγορά, Greek) and *sisämarkkinat* (Finnish).

By contrast, words of foreign origin constitute a more delicate matter – even in cases involving the Graeco-Latin heritage common to all Europe. Often, the delegates of some languages at least choose a solution other than using a word of foreign origin – for example, the term *"directive"* (in French). In most Community languages, the equivalent is easily recognisable: *directive* (English), *direktiv* (Danish, Swedish), *directiva* (Spanish, Portuguese), *direttiva* (Italian) and *direktiivi* (Finnish). Nevertheless, in Germany, Holland, and Greece an equivalent of national origin was adopted: *Richtlinie, richtlijn* and *odigía* (οδηγία).

Sometimes, Finnish and Greek remain the only languages not to have adopted a term of Latin origin. Of course, Finnish is not an Indo-European language, while Greek is the oldest language of culture in Europe. Thus, Greek does not have the same need to adopt words originating from Latin or other European languages (quite the reverse, Latin words are often calques from Greek). An example is the term *avocat général* (in French). In Italian, this becomes *avvocato generale*, in Spanish *Abogado General*, in Portuguese *advogado-geral*, in English *Advocate-General*, in German *Generalanwalt*, in Dutch *advocaat-generaal*, in Swedish and Danish *generaladvokat*. By contrast, Finnish uses the term *julkisasiamies*, while in Greek the term is *genikós eisangeléas* (γενικός εισαγγελέας). The Greek term *eisangeléas* refers to the office of public prosecutor. The Finnish *julkisasiamies* is a neologism expressing the basic idea of the concept (the literal meaning is "public representative").

The majority of brand new Community concepts were created originally in French. Sometimes, the French term expressing a concept is difficult to translate into other languages. In these cases, the original term is quoted as such. The best-known example is the term *"acquis communautaire"*. This example well illustrates the different translation strategies. The term *"acquis communautaire"* refers to the institutions and legal rules of the European Communities but – significantly – underlines their core features, including the intellectual capital of these institutions and rules.

On the basis of research carried out into Eurodicautom data, and completed by other sources, we can discern five strategies in use as to equivalents of the term *"acquis communautaire"*: the whole quotation; partial quotation; direct calque; modified calque, and simplifying neologism. Some languages propose two or three solutions.

The whole quotation (*"acquis communautaire"*) is used notably in English but also in Dutch. Italian uses a partial quotation: *"acquis"/ acquis comunitario* (*acquis* between or without inverted commas). A direct calque appears as well in Italian (*conquiste comunitarie*) and Dutch (*communautaire verworvenheden*) as in Greek (*koinotikó kektiméno*, κοινοτικό κεκτημένο). A modified calque or fairly freely formed neologism is the most common solution: *Community patrimony* (English), *patrimonio comunitario* (Italian), *acervo comunitario* (Spanish), *acervo comunitário* (Portuguese), *gemeinschaftlicher Besitzstand* and *"EG-Besitzstand"* (German), *communautair bezit* (Dutch), *EU's landvindinger; Fællesskabets politik, retsregler og aftaler; det foreliggende integrationsniveau* (Danish). In some languages can be found a translation simply signifying Community "law" or "regulations": *Einschlägiges Gemeinschaftsrecht* (German), *bestaande regeling in de gemeenschap* (Dutch), *gældende fællesskapsret* (Danish), *gemenskapets regelverk* (Swedish) and *yhteisön säännöstö* (Finnish). In English, the terms *Community law* or *body of EC law* are also in use.

This variation shows how difficult it is to bring out shades of meaning of the original French term in the other Member State languages. Danish even has four translations of the term. Some translations do not transmit the idea of accumulation of intellectual capital included in the original term. This is why it is recommended to translate the term *"acquis communautaire"* functionally, according to the circumstances and needs of communication. In texts intended for experts, it is always possible to have recourse to direct quotation of the term.[38]

3.3 Other International Organisations

Problems of terminology are the subject of discussion in all international organisations. This is notably so for organisations aiming to harmonise the legal orders of their States members. As in the case of the European Union, it is normally French and English that operate as working languages of these organisations – previously, French was often the only working language. Terminological problems exist chiefly when States members implement texts produced as a result of international cooperation: these texts then have to be translated into the national languages. Problems of this kind can also appear in the relationship between the principal working languages of international organisations – French and English – because the terminology of private international law originally developed in the frame of the first of these two languages. To take an example to illustrate this proposition: the term *"ordre public"* (in French) in the conventions of the Hague Conference on Private International Law.

"Ordre public" signifies that a court (or administrative authority) can set aside the application of foreign law if the result of applying it is established to be contrary to the fundamental values of the State where the court (or other authority) is located. In practice, this reservation is included in all international private law conventions. Over time, *"ordre public* has obtained a precise meaning, despite the fact that the term as such is semantically open. After the United States acceded to the Hague

---

38 Peyró 1999: 52–69.

Conference (1964), English became the second language of the Conference's conventions, the French and English texts being equally authentic. At this point, the question arose as to the English translation of the term "*ordre public*". The term "*public policy*" existed in legal English but the sense of this term was not the same in traditional common law as that established by the term "*ordre public*".

On comparing the various Hague conventions, it appears that three terminological strategies have been used to express "ordre public" in English. The first of these is direct quotation. For example, the Convention on the Conflicts of Laws Relating to the Form of Testamentary Dispositions (1961) prescribes, in Article 7 (English text): *The application of any of the laws declared applicable by the present Convention may be refused only when it is manifestly contrary to the "ordre public"* (inverted commas in the original text of the Convention). In the English texts of several Hague conventions, both "*public policy*" can be found as well as (between parentheses) "*ordre public*". Thus, the Convention on the Law Applicable to Matrimonial Property Regimes, Art. 14, concludes (in English) with the words: *(...) manifestly incompatible with public policy ("ordre public")*. The third strategy is explanatory translation. The Convention on the Recognition and Enforcement of Foreign Judgments on Civil and Commercial Matters of 1971 prescribes in Article 5, No 1, in French: *(...) incompatible avec l'ordre public de l'État requis*, but in English: *(...) incompatible with the public policy of the State addressed or if the decision resulted from proceedings incompatible with the requirements of due process of law or if, in the circumstances, either party had no adequate opportunity fairly to present his case*. Examination of recent Hague conventions shows that only the term "*public policy*" now appears. As an example, the Convention on the International Protection of Adults (2000), art. 21.

We can thus conclude that by semantic derivation the English term "*public policy*" has gradually obtained the same meaning as the original French term "*ordre public*". English began by using direct quotation. Later, a national term was placed beside a quotation. Then, the quotation was eliminated but the national term was provided with a supplementary explanation. Today, only the national term is included in Hague conventions. With harmonisation of the French and English meanings, the misleading nature of the latter has disappeared. This made it possible to drop the French quotation in English.

PART 3
The Major Legal Languages

Chapter 5

The Heritage of Legal Latin

1 The Importance of Roman law

Originally, legal Latin came from Roman law. In the proper meaning of the word, this latter term designates the legal system developed in the Roman Empire and which has influenced all modern systems of law. This influence was particularly profound in the countries of continental Europe and even beyond, as far as the Nordic countries, where it was likewise felt. On the other hand, "Roman law" often refers to the *jus commune*, the legal system built on the base of Roman law, in the cells of university scholars in the Middle Ages and the beginning of modern times. In this case, the terms "Roman law" and *"jus commune"* are synonymous.

Initially, Roman law was primitive and formal in character. Later, it rose to a very high level from the technical legal standpoint, thanks to the work of the profession of *jurisconsult* that gradually developed in Ancient Rome. The high point of this work occurred during the first three centuries AD. This epoch saw the birth of *jurisprudentia*, Roman legal science. The continuity of this science was assured by law schools and by legal literature. It was the work of the *jurisconsults* that formed the base on which the scholars of the Middle Ages and their successors in modern times built the system of *jus commune*. Roman lawyers approached the phenomenon of law in a rational manner. To guarantee the stability of legal relationships, these lawyers analyzed legal concepts and formed legal doctrines. This enabled Roman law to stay alive and influential long after the destruction of Rome itself.

In Antiquity, Roman legal science had still not arrived at the level of systematisation comparable to that of the end of the Middle Ages and the beginning of modern times. Nevertheless, Roman lawyers had already obtained results that later gave medieval scholars and their successors the important elements for systematizing the legal order and for forming detailed legal concepts. A good example would be the division of the legal order into public and private law.

In Western Europe, Roman law as a coherent legal system disappeared with the fall of Rome (even if that law still had a certain influence in the various western parts of the former Empire, mixed with localized Germanic customs). By contrast, Roman law was maintained at a very high level in the Byzantine Empire, which preserved the cultural heritage of Ancient Rome. In the 530s, the Emperor Justinian codified this law in a great code, which later acquired the name of *Corpus juris civilis*.

Thus was cast the basis of a supranational law, the *jus commune*, later formed in the European universities of the Middle Ages and modern times and founded on a logical system of concepts. This system still operates as a common denominator of the legal orders in the countries of continental Europe. It is likewise the case for non-European countries (notably Latin-American) that adopted their legal culture from continental Europe. The Civil Code of Brazil, for example, contains a total of 1 807 articles; some 800 of these come directly from Roman law.[1] In sum, we can say that the lawyers of continental Europe (and those from countries influenced by the law of that part of the world) speak the same conceptual language, independently of their ordinary languages (e.g., Finnish, German, Portuguese).

It is in this conceptual unity that the importance of Roman law resides, from the legal-linguistic standpoint: it is relatively easy to understand and translate a foreign legal language if the conceptual systems of both source and target languages correspond. Rodolfo Sacco, the Italian comparativist and legal linguist, rightly declares (translated here): "The majority of the immense lexical baggage that the European continent has gained is translatable by reason of its origins linked, first of all to translation from Latin to French, from Latin to German, from Latin to Italian, then to translation from French and German to Italian, Russian, Hungarian, Spanish, Polish, etc."[2]

In spite of the fact that law of English origin, the common law, is not based on Roman law to such an extent as the civil law systems of continental Europe, the Roman influence can likewise be seen there. This influence partly appears at the level of legal concepts but particularly at the level of language. The great English lawyers who gave a logical system to the common law, and who – the first to do so – expressed this system in written form, were trained in Roman law. As a result, Latin is the oldest language of systematic description of the common law. This background helps us to understand the specifics of Latin as used today in the frame of English law.[3]

2 History of Legal Latin

2.1 Latin Language in European Culture

In the Roman Empire, only a part of the inhabitants spoke Latin as a mother tongue. At the same time, Latin functioned as a *lingua franca* between the diverse populations of the Empire. It was then also often an instrument of asymmetric domination: one participant in a dialogue used Latin as mother tongue, the other as foreign language. However, in the Eastern territories of Ancient Rome the situation was different: the status of Greek as *lingua franca* was unshakeable. The boundary between the zones of dominance of these two great languages ran from north to south along the centre of the Empire: it crossed the Balkans and ran along the eastern side of the territories of today's Tunisia.

---

1   Xavier 2001: 141–142.
2   Sacco 1999: 177.
3   See pp. 229–231.

With the downfall of the Roman Empire, these different parts separated. Written culture grew weak, and numerous Germanic tribes settled on the western territories of the former Empire. As a result, Latin as a spoken language began to move further and further away from classical Latin (it is true that the spoken language already diverged from the written language in Imperial times, as is demonstrated by the vulgar inscriptions in Pompeii, for example).

Thanks notably to the Catholic Church, and despite the changes mentioned above, Latin retained its position in medieval Europe as the dominant language of all written culture, including the sciences. During the period immediately following the great migration of the Germanic peoples and the fall of the Roman Empire, this written Latin was often of poor quality. However, the Carolingian renaissance (reform of the school system by Charlemagne at the end of the 8th century) materially raised the level of written Latin. By the same token, this strengthened the general status of the language. Throughout the Middle Ages, literary works in Western Europe were regularly written in Latin. These were also many in number. Indeed, it is estimated that the number of medieval works in Latin was 50 times greater than that of works in Latin during Antiquity.[4]

From the end of the Middle Ages, scientific progress gathered speed, thanks partly to new technical inventions, notably printing. Given that science was always produced in Latin, the number of works produced in that language grew at the beginning of modern times, still more than previously. One author refers pertinently to this epoch as "an ocean of Latin literature". It can rightly be claimed that the foundations of all modern science were cast in neo-Latin: the roll includes Kepler, Newton, Galvani, Gauss, and Linnaeus, amongst others.[5]

During the Middle Ages, Latin became transformed stylistically and grammatically, moving closer to the Romance languages. One implication of this is that medieval authors made use of prepositions and subordinate clauses far more often than the authors of Antiquity. As a reaction to this transformation, from the 14th century scholars of the Humanist period restored the style and grammar of classical Latin, by imitating the Latin authors of Antiquity. As a result, Latin became more difficult than previously, even for those with a Romance language as mother tongue. Indeed, it is thought that restoring the stylistic and grammatical canons of the Latin of Antiquity brought about the demise of Latin as a tool of communication at the national and international level. Latin had become too difficult for non-Latinist scholars to have a command of it. And so it was abandoned in various countries, one by one.[6] Of course, a number of other reasons could also be listed. Outstanding among these were the strengthening of nation states, such as France, and use of the national language as a tool of their power politics.[7]

---

4   Stowasser 1998: XXIX.
5   Vossen 1980: 25–32 and Waquet 1998: 101–123.
6   Lindberg 1997: 61.
7   See pp. 187–189 and pp. 191–192.

As a result, the use of Latin as a language of science began to diminish, partially, even in the 17th century but above all in the 18th century. Following a spectacular rise to a predominant position in Europe, France sought to replace Latin with her own national language. This provoked considerable resistance, particularly in international relations.[8] At the end of the 18th century, the national languages had already *grosso modo* ousted Latin in the scientific circles of the great powers. The smaller countries, whose national languages were unable to operate as an instrument of power in the international arena, kept strictly to the use of Latin. Likewise for the former great powers that had lost their dominant position, such as Poland and Hungary, where Latin remained the language of science for a markedly longer period than in Western Europe. In international relations, French definitively ousted Latin during the 18th century, because of the position of France as a great power and of her politico-cultural penetration throughout Europe.

2.2 Latin as Lingua Franca of European Lawyers

2.2.1 Historical Overview All European legal languages are in debt to Latin, even Greek. After the transfer of the capital of the Roman Empire to Constantinople (Byzantium), the language of State power was at first Latin. The great Byzantine codification of Roman law, the *Corpus juris civilis*, dating from the reign of the Emperor Justinian, was compiled in Latin. With time, the Byzantine government and justice system became Greek as to language.[9] Nevertheless, ideological and legal-technical factors led to preservation of part of the legal terminology in the form of Latin loanwords (Latin quotations or adapted words of Latin origin), right to the very end of the Byzantine Empire. Good examples are the terms κουράτωρ (*curator*) and λεγατάριος (*legatarius*). This kind of quotation words and other Latin borrowings remained remarkably and persistently alive in the language of teachers of legal science.

It is understandable that the use of Latin was fairly quickly abandoned in Byzantium: there, the rival of that language was Greek, an even older language, enjoying a cultural status at least equal, if not superior, to Latin. By contrast, in the regions that had belonged to the Western Roman Empire, no new national written languages existed as yet. For this reason, the *leges barbarorum* (compilations of Germanic tribal laws in the period immediately following the fall of the Roman Empire) are all drawn up in Latin. Even after the birth of new languages (e.g., Spanish, Italian, French), the authority of Latin long remained markedly superior to that of those languages. As we have already pointed out, legal culture of Latin expression was also flourishing in England, despite the native character of common law.[10]

Given the conservatism of legal circles, the transition from Latin to the new national languages was particularly slow in the matter of law. This was above all

---

8   See p. 192.

9   Zilliacus 1935: 59–112.

10 See pp. 225–228.

in the case of the science and teaching of law, that is, among legal scholars and professors of law. Throughout the Western lands, theoretical legal works were normally written in Latin until the 19th century. The output of this Latin epoch of legal science is impressive. According to one research, around 4,000 new legal works were published in Latin in the 16th century. This figure does not include new editions of works from Antiquity or the Middle Ages. Moreover, it involves only the 16th century: the 17th century, and partly the 18th century, also featured in the golden age of Latin literature, while considerable output in Latin was still being published in the 19th century. This literature was widely disseminated, and carried significant influence, notably after the invention of printing. For example, in canon law 35,000 copies of the great work by Gratian, the *Decretum*, were already in print before 1500.[11]

Interestingly, Gratian's *Decretum* (which dates from around 1140) was translated into French towards the beginning of the 13th century, or even a little earlier. This translation was probably made in England, where high society at that time spoke French. Because the translator's feel for language was so good, the translation of the *Decretum* had a significant impact on enriching and generally developing the vocabulary of the French language.[12] A critical edition of the translation of Gratian's *Decretum* was recently published by Leena Löfstedt, a Finnish specialist (*Gratiani Decretum* I–V).

In international relations, Latin preserved its status as sole language of international negotiations and treaties until the 17th century, when French began to oust it.[13] This did not happen without resistance, with Latin having guaranteed the neutrality and equality of inter-State relations.

As to practical lawyering within different countries, court minutes, the records of administrative authorities, and notarial acts were drawn up, partially or wholly, in Latin, in the heart of the Middle Ages and – in some cases – until the end of the Middle Ages or the beginning of modern times. This was likewise the case for legislation. However, a great variation should be noted in Europe as to the duration of the Latin epoch and as to the extent that Latin and modern languages coexisted in each country.

From the Middle Ages, courts and administrative authorities often heard causes in the vernacular language. This was true of the *Parlement* of Paris from its establishment (around 1250) although the judgments of the court were drawn up in Latin.[14] In the same way, *law French* in England replaced Latin in the sessions of law courts in the 13th century, before their language changed gradually to English towards the end of the Middle Ages. However, throughout the whole medieval epoch judgments and orders, as well as other official English documents, were drawn up in Latin. As for legislation, in some countries the Latin period lasted until the beginning

---

11 Schoeck 1973: 578–581.
12 Löfstedt 1989: 140–141.
13 See pp. 191–192.
14 Krefeld 1985: 61–62.

of modern times. For example, in the South of France, in Provence, the language of the laws and ordinances of the Angevin princes was Latin until the French conquest (1481). At the local level, registers of municipal resolutions of several Provencal towns were kept in Latin until somewhere in the fourth decade of the 16th century – the moment when the Statute of Villers-Cotterêts (1539) began to have an effect on legal practices in the South of France.[15]

In central Europe, but also elsewhere, the status of Latin was very strong, even in modern times, by virtue of the reception of Roman law and the influence of academic authors. Italy is a good example. In the Kingdom of Naples, Latin was still being used in court minutes and other documents in the middle of the 18th century, while in Piedmont judgments were handed down in Latin until 1789.[16] Significantly, too, the Napoleonic Code was translated into Latin, besides modern languages, to ease its appropriate application in countries other than France where it had come into force. Originally, this translation was made for the Kingdom of Italy. Later, it was published in the Kingdom of Westphalia and the Grand Duchy of Warsaw.[17]

Leaving canon law aside, the Latin epoch, in legal practice, lasted particularly long in some non-German regions of the Austrian Empire, that is, in Hungary and Galizia (Galicia, Southern Poland). In these regions, in the 19th century, Latin still formed an instrument of protection against the expansion of German. Since the founding of the Holy Roman Empire (962–1806), Latin there had enjoyed the status of official language, with the same claim as German. When the Emperor of Austria tried to replace Latin with German in Hungary, the inhabitants of that country chose to keep strictly to former practices. Indeed, Latin preserved the status of an official language of Hungary until 1844. It is ironic that Latin was used in the same way as an instrument of defence in Croatia, a subject territory of the Hungarian crown, to reject the Hungarian language.[18]

In the same way again, Latin retained its status in Galizia as one of the court languages until 1848. The Emperor of Austria tried several times to impose German as the sole official language of Galizia but, thanks to Latin, the Poles succeeded in countering his plans. Thus, the trilingual character of the province was maintained in legal matters until the 1848 revolution (the Springtime of the Peoples). The rural and municipal courts operated in Polish; courts for various corporations and the aristocracy (*Fora Nobilium*) used Latin in their judgments and official correspondence (but Polish during hearings); and the Court of Appeal and specialized courts for mining affairs worked in German.[19] In these circumstances, it is understandable that the Austrian *Allgemeines Bürgerliches Gesetzbuch* was translated into Latin, in 1812.[20]

---

15 See p. 189 and Hébert 1997: 286, 292 and 294.
16 Waquet 1998: 114.
17 Mattila 2002a: 719.
18 Waquet 1998: 120.
19 Grodziski 1971: 218–219.
20 Wacke 1990: 886.

Cases exist where Latin literature of the *jus commune* epoch is important not only from the standpoint of history of law. A good example of the contemporary influence of that language is the Republic of South Africa. In that country, Roman-Dutch law has always been applied. This law – developed in the Netherlands in the 17th and 18th centuries, mixed with common law imported by the British – is still applied today, when the political power is in the hands of the African majority. This is why South African judges continuously base their judgments, in certain branches of the law, on the *Corpus juris civilis* as well as on legal works in Latin (and in Dutch, too) of old Dutch scholars, albeit in the form of translations into modern languages.[21]

2.2.2 The Periphery: Legal Latin in the Nordic Countries in the Middle Ages In the Middle Ages, use of legal Latin was not confined solely to the heart of Europe. The case of the Nordic countries demonstrates this – in spite of the fact that the Scandinavian languages have a tradition in legal dealings going back to pagan times. Indeed, legal Latin occupied an important place in these countries during the first centuries of the second Christian millenium. In Denmark, royal ordinances were promulgated in Latin.[22] In Sweden, the language of legal documents was Latin from the end of the 13th century, remaining so until the middle of the 14th century. In Finland (which then belonged to the Kingdom of Sweden), this was also the case during the first half of the 14th century. In Norway, by contrast, the position of Latin always remained weaker.[23]

Medieval legal Latin of the Nordic countries diverged little from that of the larger European countries. Texts were characterised by legal phrases, intended to give them the necessary precision, and by ceremonial formulations, intended to make them high-sounding. The language of documents was compact, which made them difficult to understand.[24]

Nevertheless, the obscurity of legal Latin of the Nordic countries should not be exaggerated. Their medieval documents are often highly readable. The sentences in these documents are quite short, and their structure is logical: the author's reasoning moves forward clearly. This especially concerns official correspondence. The following illustration presents a letter from the Bishop of Turku (in Latin: *Aboa*, Finland) to the town Council of Tallinn (in Latin: *Revalia*, Estonia) on the 12 September 1428,[25] with an English translation (made on the basis of the French translation by the author of the present work). In this letter, certain characteristics of Medieval Latin are clearly visible: the specific orthography (e.g., the letter "e" instead of "ae") and religious greetings. As to the content of the letter, this well illustrates the administration of inheritance matters on the shores of the Baltic Sea in the 15th century.

---

21 Zimmermann 1997: 537–538.
22 Karker 1983: 8, von Eyben 1989: 14–15 and Tamm 1991: 37–39.
23 Tengström 1973: 23–25.
24 von Eyben 1989: 149.
25 Hausen 1910–1933 n° 1866.

Magnus, Dei gracia episcopus Aboensis.

Amicabili et sincera in Domino salute premissa. Circumspeccionibus vestris tenore presencium intimamus, quod Gerwinus Rodhe pie memorie, condam civis Aboensis, Revalie, ut forsan nostis, oriundus, in obitu suo superstitem reliquit heredem, filium videlicet suum, Andream nomine, jam forsan viginti annos etatis habentem, quem quidam fidedigni, videlicet Tidericus de Heyden, proconsul civitatis Aboensis, et alii, anno preterito sanum et incolumem Flandrie perhibent se vidisse. Porro cum mater dicti Gerwini dicatur nunc Revalie viam universe carnis ingressa, evidens arbitramur filium Gerwini predictum in bonis avie sue succedere ipso jure. Et quia dictus Andreas pronunc ad agendum pro se personaliter non potest, justum et racioni consentaneum reputamus, ut exhibitor presencium Thorerus Pædhersson, civis Aboensis, qui vitricus dicti Andree et tutor exsistit, se de hereditate predicta et aliis ipsum concernentibus suo nomine legaliter intromittat. Quapropter circumspeccionibus vestris studiosius supplicamus, quatenus dicto Thorero in percepcione hereditatis predicte ac aliis per ipsum pro dicto Andrea, privigno suo, suo nomine nunc gerendis velitis communem justiciam exhibere. Quod in simili vel majori erga vos et vestros studebimus promereri. In Domino feliciter valeatis. Scriptum Abo profesto exaltacionis sancte crucis, nostro sub secreto.

Circumspectis viris et discretis, proconsulibus et consulibus civitatis Revaliensis, amicis nostris sinceris, detur hec.

Translation:

Magnus, Bishop of Turku, by the Grace of God.

Accept our friendly and sincere greetings in the Lord. We inform you by these presents, in leaving the matter to your discretion, that Gervin Rode, of happy memory, former burgher of the city of Turku, a native – as perhaps you are aware – of Tallinn, left at his decease an heir, namely his son, Andreas by name, aged twenty years or thereabouts, whom some trustworthy persons, namely Tiderik de Heyden, burgomaster of the city of Turku, and certain others, indicate that they saw, last year, safe and sound in Flanders. Then, it being told that Gervin's mother presently in Tallinn took the road that all flesh must follow, we deem it clear that the said son of Gervin inherits his grandmother's property by operation of law. And because the said Andreas is currently prevented from personally seeing to his affairs, we consider it just and rational that the bearer of this letter, Thorer Peterson, burgher of Turku, having become the stepfather and tutor of the said Andreas, should set about administering the said inheritance and see to other matters pertaining to him in his name. For this reason, we pray you to consider whether you would deem it just that the said Thorer enter into possession of the said inheritance and other property belonging to the said Andreas, his stepson, and take over their administration in his name. We seek, for our part, to be useful to you and the residents of your city in similar or more important matters. Go with God. Written at Turku on the Eve of the feast of the Exaltation of the Holy Cross, sealed with our seal.

To those venerable and noble men, the burgomasters and councillors of the city of Tallinn, our sincere friends.

Legal Latin to a large extent formed the stylistic basis of Nordic legal languages; this basis developed gradually from the end of the 14th century. Moreover, a large proportion of borrowings, still in use in these legal languages, is based in the final analysis on Latin. Many Latin quotation words also exist.[26]

2.3 The Language of Canon Law

2.3.1 Characteristics and Influences As already mentioned above, the *jus commune*, scholarly law of the Middle Ages and the beginning of modern times, was broadly based on canon law, the law of the Catholic Church. That is easy to understand: in the medieval universities, legal science and theology were intimately linked, and canon law was technically highly developed. Procedure for introducing evidence, for example, was particularly modern. Conversely, Roman law – laic law – had previously formed its base on canon law: Gratian's *Decretum* contained some 200 passages taken directly from the *Corpus juris civilis.* The indirect influence of Roman legal thinking was even greater.[27] For that reason, it is easy to understand that the use of Latin as the legal language of the Catholic Church, in the Middle Ages and still to modern times, was so natural that there was no need to confirm it officially.

Thus was born canon Latin. In some respects, this Latin diverged from the legal language of the Ancient Romans. The latter contained very few synonyms; the language of Roman lawyers was characterised by considerable conceptual precision, which is to say that each word corresponded to a separate concept. Legal Church Latin developed in another direction. One of the reasons for this development was the conceptual imprecision of the Germanic languages, manifest by the great number of synonyms and binary (two-word) formulas. In the Germanic linguistic zone, two conceptions of style came into collision. It was not only a matter of Romanising the stylistic elements of the Germanic languages but of a contrary influence that likewise made itself felt. Church Latin began using binary expressions, whose origin often lay in Old German (for example, *exactio et peractio* stems from the expression *twing und bann,* which roughly translates: 'order and ban'), while Germanic words were also often Latinized.[28] In sum, the Latin used by the Church gradually lost its precision since it was forced to adapt to language traditions of non-Latin peoples. The language of Church administration became rich in vocabulary but summary in conceptual precision. The language of episcopal tribunals and church notaries diverged radically from the legal language of the Ancient Romans.

The language of canon law was essentially created by the central administration of the Catholic Church. Its importance can clearly be seen in legal and administrative letters sent by the papal chancellery to different parts of Europe. Already, in the course of the 12th century, the grand total of these letters had risen to 17,000, which means that the administration had produced one letter every second day. For typical cases, exact formulas developed, included in a large number of compendia. Examples of standard openings to papal letters include *Justis petentium desideriis* ['In accordance

---

26 See pp. 136–139 and pp. 146–147.

27 Becker 1991.

28 Bader 1963: 114–117.

with the rightful wishes of the petitioners'] and *Religiosam vitam eligentibus* ['To those choosing the religious life'].[29]

Throughout Europe, the standardised language of the papal chancellery exercised an enormous influence on the legal language of the royal chancelleries, various administrative offices, notaries, and comparable organs. In the Middle Ages, the legal and administrative language of the Catholic Church was by far the most advanced in the Western world. That is why everywhere it became the ideal that people sought to follow. One author has shown that in the Middle Ages the *lettres de justice* of the king of France, for example, were drawn up according to the model given by the language of canon law.[30] With these letters, the king ordered that a legal process might be commenced, or he guided the course of a process. The royal *lettres de justice* began with the same expressions as letters from the papal chancellery, and the formulations of the measures required were often copied from papal letters. In the case of execution by distraint, for example, the phrase *que de antiqua et approbata et hactenus pacifice observata consuetudine ad ipsos pertinet* ['which, by virtue of custom, both long ago approved, and observed without dispute until today, belongs to the persons mentioned'] comes straight from the papal chancellery where it originated. That is not surprising: the medieval wills of royal notaries bear witness to the fact that their libraries were made up of legal works of canonists and canonical writing guides.[31]

2.3.2 Canonical Language Today Canon law is not a uniquely historical phenomenon. As is well known, this law still forms the legal system of the Catholic Church, today based on the *Codex juris canonici* of 1983.

A specific language is still used in Canon law. The most characteristic feature of this language is the use of Latin. Until 1917, the language of application of canon law was Latin; it was only then that the change was made to use of vernacular languages in this matter.[32] Even if the current *Codex juris canonici* – otherwise than the corresponding code of 1917 – exists, besides in Latin, in different vernacular languages, only the Latin text remains authentic.[33] This fact is likewise apparent in the General Regulations of the Roman Curia of 4 February 1992, which lays down that the dicasters of the Roman Curia draw up their acts in Latin in principle, nevertheless today being able to use the most widespread languages for correspondence, or, according to needs, for preparing documents.[34]

The Latin of canon law has specific features, analysed in detail by a German author, Klaus Mörsdorf, on the basis of the Canonic Code of 1917. Despite the fact

---

29 Hiestand 1999: 23 and 25.
30 Schmidt 1999: 365–391.
31 Schmidt 1999: 379 and 384–391.
32 Becker 1990.
33 Aymans & Mörsdorf 1991: 130.
34 Waquet 1998: 97.

that this code has already been replaced by the Canonic Code of 1983, this analysis is still revealing, and here we present certain aspects of it.

It is hardly surprising that canon law and language stick strongly to tradition. According to the instructions of the pope for drawing up the Code of 1917, the requirement was, "in conformity with the exalted value of Holy Laws, to use Latin as the legislative language, in the same way that it so successfully found its expression in Roman law".[35] According to Mörsdorf, in several cases this meant a perhaps exaggerated commitment in the code to the language of the Ancient Romans. On the other hand, modern codifications, such as the *Bürgerliches Gesetzbuch*, gave considerable impetus to the drafters of the Code of 1917. The pope's instructions required that the code be drafted *ad formam recentiorum codicum.*[36]

From the language standpoint, the Code of 1917 is a highly understandable piece of work. At times, the language of the code diverges sharply from classical Latin, less from the morphological than from the syntactic standpoint. The word order does not always respect the classical model. This is natural: between the Latin of the Catholic Church of today and the Latin of the Ancient Romans stands a distance of two millenia. At the same time, reading the Code of 1917 requires possession of a basic knowledge of theological and philosophical Latin.[37]

Over the centuries, the number of terms of canon law has grown considerably. Drafters of the Code of 1917 lacked the courage needed to abandon useless terms. For that reason, the code contains many conceptual definitions, necessitated by the imprecise nature of canonic language. In the Code of 1917, many concepts have several designations, while many terms express more than one concept. Thus, the term "natural law" appears under these forms: *jus naturale, jus naturae, lex naturalis*. Significantly, the term *jus commune* in this context means "common law of the Church". Expressions based on the word *lex* are many: e.g., *lex universalis.*[38]

Designations of different types of normative acts, from the distant past to the 20th century, give an idea of the diversity of terminology of canon law: *canon* [formerly: '(an) ecclesiastical law'; later: 'rule of canonic law'], *constitutio* [formerly: 'normative act of general character promulgated by the pope'; later, several technical meanings], *lex* ['(an) ecclesiastical law'; 'rule of canonic law'; 'law in general'], *regula* [formerly: '(an) ecclesiastical law'; later: 'legal provision', 'rule of law'], *statutum* ['(a special) ecclesiastical law', 'articles regulating an ecclesiastic community (e.g., ecclesiastic chapter)'], *decretum* [notably: 'decisions of synods', 'normative papal acts', 'normative acts of assemblies of cardinals and bishops'], *instructio* [often: 'non-compulsory direction'; occasionally: 'normative compulsory act'], *praescriptum* ['regulation of normative character'], *praescriptio* [occasionally: synonym of *praescriptum*, often: 'individual act'], *praeceptum* ['order'; occasionally: 'normative

35 Mörsdorf 1967: 24.
36 Mörsdorf 1967: 21.
37 Mörsdorf 1967: 26 and 38.
38 Mörsdorf 1967: 41–42.

order'], *edictum* ['declaration'], *ordinatio* [formerly: '(a) law'; later, occasionally: 'regulation'], *sanctio* [previously: '(an) ecclesiastical law'; later: 'sanction'].[39]

In the *Codex juris canonici* of 1983, the perspective of regulation has changed: no longer does it embrace only the ecclesiastic (*clericus*), but also the believer (*christifidelis*). This is why – as we have already mentioned – the code appears in the form of vernacular editions, although only the Latin text is authentic. Besides, the change of perspective appears from the fact of an attempt having been made to clarify the concepts of the code and the terminology that expresses them. However, criticism has been voiced to the effect that there remains too much polysemy in the language of canon law.[40]

3 Latin in Modern Legal Languages

3.1 Overview: "Latin is Dead – Long Live Latin"

3.1.1 The Situation at the International Level Over recent centuries, modern national languages have ousted Latin as the active language of lawyers. Although Latin is no longer the language of legal science, or of legal practice – leaving aside canon law – it has left important traces in modern legal languages. On the one hand, this is a matter of sentence level: the style of modern legal languages still reflects the rhythm of old legal Latin. On the other hand, a large proportion of the vocabulary of modern legal languages comes from the legal Latin used in Antiquity, the Middle Ages, or the beginning of modern times.

In the Romance languages and English, the vocabulary coming from legal Latin appears, for the most part, in quasi-original form, slightly modified. But the legal languages of other European countries (e.g., German, Greek, western Slavic languages, Nordic languages) also possess a great number of words of Latin origin. In these languages can likewise be found many loan translations (calques): Latin words used as a structural model to form new words in modern legal languages. It also has to be remembered that legal Latin has often given a new meaning to a word already existing in a modern language (the borrowed meaning of words).

But Latin elements also appear as such in modern legal languages. Modern texts contain direct Latin quotations: terms, other expressions, and maxims. This is partly a matter of rhetoric: Latin is used as a stylistic tool; an aesthetic medium. This is often explained by the need to impress the reader. Thus, by using Latin expressions and maxims, a lawyer sets out to show his professional competence in front of the uninitiated, or his colleagues. According to Ernst Kramer, Latin expressions and maxims form part of the "beloved folklore" of lawyers – folklore that law students rapidly make their own, even if Latin no longer forms part of subjects taught.[41] Learning to use Latin expressions and maxims forms part of the socializing process

---

39 Mörsdorf 1967: 54–65.
40 Aymans & Mörsdorf 1991: 129–131.
41 Kramer 1995: 141–142.

of future lawyers. However, these expressions and maxims often fulfil a more important function. They are used to convince the reader or listener of the content of the legal order or to explain a legal concept. Moreover, Latin maxims have a mnemonic importance, thanks to their often rhythmic character.

The breadth and intensity of use of Latin quotations varies from one legal culture to another. Generally, it can be said that they are more often used in legal science than in legal practice, e.g., legislation, case law, private documents.[42] In many countries (the Nordic countries, for example), legislation and case law contain hardly any Latin quotations. By contrast, other countries use these quotations more often. This is especially true of the common law countries: English and American judgments and other documents contain expressions such as *erga omnes* ['in regard to all', 'universally binding'], *inter alia* ['amongst other things'], *assumpsit* ['he undertook'; in connection with an action for failure to carry out a contractual obligation], *mens rea* ['guilty intent', lit. 'blameworthy state of mind'], *per diem* ['by the day'; referring, i.a., to a fixed daily rate of remuneration], *per stirpes* ['per branch / stirps'; in the matter of rights of succession], *stare decisis* ['to stand by decisions'; expresses the rule of precedent], *subpoena* ['under penalty of'; name given to a summons compelling an individual to appear before a court to give testimony], and so on. Examples include *non compos mentis* (Vermont Statutes: 18 V.S.A 106, § 5163), *mens rea* (US Court of Appeals for the 9ᵗʰ Circuit: USA v. Sablan 94–10533), *per stirpes* (Alaska Statutes 13.12.709; Kansas Court of Appeals *in re* Estate of Winslow 74,6663; various model wills), *stare decisis* (Alaska Supreme Court: Thomas v. Anchorage Equal Rights Commission 12/10/2994, sp – 5850).

It is clear that Latin expressions and maxims appearing in legal documents (e.g., judgments) cause difficulties from the lay standpoint but often also from that of lawyers. That is why the authorities and language specialists from various countries have been determined to limit the use of Latin in judgments. An example is the circular from the French Ministry of Justice of 15 September 1977, probably inspired by the celebrated work by Pierre Mimin.[43] This circular recommends that higher and lower courts in their judgments should replace the majority of Latin terms and other expressions with the corresponding French terms. For example,[44] *lucrum cessans* = manque à gagner ['a ceasing gain'], *de cujus* = défunt ['deceased']; *de cujus* is an elliptical expression of which the complete form is: *de cujus hereditate agitur* ['the one whose estate is at issue']. In the same way, the author of the Italian *Manuale di stile* recommends *persona che lascia un'eredità* ['person who leaves an inheritance'] in place of the expression *de cujus*.[45] A corresponding tendency is noticeable in England.[46] As a counterweight, it can be stated that German and Scottish courts are

---

42 As for common law, see Kurzon 1987: 239.
43 Mimin 1970: 58–62.
44 Troisfontaines 1981: 178–181.
45 Gutmann 1999: 85.
46 Stępkowski 2001: 105–107.

among those that consider Latin quotations permissible in documents relating to judicial proceedings.[47]

In the majority of textbooks covering legal language, the authors have taken a negative attitude towards using Latin quotations.[48] Nevertheless, exceptions can be found. For example, in their book on (Brazilian) Portuguese legal language, Regina Toledo Damião and Antonio Henriques speak in favour of Latinisms appearing in the briefs and other writings of advocates and prosecutors: *lembre-se o profissional do Direito que o latinismo é sempre oportuno, mas acompanhado de explicações de seu significado, sempre feitas com naturalidade, como se pretendessem realçar a idéia* ['the Law professional should remember that the Latinism is always timely but should be accompanied by explanations as to its meaning, always done in a natural manner, given that the aim is to conceptualize the idea behind the Latinism'].[49]

Legal Latin is used in all Western countries, at least in works by legal scholars. In Eastern Europe, it is especially interesting to note the change that has taken place in Russia in recent times. After that country's abandonment of socialism, the status of Roman law has clearly strengthened there: indeed, today it is an obligatory discipline in law faculties in Russia.[50] This strengthening is also reflected at the linguistic level. Significantly, new dictionaries of legal Latin have been published in recent years and a complete Russian translation of the Digest is being elaborated at the beginning of the third millennium.[51] By the same token, an increase in scholarly words coming from Roman law is demonstrably taking place in Russian legislative texts.[52] The strengthening of legal Latin, following the fall of socialism, is not confined to Russia alone. In Estonia, for example, a significant increase in Latin expressions and maxims has been noticeable in legal articles published in the law review *Juridica* during the period 1993–2002.[53] Russian and Estonian lawyers – along with their Polish colleagues – are in this way determined to show that they belong to the old legal-cultural community of Europe, whose traditions go back to the time of Antiquity.

Legal Latin is likewise in evidence in some non-European legal cultures which, during the colonial period or through attraction towards the West, have borrowed a good deal of Western law. In this context, they have adopted a large number of technical terms from Western languages, Latin included. An interesting example is Indonesian legal language. Here, under the influence of legal science from the Netherlands and, more recently, from America (partly also through Malaysia, where common law dominates), authors use Latin expressions and maxims to a considerable

---

47 Hennemann 1999: 413 and Robbie the Pict v. MacDonald 2001, Greens Weekly Digest, 15 June 2001, no. 764 (the author owes this information to Colin Brown and Richard Wainwright).
48 See e.g. Garner 2002: 193-195.
49 Damião & Henriques 2000: 241.
50 Sukhanov 2001: 10 and Rudokvas 2001: 8.
51 Kofanov 2001–.
52 Mattila 2002a: 722–723.
53 Ristikivi 2003: 728–729.

extent. In Indonesia, a comprehensive dictionary of legal Latin has been published: it contains around 5,000 expressions and maxims in Latin with translations into Indonesian.

> In the preface, the author refers to the fact that foreign expressions in Indonesian law received from the West (particularly the Netherlands) often stem originally from Latin words.[54] Indeed, the importance of Latin is visible in Indonesian legal literature. For example, Sunarjati Hartono has written a fairly concise work in the discipline of conflicts of internal laws. According to my calculations, the work contains – besides numerous Dutch and English quotations – 18 Latin expressions.[55]

3.1.2 The Finnish Example In clear contrast to the 17th century, practical legal documents (e.g., judgments) in today's Finland no longer have any Latin content. However, it is otherwise for legal science, notably in certain branches of law, where the country's legal scholars have recourse to Latin expressions and maxims. As a result, knowledge of these expressions and maxims still forms part of the basic professional competence of Finnish lawyers, at least as regards the most important of these.

To ascertain the extent to which Latin expressions and maxims are still used in Finnish legal literature, the author of this work – with help from two assistants – carried out research to this end. We assembled all the Latin expressions and maxims from legal textbooks and theses from the 1950s and the 1990s.[56]

The research showed that works from the 1990s included in total around 600 different expressions and maxims. Around 270 expressions and maxims appeared at least twice, around 170 expressions and maxims at least three times, and around 80 expressions and maxims at least five times. If we take three occurrences as the minimum limit of established use, the conclusion is that basic Finnish legal Latin vocabulary today consists of almost 200 different expressions and maxims. In the 1950s, the total number of Latin expressions and maxims was still about 900. Thus it can be said that the diversity of these expressions and maxims is today markedly less than forty years earlier. At the same time, it has to be admitted that in recent decades legal scholars in Finland have not entirely abandoned use of Latin in their publications – far from it!

Next, the research showed that the majority of Latin quotations were to be found in texts of certain branches of the law. The first place was occupied by civil law, both in the 1950s and the 1990s. Criminal, procedural, and international law were likewise placed high on the two lists. This, then, implies branches of the law where theoretical considerations are of great importance, or those with international features. As to this last point of view, it is worth noting that international economic law (e.g., the European Communities) does not appear high on the lists. Finnish researchers in this last law use few Latinisms, in spite of the international sources of material.

---

54 Hamzah 1985: V.
55 Hartono 1991.
56 Mattila 2000: 288–294.

3.2 Quotations

Latin quotations – expressions and maxims – constitute Latin's most striking influence on modern legal languages. In legal texts, these quotations are usually written in italics. They may have three different functions: rhetoric, display function, or expressing legal concepts.

> The work of formulating legal maxims (in Latin: *paraemia, regula, maxima, brocardus*) began in the post-classical era. The Digest contains two headings entitled *De diversis regulis juris antiqui* ['On the various rules of ancient law', D.50.17] and *De verborum significatione* ['On the meaning of words', D.50.16]. These likewise contain, besides definitions of legal terms, principles of law. Elaboration of maxims continued in the era of the glossators. Notably, it was the glossators who crystallized Roman law, quite casuistic in character, in well-wrought maxims. Therefore, many legal maxims do not come from classical Roman law. They may go back to Antiquity but, as such, they were formulated later, even today.[57]
>
> From the linguistic standpoint (as pointed out by Dennis Kurzon), Latin quotations may be grouped according to their levels of integration in modern language text. It may be a matter of an entire Latin sentence in the middle of a modern language text; of a Latin maxim as part of a modern language sentence, or of a Latin term between parentheses in a modern language sentence. Notably from the standpoint of the English language, more detailed divisions can also be presented, because the nature of that language allows a Latin expression to function in a sentence as qualifier of a noun.[58]

3.2.1 Rhetoric In the European cultural tradition, expressions and maxims from the classical languages raise the level of the text and add splendour to it. This is likewise the case for legal science. For example, authors use a Latin conjunction instead of a conjunction from their own language. A typical example taken from a recent French article (the underlining of the Latin conjunction was done by us): " ... *Une première impression serait qu'elles conviennent à des lois qui se veulent novatrices. Sed contra les réformes du droit de la famille de la Ve république n'ont été précédées d'aucune...*".[59]

Such rhetorical use of Latin is common even among lawyers from countries far removed from the heart of Europe. This is notably the case in Finland. As pointed out above, we recently carried out empirical research there on the Latin of Finnish lawyers.[60] In Finnish theses and dissertations of the 1990s, the Latin cultural expressions listed below appeared at least three times (the number of works in which there are occurrences are shown in parentheses): *ratio* [' reason'; 10], *de facto* [' in fact', 'in deed', 'actually'; 10], *e contrario* ['in the opposite (sense)', 'on the contrary'; 10], *prima facie* ['at first sight', see below; 10], *ex ante* ['from

---

57 Wołodkiewicz 2001b: 17–21.
58 Kurzon 1987: 233–240.
59 Rouhette 1999: 49.
60 Mattila 2000.

what was previously', meaning often: '(on the basis of) a forecasted estimate'; 7], *in casu* ['in the present case', 'in each particular case'; 7], *ex post [facto]* ['what was done after some other thing', often referring to a later examination; 6], *ad hoc* ['for that purpose'; 5], *numerus clausus* ['limited number'; 5], *pro et contra* ['for and against'; 5], *status quo* ['the current situation'; 5], *ultima ratio* ['the final argument'; 5], *a priori* ['from the very first', 'from what goes before'; 'from the cause to the effect'; 4], *passim* ['here and there'; 4], *a fortiori (causa)* ['with stronger reason', 'even more so'; 3], *ex analogia* ['by analogy'; 3], *genus* ['species', 'type'; 3] and *sui generis* ['of its own kind or class"; 3].

Likewise, we note that many Finnish lawyers always follow the Latin tradition in the method of referencing: & ['and'], & *al.* = *et alii* ['and others' (when only the first-named author of a collective work is mentioned)], &*c.* = *et cetera* ['and so on' (when there are several publishing houses or where these have several domiciles)], & *sqq.* = *et sequentes* ['and those following' (when the author only mentions the page on which the reference mentioned begins)], *ed.* = *edidit/ediderunt* ['edited by'], *in* ['in' (a work or article)], *in fine* ['in the end'], *passim* ['here and there' (in places in a text)], *p.* = *pagina* ['page'], *pp.* = *paginae* ['pages'].

Quite often, expressions used by authors are placed half-way between general cultural Latin and legal Latin. Let us take the expression *prima facie*. In German and Italian dictionaries of legal Latin, this expression is given the general meaning of 'at first sight', but also the meaning of 'according to the truth that comes from experience' or 'according to a principle derived from experience', notably in the expression *Prima-facie-Beweis*. Dictionaries of common law express the same idea: *prima facie evidence* is evidence that may be set aside by contrary evidence. Besides, in the Spanish-speaking world, *prima facie* is used in relation to orders that can be contested (for example, temporary detention orders). According to our empirical research, the two meanings (general and legal-technical) also appear in texts of Finnish authors.

3.2.2 The Display Function of Latin Latin possesses high status value in the Western world. That is why it has been used – and is still used – as a symbol linking legal science and practical lawyering to the common European tradition. Legal Latin maxims can often be found on the walls of courthouses. Likewise, the seals of judicial authorities are often adorned with such expressions or maxims. This is also the case for the emblems of public organs and law societies or bar associations. This is what could be called the display function of the Latin language. Examples are almost innumerable. One of these is the emblem of German notaries: *Lex est quodcumque notamus*. This means: 'All we write down is binding' or, in free translation: 'Our mark gives the force of law'. Here, the word *lex* is used in a very broad meaning, also covering clauses in private documents.[61]

A particularly fine example of the display function of legal Latin is the decoration of the new courthouse of the Polish Supreme Court, inaugurated in 1999. Some of

---

61 Bertzel 1993: 775.

the courthouse walls are flanked, on the outside, by a row of columns. The architect who planned the courthouse intended that these columns should be decorated with inscriptions that – according to ancient tradition – would indicate the ideology and use of the building. His original intention was to use maxims from Polish law currently in force. The members of the Supreme Court did not support this idea because the law in force is changeable. Thus was born the idea that the courthouse should be decorated with Latin maxims of universal and eternal character. Most of the 86 maxims used in the decoration of the courthouse are taken from the Digest or, at the very least, go back to it. For example, the first column bears the celebrated maxim against corrupt officialdom: *Qui munus publice mandatum accepta pecunia ruperunt, crimine repetundarum postulantur* ['Those who violate their public responsibility of office by taking money, are liable to criminal charges of corruption', D.48.11.9]. Some maxims come from the non-legal literature of Antiquity. Two of these have been taken from Latin sources of Polish legal history: *justitias vestras judicabo* ['I will judge your impartiality'; inscription on the court walls in Poland of old times] and *neminem captivabimus nisi jure victum* [in free translation: 'no imprisonment without due legal process'; maxim included in the privileges of Ladislas Jagellon].[62]

The display function of Latin also has a high profile in countries on the periphery of Europe, such as Finland.[63] Especially noteworthy are the old seals of the courts of appeal of Finland: SIGILLVM SVPREMI IVDICII MAGNI DVCATVS FINLANDIÆ ['the seal of the High Court (lit. 'of the Supreme Court) of the Grand-Duchy of Finland'; Court of Appeal of Turku], SIGILL. SUPR. DICASTERII WASAEI A GUSTAVO III CONST. ['the seal of the High Court (lit. 'of the Supreme Court) of Vaasa established by Gustav III'; Court of Appeal of Vaasa], SIGILLVM DICASTERII SVPREMI WIBVRGENSIS ['the seal of the High Court (lit. 'of the Supreme Court) of Viborg'; Court of Appeal of Viborg – today, a Russian city]. This also concerns epigraphs and commemorative medals. One of the walls of the old courthouse in Vaasa bears an inscription that reads as follows: GUSTAVUS III R. S. ANNO IMP. XII EXTRUXIT THEMIDIQUE DICAVIT ['erected and dedicated to Themis (goddess of Justice) by Gustav III, King of Sweden, in the twelfth year of his reign']. The medal commemorating the founding of the Court of Appeal of Vaasa bears the inscription: MISERIS PERFUGIUM MALIS PERNICIES. TRIBUNAL WASAEUM MDCCLXXV ['refuge for the wretched, damnation for the wicked. Court of Vaasa 1775']. Mention should also be made of Finnish legal publications, which can have titles such as *Defensor Legis* ['Defender of the Law'], *Bibliographia Juridica Fennica* ['Legal Bibliography of Finland', 1951–], *Encyclopædia Juridica Fennica* ['Legal Encyclopaedia of Finland', 1994–1999] or *Liber amicorum Carolo Makkonen deditus* ['Book dedicated to Kaarle Makkonen by his friends', 1986], marked by the editors: *Hoc volumen edendum curaverunt Urpo Kangas & Kaarlo Tuori* ['Publication of this book arranged by Urpo Kangas and Kaarlo Tuori'].

---

62 Wołodkiewicz 2001c: 13–14 and 17–21.
63 Mattila 2000: 281–282.

3.2.3 Legal Concepts and Principles Even after Latin was abandoned as the lawyers' living language, it has often been used to express legal concepts with precision. This has been particularly common in situations where a new legal language, the terms of which were still uncertain, aspired to creation. Here again, we can cite the history of Finnish law. Modern legal Finnish was essentially created at the end of the 19th century and the beginning of the 20th century. In legal dissertations of those times, the author would often clarify the meaning of a new Finnish term by adding the corresponding Latin term in parentheses. However, it should be emphasized that Latin quotations, to express legal concepts, are also used today, and this even in languages already long-established (e.g., English, German, French).

Apart from legal science, in some countries these quotations are also used by courts and government. This particularly applies to the *common law* countries – but not only. Let us take the case of Poland, where a group of specialists carried out detailed research on this topic. With the help of a computer, the group looked for the main Latin quotations in judgments of the Constitutional Court, the Supreme Court, the High Administrative Court and certain courts of appeal, from 1971 to 2001 (in all, some 35,000 judicial decisions). By virtue of this method, it was possible to establish a list of the most common expressions and maxims, with information on their frequency.[64]

The ten most popular expressions are (the number in parentheses): *ratio legis* ['the reason of a law; the occasion for making a law'; 411]; *lege non distinguente*; the end left off the maxim: *nec nostrum est distinguere* ['what the law does not take notice of (lit. 'distinguish'), we, too, should take no notice of'; 77]; *jus* ['the law'; with epithets, 61]; *res judicata* ['a matter adjudged', 'a thing or matter settled by judgment'; 'final (non-appealable) judgment'; 'rule that final judgment constitutes an absolute bar to a subsequent action involving the same claim'; 50]; *quo ad usum* ['with a view to usage (in company law); 49]; *erga omnes* ['in regard to all', 'universally binding'; 47); *in rem* ['against a thing (in property-law actions)'; 39]; *ad rem* ['with regard to a thing/ matter'; 37]; *jus ad rem* ['a right to a thing'; 37]; *contra legem* ['against the law'; 29]. In a parallel direction, the ten most popular maxims are: *lex retro non agit* ['the law does not operate retroactively'; 140]; *in dubio pro reo* ['in case of doubt, in favour of the accused/the defendant'; 110]; *nullum crimen (nulla poena) sine lege (poenali)* [in free translation: 'the only crimes, the only penalties are those prescribed by law'; 47]; *pacta sunt servanda* ['agreements/ contracts should be respected'; 37]; *clara non sunt interpretanda* [in free translation: 'transparent text requires no interpretation'; 29]; *nemo plus juris in alium transferre potest, quam ipse haberet* [in free translation: 'you cannot transfer to someone else a greater right than you yourself possess'; 27]; *superficies solo cedit* ['the surface yields to the soil', meaning: 'Whatever is attached to the land forms part of it'; 26]; *ne bis in idem* ['not twice for the same'; 23]; *in dubio pro fisco* ['where in doubt, in favour of the fisc; 21]; *exceptiones non sunt extendendae* ['exceptions should not be broadly interpreted' 19]. The second research enabled a finding that the ombudsman

---

64 Wołodkiewicz 2001c: 10–11.

of the Polish Republic likewise uses Latin quotations. He makes notable recourse to the maxim *pacta sunt servanda*. This normally concerns cases where the ombudsman declares that the public authorities should respect their obligations. The maxim *lex retro non agit* is also quite common. Moreover, the ombudsman's decisions contain maxims such as: *nullum crimen sine lege, exceptiones non sunt extendendae, ignorantia juris nocet* ['failure to know the law stands one to disadvantage'], *dura lex sed lex* ['the law is hard, but it is the law'], *clara non sunt interpretanda* (see above).[65]

Latin expressions and maxims have been – and still are – particularly common in cases where there is a desire to guarantee their international understandability. As regards Central Europe, the example of the *Allgemeines Bürgerliches Gesetzbuch* (1811) can be mentioned. When this code was translated into the various languages of the Austrian Empire (of which several were only quite recently in use for legal matters), after the main terms translated were added the corresponding ones in Latin.[66]

Today, practical lawyers seeking to guarantee the international understandability of legal texts use Latin quotations notably in two cases: international organisations, and international commercial arbitration. In Article 33, paragraph 2, of the arbitration rules of the United Nations Commission on International Trade Law (UNCITRAL), for example, appears the expression *ex aequo et bono:* "The arbitral tribunal shall decide as *amiable compositeur* or *ex aequo et bono* only if (…)". Other examples of Latin expressions often used in these contexts include *aequitas mercatoria* ['commercial fairness'] and *bona fides* ['good faith'].[67]

As for legal science, new legal phenomena of an international character often acquire a Latin name. For example, the new unified European law (notably through the activities of the European Union) is sometimes termed *jus commune novum,* ['the new common law'] and a company formed under community legislation is designated *societas Europaea* ['European company'].

Likewise, it may occur that Latin is used for mutual intelligibility within one and the same State. This is so where diverse legal traditions are found in the territory of a single State. Canada offers a good example. Here, the law is influenced both by common law and by law of French origin. Quebec's *Code Civil* has been translated into English, as foreseen by the country's linguistic legislation. The preamble to the Code in French appears in the following terms: "(…) *Le code est constitué d'un ensemble de règles qui, en toutes matières auxquelles se rapportent la lettre, l'esprit ou l'objet de ses dispositions, établit, en termes exprès ou de façon implicite, le droit commun.*(…)". As for the English version, this is formulated as follows: "(…) *The Civil Code comprises a body of rules which, in all matters within the letter, spirit or object of its provisions, lays down the jus commune* [sic!]*, expressly or*

---

65 Marquez 2001: 227–244.
66 Wacke 1990: 886.
67 Meyer 1994: 14.

by implication.(...)".[68] The use of the Latin expression in the English version is explained by the fact that the literal translation of the term *droit commun* would be *common law* – a term quite misleading in this context: the common law refers to law of English origin.

When Latin is used to express legal concepts, great liberties are often taken from the standpoint of Latin grammar. The part-of-speech classification is often changed. This is especially typical of common law. Let us take the word *assumpsit*, used today as a noun. Literally, the word means 'he undertook', 'he promised'. Formerly, *assumpsit* made reference to an action based on contract. Today, this expression means 'a promise or engagement by which one person assumes or undertakes to do some act or pay something to another'.[69] Another similar example is *affidavit*. This Latin word means literally 'he affirmed' and has the legal meaning of 'a written or printed declaration confirmed by an oath'. The phenomenon in question is also no stranger in continental Europe. The word *fiat* means literally: 'let it be done'. In Spanish legal Latin, this has obtained the meaning of 'order by which something should be performed' and of 'approval of the entry into force or realisation of a fact'.[70]

As for Latin maxims expressing legal principles, these are as common as Latin expressions. Arbitral decisions often contain maxims such as *pacta sunt servanda* ['agreements should be respected']; *verba ita sunt intelligenda ut res magis valeat quam pereat* ['the words (of a contract) should be understood in such a way that the agreement should be valid rather than void']; *qui elegit judicem elegit jus* [in free translation: 'choice of judge also implies choice of law'].[71] In the practice of the board of appeal of the European Patent Office appears: *tu patere legem quam fecisti* [' you have to bear the contractual clause (lit. 'the law') that you made (yourself)'] and *qui tacet consentire videtur* [in free translation: 'silence implies consent'].[72] Importantly, Latin legal maxims often appear in shortened form. Only the first word, or the first few words, of the maxim in question are taken, to form a kind of linguistic code. For example, the maxim *pater (is) est quem nuptiae demonstrant* [in free translation: 'marriage makes the father (of a child) presumed', literally: 'the (identity of the) father (of a child) is demonstrated (implied) by the fact of marriage'] is sometimes expressed in shortened form. A lawyer might say, for example: "That is clear by virtue of the principle *pater is est*."

In this context arises an entirely different question, discussed notably in Germany: do legal principles expressed through Latin maxims still correspond to the content of current law? From this standpoint, the following are some of the maxims that have been examined: *falsa demonstratio non nocet* ['a false description does not injure/vitiate'], *ambiguitas contra stipulatorem* ['ambiguity (in a document) should be

---

68 Gémar 1995: 202.
69 Black's Law Dictionary 2000.
70 Martín & al. 1996: 10.
71 Meyer 1994: 14.
72 Knütel 1994: 251–253.

interpreted to the disadvantage of the drafter], *lex specialis derogat legi generali* ['a specific law derogates from general law'], *singularia non sunt extendenda* ['specific rules should not be interpreted extensively'] and *cessante legis ratione cessat lex ipsa* ['once the reason for a law ceases, so does the law itself']. Amongst these maxims, *falsa demonstratio non nocet* appears, amongst others, in Swiss legislation on contractual obligations.

In general, these maxims are not quite exact, from the standpoint of current law. That is understandable: it is a matter of principles of law, to which there are always exceptions. That is why Latin maxims are considered to have a persuasive function: they provide a basis on which to reinforce principles that only appear in a sporadic manner in positive law. Moreover, thanks to Latin maxims it is easy to raise these principles to the international level.[73] Latin-American authors also emphasize their persuasive function. In Brazil, one author characterizes Latin maxims as a kind of compass indicating the proper direction in legal interpretation.[74] However, the direction indicated by this compass may be ambiguous. The maxim *ambiguitas contra stipulatorem*, for instance, has been interpreted in two opposite ways in common-law countries and in continental countries: either against the creditor or against the debtor, according to the understanding of the word *stipulator*.[75]

3.3 Terms of Latin Origin in Modern Legal Languages

3.3.1 The Common Heritage of Words The Latin heritage in modern legal languages also shows itself in terms of Latin origin, adapted to the rules relative to word formation and orthography of the particular language. It is true that in the Romance languages and English these terms are formed, in part, in a natural way: the Romance languages gradually became different from Latin, while the English language became Gallicised in the Middle Ages. But, even in these languages, a considerable part of the vocabulary and phraseology used in legal contexts comes from legal Latin of the Middle Ages and modern times. In that legal Latin, a large number of neologisms were created.

This legal-linguistic Latin heritage is largely common to the whole of Europe. Let us take the word *codex*. This appears, in modified national form, throughout Europe: *code* (English, French), *codice* (Italian), *código* (Spanish, Portuguese), *kodeks* (Polish), *kod/kodeks/kodex* (Scandinavian languages), *koodeksi/koodi* (Finnish). Finnish is a non Indo-European language, very different from the Indo-European languages as to grammar and word formation. But, in spite of that, the language of Finnish legal scholars contains a large number of words of Latin origin. It is enough to consult the index of the *Encyclopædia Juridica Fennica*. Let us take the letters 'b','d' and 'f': *bilateraalinen* (*bilateralis*), *defensiivinen* (*defensivus*), *deklaratiivinen* (*declarativus*), *delegointi* (*delegatio*), *delikti* (*delictum*), *denuntiaatio* (*denuntiatio*),

---

73   Kramer 1995: 141–158.
74   Xavier 2000: 213–214.
75   Ferreri 2000: 184–200 and 2003: 117–139.

dereliktio (*derelictio*), *derogaatio* (*derogatio*), *diaari* (*diarium*), *dilatorinen* (*dilatorius*), *direktio* (*directio*), *disponointi* (*dispositio*), *dissimulaatio* (*dissimulatio*), *domisiili* (*domicilium*), *fideikommissi* (*fideicommissum*), *fidusiaarinen* (*fiduciarius*), *fiktio* (*fictio*), *foorumi* (*forum*).

3.3.2 The Danger of Mistakes and Misunderstandings The common language heritage, coming from the Latin language, considerably facilitates communication between lawyers from various countries. At the same time, it has to be firmly said that it can cause the danger of mistakes and misunderstandings. It often occurs that variants of Latin origin that look alike, or expressions translated directly from a foreign language (in the final analysis, from Latin), mean different things in different linguistic zones.[76] The most difficult cases are those where the interpretation of a legal text permits several meanings. An example is words referring to the various courts of law.[77] – We shall see below that, besides adapted words of Latin origin, direct Latin quotations can likewise cause mistakes and misunderstandings.[78]

3.4 Calques and Borrowed Meanings

As already mentioned, a calque (loan translation) signifies that a new word is formed in the target language by imitating the elements of the original word in the source language. A borrowing of meaning signifies that a word already existing in a language obtains a new meaning – normally more abstract than previously – under the effect of a foreign language. These phenomena already occurred on a massive scale in Antiquity, from Greek to Latin. For example, *unio*, in the Christian sense ('religious unity' and 'community') was adopted in Latin according to the model given by *hénosis* ('ἕνωσις), created on the basis of the noun of the number 'one'.

Later, these two forms of influence appeared in abundance in relationships between legal Latin and the modern legal languages of Western and Central Europe. Above all, it was legal German that gained a wealth of legal neologisms, based on models provided by legal Latin. Moreover, old words in German often obtained a new legal meaning under the influence of Latin. From legal German, these words were transmitted into the legal languages of the Nordic countries and Central and Eastern Europe. Often, the same word can be both a calque and an example of borrowed meaning. Let us take as an example the expression *onus probandi*. This metaphorical expression, coming from the lawyers of Ancient Rome, exists throughout Europe, in the form of a calque.[79] At the same time, *onus probandi* is an example of borrowed meaning. In each of these languages, the word meaning a concrete burden has obtained an abstract sense of obligation.

---

76 Burr & Gallas 2004: 232.
77 See pp. 264–265.
78 See p. 155.
79 See p. 76.

Another similar example is *fons juris*, likewise dating from the days of Antiquity. Livy uses the expression *fons omnis publici privatique juris* in referring to the Law of the XII Tables. In all modern legal languages, this expression is very common: πηγή δικαίου (*pigí dikaíou*, modern Greek), *fonte del Diritto* (Italian), *fuente de(l) Derecho* (Spanish), *source du Droit* (French), *source of law* (English), *Rechtsquelle* (German), источник права (*istochnik prava*, Russian), *źródło prawa* (Polish), *rättskälla* (Swedish) and *oikeuslähde* (Finnish). In this expression, a word referring to a natural phenomenon (the flow of water from the ground) has obtained in the various languages, according to the Roman model, an abstract meaning referring to entities from which the law emanates.

Calques concern not only nouns. The so-called "legal pronouns" also mainly come from Latin: *supranominatus* ['named above'], *infranominatus* ['named below'] *dictus* ['the said']. Verbs and adverbs, too, should not be forgotten: e.g., *notum facere* ['to make it known (that)'], *manu propria* ['by one's own hand'].[80]

3.5 Stylistic Reflections of Legal Latin

3.5.1 The Influence of Legal Latin on Modern Legal Languages Besides vocabulary, the modern legal languages of Europe have inherited many of their stylistic properties from legal Latin. This comes as no surprise, because legal Latin and modern legal languages have coexisted for several centuries in the legal life of different countries. This was also the case in the Nordic countries. In Denmark, for example, medieval statutes were long written in Latin but were later rapidly translated into Danish, the language of the people. The stylistic characteristics of legal Latin were highly important in these translations. In addition, other Danish documents were drawn up in Latin until about 1400.[81]

It has to be remembered that the relationship between Latin and popular languages has always been reciprocal. The Germanic languages strongly influenced Medieval Latin, as much from the standpoint of vocabulary as of style. This notably concerned the use of metaphors and rhythmics. For example, the German tradition of alliteration was taken up by medieval legal Latin: *expressio unius exclusio alterius* ['Including one means excluding the other'].[82]

At the same time, the Nordic countries provide an example of the fact that the influences of legal Latin on legal languages in process of formation have often been indirect. The Nordic countries imitated the Low German (*Niederdeutsch*) document style of the Hanseatic city chancelleries – but, in the final analysis, the Hanseatic style goes back to medieval legal Latin style.[83] The language of old Danish documents, for example, often followed Germano-Latin models to such an extent that the reader unfamiliar with these models was unprepared to understand the language. Somewhat

---

80 Holm 1970: 126.
81 von Eyben 1989: 14–15.
82 Tiersma 1999: 22–28.
83 Wellander 1974: 13.

later, Latin left its mark on legal Danish through the medium of German legal science, notably in the field of administrative law. As Leif Becker Jensen noted,[84] it was a matter "of a highly specific cocktail of Danish, German and Latin rhetoric" (*særegne cocktail af dansk, tysk og latinsk retorik*). This style, dominated by the tradition of legal Latin, is called, particularly in Nordic countries, 'chancellery style'.

3.5.2 Characteristics of Chancellery Style   Throughout Europe, certain typical features made chancellery style difficult to understand.[85] First in order of mention is that authors in this style wrote extremely long sentences, often called 'periods', interrupted by numerous subordinate clauses. According to this ideology of writing, every detail (e.g., conditions, exceptions, etc.) relating to the theme of a periodic sentence should be included in this sentence itself, to avoid omissions, mistakes, and misunderstandings. Chancellery style is also characterized by the use of complicated structures at the beginning of sentences, as well as by use of the passive, legal pronouns (e.g., the said) and heavy verbal nouns. In the background of grammatical features of modern legal languages, even non-Romance, can often be distinguished the Latin subjunctive and *ablativus instrumentalis*.[86] It should likewise be mentioned that certain modern legal languages, such as legal Spanish, use double negatives and other inverted means of expression, typical of legal Latin.[87]

> It is characteristic of Latin to express something positive by denying its opposite (litotes): *non ignoro* ['I am not unaware, *i.e.* I know']. Thus, the classical Finnish author Matthias Calonius (1738–1817) often wrote *haud raro*. For example: *Sed accidit haud raro ut duobus vel pluribus eodem infortunio pereuntibus...*[88]

It is worth mentioning that the passage of Latin into modern legal languages accentuated the heaviness of chancellery style. Latin is a synthetic language that enables authors to express themselves laconically, by virtue of the system of cases, notably the ablative. Latin's laconic mode of expression is further reinforced by the frequent omission of conjunctions. Translating a Latin sentence into a modern language often results in verbosity.

3.5.3 The Abandonment of Chancellery Style   The features typical of chancellery style became particularly accentuated, in the legal and administrative languages of Europe, towards the end of the Middle Ages and the beginning of modern times. Some researchers explain this by the strengthening of State power and the increasing complexity of society at that time. These phenomena called for centralized government. A strong central power, far from the citizens, was born. Such an exercise of power presupposed creation of a language more abstract than previously: laws

---

84   Jensen 1998: 31.
85   Myklebust 1996: 19–27.
86   von Eyben 1989: 25 and 44.
87   Martín *et al.* 1996: 56–59.
88   Calonius 1908: 553 *in fine*.

and regulations had to be written in a general way so that they could be applied to individual matters in different parts of the country.[89]

Next, it has to be remembered that chancellery style developed at a time when written culture was a privilege of social elites. The goal of simplicity of language was foreign to the tradition of legal Latin. Rather, lawyers sought to attain linguistic and legal elegance, *elegantia juris*, when writing Latin. To achieve this, they used extremely long sentences, in harmony with the inherent rhythmics of the Latin language. This tradition was transmitted to modern legal languages and has continued until our own times. Long sentences have been typical of legal languages throughout Europe.

However, the style of legal and administrative language has begun to change in recent decades. In various countries, the synthetic style is in course of disappearing from the language. One important reason for this development is the lightning growth of the civil service. Nowadays, legal and administrative language is often used by bureaucrats lacking specific legal training and who are unaware of the tradition of chancellery style. Besides, the demands of democracy have to be taken into consideration: administrators should be better placed than previously to justify their decisions, and this is reflected at the language level. It is a requirement that citizens themselves should be able to understand documents that express the grounds of decisions involving the exercise of power.[90]

Some specialists see problems in this development. They emphasize that certain features of chancellery style are positive. According to them, legal and administrative language should not become like spoken language in every respect. It is necessary to formulate a compromise in which the logicality and lucidity of thought, which are typical of chancellery style, combine with the clarity of means of expression of the spoken language.[91]

4 The Communication Value of Legal Latin

4.1 A Caveat on Variants of Legal Latin

As we have just seen, lawyers from various countries still use direct Latin quotations. It is natural to think that this use noticeably facilitates international cooperation between lawyers, and with increasing intensity in our time. That is clear to see in legal science of various countries. To describe legal Latin, one author coined the metaphor of the "lingua franca of the world's lawyers". Another referred to the former *jus commune* of Europe: it was this law that gave today's lawyers the legal Latin maxims guaranteeing respectively the unity of the European legal orders and international intelligibility between jurists. Indeed, according to one author, over recent decades legal Latin terminology has acquired growing importance from the

---

89 Jensen 1998: 31–33.
90 Myklebust 1996: 26.
91 Myklebust 1996: 27.

standpoint of reciprocal message understanding between lawyers. He emphasizes that Anglo-American legal language is very rich in legal Latin. Finally, legal Latin eliminates translation problems and linguistic disagreements: a dead language is hardly polysemic.

However, lawyers with wide international experience have noted that it is not always easy to understand the legal Latin of foreign colleagues. Jean-Claude Gémar states that "[e]ach language... possesses its own Latin, and its own way of using it",[92] while Pascale Berteloot writes that one should be under no illusions about (legal) Latin as a *lingua franca*.[93] The same expressions and maxims are not used in all countries, and their meaning is not necessarily the same. – This discussion is described in the article by Mattila (2002) which includes detailed references.[94]

Besides, many of today's lawyers lack the necessary qualifications for a linguistic grasp of Latin expressions and maxims: they do not read ordinary Latin. This means that they are unprepared to understand an expression or a maxim written in a form that even slightly differs from one learned by heart. If, for example, a lawyer with no command of ordinary Latin has only learned the expression *nudum pactum* by heart, then he is not capable of recognizing the form *nudo pacto*. Understanding legal Latin is also made more difficult by the fact that it is often used as a sort of code, impossible to decode by purely language means.[95]

This use as a code is especially typical of common law Latin. Very often, the first word (or the first two or three words) of an old Latin sentence is used to express a legal notion. A good example is *nisi prius*. The literal translation 'unless before' gives no idea of the sense of these words. According to English and American legal dictionaries, it originally involved a situation where jury members only had to come to London *if* proceedings had *not* already been commenced in the country *beforehand*. Today, *nisi prius* is used to indicate that it is a matter of proceedings at first instance with a jury present. As a result, a *nisi prius* court is a lower-instance court that tries cases with juror participation.

A particular problem appears in the shape of oral use of legal Latin expressions and maxims. In different countries, the Latin accents (e.g., German, English, French, Italian, Nordic, Polish) differ widely. That makes it difficult to understand spoken Latin expressions and maxims, even where the listener knows them in writing. This is particularly so for the Latin of Anglo-Saxon lawyers (common-law lawyers). They pronounce Latin almost as they would their own language (the so-called Anglo-Latin). However, among young American lawyers there is a tendency towards classical pronunciation.[96]

Under these conditions, it would be important to know, from the standpoint of international communication among lawyers, how widely and on which points expressions and maxims in use in various countries differ in reality. Given the

---

92 Gémar 1995: 98.

93 Berteloot 1999.

94 Mattila 2002a.

95 See p. 145.

96 Tiersma 1999: 53–55, and Black's Law Dictionary, pp. vii–x (The Pronunciation of Latin). See below pp. 239–240.

absence of earlier studies, the author of these pages and his research assistants carried out – on the basis of specialist dictionaries – an empirical research on this topic, published in French.[97] In this research, a sort of *tertium comparationis* appears in the shape of legal Latin dictionaries from German-speaking countries. The research compared their content with that of three groups of dictionaries, chosen on the basis of the division of legal orders into major legal families. The first group consists of Anglo-American dictionaries, the second of dictionaries published in Romance languages, and the third of Polish dictionaries. They thus represent the common law and the civil law (Romano-Germanic) legal families, the latter in two variants: the laws of Romance-language countries and the laws of Central Eastern Europe. The purpose of the research was to find out to what extent these dictionaries are made up of the same expressions and maxims; to what extent the meanings given to these expressions and maxims are the same; and to what extent their exterior form is the same. The results of the research are as follows.

4.2 International Coherence of Legal Latin

4.2.1 Major Legal Families and Legal Latin Our research shows that part of legal Latin is of international character. This is particularly visible within the civil-law legal family. The majority – in one dictionary, practically all – of the expressions and maxims included in German-language dictionaries were found in at least one dictionary from the Romance countries. Undoubtedly, the heritage of the European *jus commune* explains this observation.[98] Until the end of the 18th century, legal science in continental Europe was supranational. Legal scholars of the countries of this region studied and developed, in Latin, a common legal system, independently of State borders.

Additionally, a partial coherence – though to a lesser extent – exists between the common law countries and the civil law countries: one-fourth of the Latin expressions and maxims in German-language dictionaries were found in common law dictionaries. We have to remember that England, in spite of its native positive law, was never completely left out of the common legal science of continental Europe. This common science had an influence in England, notably through the agency of Canon law and the *lex mercatoria*.[99] For that reason, a large part of Western legal thought is common to both the civil law countries and the common law countries. Expressions and maxims belonging to this common heritage can be used in any Western legal culture. On the other hand, till the middle of the 20th century continental legal thinking had a fairly strong influence on the United States. Nowadays, we should also recall the convergence of common law and continental law, by virtue of the activities of the European Union and the universal reception

---

97 Mattila 2002a.
98 Knütel 1994: 244–276 and Berman & Reid 1995: 3–34.
99 Berman & Reid: 11–12.

of legal institutions developed in the United States. This implies that legal Latin is crossing the boundaries of legal families more easily than previously.

By way of exception, certain civil law countries also previously received common law institutions, sometimes adopting their Anglo-Latin title. Thus, the institution of *habeas corpus* was included in the Brazilian Constitition of 1891, under the same name. Today, Article 5/LXVIII of the 1988 Constitution has the following tenor: *conceder-se-á habeas-corpus sempre que alguém sofrer ou se achar ameaçado de sofrer violência ou coação em sua liberdade de locomoção por ilegalidade ou abuso de poder* ['*habeas corpus* is always granted when someone suffers or is under threat of suffering violence or restraint on freedom of movement, by reason of an illegal act or abuse of power']. The term *habeas corpus,* included in the Constitution, is of course reflected in documents referring to it, for example in forms concerning the release of a person illegally detained (*habeas corpus liberatório*).[100]

The other side of the coin is that the content of Anglo-American dictionaries of legal Latin is largely (three-fourths) original in comparison with those of the German linguistic zone. It is symptomatic that these last-mentioned dictionaries contain entries provided with the note *im angloamerikanischen Recht* ['in Anglo-American law'], for example in the case of the expression *amicus curiae*.[101] The concept expressed by this term is unknown in continental laws.

In sum, our research discloses considerable divergence between different legal cultures as to the coherence of legal Latin. Legal Latin dictionaries published in the Romance countries and Poland include three times more expressions and maxims in common with dictionaries of the German linguistic zone than with dictionaries from the Anglo-Saxon countries. As a result, a firm basis exists to distinguish between common law and civil law as regards legal Latin.

A special group is based on mixed law, such as Quebec. Legal Latin in these laws comes from two legal cultures. André Mayrand points out (translation here), in the foreword to his dictionary of legal Latin, that "[b]y a curious turnabout, Latin expressions and maxims have crossed the Atlantic from England, to find their way into Quebec's civil law, bringing common law notions with them (e.g. *res ipsa loquitur*)".[102]

By contrast, the division of the civil law (continental family) into the laws of Germanic countries and those of Romance countries is far more problematic as far as concerns legal Latin (not to mention the distinction between laws of Germanic countries and that of Poland): the greater part of Latin expressions and maxims in German-language dictionaries were found in dictionaries from the Romance countries. However, our research seems to indicate that legal Latin of the Spanish-speaking world and that of the French-speaking world are quite original compared with the legal Latin of Central Europe; the jurists of these countries hardly use any

---

100 Damião & Henriques 2000: 64, 207–210 and Xavier 2000: 154.
101 See p. 230.
102 Mayrand 1985: VIII.

Latin sources (e.g., dictionaries) from the German-speaking countries. The high percentage of expressions and maxims crossing the Romance-German cultural border is basically explained by the Italian dictionary used in this comparative study. That was hardly pure chance. In Italy, German legal science (including both research into Roman law and legal Latin) served as a model for national research in the 19th and 20th centuries. Old cultural liaisons had existed between Germany and Italy since the days of the Holy Roman Empire, which at least partially explains this influence. Let us also remember that Northern Italy long formed part of the Austro-Hungarian Empire, until the end of the First World War.

The fact that a part of legal Latin is essentially national in character is well illustrated by the maxim *lex retro non agit* ['the law does not operate retroactively'], used in the frame of Polish legal culture. This maxim was not formulated by the Romans (although it is certainly based on Roman law). Apparently, it is purely Polish. According to one Polish author, the maxim *lex retro non agit* appears in no dictionary of legal Latin outside Poland; Anglo-American lawyers, for example, refer to the same phenomenon by the expression *ex post facto law*. The maxim *lex retro non agit* was probably formulated by a Polish specialist in Roman law, Stanisław Wróblewski, at the beginning of the 20th century. Today, it is the most popular maxim in Polish legal circles: for the period 1971–2001, it appears 140 times in Polish judgments, notably in judgments of the Constitutional Court, but also in those of the High Administrative Court and courts of appeal.[103]

4.2.2 Coherence of Legal Latin in Dictionaries of the Same Linguistic Zones An indirect result of our research is that the content of legal Latin dictionaries is not the same within the same linguistic zones – even where the target readership of these works is the same. In this regard, the variation between the two sub-families of civil law (the laws of Germanic countries and those of Romance countries) is practically no greater than the variation within linguistic zones in continental Europe.

This variation within the same linguistic zones, even the same countries, is very likely explained by the fact that two centuries have already passed since the final high point of Latin-language legal literature. The treasury of legal literature in Latin is enormous – and, at the same time, highly varied. The language of a classic legal Latin work, like that of an encyclopaedia or dictionary in Latin, reflects, besides common tradition, the national legal order and the author's individual taste as to Latin style. Even if all the legal scholars represented *jus commune* thought, they each wrote in their own way, in the frame of the rules of the Latin language. After the introduction of national languages into internal and international legal life in Europe, authors of legal Latin dictionaries assembled, in the treasury of legal Latin, expressions and maxims that they considered relevant (sometimes, they themselves invented new Latin expressions and maxims).

The authors had to feel their way to assemble these expressions and maxims: no research existed on the frequency of each expression or maxim in contemporary

---

103 Wołodkiewicz 2001a: 154–155, and Wołodkiewicz 2001c: 10–11.

texts. The expressions and maxims that the authors included in their dictionaries were therefore chosen somewhat at random; according to the authors' personal preferences. Moreover, the way in which these expressions and maxims have been handed down from generation to generation to our own times is likewise random. We can thus understand why dictionaries of legal Latin so often differ, even within a single linguistic zone, indeed even in a single country.

4.2.3 Risk of Mistakes and Misunderstandings We also observed that, where the same expression or maxim is included in legal Latin dictionaries from different countries, the meaning given is often identical, or at least similar. In this perspective, legal Latin is not without value in international communication between lawyers. Nevertheless, differences in meaning likewise exist. An expression or maxim included in legal Latin dictionaries from both common law countries and civil law countries sometimes has a different meaning in both cases. As for the hard core of legal Latin in these countries, this risk appears to exist, in the light of our research, in 5 to 10% of cases.

> One example that well illustrates the differences in meaning is the word *exitus*. In the laws of the German linguistic zone (as, for example, in the Nordic countries), *exitus* means, exclusively or mainly, 'decease'. But common law authors give it the sense of 'children' ; 'offspring'; 'the rents, issues, and profits of lands and tenements'; 'an export duty'; 'the conclusion of the pleadings'.[104] They do not even mention 'decease'.

We should also stress that the risk exists within each country. Concise dictionaries are particularly incomplete in this respect. The author often defines a legal Latin expression in a very limited context (for example, *a die* only in the case of debt) while the field of application of the expression is in reality clearly wider. By way of example, the word *denuntiatio*. In classical Latin, this word referred to any announcement or notification (also Senate decrees). Even today, *denuntiatio* sometimes means, in a general way, 'announcement'. However, over the centuries specific meanings have developed, such as – in France – 'notice of assignment of debt' (in private law) or 'report of an offence' (criminal law), often without an epithet. Some small dictionaries of legal Latin contain only one or two of these meanings.

4.2.4 External Variation in Expressions and Maxims Understanding Latin expressions and maxims is often handicapped by the fact that their appearance can vary. Identifying expressions and maxims is made difficult by several factors which result, amongst other things, from the fact that Latin is a synthetic language. These difficulties would originate in the distinction between singular and plural of nouns (e.g., *pactum – pacta*), in cases (e.g., *nudum pactum – nudo pacto*), in prepositions or synonyms (e.g., *argumentum ad absurdum – argumentum in absurdum*), in

---

104 Black's Law Dictionary 2000.

word order (e.g., *compositum mixtum – mixtum compositum*), and in incomplete or elliptical forms (e.g., *lex loci regit actum – locus regit actum*).

The sole fact of ignoring that today's Italian and German authors hardly ever use the letter 'j' (a neo-Latin creation) can cause difficulties: *jus* is always written *ius*, so that the word appears in dictionaries under the letter 'i'. By contrast, Anglo-American and French authors normally use the letter 'j'. In the Spanish-speaking world, both orthographies are current. – For the sake of simplicity, only "j" is used in the present work.

Another, general, orthographic difference concerns the use of medieval forms (for example, *conditio* instead of *condicio*). It is useful to know besides that German Latinist authors use the comma somewhat as in German, and that a Latin expression is sometimes written in a single word, sometimes in two or several (*usus fructus – ususfructus*, *sub poena – subpoena*).

Our research shows that the appearance of expressions and maxims varies, in the ways indicated above, in some 10% of cases. One surprising finding: this variation is not dependent on linguistic zones. Within each linguistic zone exist variations as important as between different linguistic zones. In some cases, legal Latin dictionaries give two or three variants. But that is exceptional: normally, a single variant of an expression or a maxim is included in legal Latin dictionaries. From the reader's standpoint, a problem therefore exists.

Sometimes, the same maxim can appear in five variants: *Quod ab initio non valet in tractu temporis non convalescet* ['what is valueless (lit. 'invalid') from the start does not appreciate (lit. 'become valid') with time']; *Quod ab initio non valet in tractu temporis non convalescit*; *Quod ab initio vitiosum est, tractu temporis convalescere non potest*; *Quod initio vitiosum est, non potest tractu temporis convalescere; Quod nullum est nullo lapsu temporis convalescere potest.*

4.3 Mitigating Problems

In sum, evaluated on the basis of dictionaries, legal Latin can be said to be not very coherent as to the major legal families, even not always within each linguistic zone or country. How, then, to remedy this shortcoming, to raise the communicative value of Latin in international relations, and avoid mistakes and misunderstandings? In principle, two possibilities exist: to reinstate knowledge of Latin as a language; and to undertake lexicographical work internationally.

As to the first possibility, it is probably realistic to suppose – in spite of representations eloquently emphasizing the importance of Latin from the standpoint of the capacity for logical reflection[105] – that, in the future as today, only a part of lawyers participating in international cooperation will have a good command of Latin. On the other hand, as mentioned earlier, a Latin expression or maxim can have a specific legal meaning that it is quite impossible to deduce from ordinary Latin. That is why the author of this book has proposed that an international legal Latin

---

105 Fricek 1981: 260–267.

dictionary be compiled, bringing together the expressions and maxims actually in use in various legal cultures, indicating their meaning in each of these cultures.[106] By virtue of such a dictionary, a lawyer would easily be able to clarify the meaning that foreign colleagues intend to give to expressions or maxims that they are using.

5 Dictionaries of Legal Latin

For the reasons indicated above, it is always important to verify the meaning of a Latin expression or maxim in an appropriate source. If possible, a specialist dictionary should be used from the same legal culture that the text comes from or in which the expression or maxim in question appears. The list below sets out the most important dictionaries from the main Western legal cultures (those of certain countries with lesser-known languages are mentioned in the article by Mattila 2002a).

It must be stressed that the various dictionaries do not give preference to the same elements of legal Latin. Some of them only contain terms and other expressions, some others also comprise maxims. In most cases, the accent is placed on expressions and maxims used nowadays, but nearly all the dictionaries also contain purely historical expressions. It is worth mentioning that the (Greek) dictionary of Athanásios Lamprópoulos and Fótios Karagiánnis includes an appendix relating to the legal Latin of Byzantium (pp. 119–136).

English linguistic zone. Black's Law Dictionary (7th ed. St. Paul, Minn.: West Publishing 2000; a very large number of Latin expressions and maxims). – *Jowitt's Dictionary of English Law I-II* (London: Sweet & Maxwell 1977; a very large number of Latin expressions and maxims). – *Latin Words & Phrases for Lawyers* (publ. Datinder Sodhi, editor-in-chief R. S. Vasan. New York: Law and Business Publications 1980). – *Trayner's Latin Maxims*. 4th ed. Edinburgh: W. Green / Sweet & Maxwell 1993. – Russ VerSteeg, *Essential Latin for Lawyers*. Durham (North Carolina): Carolina Academic Press 1990).

French linguistic zone. Albert Mayrand, *Dictionnaire de maximes et locutions latines utilisées en droit* (3e éd. Cowansville/Québec: Editions Yvon Blais 1994). – Yves Merminod, *Expressions et proverbes latins. Adages juridiques* (Neuchâtel: Ides & Calendes 1992). – Henri Roland & Laurent Boyer, *Locutions latines du droit français* (Paris: Litec 1998). – Henri Roland & Laurent Boyer, *Adages du droit français* (Paris: Litec 1999). – Wallace Schwab & Roch Pagé, *Les locutions latines et le droit positif québécois. Nomenclature des usages de la jurisprudence* (Dossiers du Conseil de la langue française. Études juridiques 7. Éditeur officiel du Québec 1981).

German linguistic zone. Klaus Adomeit, *Civis Romanus. Latein für Jurastudenten* (2 Aufl. Berlin: Berlin Verlag 1999). – Nikolaus Benke *et al.*, *Juristenlatein* (2 Aufl. Wien, München & Bern: Manz, Beck & Stämpfi 2002). – Jochen Bruss, *Lateinische Rechtsbegriffe* (2. Aufl. Freiburg &c.: Haufe Verlagsgruppe 1999). – Jo-

---

106 Mattila 2002a: 754–755.

hanna Filip-Fröschl & Peter Mader, *Latein in der Rechtssprache. Ein Studienbuch und Nachschlagewerk* (2. Aufl. Wien: Braumüller 1993). – Rolf Lieberwirth, *Latein im Recht* (4. Aufl. Berlin: Verlag Die Wirtschaft 1996). – Detlef Liebs, *Lateinische Rechtsregeln und Rechtssprichwörter* (6. Aufl. München: Beck 1998).

Spanish and Portuguese linguistic zone. Guillermo Cabanellas & Luis Alcalá-Zamora y Castillo, *Diccionario enciclopédico de derecho usual I–VIII* (16ª ed. Buenos Aires: Editorial Heliasta 1992; a very large number of Latin expressions). – Guillermo Cabanellas, *Repertorio jurídico de principios generales del derecho, locuciones, máximas y aforismos latinos y castellanos* (4ª ed. ampliada por Ana María Cabanellas. Buenos Aires: Editorial Heliasta 1992; a very large number of Latin expressions and maxims, systematically assembled). – Nelson Nicoliello, *Diccionario del latín jurídico* (Barcelona: Bosch & Faira 1999). – Ronaldo Caldeira Xavier, *Latim no direito* (5ª ed. Rio de Janeiro: Editora Forense 2000).

Italy. Umberto Albanese, *Massime, enunciazioni e formule giuridiche latine* (Milano: Hoepli 1997). – Italo Bellina, *Salvis juribus. Il latino degli avvocati* (Torino: UTET 1992). – Paride Bertozzi, *Dizionario dei brocardi e dei latinismi giuridici* (IPSOA Editore 1994). – L. De-Mauri, *Regulae juris* (Milano: Hoepli, ristampa 1984). – *Dizionario giuridico romano* (III ed. Napoli: Edizioni Giuridiche Simone 2000). – *Il latino in tribunale. Brocardi e termini latini in uso nella prassi forense* (Napoli: Edizioni Giuridiche Simone 1999). – Edoardo Mori, *Dizionario dei termini giuridici e dei brocardi latini* (Piacenza: Casa editrice La tribuna 1999).

Russia. F. Dydynskii (Ф. Дыдынский), *Latinsko-russkii slovar' k istochnikam rimskogo prava* (Латинско-русский словарь к источникам римкого права. Moscow: Izdatel'stvo "Spark" 1896, reprod. 1997). – M. Gamzatov (М. Гамзатов), *Latinsko-russkii slovar' iuridicheskikh terminov i vyrazhenii dlia spetsialistov i perevodchikov angliiskogo iazyka* (Латинско-русский словарь юридических терминов и выражений для специалистов и переводчиков английского языка. St. Petersburg: Izdatel'stvo Sankt-Peterburgskogo universiteta 2002). – B. S. Nikiforov (Б. С. Никифоров), *Latinskaia iuridicheskaia frazeologiia* (Латинская юридическая фразеология. Moskva: Iuridicheskaia literatura 1979). – G. V. Petrova (Г. В. Петрова), *Iuridicheskie terminy i vyrazheniia. Kratkii latinsko-russkii, russko-latinskii slovar'* (Юридические термины и выражения. Краткий латинско-русский, русско-латинский словарь. 2nd ed. Moscow: Izdatel'stvo URAO 2004). – E. I. Temnov (Е. И. Темнов), *Latinskie iuridicheskie izrecheniia* (2e éd. Латинские юридические изречения. Moskva: Ekzamen 2003). – Besides these, several manuals of legal Latin with a Latin vocabulary.

Greece. Kalliópi Bourdára (Καλλιόπη Μπουρδάρα), *Lexilógio latinikón nomikón orón* (Λεξιλόγιο λατινικών νομικών ορών. Athína: Sákkulas 1994). – Athan. Lamprópoulos (Αθαν. Λαμπρόπουλος) & Fótios Karagiánnis (Φώτιος Καραγιάννης), *Latinoellinikó lexikó nomikón orón* (Λατινοελληνικό λεξικό νομικών ορών. Athína: Sákkulas 1992).

Chapter 6

Legal German

1 History of Legal German

1.1 The Period of Barbarian Laws

After the fall of the Roman Empire, the Germanic tribes assembled their legal rules in laws called by Latin authors "barbarian" (*leges barbarorum*), e.g.: *lex Salica, lex Ribuaria*. This involved somewhat primitive compilations from the standpoint of legislative technique, characterised by considerable casuistry. For example, theft was not approached uniformly in the *lex Salica*. Indeed, the distinction was drawn between theft of a pig, a calf, a dog, a chicken, and so on. As to theft of a pig, this law contained no less than 16 legal provisions.[1]

The barbarian laws were drawn up in Latin. The same was also the case for other legal documents in the German linguistic zone from the great migrations to the 13th century. This heritage is still reflected today. German-speaking lawyers nowadays use loanwords dating from that era, or even from earlier times. For example, the word *Pacht* ['lease'] was formed on the basis of the plural of the word *pactum* as long ago as the Germanic era.[2] When the customary laws of the Germanic peoples were expressed in Latin, their original style necessarily had repercussions on the means of expression used in translations. In consequence, the Latin language of the Germanic laws of the Middle Ages was a mixture of Germanic and Roman styles.

According to some sources, from time immemorial German had been the spoken language of legal proceedings on German-speaking territories.[3] In court sittings, German judges always used the vernacular (vulgar tongue). In the Middle Ages, this meant using different dialects of Old German.[4] However, it is not known for sure how the content of laws expressed in Latin was communicated to an illiterate people.

1.2 Linguistic Conditions in the Holy Roman Empire

1.2.1 Nature of the Empire At Christmas in the year 800, the Pope crowned Charlemagne Roman Emperor. When Charlemagne's empire was later divided, the

---

1   Kaufmann 1984: 19.
2   Wacke 1990: 880.
3   Wacke 1990: 881.
4   Bergmans 1987: 99.

tradition continued: Otto I obtained the centre of the Empire (today's Germany and Northern Italy) and in turn was crowned Roman Emperor in 962. Thus was born the (Germanic) Holy Roman Empire (*Heiliges Römisches Reich Deutscher Nation, Sacrum Romanum Imperium Nationis Germanicae*). This involved a fusion of the German throne and "the Roman Empire".

It has been said that this brand new Empire was neither holy, Roman, nor a real empire. The lawyer and historian Samuel Pufendorf (1632–1694) described it as a "monster". According to him, the Germanic Roman Empire, consisting of over 300 regional States and 400 still smaller pieces, was *irregulare aliquid, monstro simile* ['something misshapen, like a monster'].[5] Over time, the Empire grew increasingly powerless in relation to the regional power centres: it was more a symbolic facade than a genuine political power. The power of the emperor diminished and that of the regional princes flourished. However, the Holy Roman Empire long had considerable importance in the judicial domain (notably through the *Reichskammergericht;* see below). Formally, the Empire lasted until 1806.

1.2.2 Status of Latin and German Latin and German (in reverse order, in some contexts) served as official languages for the Holy Roman Empire for the whole of its existence. The same was also the case for the Imperial Diet and the Imperial Court (*Reichskammergericht*). Vienna in particular cultivated Latin, along with German. Under medieval conditions, it was thought natural that the emperor should have a command of the language of the Church. He also heard proposals from his council in Latin, giving his responses in the same language. After the Reformation, the protestant States used the new German written standard (*Hochdeutsch*) since Low German was no longer accepted in the Diet. An example of the equality of Latin and German as official languages of the Empire appears from the *Reichspolizeiordnung* (1530), according to which the estates had to lodge their complaints in Latin or in German. Needless to say, the deputies from non-German-speaking regions of the Empire used Latin in the Diet.[6]

These principles were followed until the Empire came to an end, which formed an obstacle to the use of modern foreign languages in State contexts. Despite the spread of French from the 17th century as the language of education of young aristocratic Germans, the business of Empire would always be attended to in Latin or German. This provoked serious conflict with French diplomats in the late 17th and early 18th centuries.[7]

---

5   Cohn 1968: 23.
6   Hattenhauer 1987: 6–10.
7   See p. 192 and Hattenhauer 1987: 12–13.

1.3 The Flowering of Old Legal German

As already mentioned, Latin and German provided the official languages of the Holy Roman Empire throughout the entire history of this State edifice. However, the proportional importance of the two languages was not stable.

From the 13th century, German, that is, the various dialects of Old German, overtook Latin as the language of law. After the middle of that century, the use of German spread to all areas of legal life (e.g., laws and decrees, judgments, private documents). Gradually, German began to oust Latin in the imperial chancellery, and the first law in German, the *Mainzer Reichslandfrieden*, was given to the Empire in 1235 by Frederick II.[8] In addition, many legal documents of the period were bilingual: these were drawn up in Latin and in German.[9] This use of German continued until the reception of Roman law (see below).

Old legal German, based on various dialects, was not uniform: several regional variants existed and it was also socially conditioned. Some of the vocabulary from this language is still in use, e.g.: *anfechten* ['to annul'], *bescheinigen* ['to certify', 'attest in writing'], *erweisen* ['to demonstrate', 'prove'], *verantworten* ['to be answerable for', 'guarantee', 'commit (oneself) to'; 'accept the consequences'].[10] The legal German of the Middle Ages was concrete on the one hand, and rich in vocabulary on the other. These two features somehow formed both sides of the coin: the level of abstraction of medieval legal German was low, which necessitated a large number of words to describe concrete cases. The number of words needed was further increased by the Germanic tendency to repeat important points in texts by using synonyms or quasi-synonyms.

1.4 Linguistic Consequences of Reception of Roman law

1.4.1 Reasons for Reception The incoherence of the Holy Roman Empire in large part influenced the evolution of German law, in particular the reception of Roman law.[11] Because of its weakness, the Empire possessed no uniform legal system created by the imperial legislator. The laws of German territories, created by the princes, were local: they were often vague and incomplete. These local statutory laws, and traditional customary laws, did not correspond to the needs of a German society characterised by rapid progress. There was a need for a more advanced legal system, applied independently of the frontiers of the principalities forming the Empire.

Indeed, such an advanced system already existed. The European universities, promoted by the Catholic Church, taught Roman law. This formed an exhaustive system, formulated scientifically, with well-established rules. Clearly, this did not involve classical Roman law but *jus commune* (in German: *Gemeines Recht*), created

---

8   Lohaus 2000: 29.
9   Hattenhauer 1987: 6.
10   von Polenz 1991: 215.
11   Foster 1996: 14–17.

by medieval lawyers.[12] The *jus commune* was supranational in character and its authority was underwritten by the Church: it was in harmony with Canon law, itself largely created on the basis of Roman law. At the same time, this last amounted to an ideologically appropriate solution for the Empire: given that it was the "Roman Emperor" who ruled over the German territories, it was also natural that Roman law should form the legal order of the Empire. This law accentuated the status of the Empire as a continuation of the original Roman Empire.

Further, we should bear in mind progress in law teaching. In the Middle Ages, the German universities belonged to a great supranational system: the first professors of law at these universities had been trained in Italy, in Roman law. Even in 1200, the number of students of law in Bologna was considerable, not to mention later times in the Italian universities. Among the students were many Germans, who brought back to their native land Roman law learned in Italy. The primitive commentaries on local German laws could not match the refined legal doctrines of the Italian universities. The professors, too, often moved from country to country during their career. All this brought about the intellectualisation of German law, which in turn brought about the need for judges with a theoretical training in law.

Finally, the reception of Roman law was prompted by the judicial system of the Empire. The judges of the higher German courts were lawyers with a university education. In 1495, an imperial court (the *Reichskammergericht*) was set up. Half the judges appointed to the court were noblemen, the other half doctors of law. The *Reichskammergericht* applied Roman law (also partly Canon law). Its establishment meant recognition by the imperial power of Roman law as the basis for German common law (*Gemeines Recht*). Beneath the *Reichskammergericht* stood the lower imperial courts, which also applied Roman law. These new courts were more interesting, from the standpoint of the inhabitants of the country, than the former courts whose judges lacked theoretical training in law. Further, people often appealed to the Church courts with their Romano-Canonical procedure.

As the application of Roman law spread in the German justice system, judges without legal knowledge began asking legal scholars for opinions. Case files were sent to the universities (a practice called *Aktenversendung*). In consequence, the law faculties in Germany provided a kind of higher court service, particularly in the 16th and 17th centuries. The judicial process, properly speaking, became an illusory procedure. At the same time, the status of judges lacking knowledge of Roman law weakened (they gradually disappeared), while that of the law professors strengthened. The opinions of the legal scholars were also published. Thus was born *usus modernus Pandectarum*, in the 17th century called *usus modernus juris Romani in foro Germanico*.[13] The former local law was not entirely neglected but its importance was reduced by an important rule of evidence: anyone relying on a local legal rule had to prove it (which was not easy under the conditions of the period).

---

12 See pp. 125–126.
13 Dahm 1963: 105.

1.4.2 Consequences of Reception The reception of Roman law profoundly influenced German law, conferring on it an abstract and conceptual character. Until reception, the judge's task had merely required some life experience and a feel for justice. Now, this had become a technical art to be learned more formally. As a result, the profession became one for lawyers with a university education. In this way, justice was no longer based on the conviction of lay judges but rather on the authority of the *Corpus juris civilis.* This would pave the way for the technical development of the law, and its codification.[14]

As we have seen, Roman law was received in Germany in the form in which it was taught in the medieval universities (and applied in the higher courts). We should highlight the great importance of Canon law in this context, particularly in the field of the law of inheritance and succession. The idea of appealing a judgment and the written procedure also came from Canon law. On the other hand, Germany did not receive Roman law in its entirety. Reception focused on private law. However, it was very important in the fields of law of contracts, the law of damages, and law of property. All this shows the extent to which Roman law was used in Germany at the beginning of modern times. That influence proved to be deep and durable, as we shall see.

1.4.3 Linguistic Consequences of Reception Following the reception of Roman law in Germany at the end the Middle Ages and the beginning of modern times, Latin was there raised once again to the rank of dominant legal language. This was facilitated by the fact that a unified German language still did not exist. Under these conditions, Latin regained its status as judicial language, largely displacing German.[15]

To the extent that legal German remained in use, it contained a large number of learned words and loanwords of Latin origin. For example, the meaning of the word *reht* (*Recht*) broadened, in line with the word *jus*.[16] The strengthening of Roman legal thinking also implies that legal Latin in Germany was beginning to become more abstract and precise. From the end of the 15th century, German legal terminology was systematised and partly Latinised, in the wake of reception of Roman law there. During the reception period, Latin gave some 80% of loanwords in German.[17]

To reduce the disadvantages of Latinisation of legal circles, a movement began to write works in which the new legal system of Roman origin was presented to the people in vernacular language and in simplified form. Popular works appeared in German on Roman private law and related procedural law. One work worthy of mention is the *Klagspiegel,* published in 1516 by Sebastian Brandt (originally, this work dates from 1480), which also contains forms of procedure. Another celebrated work, aimed at the German people, is Ulrich Tengler's *Laienspiegel.*[18]

---

14 Dahm 1963: 99.
15 Schmidt-Wiegand 1990: 348–349.
16 Letto-Vanamo 1999: 28–29.
17 von Polenz 1991: 215–220.
18 Kaufmann 1984: 27.

Indeed, in the Germany of the late Middle Ages and early modern times, the choice of language for a legal text depended on who the text was aimed at. For example, criminal legislation and laws on public order were intended to be observed by the people. In consequence, they were prepared in German. Notable examples include the *Karolina* (*Constitutio Criminalis Carolina*, 1532) and the *Reichspolizeiordnung* (16th century).[19] The *Karolina* in particular is considered to be a splendid language product, quite comparable to Martin Luther's German translation of the Bible. On the other hand, in addition to the original Prussian *Landrecht* in German (1620), a Latin version was devised, since a Polish court in some cases examined disputes under appeal relating to it.[20]

German lawyers in early modern times adhered to Latin. They did so long after the language had been dropped in other fields. The transition in the 17th and 18th centuries was gradual. Legal language at the time was a mix, in judgments as in legal science.

To illustrate, a passage from a 1625 judgment: *Quae sententia etiam postea ex sententia Scabinorum Hallensium 3. Jan. Anno 1625; Dass es eingesanter Leuterung ungeacht, bey dem am 17. April anno 1618 publicirten Urtheil allenthalben billich bleibet. V.R.W. confirmata, tandem vires judicata accepit.* Again, an early 18th century study on Bavarian civil law contains the following explanation: *Die Doctrinal-Auslegung wird auch Mentalis oder Logicalis genannt, weil sie eigentlich ad Logicam gehört, und von Eclecticis darinn abgehandelt zu werden pflegt. Man theilt sie in Declarativam, Extensivam (und) Restriktivam.*[21]

By the mid 18th century, the situation still remained the same: German-language legislation was full of linguistically-mixed texts, with many Latin quotations. This is clearly shown by the *Codex Max. Bavaricus* (1756, book IV, chapter 15, article 12): *unter folgenden drei Requisitis: weder Mora noch Culpa aut Facto Debitoris.*[22]

1.5 Influence of Legal French

In the 17th century, France became the dominant superpower, spreading its culture and language to other countries, including the Holy Roman Empire.[23] The German upper class then largely became trilingual (German, Latin, and French). In addition, Spanish or Italian was used in particular situations. Words of foreign origin naturally abounded under these conditions. Indeed, one author declares that the influence of French on German was stronger in the late 17th and early 18th centuries than that of English today.[24]

---

19 Kaufmann 1984: 174.
20 Wacke 1990: 884.
21 Kaufmann 1984: 174.
22 Behrends 1990.
23 See pp. 191–193.
24 von Polenz 1994: 49–76.

The position of the French model was also in evidence in legal matters. Despite the fact that only Latin and German enjoyed the status of official languages of the Holy Roman Empire, French was also of significant importance there. A large number of loanwords from French found their way into legal German: in the mid 17th century, the number of French loanwords was already comparable to that of Latin loanwords.[25] This comes as no surprise if we bear in mind, for example, that France's commercial legislation was translated word for word into German, in Prussia, and entered into force there as such.[26] At the same time, French played an important role in the foreign affairs of central European States. French was the internal language of the Prussian Ministry of Foreign Affairs, while in some cases treaties between two or more German-speaking States were concluded in French.[27]

1.6 The German Enlightenment and Legal Language

1.6.1 The Requirement for Understandability of Legal Language Baroque taste demanded that everything should be ornamented. This was also evident in German legal language, where words abounded. Binary formulas were no longer enough; the same thing was said at least three times, and in different ways. According to one researcher, lawyers beat all other scholars, including theologians, in the art of ornamenting language. Sentences in legal texts were to grow to absurd lengths.[28] At the same time, the number of legal terms was immense, due to the linguistic heritage of Old German and the legal fragmentation of German-speaking territories. For example, the Latin word *pignus* [main meanings: 'pledge', 'guarantee', 'surety'; 'proof'] had fifty [!] German equivalents.[29]

The values underlined by the Enlightenment provoked a reaction. The philosophers of the 18th century considered the ideal citizen to be active, aware of his rights, rather than the passive subject of former times, the object of administrative measures. For this reason, one right stressed was that of citizens themselves to obtain by their own means information on the legal rules in force in society. The intention was no longer to leave those with business before the courts "in the hands of unscrupulous lawyers, invoking Roman law". Cultivated citizens had to know their rights and duties. Thus was born the requirement for clear legal language and the drafting of intelligible codes. Legal language had to be concise, simple, and understandable. It also had to be as brief as possible, in the image of military orders.[30]

An attempt was also made to specify what was required. To guarantee that legal language could be understood, legal texts had to be clearly constructed, mysterious abbreviations and complex sentence structures abandoned, the use of Latin curtailed,

---

25 von Polenz 1994: 78–79.
26 Hattenhauer 1987: 86–87.
27 Brunot VIII 1935: 812.
28 See p. 38.
29 Bader 1963: 125–127.
30 Hattenhauer 1987: 34–35.

and words of foreign origin replaced by genuinely German words. It is also interesting to note that even in those days problems caused by subordinate clauses in legal sentences were under discussion. Ernst Klein, a notable author of Prussian legislation, stated that subordinate clauses were always signs of weakness of logic in the text.[31]

1.6.2 Germanisation of Legal Language One of the essential requirements of the philosophers of the Age of Enlightenment in the matter of linguistic policy was that Latin should be dropped. Before them, Hermann Conring (1606–1681) had already declared (in Latin, of course!): *Si lingua utaris aliena aut solis doctis nota, injurius es in populum* ['If you use a foreign language or one known only to the learned, you are doing a (great) wrong to the people'].[32] Part of the background to this requirement was formed by the internal decay of the Holy Roman Empire in the 17th century, following the Thirty Years' War. To regain national unity, the German language was needed as a cohesive factor. This necessitated pushing aside over-strong language influences from abroad (*Überfremdung*: 'foreign infiltration').

However, legal circles were initially cautious towards Germanisation of their language. Why abandon the language of Virgil, Seneca, and Tacitus, so rich and relevant in expressing legal concepts? Because of resistance from lawyers, the situation remained essentially unchanged until the mid 18th century. Scholars were still writing in Latin, considering that the German language was unusable for the study of legal matters.[33] The period of Latin domination lasted particularly long in administrative language, despite criticisms raised as early as the 16th century. As chancellors, ministers, or States councillors, lawyers held fast to Latin, the badge of their high status.

In spite of all, symptoms of change were on the increase. At the end of the 17th century, some courts, such as the *Reichskammergericht,* had already begun to draw up their judgments in German. In the same way, notaries of somewhat more modest status moved over to using German. We should also recall that part of the legal Latin terminology had already been translated into German in the humanist period (*proprietas – Eigentum,* 'property'; *possessio – Besitz,* 'possession'; *ususfructus – Nießbrauch,* 'usufruct, use'; *fidejussor – Bürge,* 'surety (person)'; *societas – Gesellschaft,* 'company or partnership'; *bona fides – guter Glaube,* 'good faith').[34]

Change was also in evidence in legal science. One illustration is the choice of language of works presented at the book fairs in Leipzig. In 1701, the percentage of books in Latin stood at 55%. In 1740, the figure had fallen to 27%. In 1770, only 14% of works presented were in Latin.[35] Even if these figures do not specify the share of legal works, they certainly amount to a sign of evolution in this respect, too.

---

31   Hattenhauer 1987: 47–50.
32   Wacke 1990: 884.
33   Hattenhauer 1987: 22.
34   Behrends 1990.
35   Becker 1990.

However, it is worth recalling that legal theses were largely published in Latin until the mid 19ᵗʰ century in Germany, as elsewhere.

At the end of the 18ᵗʰ century, the proportional importance of Latin and German in German legal circles already stood in reverse compared with the previous situation: German had become the main language of German legal culture, while Latin constituted only a subsidiary means of clarifying new or difficult terms. For example, the enlightened lawyer and economist Joseph von Sonnenfels (1733–1817) only used Latin where German might cause difficulties of interpretation.[36] In spite of this, the number of words of Latin origin still stood large in legal documents.

Under these conditions, binary formulas fulfilled an important function by facilitating understanding of terminology: purely German words clarifying the meaning of words of foreign origin or vice-versa – in professional communication – as for example for *publice und öffentlich* ['publicly'], *Bestätigung und Approbation* ['confirmation', 'acknowledgement', 'approbation'], *exequiren und vollstrecken* ['enforce', 'execute'], *bona fide und unter gutem Glauben* ['in good faith'], and for *Curator und Sachverwalter* ['guardian', 'trustee']. Synonyms could also appear between parentheses: *Vermächtnis (Legat)* ['bequest', 'legacy dealing with a particular good or right'].[37]

According to more radical demands, legal German had to be entirely cleansed of words of foreign origin. Apart from words deriving from Latin, the radicals wanted to abandon words coming from French. From this last, German had indeed adopted a good deal of vocabulary, with French at that time dominating in cultural and diplomatic affairs. What was therefore needed was a methodical Germanisation (*Eindeutschung*) of the German language. Opinion confirmed that there was absolutely no need for loanwords, since any and every subject could be dealt with in depth simply by using purely German words. According to extreme opinion, genuinely German expressions were clearly superior to those of Latin origin. Christian Wolff (1679–1754) considered that German was more suitable than Latin for scientific use, and that German had the versatility to express things which appeared barbaric when presented in Latin.[38] Germanisation presupposed formulation of new words of a scientific nature – artificial words (*Kunstwörter*).

1.6.3 Linguistic Importance of the Major Codifications In the Age of Enlightenment, a new notion was born: the world had to be conceptualised as a rational system, functioning with virtually mathematical accuracy. In legal affairs, the major systematic codifications were an expression of this notion. Instead of the dead weight presented by history, the law had to contain "rational" solutions. The basic idea of the legislative codifications of the Enlightenment was not to form a collection of legal rules previously applied. Rather, the intention was to create "natural" solutions.

---

36   Hattenhauer 1987: 38.
37   Wacke 1990: 883–884.
38   Hattenhauer 1987: 32.

This is why the legislative works of the period are called "codifications of natural law". Setting these in force meant setting aside the *jus commune* of Roman origin.

The Holy Roman Empire was no longer in a fit state to codify the law of German territories. The works of codification were therefore carried out at a lower level, in the regional States of the Empire. The enlightened sovereigns of these States set about elaborating codes inspired by natural law, to produce legal rules corresponding to the needs of citizens in everyday language. Thus were born the *Allgemeines Landrecht für die preußischen Staaten* (ALR, 1794), an exhaustive codification of Prussian substantive law (covering constitutional and administrative rights as well as private law), and the *Allgemeines Bürgerliches Gesetzbuch* (ABGB, 1811), a codification of Austrian civil law. On the other hand, the new French codes, particularly the Civil Code, came into force in some western parts of the Holy Roman Empire, due to the growth of French influence under the reign of Napoleon. On the substance of criminal law, an example is the Bavarian *Kriminalgesetzbuch* (1813).

The German codes of natural law sought to improve legal protection of citizens. All citizens were to know their rights and duties. For that reason, these were to appear clearly and precisely in legal provisions. At the same time, the popular character of laws implied extended casuistry: regulation of German natural law codifications was highly detailed, in comparison with that of the German Civil Code (*Bürgerliches Gesetzbuch*, BGB) a century later (1900). The ALR contains 32 articles on the sole question of building accessories (the number of corresponding articles is only two in the BGB). For example, problems over keys, locks, wallpaper, are separately regulated.[39] That explains why the *Allgemeines Landrecht* has sometimes been described as a "monstrously long law".[40]

The natural law codes sought to guarantee the greatest possible level of understandability. Their language was natural and their style clear, paternal, and pedagogical. According to one author, these codes restored the honour of German legal language.[41] However, the search for clarity implies a certain lack of legal precision in the legal provisions of the codes.

The *Allgemeines Landrecht* is the first German-language codification aimed at educated non-lawyers and which is convincing from the standpoint of the language used.[42] Indeed, the ALR is a breakthrough in German legislative language, a linguistic cultural achievement that considerably influenced all later German-language codes. It has even been compared with Martin Luther's translation of the Bible.[43] The popular nature of the *Allgemeines Landrecht* appears in the limited number of words of foreign origin. Legislative proposals of the mid 18th century contain a good deal of Latin in parentheses. For example, since German legal terminology was as yet not established, to translate the expression *ex statu familiae,* a relative clause

---

39   Kaufmann 1984: 32–34.
40   Markesinis 1997: 3.
41   Schmidt-Wiegand 1990: 349.
42   Hattenhauer 1987: 56.
43   Wacke 1990: 884.

consisting of 14 German words was required.[44] However, the final code largely made the transition from Latin to German. Before the ALR was set in force, the percentage of terms of foreign origin in Prussian provisions relating to divorce stood at around 4.4%. With the ALR, this percentage fell to 0.8%. To further illustrate, the corresponding figure was 0.5–1% in the 20th century.[45]

1.7 Legal Language of a Unified Germany

1.7.1 Rejection of Foreign Language Elements In the 19th century, Germany was unified and rose to the position of a great power. National language is an important reflection of nationalism. It is thus easy to understand that the awakening of national sentiment would translate itself into the care given to the German language, even to the requirement of its disciplined use (*Sprachzucht*).[46] Cleansing the German language of foreign influences had already begun some time previously, and intensified with strengthened nationalism. Many neologisms were introduced in the various specialisms. For example, in the field of transport over 1300 technical terms were Germanised during the period 1886–93.

Needless to say, Germanisation of technical terminology also affected legal matters. During the 19th century, the number of words of foreign origin fell from 4–5 to 0.5%. Examples could easily be presented from almost any branch of law: *Alimentation – Unterhalt* ['support', 'maintenance']; *Desertion – Verlassung* ['desertion']; *Citation – Ladung* ['request to appear', 'summons']; *Kopie – Abschrift* ['copy'].[47] The *Bürgerliches Gesetzbuch,* BGB (1900) almost completely Germanised the terminology of German private law. This was one of the main reasons for the reputation of the language of the code as "paper German" (*Papierdeutsch* = a kind of German that no one would use orally).[48] In spite of all, German lawyers grew accustomed to the new language. The feeling that the vocabulary of the BGB was artificial and forced gradually ebbed away.[49] At the same time, the terminology of the BGB fuelled ordinary German through use of the language by the authorities: common parlance adopted legal terms in a more general sense.

In the 20th century, the era of National Socialism saw a change in attitude towards words of foreign origin. Adolf Hitler, in other ways highly chauvinistic, was very fond of such words.[50] According to Viktor Klemperer, who studied Hitler's motives, this involved mass psychology: *"Das Fremdwort imponiert, es imponiert um so mehr, je weniger es verstanden wird"* ['Foreign words are impressive, and the less they are understood, the more they impress']. Although some criticisms were levelled against words of foreign

---

44 Hattenhauer 1987: 52.
45 von Polenz 1994: 384.
46 Hattenhauer 1987: 79.
47 von Polenz 1999: 486–487.
48 Bergmans 1987: 99.
49 Hattenhauer 1987: 85.
50 von Polenz 1999: 281.

origin under the National Socialist regime, these were racist in nature (e.g., use of the language of Jews).

As for style, legal German's means of expression once again changed towards the abstract in the 19th century. The popular language of the Enlightenment was no longer in fashion. This was for a number of reasons.[51] Above all, we should recall the ideas promoted by the great 19th century German schools of law. These, then, merit a brief presentation.

1.7.2 The 19th Century Schools of Law In 19th century Germany, notions of natural law gave way to the Historical School of law. In the background stood the romantic currents generally prevailing in German culture. These prompted the idea that the law is an organic entity of each particular society. Previously, the universal character of law had been underlined: it was common to all humanity. According to the new ideology, the law is fashioned by the separate heritage of a people. Paradoxically, the thinking of the Historical School of law led to a fresh strengthening of Roman law. The explanation is simple: Roman law was considered to be an essential part of the German legal heritage because it had decisively contributed to the development of national law. *Pandektenwissenschaft*, admired throughout Europe, was born. Apart from Germany, this was of great importance in countries such as France, Italy, and Austria. The most celebrated representative of this school is Friedrich Carl von Savigny (1779–1861). His work *System des heutigen Römischen Rechts* ['System of the Modern Roman Law', 1840–1849] played a role of prime importance both in Germany and elsewhere.

The thinking of the Historical School of law provoked a reaction: once again, the importance of State power as creator of the law began to be underlined. Legal positivism, according to which written laws are the sole or at least the main source of law, spread. Previously, the representatives of natural law and the Historical School of law had discussed the characteristics of "true" law. The positivists no longer put this question; purely formal criteria were enough to justify the validity of a legal rule. They were able to rely on Montesquieu's doctrine of separation of powers, with its distinction between the legislative, executive, and judicial powers. Moreover, they stressed the supremacy of legislative rules, which could be expressed clearly and without contradictions, contrary to legal rules of other types.

As to the doctrine of *Begriffsjurisprudenz* (for which several English translations have been proposed: 'conceptual jurisprudence', 'conceptual legal dogmatics', 'legal conceptualisation', 'analytical jurisprudence'), this maintained that the legal order was a system formed by legal concepts. This is why legal reasoning was to be based on the grounding of concepts in the system. Each concept was to find its right place in the legal system, thus enabling an overview of legal effects. According to the representatives of this doctrine, a logical and exhaustive system of legal concepts allowed sure and simple resolution of disputes: it was enough for the lawyer to

---

51 Hattenhauer 1987: 63.

link the facts of a particular dispute to the system of concepts to produce an almost automatic resolution.

Interessenjurisprudenz ['Jurisprudence of interests'] and the *Freirechtsschule* ['Free Law School'] were born in turn as reactions against *Begriffsjurisprudenz*. The representatives of the first school underlined the importance of legislative aims standing in the background of legal rules, in legal interpretation. As for the *Freirechtsschule*, this maintained the independent character of application of law in relation to written law. The two schools shared the idea according to which legal rules were merely a means towards attaining social ends. They were not to be revered as fetishes. However, it was *Pandektenwissenschaft* and *Begriffsjurisprudenz*, discussed above, that most strongly influenced the language of the *Bürgerliches Gesetzbuch*, the legislative masterpiece of modern Germany. This language also merits our attention.

1.7.3 The Bürgerliches Gesetzbuch   The German Civil Code (*Bürgerliches Gesetzbuch*, BGB, 1900) constitutes a breakthrough of utmost significance in the development of German law. It involves the most celebrated piece of German legislation. The internal logic of the code is excellent (in the image of the natural sciences) but its content is not easily understood from the reader's standpoint. The *Bürgerliches Gesetzbuch* is a monument of refined legal scholarship; it was written, not for laymen but for judges versed in law.

One feature of the code is its conceptual hierarchisation, "pyramids of concepts"; this has aroused great admiration, but also great irritation. Some of the basic concepts include "*Rechtsgeschäft*" (a notion unknown in common law which reflects in the multitude of translations proposed: 'legal act', 'juristic act', 'act in law', 'legal transaction', 'transaction', 'juridical act'), "*Willenserklärung*" (again, the same difficulty: 'declaration of intent', 'declaration of intention, 'declaration of will', 'declaratory act', 'act of a party', 'act and deed') and "*Schuldverhältnis*" ('legal relationship between creditor and debtor', 'obligation', 'obligation of debtor to creditor', 'debt relationship'). Many articles can only be understood when placed side by side with other articles located elsewhere in the code. The authors of the code also sought to use each legal term in a single meaning. At the same time, sentence construction often determines the question of burden of proof.

The extreme conceptualism of the *Bürgerliches Gesetzbuch* expresses the heritage of the renowned schools of the 19th century, *Pandektenwissenschaft* and *Begriffsjurisprudenz*. Among the ideas standing in the background to the code are those of Philipp Heck (1858–1943), Gustaf Hugo (1764–1844) and Friedrich Carl von Savigny (1779–1861). The power of the BGB lies in the formalism of its rules, the balance of its structures, and the general principles of civil law. This explains why the code has remained in force despite the great social and economic changes of the 20th century. It has also been usable under extreme conditions, such as during the hyperinflation that followed the First World War. We should also recall that the BGB was long in force in the German Democratic Republic, before promulgation of the East German Civil Code in 1975. It is also above all the technical and abstract character of the BGB that explains its reception in far-off countries such as Brazil and Japan.

All this is also clearly visible at the language level of the BGB. Although the language is simple and precise, at the same time it is highly technical. Abstract terms abound in the code. Understanding these presupposes a knowledge of the legal structures to which they belong; they are hermetic from the standpoint of the uninitiated. Despite the clarity of style of the BGB, reading the code requires possession of legal knowledge. Paradoxically, the hermetic nature of the BGB was in part aggravated by its authors' aspirations to ensure the quality of its language. The care taken to put aside verbosity and subordinate clauses led to highly abstract language, with a noun-heavy style and dense sentences. For this reason, the BGB cannot be considered a popular legislative work, despite all the steps to ensure its language quality. It is dry and without fantasy. It could never provide a model for a novel. It clearly differs from the French Civil Code, which provided such inspiration for Stendhal.[52]

> Article 164 well illustrates the BGB's highly abstract and hermetic manner of formulating legal rules: *Tritt der Wille im fremden Namen zu handeln, nicht erkennbar hervor, so kommt der Mangel des Willens, im eigenen Namen zu handeln, nicht in Betracht.* The literal translation of this article goes as follows: 'If an intention to act in the name of another does not manifestly appear, then the absence of intention to act in one's own name is not taken into consideration'. Put plainly, this means: If the agent has not clearly acted (i.e., clear to an onlooker) as an agent, then he cannot claim an intention only to act as agent but becomes personally bound by the legal act in question.

In recent decades, the German Civil Code has become even more hermetic. This is explained by the fact that some phenomena that the law regulates have become more complex. In consequence, the formulations of the code are even more complex than before. Understanding them presupposes still more legal training. When the *Allgemeines Landrecht für die preußischen Staaten* was promulgated two centuries ago, the target reader of the code was the layman untaught in legal science. Today, the position is as it was under the reign of scientific Roman law – once again, the readers of German civil legislation are lawyers with a theoretical training in law.[53]

1.7.4 Efforts to Spread Legal German　All the great powers have actively sought to spread their languages to neighbouring territories, even throughout the entire world. That was already done by the ancient Romans. European linguistic imperialists whose efforts have been successful include the Romance countries, the English, and the Russians. A unified Germany was no exception in this regard, although her success has been far more modest. This was also true of Austria.

In the 18th and 19th centuries, the linguistic policy of the German-speaking countries was chiefly visible within those countries and in their surrounding regions.

52　Hattenhauer 1987: 80 and von Polenz 1999: 486–487.

53　von Polenz 1999: 486–492.

In Austria, the liberal linguistic policy came to a close with the edict of 1784 declaring German to be the official language on the territories of the Hungarian crown.[54] In the 19th century, Germany wanted to Germanise the Slavic regions belonging to it (in Eastern Germany and on the territory of today's Poland). To this end, the *Gerichtsverfassungsgesetz* (1877) prescribed that German was the sole judicial language of the country (Art. 184). This provision was directed mainly against the principal Slavic language of Eastern Germany: Sorabian. As is well known, the results of Germanisation were generally not long-lasting, due to the fall of the Austrian and German empires. This also applies to efforts to spread German in Africa, where the German colonial period was somewhat short.

1.8 The Period Following the Second World War

The post-World War II period is characterised both in Germany and in Austria by a reaction against the excesses of the National Socialist era. Under post-war conditions, efforts to force the spread of the German language were no longer possible. Indeed, the Germans no longer wanted to do so. As to German vocabulary during the same period, to some extent concessions were made regarding purity of the language, so strongly stressed during the time of *Eindeutschung*. For example, the famous Duden dictionary once again gives the word *Pronomen* (the genuinely German synonym: *Fürwort*). This is also evident in legal circles. One specialist, Andreas Wacke, finds the word *Prozeß* more natural than the word *Rechtsstreit* contained in the German Civil Code, which is difficult to pronounce.[55]

The relaxation of nationalist linguistic policy also prepared the way for Anglo-American influence in legal language. Words such as *franchising* are used. The stress on care for the quality of legal language is being transferred from criticism of words of foreign origin to the problems of sentence structure (e.g., doing away with over-long sentences). The aim is so far as possible to ensure the democratic character of the language of State institutions. At the same time, there is an awareness that the ideal of a generally comprehensible legal and administrative language, typical of the Age of Enlightenment, is an unattainable Utopia in the frame of the complex State of today.

2 Characteristics of Legal German

2.1 Overview: Lexical Richness and Conceptual Distinctions

2.1.1 Wealth of Terms In comparison with other legal languages, legal German is considered exceptionally rich in terms. This is explained by a number of reasons. Germanic language tradition is wordy, which is partly explained by the numerous prefixes (*ver-, ent-, un-,* etc.) that can be attached to words, and

---

54 von Polenz 1994: 51–52.
55 Wacke 1990: 885.

by the ease of forming compound words, often of great complexity. The word *Isolierglasscheibenrandfugenfüllvorrichtung* appeared in a German judgment, probably setting a record for length. At the same time, legal thinking based on conceptual analysis requires a large number of clearly distinguishable expressions. All this signifies that legal German consists of very many terms. For example, the generic term *Verstoß* ['violation (of the law)'] covers 49 [!] detailed terms, distinguished by the degree of culpability of the perpetrator and by the character of the rule violated.[56]

Wealth of terms is surely one of the main explanations for the fact that the reasoning of German lawyers is still in reality based on *Begriffsjurisprudenz*, despite criticisms levelled against it for over a century. German lawyers benefit in their reasoning from the many key-words whose true content is heatedly discussed by legal scholars. According to Bernhard Bergmans, German lawyers seek to reveal a hidden reality by using relevant words, rather than finding words to express a reality already revealed. In German legal culture, the word creates the meaning, not the other way around.[57]

2.1.2 Pure German Word-forms With the *Eindeutschung* policy, the appearance of German legal terms today is essentially national: normally, these terms are not words of foreign origin (e.g., Latin, French). However, the impression created by the external aspect of words is misleading because these words contain an enormous number of Latin calques. As already mentioned, a significant Roman heritage lies beneath the surface of legal German. In reality, *Eindeutschung* largely involved the creation of calques based on legal Latin. In this way, Roman legal thinking received a German language form. "Today, those who command the language of Roman lawyers still hear the echo of Latin in German words": e.g., *jus civile – bürgerliches Recht, onus probandi – Beweislast*.[58] This Roman foundation is beneficial from the standpoint of international communication. Retranslating German legal terms into Latin provides the keys to understanding the laws of Germany's Romance neighbours.[59]

In general, it is impossible to understand the birth of legal German without being familiar with the fact that German and Latin legal cultures have lived for centuries in symbiosis, intertwined. The creation of German legal language amounted to the final phase of the nationalisation of legal Latin, the pan-European language. However, it is worth recording that in this nationalisation exist differences in degree within the German linguistic zone. In Switzerland, a multicultural country, the use of words of foreign origin is still more common than in Germany. The number of these words is two times greater in the Swiss Civil Code (*Zivilgesetzbuch*, ZGB) than in the

---

56 Bergmans 1987: 100–102.
57 Bergmans 1987: 102.
58 Hattenhauer 1987: 67.
59 Wacke 1990: 886.

German Civil Code.[60] This is already evident in the titles of these codes (the word "civil"): *Zivilgesetzbuch* (Switzerland) – *Bürgerliches Gesetzbuch* (Germany).

In spite of the policy of *Eindeutschung*, legal German (in Germany, too) still contains a certain number of words of foreign origin. Apart from Latin, these often come from Renaissance Italian, especially in the field of commerce: e.g., *Bank, Konto, Risiko, Giro, Indossament*. Some French words are also alive today, from the era when French dominated in Germany. An illustration is the terminology of International law, influenced by French as the language of diplomacy: e.g., *Konvention, Konstitution, Föderation, Intervention*. Self-evidently, the majority of words received from Italian and French go back to Latin in the final analysis.[61] Today, loanwords in German legal language regularly come – as elsewhere – from English (e.g., *franchising, leasing*).

2.1.3 Abstract Character At sentence level, legal German is often characterised as clumsy and complicated. Large numbers of epithets building up in front of substantives are still typical. An expressive example: "*...eine unter Hinzurechnung der Zusammenhangstätigkeiten bei Berücksichtigung einer sinnvollen vernünftigen Verwaltungsübung nach tatsächlichen Gesichtspunkten abgrenzbare und rechtlich selbständig zu bewertende Arbeitseinheit der zu einem bestimmten Arbeitsergebnis führenden Tätigkeit eines Angestellten*".[62] The literal translation (my own) goes: '... a unit of work relative to the activities of an employee that lead to a certain working outcome, to be delimited according to factual aspects and to be independently considered from the legal viewpoint, including connected activities, taking into account reasonable and judicious administrative use'.

As mentioned, complicated legal German has pertinently been called *Papierdeutsch*. It is logical to think that the complexity of the language is explained by the abstract character of German legal thinking. However, this conclusion can be relativised. It largely involves a feature typical of all modern law. That is why any and every legal language is today clumsy and complicated.

2.2 International Coherence

2.2.1 Geographical Overview Legal circles use German in several countries. Apart from the Federal Republic of Germany, it enjoys official status in Austria and Switzerland. The latter country has three other legal languages (French, Italian, and Rhaeto-Roman [Romansch] – the last of these enjoys a special position) but German is the dominant language at the level of the Confederation. Moreover, German possesses an official status in some eastern parts of Belgium and in the North of Italy (Alto Adige / Südtirol [South Tyrol]). Despite the fairly small number of German-speaking South Tyroleans (some 300,000 persons), advanced autonomy has ensured

---

60 Wacke 1990: 886.
61 Wacke 1990: 879–880.
62 Hennemann 1999: 413.

special care taken of German as a legal and administrative language of the region. South Tyrolean specialists have developed the German terminology of the region in such a way that it is possible to use it to express every Italian legal institution. By the comparative method, they have sought to know if a particular Italian legal concept could be expressed by a term already adopted in Austria, Switzerland, or Germany, without the danger of misleading conclusions. In cases where that was not possible, the South Tyroleans have introduced an Italian loanword or a neologism created on the basis of the German language.[63] As a result of this work, a bilingual dictionary of the legal and administrative language of South Tyrol was published.[64] This contains legal-administrative terms in German and Italian, with definitions in the two languages.

In the following paragraphs, we will examine in further detail the legal German language of Austria, whose relationship with that of Germany is dealt with in a recent thesis (Lohaus 2000). This thesis forms the basis of the examination below. The legal German language of Switzerland would also be a highly interesting subject for examination, but unfortunately the author has not found specific studies in that regard.

2.2.2 Austrian Legal German

History. In the Middle Ages, German was still not a unified language. For example, letters from the chancellery of the Holy Roman Empire were drawn up in various dialects. At the close of the Middle Ages, a Bavarian-Austrian standard widely used (*Gemeines Deutsch*) had developed in the southern parts of the German linguistic zone. The Reformation had for its part aggravated the linguistic divergence between the Lutheran and Catholic German regions. In consequence, the central regions of Germany introduced a standard created by Martin Luther (*Lutherisch-Deutsch*), as a counterbalance to the southern standard. As a reaction, the Jesuits directing the Counter-Reformation energetically supported the development of a separate South-German language, Catholic in character and chiefly used in chancelleries.[65]

Despite this, however, the end of the 18th century saw the introduction of the German-language variant of Lutheran origin in the Catholic southern German States. In the background to this solution stands German national sentiment: the conviction according to which there exists a single German cultural nation – a conviction strengthened to compensate for the weakening of the Holy Roman Empire. At the language level, the struggle against Latin was the first consequence of this national sentiment. The second was unification of the written language: the politically fragmented country should at least be unified at the language level. For that, a modern solution was found: the written language of the central parts of Germany, further refined after Luther and sometimes called *Meißnisch*. By contrast, the southern variant of German (*Gemeines Deutsch*) had become weakened by the

---

63   Mayer 2001: 673–675.
64   Mayer 1998.
65   Lohaus 2000: 31–32.

very strong position of Latin and by association of that variant with the language of Catholic clerics (*Jesuitendeutsch*); the Church received severe criticism in the Age of Enlightenment. The final decision to choose the central German variant in Austria was taken by the enlightened sovereigns Maria-Theresa and Joseph II, with their positive attitude towards linguists who favoured unification of the German language. This development later led to Austria's accession in 1901 to the Convention of German-speaking countries on German orthography.[66]

However, language unification was still not quite complete. A sharp rivalry arose between Prussia and Austria, who had acquired the position of dominant German-speaking States. This is why Austria remained outside the *Deutsche Bund*, founded in 1815. She formed a separate great power, largely consisting of non-German-speaking regions. Under these conditions, she did not join the German Empire in 1871. This peculiarity explains the characteristics of legal and administrative language in Austria: she has long possessed her own judicial and administrative system, whose terminology was created in the 19th century, above all without the influence of the *Eindeutschung* movement so strong in Germany at the time. Austria often introduced terms that were unknown in Germany and the meanings of the same terms could be divergent.[67] This terminological divergence was promoted by the fact the German ruling classes in Austria were permanently in contact with the non-German linguistic groups of the Empire. In consequence, a cultivated use of the German language developed, with no basis in genuine German dialects. This was called *Schönbrunnerdeutsch* (after the imperial palace) or *Hofratsdeutsch* (after the title of a high imperial functionary).

Following the fall of the Austrian Empire, the inhabitants of Little Austria, the German-speaking rump-state, felt that the country was no longer viable and that it would be better worth becoming part of Germany. The great powers, having won the war, rejected this idea in the Versailles peace treaty. Frustration became manifest in Hitler's *Anschluß* ['joining, accession'], which later brought so much misfortune on the country. After the horrors of the National Socialist era, the will to unite with Germany died away. The conviction that Austria is a separate country, "the Austrian idea", was – and remains – also visible at the language level, at least symbolically. It is worth mentioning that a large dictionary, *Österreichisches Wörterbuch*, taking careful account of the peculiarities of the German used in Austria, had already been compiled in the early 1950s. Even the word *Deutsch* ['German'] was then avoided: immediately after the Second World War, nobody spoke in schools about teaching "German" but about "the language of instruction".[68]

Features. Basically, the variants of legal German in Germany and Austria are identical. This is notably explained by the fact that the legal thinking of the two countries is based on the same traditions. Apart from the foundations laid by the German-style *jus commune* (*Gemeines Recht*) several centuries ago, the main item

---

66   Lohaus 2000: 35–42.

67   Lohaus 2000: 49–50.

68   Lohaus 2000: 53–58.

to mention is the influence of representatives of *Pandektenwissenschaft* of the *Reich* invited to the Austrian universities in the 19th century: the conceptual language of these professors remains the *lingua franca* of all German-speaking lawyers.[69]

Thanks to this conceptual identity, legal terminology is essentially similar in Germany and Austria. Of course, some divergences exist. Marianne Lohaus points to some 650 Austrian terms that differ from the corresponding terms in Germany (listed in the appendix to her book). In comparison with the number of legal terms in the Köbler legal dictionary (around 5,000), the percentage of legal terms diverging in Germany and Austria is therefore 13%. These are clearly more numerous than specifically Austrian words in the everyday German language in Austria (2%). That is easy to understand because it is precisely the fact that a country forms a separate political entity that is apt to produce country-specific legal terms.

Terminological differences appear in all branches of the law. For example, the semantic domain of the word *Mord* differs in Austria and in Germany. The majority of specifically Austrian terms appear in administrative law and in administrative procedural law. They also figure largely in matters of civil law and civil procedural law. A good example is the designations of various courts. In Austria, the courts of first instance are called *Bezirksgericht* and the Supreme Court *Oberster Gerichtshof*. In Germany, by contrast, the corresponding names are *Amtsgericht* and *Bundesgerichtshof*. In the same way, legal aid in Austria is called *Verfahrenshilfe* and in Germany *Prozesskostenhilfe*. Differences also exist as to methods of appeal. In civil matters, Austria uses the term *Rekurs*, while Germany the term *Beschwerde*.[70]

Influence of the European Union. It can generally be said that Austria's accession to the European Union caused only minor changes in the country's legal and administrative language. One important reason for this is the fact that the law is normally harmonised in the Union by directives, with their character of framework-laws. This allows preservation of traditional Austrian terminology because the final rules are formulated in Austria. If the Union used more regulations of direct application, then the changes in legal and administrative terminology in Austria would be more significant: Union regulations use the terminology of the Federal Republic of Germany.[71] In addition, on acceding to the Union, Austria received permission to stick to traditional Austrian words for agricultural products (*Austriazismenprotokoll*). To illustrate, the word *Ribisl* instead of *Johannisbeere* ['(red)-currant']. These words obtained the same status as the corresponding words used in Germany. Given that the number of these Austrian words amounts to a mere 23 in the *Austriazismenprotokoll*, it can be said that this essentially involves a symbolic gesture: an international treaty declares for the first time that differences exist between the German in Austria and that in Germany. The guide *Ausdrücke des öffentlichen Bereichs in Österreich* provides a clearer idea of these differences. "Expressions in the public sector in

---

69 Lohaus 2000: 86 and 211.
70 Lohaus 2000: 117–125 and 144–145.
71 Lohaus 2000: 9–11 and 216.

Austria", published by the translation service of the Commission of the European Communities, contains 1125 entries.

3 International Importance of Legal German

3.1 General Position of the German Language

Historically, the German language was an important means of communication in the regions surrounding the Baltic Sea (notably in the Hanseatic era) and in Eastern Europe. It also had a solid population base: in 1800, German was the largest language in Europe, according to linguistic statistics. Further, in the late 19th and early 20th centuries, German enjoyed the status of official language in a substantial part of Europe. At that time, the Austrian and German Empires had reached their high point: a large number of the peoples of Central and Eastern Europe were in the immediate sphere of influence of the German language. This influence also made itself felt in the West: at that time, Alsace and Lorraine belonged to the German Empire.[72]

One of the ways in which this domination manifested itself was in German language studies. Towards 1800, the language was widely studied in England. One hundred years later, towards 1900, it was by far the most popular foreign language in France. The attraction of German reached its height immediately before the First World War. It then occupied third place in the world as to foreign language studies. In Northern and Eastern Europe, German was – depending on the country – the first or second foreign language.[73]

After 1918, the position of German was to weaken considerably. Germany and Austria had lost the war and several non-Germanic nation-States sprang up on territories that had belonged to these empires (Poland, Czechoslovakia, Hungary, the Balkan States). In these States, German no longer possessed the status of official language. The excesses of National Socialism and defeat in the Second World War accelerated this development. The cultural attraction of German diminished and the eastern regions of the country had been annexed to Poland and the Soviet Union.

Following this development, the German language was to find itself with an international position clearly inferior to that of English and French. This is true for the use of German in the frame of the European Communities and for studies of the language in schools throughout Europe. In English-speaking countries, even during the period between the two World Wars, studies of German had been replaced by studies of French and Spanish. However, at that time German still occupied an important position in the North of Europe, although there, too, a downward trend was perceptible at the end of the 20th century. Today, German as a foreign language in European schools stands clearly after English and French. The respective figures are: 6.3 / 3.1 / 1.[74]

---

72 von Polenz 1999: 191–193.
73 von Polenz 1999: 196.
74 von Polenz 1999: 197.

In spite of all, German remains an important language. Excluding German speakers in Russia, Europe today has some 90 million people who use German as a first language (notably in Germany, Austria, and Switzerland) and 10 million who use it as a second language; the corresponding figures worldwide are 120 and 40 million. The number of students who study German is estimated at 15 to 20 million. If choosing as a criterion the economic weight of countries where a language is spoken, then German occupies third place worldwide, after English and Japanese. German remains a language of international communication in certain countries bordering on Germany (the Netherlands, Flanders in Belgium) and in many eastern regions of central Europe. After the revolution of 1989 and 1990, the position of German has strengthened in these regions – but not quite to the extent foreseen in the early 1990s.[75]

3.2 German as a Legal Lingua Franca

3.2.1 International Radiation of Laws of German-speaking Countries   The international importance of legal German is largely explained by the spread abroad of the laws of German-speaking countries. These laws have had a great influence in Europe, partly also in other continents. This was already the case in the Middle Ages, notably in the Baltic countries, the Nordic countries, in the eastern part of Central Europe, and in Eastern Europe. These are the regions where Germany's political, economic, and cultural influence has been greatest for centuries. At the time of the Hanseatic League, German law commanded great authority in the Nordic countries, as well as the Baltic countries.[76] For example, in the Middle Ages the law of Magdeburg was applied in Vilnius (Vilna), in Lithuania. In the same way, Ukrainian documents from the 16th to the 18th centuries refer to the *Sachsenspiegel* code as a valid source of law.[77] In partitioned Poland, the legislation of Prussia and Austria was applied.[78]

The great codifications of the 19th and 20th centuries were of particularly great importance from this standpoint. The system of concepts of the *Bürgerliches Gesetzbuch* was adopted in the corresponding code of Japan (1898), as was also the case for the civil codes of Brazil (1916), Siam (1924–1935), China (1930), and Greece (1940). The influence of the BGB also made itself felt in Hungary, in Turkey, in Mexico, and in Peru. Further, it is worth noting that the structures of the civil codes of the Soviet republics in the 1920s followed the example of the BGB.[79]

The Swiss Civil Code (in German *Zivilgesetzbuch*, ZGB, 1907) is constructed using the legislative technique of popular character, dating from the Age of Enlightenment, underlining the understandability of legal provisions. This code has

---

75   von Polenz 1999: 190–202.
76   Ebel & Schelling 2001: 37.
77   Dahm 1963: 100.
78   Bardach & *al.* 1976: 347–454.
79   Cohn 1968: 25 and Foster 1996: 23.

also been used as a model abroad. In Turkey, a code that imitates it almost word for word came into force in connection with the reforms of Kemal Atatürk.[80] In addition, the specialists charged with preparing the Finnish Inheritance Code (*perintökaari*, 1965) carefully studied the corresponding provisions of the Swiss Civil Code. Further, the basic structure of specific rules on agricultural succession of the Finnish Code (added in 1982) are in line with those of the Swiss system (*Zuweisung, attribution globale directe*).[81]

A new wave of German legislative influence has been felt following the transition of the European socialist countries to the market economy system in the late 1980s and early 1990s. At that time, these countries also largely sought legislative models in the German-speaking countries. This involved the former people's democracies (e.g., the Czech Republic) and some former republics of the Soviet Union.

Even more than legislative models, legal science of the German-speaking countries enjoys a global reputation. One illustration is the Nordic legal cultures. At the beginning of modern times, the *jus commune*, largely prepared and polished in Germany, exercised great influence in the Kingdom of Sweden (then including Finland). It is understandable that this appeared first of all in the universities. Gradually, university teaching of the *jus commune* spread to the courts of appeal and even to the courts of first instance there. Some great Swedish lawyers of the 17th century were of German origin, which greatly contributed to the generalisation in Sweden of the *jus commune* developed in Germany.[82] Later, notably in the 19th century, German legal thinking was also of great importance in the Nordic countries. As already pointed out, Germany in the late 19th and early 20th centuries was the dominant country of legal science to which junior university jurists from the Nordic countries made their way for postgraduate studies. With them, several waves of German legal thinking penetrated the Nordic countries, Finland in particular, until the Second World War.

Naturally, the position of German legal science as a model was not restricted to the Nordic countries alone. We have already recalled the German contribution to the *jus commune*. Thanks to the common language, Latin, German works of the period were read throughout Europe. In the same way, the 19th century was the golden age of modern German legal science, when its influence made itself felt in all corners of Europe. The *Pandektenwissenschaft* inspired scholars the world over. The tradition of following the progress of German legal science continues in many countries. For example, legal scholars in Southern Europe quite often have at least a passive knowledge of the German language. A more exotic example comes from the Korean Republic (South Korea), which recently adopted German doctrines of administrative law.[83]

---

80 Zweigert & Kötz 1996: 175–176.
81 Mattila 1979: 123–126.
82 Mattila 2000: 276.
83 Seok 1991.

A singular influence of German law appeared in the period of National Socialism. A large number of scholars, often of Jewish origin, left the country. The law faculties in Germany thus lost a third of their professors due to emigration, redundancies, and bans, not to forget those who later lost their lives. In their new homelands, notably the United States and England, the immigrant scholars added German colour to the common law as teachers of law.

3.2.2 International Importance of Legal German In the Middle Ages and early modern times, European scientific authors all used Latin. From the Age of Enlightenment, they increasingly used French. Until about 1800, French was considered the language of scientific progress in Germany, too (for example, English research was often read in Germany in the form of French translations). As almost always occurs, linguistic changes were slow in German scientific circles: German-speaking scholars published their studies in two or even three languages (German/Latin, French/German/Latin).

During the period 1794–1814, France occupied German territories. This fact caused a reaction against the French language: German scientific circles began to use German in their studies. Towards the end of the 19th century, this phenomenon gathered speed through the spectacular success of German science, which rose to a dominant world position in many disciplines. The high point of German as an international scientific language is placed around 1920. For example, during the 1920s and 1930s, German was still the main language of international congresses in physics and linguistics. After that, researchers from various disciplines moved increasingly towards the use of English.[84] The position of German as an international scientific language basically weakened after the Second World War. In spite of that, a considerable section of Western researchers are still able to read in German. According to one survey, almost half (44.9%) of British researchers have at least a passive command of the language.[85]

The great importance of German science was also in evidence in the legal sphere: at one time it was simply accepted in many European countries that legal scholars – like theologians for example – should have some command of German (passive in all cases). This notably concerned the Nordic countries and the eastern part of Central Europe, but partly also some countries in Western and Southern Europe. Today, the situation has changed.[86] Nevertheless, law researchers generally have a knowledge of German in the countries mentioned.

Legal science is more closely linked than the natural sciences to the culture and language involved. This explains the fact that at the beginning of the 1990s German lawyers still published some 80% of their scientific articles in German and only 20% in other languages (8% in English). As for books, the dominance of German was even clearer: 85% of legal books were published in German and 15% in other

---

84   von Polenz 1999: 217–218.
85   Skudlik 1992: 397.
86   Hattenhauer 2000: 550.

languages – 4% in English.[87] If a foreign lawyer wants to follow the progress of German legal science – often at the head of international progress – then a command of German is necessary.

In the field of diplomacy and international treaties, the position of German is traditionally weaker. The Holy Roman Empire stuck to Latin in its diplomatic relations. Until 1918, Latin was the official language of correspondence at the Court of Vienna.[88] From the 17th century, French began to oust Latin in the field of diplomacy. As for international treaties, however, German is not deprived of all tradition. It was used in relations between German-speaking States and their neighbours (the Nordic countries, the eastern part of Central Europe, and Eastern Europe, notably the Russia of Peter the Great). In some cases in the 16th century, German was also used in treaties between the Nordic countries, and between the Nordic countries and Russia.[89]

In contrast to French and English, German is not an international language outside Europe. This is evident in international organisations. German possesses official status in only three global organisations; it is one of the working languages in only one of these organisations.[90] Within Europe, the situation is different. German possesses full status as an official language in 12 European organisations; it possesses partial official status in 18 cases. Nevertheless, the fact has to be borne in mind that in practice French and English occupy the dominant positions in almost all organisations.

This last comment also concerns the European Union. In 1994, only 6% of Union civil servants mainly used German in oral communication. The number of civil servants using German but with another mother tongue was smaller still: 3% (basically Dutch-speaking and Danish). In communication with spheres outside the Union, German was resorted to in only 1% of cases.[91] As a counterbalance, the existence should be noted of a large number of German-language legal reviews regularly followed abroad. In the matter of Community law, these include *Europarecht, Europäische Zeitschrift für Wirtschaftsrecht, Zeitschrift für europäisches Privatrecht* and *Zeitschrift für europarechtliche Studien.*

3.2.3 An Example: Legal German in Finland
Medieval Low German. German has a long tradition as a legal language in Finland. At one time in North Germany, people spoke Low German, a close relative of Dutch. In the Hanseatic period, notably in the 14th and 15th centuries, Low German became the *lingua franca* of the regions surrounding the Baltic Sea. It was used – apart from Latin – in relations between the various States and the various merchant cities of these regions, as well as in the administration of the Hanseatic cities. This was also

---

87 Skudlik 1992: 398.
88 von Polenz 1999: 221.
89 Ammon 1992: 424–431.
90 Ammon 1992: 434.
91 von Polenz 1999: 225.

the case for Finland.[92] In the Middle Ages, two main merchant cities were situated in Finland: Turku (in Swedish: Åbo) and Viborg (today, the Russian city of Vyborg). Traders of German origin occupied an important place among the burghers of these cities, notably during the periods when a king of German origin reigned in Sweden (to which Finland then belonged). At the end of the 14th century, Turku counted 27 municipal councillors of German origin; Councillors of Swedish-Finnish origin were only 14.[93] The law at that time required that at least half the municipal councillors of the merchant cities should be of German origin. Between 1430 and 1440, all the burgomasters of Turku were of that origin.[94] Indeed, traders of German origin occupied a corresponding position throughout the regions surrounding the Baltic Sea, for example in Tallinn (Estonia) and Danzig (Gdańsk, Poland). The Hanseatic League lost its status in the 16th century, and the situation of burghers of German origin then experienced a weakening in these regions.

This context explains why many legal documents in medieval Finland were drawn up in German. The variant of German used in almost all these documents was Middle Low German (*Mittelniederdeutsch*), with a Baltic character.[95] These documents are mainly placed – using modern terms – in the fields of public and private international law. Most commonly, this involved correspondence with the Tallinn municipal council. Many letters concern commercial blockade or obstacles to trade, as well as creating alliances or coalitions or repelling pirate attacks in the Gulf of Finland. As to private matters, a large number of documents can be found relating to international inheritance issues. Further, documents also exist concerning mortgage or sale of real property located in Finland or some other legal relationship connected with Finland (e.g., receipts, proxies).[96]

By way of example, a power of attorney given in Viborg on the 13 July 1430. This power of attorney well highlights the features of Low German used in Finland, as well as the medieval style used to draw up a legal document. In the translation (by the author of the present book), the Finnish and Germanic names have left been intact, given that modernisation of their orthography is highly doubtful.

> Witlik sy alle den ghenen, de dessen breff seen edder hören lesen, dat ik Hinrik Rasse van Kangasala mektigh vnde myndugh makede dessen jeghen wordeghen brefujsare, Hannes van Hamelen, borgare to Abo, in to manende vnde vp to börende van den lüden to Sweykala bü, de my beroüeden vnde mynen selschapp; vnde dessen weren höuetlüde also Mykkule, de ander Ywasche, de dridde Koske; desse dre houet lüde myt syner selschap beroüeden my liiij march Rigiske vnde sloghen wns wnde hangeden wns in deme rök vnde plaghede vns oüel. To desses breues mere betuchnisse vnde warheit so bid ik desse beterue lüde Lasse Olafsöne, Staffan Helgesöne, Henyngh Bernefyr, Mathis Lafrensöne,

---

92 Kallioinen 2001: 76–77.

93 Ruuth 1916: 26–27.

94 Ruuth 1916: 60–61.

95 Kantola 1987: 67–70.

96 These documents are included in the collection *Finlands medeltidsurkunder* 1910–1933.

Sweyka Pawel vnde Thomas Wiggere, dat se synen ingheseghel vor dessen breff hanghe. Ghescreuen na godhes bort mcd° vppa dat xxx jar, xiiij dagha na sancte Peters vnde Pauels dagh etc. To Wyborg is dyt breff ghescreuen etc.

Be it known to all persons who shall see these presents or who hear the reading of it that I, Hinrik Rasse of Kangasala, have charged and authorised this person (on the premises), Hannes van Hamelen, burgher of Turku, on presenting this document, to require and receive indemnity from the men of the village of Sweykala who robbed myself and my companions; and they were led by Mykkule, in second place by Ywasche, in third place by Koske; these three principal perpetrators with their accomplices robbed me of 54 Riga marks and did beat us and did leave us hanging in the smoke and did cruelly torture us. In faith of which and for greater surety of the authenticity of these presents, I ask these honest men Lasse Olafsöne, Staffan Helgesöne, Henyngh Bernefyr, Mathis Lafrensöne, Sweyka Pawel and Thomas Wiggere to affix their seals to this document. Written *anno domini* 1430, the 14ᵗʰ day after the feast of Saint Peter and Saint Paul, etc. This document was written at Viborg etc.

The 19ᵗʰ and 20ᵗʰ centuries. Following the final demise in the early 19ᵗʰ century of the legal culture of *jus commune,* expressed in Latin, German law and German-language legal science had a strong influence in Finland. An example will illustrate: right up until today, Finnish *travaux préparatoires* normally include a comparative overview on German law. In the late 19ᵗʰ and early 20ᵗʰ centuries, junior university jurists of the country regularly carried out postgraduate studies in Germany. In consequence, they introduced to Finland the latest currents in legal science, such as *Begriffsjurisprudenz* or *Interessenjurisprudenz*, both already mentioned above. At the language level, this meant that the traditional style of Finnish lawyers quite closely imitated that of German lawyers. Until recent decades, Finnish legal documents were constructed according to the German style. On the one hand, they were systematically arranged, but on the other their language was somewhat clumsy and abstract.

In the same way, in the 19ᵗʰ and early 20ᵗʰ centuries Germany served as a direct model for developing the vocabulary of legal Finnish. *Eindeutschung* offered both the ideological foundation and the concrete model for the Finnification of legal terms. For example, in 1899 a Finnish author published a Finnish translation of Rudolph Sohm's celebrated work, *Institutionen des römischen Rechts*. According to the introduction to the translation, one of the translator's motives was to create Finnish terminology of legal science. Indeed, the appendix includes a German-Finnish lexicon of legal terms.

To sum up, legal German is one of the main keys to understanding the development of legal Finnish. This is why it is useful, still today, for Finnish legal scholars to have a command of German. In fact, many lawyers do know German, at least passively. Illustratively, some legal theses in Finnish in the 1990s were provided with a *Zusammenfassung* in German, although most lawyers publishing a thesis chose a *summary* in English. However, it is true that the position of German among Finnish lawyers has weakened over recent decades and that young Finnish lawyers' knowledge of German is often insufficient. This puts at risk their understanding of the historical roots of the Finnish legal system.

Chapter 7

Legal French

1 History of Legal French

1.1 National Supremacy of the French Language

1.1.1 The Struggle with Latin

Beginnings. The oldest monuments of the Romance languages go back to the end of the first Christian millenium and the start of the second. Most of these monuments were administrative or judicial. In 842, the Oath of Strasbourg was sworn in two languages; one of these was the primitive form of Old French. This compares with the *Placito de Capua* (960) and the *Placito de Sessa Aurunca* (963) in Italy. Somewhat later, in the 12th century, the *Noticia de Torto* was drawn up in Portugal; the same century also produced texts in Provençal and Catalan.[1]

In general, the use of vernacular languages in the chancelleries of States and principalities of Europe began spreading in the 12th and 13th centuries. This was also true of French. Philip the Fair (1268–1314) introduced French to the royal chancellery, and following the king's example this usage spread to the chancelleries of dukes and counts, city administrations, and private documents. At the same time, the king stressed the importance of generally dropping Latin from the administration of law and government. Early in the 13th century, French was widely in use in northern France. In the middle of the century, French was already an established language for legal documents, at least in part of the French-speaking regions in the north of France. In the cities there, over 2,000 documents were drawn up in French during the 13th century. From then on, local customs were also registered in French. By contrast, Latin dominated in the chancelleries of the Midi until the reign of Louis XIV.[2]

French was also in evidence in the courts. In northern France, judicial matters were already being pleaded in French in the Middle Ages. This was also the case for the higher courts. The *Parlement* of Paris, the royal court, going back to the King's Council, began its activities as a specialised court organ in the mid 13th century. Sittings of the *Parlement* were held in French from its foundation, and its judgments were delivered in the same language. In connection with some matters, the *Parlement* had to formally forbid advocates from pleading in Latin. Even those representing the University of Paris had to use French. However, judgments were recorded in

---

1   Duarte & Montserrat 1998: 44–45.
2   Didier 1990: 5–6.

Latin. This was necessary to ensure that judgments could be enforced throughout the country, since as a whole the peoples of the realm did not understand French at the time. Witness statements were also recorded in Latin. To be sure, though, from 1510 these had to be read to the accused in French.[3]

The strengthening of the king's position largely explains the consolidation of French as the administrative and judicial language of the realm. The radical expansion of French began after the Hundred Years War (1337–1453), which had considerably increased the power of the king of France. Thanks to permanent taxes and a centralised administration, the king was able to place vassals under tighter control than previously. Conditions then coincided to bring about the birth of a powerful kingdom. The king and his councillors had well understood that the linguistic unification of the kingdom was highly useful from the standpoint of the exercise of power. In consequence, they applied themselves with energy to spreading the use of the French language. To facilitate and support this action, the king had Greek and Latin classics translated into French.[4]

To sum up, the conclusion is that the legal and administrative language of Paris had begun to challenge Latin earlier than any other language for special purposes. This is why government and the courts played a role of prime importance in the development of French. A large part of their vocabulary was gradually transmitted to ordinary language. French orthography also largely goes back to the practices of administrative and judicial organs.

Modern times. The Reformation had the effect of unsettling the position of the Catholic Church. Thus, the status of Latin weakened still more than before. Paradoxically, the Humanists contributed to this trend through their enthusiasm for Latin. They set up as an absolute model the style of the Roman authors of the classical era, which crippled the use of Latin for everyday ends. Indeed, French finally ousted Latin in government and the courts during the 16th and 17th centuries. It was introduced into all spheres previously reserved for Latin only.

This development was accelerated by new language legislation, consisting of a series of royal decrees, directed against Latin and the traditional languages of the provinces. This series of decrees reached a peak with the Decree of Villers-Cotterêts, promulgated by Francis I in 1539. According to the Decree, judgments and various procedural acts were to be pronounced, recorded, and delivered to the parties in "the French mother tongue and not in any other form". In 1629, French also became the language of Church courts.[5] At the same time, it became generally stronger as the language of culture. Apart from literature, the requirement was that French should conquer the sciences. In the mid 16th century, the first conference in French took place at the *Collège de France*.

Amongst universities, the change was slower (as elsewhere in Europe). In the mid 17th century, French law faculties were still using Latin – the traditional language of

---

3   Krefeld 1985: 61–63.
4   Haas 1991: 15–17.
5   Haas 1991: 17–20.

Roman law, the *jus commune*, and canon law. In 1679, Louis XIV had French law (that is, royal decrees and customs) included in law faculty programmes throughout the land. Somewhat later, he ordered that the professors should teach this law in French.[6] In reality, teaching of French law in French was only truly launched in the 18th century; legal theses were still being drawn up in Latin in the 19th century.

1.1.2 Discarding Regional Languages The main aim of the decrees of the late 15th and early 16th centuries was to evict Latin in favour of French. Mention has already been made of the Decree of Villers-Cotterêts (1539). However, the Decree speaks explicitly of the "French" language, whereas the Decree of Lyon (1510) still referred to the language of the *pays*[7] – a word that could refer to the traditional provinces of the country. This change shows that, apart from evicting Latin, the Decree of Villers-Cotterêts aimed to discard other languages of the realm, notably those of the Midi. Given that judgments and other legal documents had to be drawn up in French, the old languages of the various provinces were excluded. In particular, the Decree of Villers-Cotterêts signalled the end of the use of the Romance languages of the Midi.[8] French had become the sole language of government and the courts. It thus comes as no surprise that at first the decree provoked strong protests in the non-French-speaking regions of the realm.

On these lines, government and the courts played an important role in making French the language of regions conquered by the French crown. For example, the *Parlement* of Pau, a royal court set up in 1620 to deliver justice in the territories of the ex-kingdom of Navarre, had to use only French. In addition, in 1684 the king ordered that all legal business in the city of Ypres in *Flandre Maritime* should be pleaded in French. In Alsace, too, all judgments and other legal documents had to be drawn up in French from 1685.[9]

However, the linguistic change of conquered territories only proceeded slowly. The regional languages remained very much alive among the people. In practice, they still played an important role, despite the fact that administrators were already able to express themselves in French. For example, the local administration in Alsace functioned in German until the Revolution. At the time of the Revolution, the kingdom numbered about 25 million inhabitants. Some 6 million of these did not understand French at all, another 6 million only understood it as a basic level, while a mere 3 million had a firm command of the language; and about 10 million inhabitants had a passable knowledge of French.

During the Revolution, the French language and progress in society were ideologically linked because the bourgeoisie had already generally adopted the use of French by the end of the 18th century. Revolutionary decrees obliged civil servants to use French and to draw up all public documents in it. French was also favoured by

---

6   Krefeld 1985: 63.

7   Didier 1990: 8.

8   Haas 1991: 18.

9   Didier 1990: 10–11.

the fact that the Revolution became militarised and changed into Bonapartism: a very large number of men spent years in an army led and administered only in French. Later, popular education was to be exclusively organised in French. Compulsory military service and the progress of the press also encouraged the linguistic unification of the country – just like construction of postal services and the rail network: it increased the movement of populations and consolidated the central administration of the country.

In spite of these measures, in the 1860s many French people still did not properly understand the main language of the country. Today, all French people have a good command of French but about one-third of them speak a regional language in addition to the national language.[10]

1.1.3 Quality Assurance of Legal Language   From the end of the 15th century, a linguistic awareness developed in France: people began to understand the value and significance of French, the national language. In the 16th century, French was already a fairly well established language as to style and vocabulary. However, in the courts and government offices it had differentiated itself as a particular language genre – legal French – with its own terminology. Legal French gradually became petrified and increasingly difficult to understand from the standpoint of the uninitiated. Even by the reign of Francis I, legal texts had grown dull and heavy through the use of obscure language, largely due to archaisms.[11] This provoked parodies on legal French, such as the celebrated work *Pantagruel*.[12]

Care for quality assurance of the French language began in the 17th century with the foundation of the *Académie Française* in 1635. This defined French "good usage", based on a conception of the style of high society. The *Académie Française* aimed to strengthen this conception, energetically underlining the requirement for linguistic aestheticism. Thus rhetoric became an end in itself. Pretty, charming words formed the ideal, rather than clear and effective ones. Lawyers could not have attained this goal even if they had wanted to. In particular, replacing one word by another to avoid tautology and textual monotony, remained an idea foreign to lawyers: synonyms are often dangerous in legal contexts.[13] A gulf thus opened up between the style of lawyers and that of the literary elites. The *Académie* looked down haughtily on the language of courts and government offices. It found the style of law courts out of fashion, over-technical, and bourgeois, even incomprehensible. This led lawyers to dig in behind their traditional language more strongly than before.[14]

1.1.4 Style of Judgments   The *Parlement* of Paris often gave reasoned judgments in the 13th century but abandoned this practice in the following one. Until the

---

10   Haas 1991: 24–29.
11   Haas 1991: 15.
12   See p. 43.
13   See p. 112.
14   Krefeld 1985: 65–68.

Revolution, French judgments thus lacked grounds. At least two reasons lie behind this. Firstly, the *Parlement* of Paris was a high court, and strengthening its position brought about power struggles with the king. These struggles would have been aggravated by explicit presentation of grounds for judgments, which the king might have felt provocative. Secondly, a class of judges conscious of their worth came on the scene in France. Requiring grounds would have been insulting to the authority of senior judges. As a result, publication of decisions was considered useless, and even banned.[15]

During the Revolution, judges began motivating their decisions again but the grounds were laconic, even formal. Judges wanted first and foremost to show their loyalty to the revolutionaries and their new legislation. That is why court reasoning consisted essentially of articles of law; presenting grounds of any other kind would have been dangerous. According to the new ideology, in a judge's work the question did not even arise of independently creating law – it involved solely the mechanical application of statutes. This is why French judges developed a style of formal grounds: they refer only to statute articles, thus concealing the creative aspect of their activities, the formation of law by cases.[16] This style remains typical of French courts. Statute articles occupy a central place in the grounds of judgments; grounds of other kinds are less common. The fact that the Civil Procedure Code requires judgments to be reasoned is not reflected in the content of the grounds.

1.2 Globalisation of Legal French

1.2.1 Diplomacy During the Middle Ages and indeed up to the 17th century, Latin was the main language of inter-State relations. Bilateral and multilateral treaties were drawn up in Latin. Following the rise of France to a dominant position of great power, she sought to spread the use of French in the international arena, not only as a language of culture but also as a language of diplomacy and international law.[17]

The conviction according to which France should only negotiate in French had already sprung to life in the 16th century. In the following century, the French began applying it: France was now an international heavyweight, and the French language widespread. We should remember, too, that French had possessed the status of administrative and judicial language in medieval England, and that it had a long tradition in Holland through the influence of Wallonia.

At the same time, the ability of Latin to respond to the requirements of modern times had been weakened by the ideology of the Humanists, for whom the classical authors of Rome formed the absolute style-model. Nor should we forget the problems of comprehension caused by spoken Latin: a foreigner might take a greeting from an Irishman in Latin as a greeting in Irish. This led Samuel Sorbière to the following

---

15 Krefeld 1985: 85.

16 Krefeld 1985: 84–92.

17 As for the globalisation of legal French, see Brunot 1917: 387–430, Brunot 1927: 387–431, Brunot 1935: 811–833, also Picoche and Marchello-Nizia 1994: 141–177.

comment on the Latin of the English: "The English explain themselves in Latin with a particular accent, and with a pronunciation that makes it no less difficult than their language".

Around 1640, those corresponding with the Court of France in French included a number of German princes, the Queen of England, and the Estates-General of Holland. The French themselves naturally drew up their diplomatic letters in the same language. On the other hand, the King of Spain used Spanish, while the Italians generally used Italian. Latin was used, for example, by the Holy Roman Empire, some German princes, the Nordic countries, and the King of Poland. The Swiss, in particular, communicated their diplomatic messages in German. A French ambassador of the time wrote that it was not possible properly to perform ambassadorial duties in the Nordic countries without knowledge of Latin and German. Still at that time, conversations at table were often conducted in Latin.

It was chiefly in relations between France and the Holy Roman Empire that conflicts arose over the language of diplomacy. The Holy Roman Empire was clamouring for the use of Latin, while ambassadors of France were presenting documents in French to the Empire's representatives. Similar conflicts made themselves apparent in other contexts, too. An example is the dispute over the drafting language of powers plenipotentiary during negotiations for the Peace of Nijmegen (1677). The Danish ambassador considered that he had the right to give his powers plenipotentiary in Danish if the French representatives gave theirs in French; if the Danish ambassador gave his powers in Latin, the representatives of the King of France ought to do the same.

Gradually, the Holy Roman Empire gave way to France: the Convention of Vienna (1736) and the Treaty of Aix-la-Chapelle (1748) had already been drawn up in French. To save the Germans' face, a clause was included in these treaties to the effect that the use of French was not to be considered a precedent; theoretically, Latin still enjoyed priority. From 1676, all ambassadors of France spoke French in their countries of accreditation. To illustrate the ever-growing strength of French, the language of diplomatic literature of the 17th century also provides a striking example: when a Dutch diplomat wrote a manual for use by ambassadors, it was published in French. The same was the case for a major collection of international treaties published in 1700.

French even spread to international treaties to which France was not a party. Examples include treaties signed by Holland, Prussia, Russia, the Sublime Porte (Turkey) and Great Britain. Furthermore, French was the language of treaties between Prussia and other German-speaking States, while some German ambassadors corresponded with their ministries in French. Analogically, British diplomats used French in relations with various countries. In the wake of this development, international treaties in Latin became increasingly rare during the 18th century. Isolated treaties were still, it is true, concluded in Latin. Long tradition and established contractual formulas spoke in its favour. Latin was neutral, thanks to its being a dead language. Further, Latin was fairly widely understood, although diplomats' knowledge of it had begun to weaken. In short, the position of French was growing ever stronger.

The dominance of French was so strong that it was used in cases where action was directed against France or even in cases involving her defeat. Indeed, the Treaty of Kalisz (1813), concluded by Russia and Prussia against France, was drawn up in French. Later, at the Congress of Vienna (1815) following the defeat of France, French remained the sole negotiating and Treaty language. The solution remained the same in 1871, during peace negotiations following the Franco-Prussian War, which France lost: Otto von Bismarck used French.

The first signs of a contrary tendency appeared at the end of the 18th century. The United States decided immediately following their independence to use only English in their diplomatic relations. They accorded reciprocally, it is true, the same right to representatives of foreign States in Washington. In the same way, William Grenville (1759–1834), appointed British minister for foreign affairs, replaced French with English in Great Britain's diplomacy. At the end of the 19th century, national sentiment also arose in some countries of continental Europe. Despite the fact that Bismarck had carefully avoided humiliating France in 1871 (as we have just seen), he introduced the use of German in German foreign affairs. During the 20th century, English began seriously to threaten the position of French in international relations, and it gradually acquired dominance in this field. Nevertheless, French is far from having disappeared from diplomatic use (see below).

1.2.2 Colonisation

Canada. In the 16th century, France became a colonial power. From the beginning of the century, she founded permanent colonies in North America. Early in the 18th century, French possessions then covered a large part of the continent. French-speaking colonisation in Canada survived in the era of English power. (French remains the dominant language of Quebec, and is also widely used in other Canadian provinces – notably New Brunswick and Manitoba).

In this respect, three periods can be distinguished: French Canada (1534–1760), British Canada (1760–1867) and "Canadian Canada" (1867–). The history of legal language there is closely linked to legal translation – first in a negative sense and later in a positive sense. Before the British conquest, Canadian French was of high quality, independently of the fact of knowing whether the laws and decrees applied in Canada were prepared in France or in America. After the British conquest at the end of the 18th century, poor translators corrupted the language.[18] Nowadays, the situation is quite different, as we shall see.

At the end of the 18th century, public law and the judicial system in Quebec were anglicised. This necessitated rapid translation into French of a large number of laws and other legal English texts, since these were to be applied *vis-à-vis* the French-speaking population. The work of translation became continual because the laws were prepared almost exclusively in English until 1867. The translators had

---

18 Gémar 1995: 7–13.

no specialist training for this kind of work. In consequence, results were poor from the standpoint of quality of French. The fastidiousness and repetitiveness of legal English was clearly evident in the legislative French of Quebec. For example, a law of 1774 contains formulations such as *il sera levé, perçu et payé à Sa Majesté* ['it shall be raised, levied and paid to His Majesty'] (repetition of synonyms) and *en vertu de tout acte ou tous actes du parlement* ['in virtue of all or any act or acts of Parliament'] (a combination of singular and plural).

During the period between the early 1790s and the mid 19th century, legal French in Canada clearly moved very far from that in France. Although some translators proved an exception to the rule, in general French-Canadian legal language became increasingly English, as indeed did the ordinary language. The problem was aggravated by the fact that legal English expressed a completely different legal culture. French-Canadian legal texts of the period were full of Anglicisms. Here are some examples: *acte* in the sense of '*loi*' (Engl. act/statute); *délai* in the sense of '*retard*' (Engl. delay); *évidence* in the sense of '*preuve*' (Engl. evidence); *offense* in the sense of '*infraction*' (Engl. offence).[19]

It seemed that the Act of Union of 1840 had given a mortal blow to the French language in Canada: the law prescribed that English was the only official language of the country. However, the Act of Union provoked a strong resistance on the part of French speakers – a resistance that fairly rapidly led to recognition of French on the part of the public authorities. English as the exclusive official language of Canada came to an end by 1848. Strengthening the position of French started with using it in legal matters. This gradually spread to other areas of public life.[20] The language rights of French speakers were recognised for the first time in the Constitution of 1867 on which the Canadian federal state was founded. With the Peaceful Revolution of the 1960s, the status of Quebec consolidated. The importance of legal translation then began to lessen, thanks to autonomous preparation of laws in French in the province. Recently, the Quebec legislature three times (1969, 1974 and 1977) reinforced the status of French in the province. Today, it is the only official language in Quebec.[21] Consequently, the Quebec National Assembly adopts all its laws in French.

To clarify, French and English both enjoy the status of official languages in Canada – but only at the level of the federal government (in Ottawa) and its institutions. Needless to say, legal texts of the Canadian parliament are always translated into both languages. However, at the level of provincial and territorial governments, New Brunswick is the only English-majority province that has promulgated a specific law on official languages. In spite of that, other Canadian provinces and territories translate some of their legislative texts into French (this is done systematically in Ontario and more selectively elsewhere, notably in the Yukon). In 1985, the

---

19   Gémar 1995: 9–10.
20   Gémar 1995: 40–42.
21   Gémar 1995: 42–45.

Canadian Supreme Court obliged the government of Manitoba to publish the laws of the province in French, in addition to English.[22]

As for preparing Canadian laws (at federal level), the texts of the two versions, English and French, of legislative drafts are worked out simultaneously. This, then, follows the principle of co-drafting legislative texts. The advantage of doing so is considerable: the quality – high or low – of the original draft is more easily revealed by comparing the two language versions than by examining a single version. Terminological work and the principle of co-drafting have freed Canadian French from the patronage of English. At the same time, French is generally enriched. As Jean-Claude Gémar puts it,[23] young nations are less inhibited about dealing with the obsolete in national language usage (as is also visible in the English of the United States and the Portuguese of Brazil, for example). In the case of French, a creative attitude is particularly well-founded. For several centuries, the natural development of French was somewhat slow, due to exaggerated linguistic conservatism. Canadian legislative work brings fresh elements into the French language because the specific conditions imposed by bilingual texts oblige the Canadians to be creators, surrendering the mental comfort created by preserving what is old and certain.

Africa. In the 19th century, French colonial power extended its empire, notably in Africa. As a result, French spread among the upper classes of the countries concerned, partly also in other social classes, both in North Africa and in Black Africa.[24]

1.2.3 Radiation of French Legal Culture Since medieval times, French legal science has figured largely in creating a uniform legal culture in Europe (initially, in Latin). The University of Paris was founded early in the 13th century. In the Middle Ages, the professors of the university contributed greatly to the development of Canon law and *jus commune*. Further, they added impetus to the theory of international private law, expecially in the 16th century. Later, the international influence of French legal science grew still further: as we shall see, a very large number of French legal works were translated into Italian in the 19th century.

In common with legal science, French legislation has also exercised a significant global influence. From the early 19th century, several foreign countries have received French codes. This particularly concerns the Civil Code (1804), the monumental expression of the new values supported by the bourgeoisie that had assumed power. The Civil Code became all the more attractive as a high-quality product from the legislative drafting standpoint. For these reasons, the French Civil Code served as a model for corresponding codes in various countries throughout the world (in some cases, it was implemented as such). Examples in Europe include the Rhineland, Belgium, Luxembourg, Italy, Spain, Portugal, the Netherlands, Poland, and Rumania. In America, the same applies for Quebec, Louisiana, and several Latin American countries. As for Africa, illustrations include Egypt, Ethiopia, and the countries of

---

22 Gémar 1995: 80 note 80.

23 Gémar 1995: 36.

24 See pp. 211–213.

the Maghreb. Nevertheless, the intenational influence of French legislation is not restricted to the Civil Code.[25] For example, in Japan the models of the Criminal Code and the Criminal Procedure Code in the 19th century were French.

French legal culture has also helped progress the development of foreign laws in other ways. For example, French administrative justice essentially contributed to the birth of German administrative legal science in the late 19th century. This chiefly involves general principles of this law, created in France by the *Conseil d'État*. Otto Mayer, the great German scholar (1846–1924), first wrote a survey on French administrative law. It was only after the survey was published that he wrote a similar work on German law, strongly influenced by French law.

French legal science, legislation, and jurisprudence were considered models to follow in other countries. This fact has inevitably contributed to the expansion of French, as an original language of influential legal culture. Thanks to this expansion, French was normally the international language of communication of lawyers from different countries in the 18th and 19th centuries. For example, in the late 19th century a debate took place on the constitutional status of the Grand Duchy of Finland in its relations with the Russian Empire. On the international stage, the contributions to this debate were formulated in French. The position of French remains fairly strong in lawyers' international communication, despite the triumphal march of English in recent times.[26]

1.3 An Example: Legal French in Finland

Apart from international relations in the full sense, French in its heyday could also serve as a tool of legal communication within large multinational countries outside the French linguistic zone. Here, too, we can cite the case of Finland.

This concerns the beginning of the era when Finland was an autonomous Grand Duchy, attached to the Russian Empire. In relations between the Empire and the Grand Duchy, Tsar Alexander I systematically used French during his reign, which lasted until 1825 (his successors preferred to use Russian). At that time, Alexander notably established the Regency Council of Finland, later designated the "Senate". The Regency Council was established by a regulation drawn up in French, dealing in detail with matters relative to its structure and functions (*Règlement de Sa Majesté l'Empereur Alexandre I:er, Autocrate de toutes les Russies &c. &c. &c. pour l'organisation du Conseil de régence dans le grand Duché de Finlande, à Peterhoff ce 6 août 1809*); the Russian, Swedish, and Finnish versions of the document only have value as translations.

Articles 32 to 40 of the second chapter of this regulation concern the Regency Council's Justice Division, competent to decide on judicial matters as final instance (in effect, the organ that immediately preceded today's Finnish Supreme Court). Some of these articles are very lengthy but are divided into paragraphs. The regulation of

---

25 Sacco 1995: 515–523.
26 See pp. 216–219.

1809 confirms, among others, the principle according to which the Justice Division, in its capacity as supreme court of Finland, should decide judicial matters in line with the proper laws of the land (that is, according to legislation of Swedish origin in force in the Grand Duchy, and not according to Russian legislation). The regulation goes on to describe in detail the matters that can be brought before the Division. It even contains a provision on counting votes in case opinions of judges were split (Art. 39). Thus the organisation of Justice at the highest level in Finland goes back to a document originally drawn up in French.

The use of French in Finland as a language of governmental power under the reign of Alexander I was not limited to the regulation of 1809. For example, contributions to the Finno-Russian discussion on reform of the Finnish Constitution, in the period just before and after 1820, were partly formulated in French.

The same was true of presentation notes of the Finnish Secretary of State, drawn up for use by the Tsar. The Secretary of State was a high-ranking Finnish civil servant based in St. Petersburg, to explain Finnish affairs to the Tsar, before the imperial decision was taken. To that end, under Alexander I the office of the Secretary of State drew up presentation notes in French, sometimes running to dozens of pages. If Alexander agreed with the Secretary of State, he wrote in his own hand on the first page of the note, the French word *approuvé*, followed by his signature (very elegant, moreover!) in Latin script.

The Tsar personally decided administrative matters of various kinds, such as nominating civil servants and judges. He also issued decrees on anticipated interpretation of laws, in line with the traditional power that had belonged (in Finland, too) to the King of Sweden, transferred to the Tsar of Russia after Finland was annexed to the Russian Empire as an autonomous Grand Duchy. For example, on the 13th November 1812, he issued a decree (N° 67), at the request of the Turku Court of Appeal (in the decision: *Haute cour de justice d'Abo*), in the matter of the deadline for appealing Governors' decisions on the right of possession and compensation of certain farms whose right of ownership belonged to the State. To illustrate the style of French of legal documents drawn up in Finland and St. Petersburg in the early 19th century, we quote a passage from the presentation note on the basis of which the Tsar issued the decree:

> ...: *que la Haute cour de justice d'Abo a demandé 1 dans quel espace de temps doit être formé auprès de la Haute cour l'appel de la décision portée par les Gouverneurs sur les contestations qui se sont élevées à l'égard du droit de possession et de rachat des terres connues sous le nom de Rusthåll avec leurs dépendances, données à titre d'amodiation par la Couronne, à charge d'équipes des cavaliers pour son service, cette question étant occasionnée par la raison qu'il n'a été donné aucune ordonnance fixe et particulière à ce sujet, et qu'il a été communiqué aux parties plaidantes des instructions différentes, 2 (...)*

...: that the High Court of Justice of Abo [Turku] has asked 1. What time should be allowed for lodging with the High Court an appeal against the decision brought by Governors on the disputes raised with regard to the right of possession and compensation of lands known by the name of *Rusthåll* with their outbuildings, given by the Crown [to the possessors] absolutely, on condition that they equip troopers for Crown service, this question being occasioned by reason that no clear and specific regulation has been given on the matter, and that different instructions have been communicated to the parties pleading, 2 (...). – [Author's translation]

1.4 Defending the Position of French

During the Age of Enlightenment, the French language had become so widespread among the upper classes in European countries that the expression "French Europe" was used. However, even by the early 19th century, pessimists believed that the universality of French could not last long. The social radicalism of the Revolution and the policy of conquest in the Napoleonic era were apt to lessen the popularity of French in Europe. The cosmopolitan intellectuals of the Age of Enlightenment had become passionate nationalists of new nation-States. During the Revolution, the British in particular considered that the dominance of the French language further strengthened the already overly strong influence of France and helped spread undesirable political ideas in Europe. Therefore a fight had to be maintained against the language.[27]

The political dominance of France collapsed with the defeat of Napoleon. At the same time, the population of France was falling proportionately by comparison with some other European countries. In consequence, the French language began to beat a retreat in Europe during the 19th century. As a counterbalance, the importance of English and German was on the rise, both in matters of science and technology as well as those of commerce. In the main, it was the British who took over world commerce. The French language lost status and became (though major) a language like others in Europe, whereas it had previously been the common language of all Europe. On the other hand, in the late 19th century all the natural languages had to defend themselves against artificial languages (e.g., Valapük 1880, Esperanto 1887). The search was then on to develop these languages, to create a neutral tool of international communication. The hope was in this way to prevent world dominance by one natural language and prevent the countries using that language from manipulating other peoples.[28]

The European powers began their second colonial expansion in the late 19th century, conquering new colonies beyond Europe. In 1884 and 1885, the colonial powers organised a conference in Berlin to consolidate the partition of Africa between them. France and Belgium took part in the congress, which opened new possibilities to maintain and strengthen the international position of the French language. Under the new ideology, French should be spread as quickly as possible as a language of daily life of the indigenous populations of colonised countries. The belief was that the future of French would in this way be better guaranteed than by propagating it among European elites as a tool of international communication. French enrooted among the colonial peoples was sustainable but if learned only at school, as in

---

27 Baggioni 1996: 793.
28 Baggioni 1996: 794 and 796.

the case of the European elites, it would soon be ousted by another international language.[29] Today's community of French-speaking countries, "Francophonia", is essentially the creation of that linguistic policy.

2 Characteristics of Legal French

2.1 The Link between Related Languages

2.1.1 The Romance Languages Legal French maintains close relations with other Romance legal languages, as much through linguistic affinity as through the common legal heritage.

In medieval Europe, two factors apt to unify the law stood out: the Canon law of the Church and the secular *jus commune*, based on Roman law codified in the Byzantine Empire and taught in the universities.[30] These were supranational systems of law. Apart from Germany, the Romance countries formed the core of a uniform culture of Canon law and *jus commune*. This is why the basis of legal thinking and the manner of systematising the legal order remain essentially the same in these countries. Later, the cultural dominance of France and the fact that French law might serve as a model abroad, combined to reinforce this uniformity. As we have seen, the French Civil Code (1804) provided a model or blueprint in various countries of the world. In some countries or some regions, it was even implemented as such, or virtually so.

French legal influence was particularly strong on the Italian peninsular. Even in the 17th and 18th centuries, the Italians were diligently following the progress of French legislation. Legislators of the peninsular's principalities took the decrees of the King of France as models. At the same time, classic authors of French legal science, such as Jean Domat (1625–1696) and Robert Joseph Pothier (1699–1772) were highly popular among Italian lawyers, in the form of Italian translations. In consequence, the vocabulary of Italian law and of Italian legal science clearly developed in the direction indicated by French models. As the legal historian Piero Fiorelli points out, new Italian legal terms often came from France: *Molta parte di questi vocaboli sono francesismi o anche franco-latinismi* ['Many of these words are gallicisms or even franco-latinisms'].

French influence became still stronger under the effect of the Revolution and the work of Napoleon. An example that well illustrates this subject comes from the Italian regions annexed to the French Empire (Piedmont, Parma and Piacenza, Liguria, Tuscany, Umbria, Lazio, and Corsica), where decrees and administrative circulars were published in both French and Italian. In the other regions, these decrees and circulars were published in the form of Italian translations. The effect in Italy of French legal science was still greater. In the 19th century, Italian translations

---

29 Baggioni 1996: 795.
30 See pp. 125–126 and p. 133.

were made of no less than 1,315 French legal works (note, by way of comparison, that the corresponding number of German legal works translated was 582 and that of English legal works 191). Italian lawyers were particularly interested in French legal science on the eve of the political unification of Italy.[31]

It is remarkable that during the 19th and 20th centuries legal French also produced a great effect in Rumania – a country long isolated from the culture of Western Europe. Explanations are twofold. On the one hand, written Rumanian in the modern sense was created following the country's independence and unification (1859), under the impetus of other Romance languages, notably French. On the other hand, it was France that also inspired reforms in the legal order of Rumania. The Rumanian Civil Code (1864) is an almost direct copy of the French Civil Code. It was not even repealed during the Socialist period and still remains in force.[32] The terminology of Rumanian civil law, still in use today, was created during preparation of the Civil Code of 1864. Indeed, the French and Rumanian languages are in no field closer to one another than in legal science and legal matters in general. Rumanian civil law terminology in particular is essentially based on the French example. A speaker of French easily recognises Rumanian terms in any article of the 1864 Code, e.g.: *petiţie, creanţă, creditor, debitor, obligaţie, proprietate, uzufruct, servitute, succesiune, acceptare, repudiere, legat, donaţie, convenţie, quasi-contracte, quasidelicte, nulitate, interpretare, solidaritate, subrogaţie, validitate, titlu, divizibil.* It is particularly important that the meaning of these terms is the same as in France, because the legal rules of the Rumanian Code are formulated in accord with the French Code.[33]

To sum up, we can conclude that legal French language and the legal languages of other Romance countries are quite close to one another. First of all, a large part of the legal terminology, both in France and the other Romance countries, comes from the Latin of Roman and medieval legal science. Further, many French legal terms were adopted in other Romance countries: this essentially involves variants of the same word-stems from Latin. Secondly, the conceptual system that these terms express is built on a common base: the legal order is understood and systematised in the same way in all Romance countries. For this reason, the similarity in appearance of legal terms in these countries is not in general misleading: all variants of the same word-stem express the same concept. Naturally, exceptions to this rule exist, some of them significant.

2.1.2 Legal English The royal courts of medieval England used a French variant called *law French*, developed on the basis of Norman French (and later Parisian). The French language arrived in England with William the Conqueror. It was used

---

31   Fiorelli 1994: 582–583, especially notes 40 and 41, and Fiorelli 1994: 589, especially notes 68 and 69.
32   Stângu 2000: 73.
33   Stângu 2000: 80–81.

as a judicial language in the 13th and 14th centuries especially.[34] The foundations of English common law were therefore laid in the days when the most important courts in the land were using French. At the same time, because of the Norman Conquest the majority of modern English vocabulary relating to any abstract matter comes from French and, in the final analysis, from Latin. All this implies that legal English and legal French largely use the same vocabulary. Often, legal terms from these languages appear perfectly identical (for example, the word *jurisprudence*).

On the other hand, the concepts expressed by *law French* were created in England under particular conditions. For this reason, the legal system developed in medieval England is highly original compared with the continental systems.[35] The legal systematics and conceptual apparatus of common law differ considerably from those of the civil law countries. In consequence, the relationship between legal English and legal French is complicated. Many misleading elements occur in this relationship: terms that appear identical do not necessarily express the same concepts.

The French term *équité*, appearing in English in the form *equity*, is a classic example. In legal French, the word means 'natural justice able to take its source beyond the rules of law in force'.[36] An English lawyer, too, may sometimes use *equity* in this sense. However, the term normally has a technical meaning that originally comes from the thinking of natural justice but that today is wholly differentiated from it.[37] Since this technical meaning can only be understood in the frame of the common law system, *equity* is an untranslatable term in the legal languages of civil law countries.

On that account, translators of legal texts between French and English should be especially cautious in drawing conclusions on the basis of the similar appearance of the terms of these two legal languages. Even if the meaning of English and French terms is often the same, in many cases this appearance is misleading.

2.2 International Homogeneity of Legal French

2.2.1 Belgium The legal languages of independent countries always diverge to some extent, even within the same linguistic zone. The differences between the legal languages of France and Belgium are fairly small. In an article on Belgian legal French, a Belgian specialist asks: "Is Belgian legal French *in all respects* the same as French legal French?" (my italics). The formulation of this question shows that differences are the exception. For example, the names of certain State organs. Again, some terms in Belgian judicial language are no longer used in France; they have an archaic ring to the ears of a lawyer from France. Apart from historical reasons, the homogeneity of the legal languages of France and Belgium can be explained by the fact that legal science in the French-speaking part of Belgium has tended until

---

34 See pp. 226–228.
35 See pp. 106–107.
36 Barraine 1974: 204.
37 See p. 223 and pp. 251–252.

recently to look for inspiration almost exclusively to the legal culture of France, and not to the legal culture of Dutch-speaking (Flemish-speaking) Belgium, not to mention that of the Netherlands. However, it seems that the situation may be changing: law students in the French-speaking part of Belgium have begun to take an interest in the legal language of Flanders.[38]

2.2.2 Switzerland In comparison with Belgium, the situation in Switzerland differs. The legal French of Switzerland is partly original in relation to the legal French of France because the legal traditions of the Confederation are essentially Germanic, while the country's main language is German. For example, the Canton of Geneva only joined the Confederation in 1814/1815. The originality of Swiss legal French can be seen as much in matters of style as of terminology.

In practice, German is the language of preparation of laws of the Confederation, that is, the Swiss federal State. When the French versions of the first pan-Swiss codes were formulated, at the end of the 19th century, the aim was to follow as faithfully as possible the traditions of French legal language. The Swiss Civil Code (in German: *Zivilgesetzbuch*) was translated into French by Virgile Rossel, the statesman, lawyer, and writer trained both in French and German law. As a language model, he took the Napoleonic Code and the language of French legal science. According to him, the French version of the Swiss Civil Code should not be formulated in "Gallicised German" but in language that citizens could recognise as their own. The objective was not external concordance but concordance of content of legal rules. This is why Rossel was determined to avoid direct calques from German and to use, as far as possible, established French legal terms. For example, in the French version of the Swiss Civil Code the term *Mündigerklärung* ['declaring a person to be of age'] is not *déclaration de majorité* [lit. 'declaration of majority'] but *émancipation*. This cultural adaptation was of great help in introducing the legislation of the Confederation into French-speaking Switzerland.[39]

At the beginning of the 21st century, over one hundred years have passed since the birth of pan-Swiss legislation. The fusion of both Germanic and Romance legal cultures is today a reality. As Claude Bocquet puts it, this has partly led to legal circles in French-speaking Switzerland imitating the language of the dominant Germanic legal culture. Lawyers charged with translating federal laws have been inclined to believe that concordance of content of the German and French variants of laws can only be guaranteed by literal translation of terms.[40]

An example will illustrate this change in translation ideology in French-speaking Switzerland. French legal culture does not recognise the concept expressed by the German term *die beschränkten dinglichen Rechte* ['limited property rights', 'limited real rights', 'restricted rights *in rem*']. Indeed, this term goes back to the thinking of the German Pandectists of the 19th century. In France, the concept of law of property

---

38   Verrycken 1995: 372–375.
39   Dullion 1997: 376–387.
40   Bocquet 1994: 49–50.

is differently divided. This is why the original articles of the Swiss Civil Code speak, in the case of *beschränkten dinglichen Rechte*, about *autres droits réels* ['other property rights']. Later, however, after strengthening of the translation ideology underlining the importance of direct calques, a literal translation of this term was created. The French version of the law (1989) modifying the Civil Code's provisions on leasing prescribe that: *Lorsque le bailleur accorde à un tiers un droit réel limité et que cette opération équivaut à un changement de propriétaire, les dispositions sur l'aliénation de la chose louée sont applicables par analogie* ['When the lessor grants to a third party a limited property right and this operation is equivalent to a change of owner, then the provisions on alienation of the property leased are applicable by analogy'].[41]

The attitude of French language specialists towards neologisms is cautious. In spite of that, the above example shows that the autonomy of Swiss law sometimes requires, in line with the prevailing ideology, adoption of original terms in order to express that autonomy. Cases also exist where the meaning of legal terms differs between Switzerland and France. For example, the term *nantissement* ['security', 'pledge', 'lien'] refers to all liens on personal (movable) property in France, whereas in Switzerland it involves a specific type of lien on personal (movable) property. The probability is that as a result new legal terms will also be created in French-speaking Switzerland. According to Pierre Tercier, French-speaking Swiss lawyers should always be able to express the original character of their law. This means that a certain number of neologisms are inevitable. At the same time, however, Swiss lawyers should first ascertain that it is impossible to express the particular Swiss legal institution by an established French term.[42]

Apart from questions of terminology, the fusion of the Germanic and French legal traditions is also in evidence in decisions of the Swiss Federal Court. These decisions correspond in their basic structure to the French tradition. However, as to syntax, arranging the text in numbered paragraphs in accordance with the progress of the argumentation, and dialogue between legal scholars and the judges, the decisions of the Swiss Federal Court follow the Germanic tradition.[43] These features characterise decisions originally delivered by the Court in both German and French.

In spite of this fusion, divergences between the legal French of France and Switzerland are "fewer than it would seem".[44] In the case of some cantons, it can be otherwise. German speakers form the great majority of the population in the Canton of Berne. That explains the fact that the legislative language of Berne at one time contained many German words, direct calques from German, and French neologisms freely constructed under the inspiration of German words. Today, the aim is to improve the linguistic quality of French versions of the laws of the canton. On the other hand, a great variation exists as to the names of the authorities of

41 Bocquet 1994: 50–52.
42 Tercier 1999: 267–269.
43 Ballansat-Aebi 2000: 719–720.
44 Tercier 1999: 268.

the various cantons. Federal legislation designates the supreme organs of executive power in the cantons as *Kantonsregierung /gouvernement cantonal* but at the level of individual cantons several names are both in German and in French, e.g.: *Conseil d'État, Conseil-exécutif, Gouvernement, Staatsrat, Regierungsrat*.[45]

2.2.3 Canada Canada supplies the most significant differences in legal French in use by comparison with France. As the brief overview on the history of legal French shows, Quebec is a province where common law of English origin intermingles with law of French origin to form a coherent whole.[46] The legal system of Quebec is a mixed-law system: the public law of the province comes from common law but its private law is mainly continental in character. To ensure the continuity of civil-law legal culture in Quebec, lawyers called to the bar in the province have to to fulfil a training requirement in that culture. Further, a French-style notarial profession is an important element in the Quebec legal system; this is unknown in common law countries. The hierarchy of sources of law also has a typically Continental flavour.

The mixture of law of French origin with common law has had interesting and significant consequences from the standpoint of Quebec legal French. Indeed, it has given rise to the need to express traditional common law concepts in French, and – *vice-versa* – traditional concepts of French law in English. The problems connected with this have been gradually resolved.

In some cases, traditional terms from French law have obtained in Canada a meaning different from that in France. However, this solution is not desirable because it can cause mistakes and misunderstandings, notably in communication with France. In other cases, Canadians have used a particularly interesting method. At the time when English common law was created, legal circles in the country were using French.[47] Thus, institutions peculiar to common law were from the very outset expressed in French. By then highlighting the original form of common law terms, it is possible to fashion terms that are authentically French, with a character at once old and new. For example, the term *chatel* ['a type of personal [movable] property'], in English *chattel*.[48] This terminological work has enabled compilation in Canada of legal dictionaries and vocabularies containing, in French, the terminology of various branches of common law (for example, law of property, trusts, torts).

> The mixed character of Quebec legal French is also in evidence in the fact that Latin maxims appearing in this form of French come both from the traditional Latin of common lawyers and from the Latin used as established in France.[49]

---

45   Bocquet 1994: 54–57.
46   See p. 193.
47   See pp. 226–228.
48   Snow 1999: 191.
49   Schwab and Pagé 1981: 233.

2.2.4 Africa The peoples of sub-Saharan Africa have traditionally observed a variety of customs (customary laws). The French colonial power codified some of these. However, customary laws can only produce a small part of the legal rules needed in a modern society. For this reason, they were completed by European law, that is, by French law. At the same time, the colonial power put an end to customary rules of law to the extent that these were considered in contradiction with the fundamental values that Europeans supported. This was especially the case for criminal law. At the end of the Second World War, the French Criminal Code was applicable throughout the regions of Africa ruled by the French. The Africans also had the possibility to submit themselves entirely to French justice, in terms of the legal order as a whole. Nor should we forget that the legal elites of Africa received their professional training in France.

This background explains why the French used in Black Africa is essentially the same as that in France. In the main, this also applies to North Africa, with its Islamic tradition, although Arabic quotations may exist in the legal French of the Maghreb, notably in traditional branches of the law expressing concepts from the sharia. Needless to say, local traditions and conditions are also reflected in African legal French.

2.3 Origin of Vocabulary

Since the traditions of legal French go back a long way, several layers of vocabulary can be distinguished. In legal French, the heritage of Antiquity is even more evident than in ordinary French. Apart from Latin, legal French terms of today have a background of classical Greek and some modern languages. The most recent layer is formed by loanwords from English.

Clearly, French – as a Romance language – has inherited part of its legal vocabulary by the natural route. This involves words transmitted from Antiquity by continuous tradition. Examples of basic legal terms include, e.g.: *loi* (Lat. *lex*), *législation* (Lat. *legislatio*), *juge* (Lat. *judex*), *justice* (Lat. *justitia*), *délit* (Lat. *delictum*), *société* (Lat. *societas*).[50]

However, the later use of Latin in legal circles in Medieval and modern times has been of great importance. In this way, French acquired from scholarly Latin both terms and the meaning of terms. Examples include *contumace* ['contumacy', 'contempt', 'non-appearance in court', Lat. *contumax*], (*testament*) *nuncupatif* ['orally declared (will)', Lat. *nuncupare – nomen capere*], *traduire en justice* [' to proceed against sb.', 'to sue sb. at law', Lat. *traducere*].[51] These borrowings go back to different eras and sources (late Latin, canon Latin, scholarly Medieval Latin, the Latin of the Humanists). Thus, from Medieval Latin come the terms *collatéral* ['collateral (e.g. heir)', Lat. *collateralis*], *curatelle* ['guardianship'; 'trusteeship', Lat. *curatela*], *habilitation* ['enabling', Lat. *habilitatio*] and *légiste* ['jurist', 'legal

---

50 Cornu 2005: 141.

51 Krefeld 1985: 207–209 and 220.

specialist', Lat. *legista*] which is notably found in the expression *médecin légiste* ['medical expert (at trials)'].[52]

On the other hand, the influence of Latin – and Greek – on the vocabulary of legal French today appears in the form of neologisms which were never used in Latin or Greek but directly in French.[53] From amongst these neologisms we offer *autogestion* ['self-regulation', 'self-management' (participation of the personnel in the administration of a business), Gr. *autos* and Lat. *gestio*] and *monoparental* ['single-parent', 'one-parent', Gr. *monos* and Lat. *parens*], which notably appears in the expression *famille monoparentale* ['single-parent family', 'one-parent family']. Today, legal neologisms of Graeco-Latin origin often come into French through English. The United States is known to be the chief manufacturer of many neologisms on the basis of the classical languages.

Indeed, terms of Greek origin make up the largest group of loanwords in legal French, after words of Latin origin. This Graeco-French vocabulary covers not only Constitutional law (*démocratie* ['democracy'], *politique* ['policy'; 'politics']) but also other branches of the law, e.g.: *hypothèque* ['mortgage'], *emphytéose* ['hereditary lease'], *antichrèse* ['antichresis', 'assignment of the revenue from real estate as a security for a debt'], *chirographaire* (for example in the expression *créance chirographaire* ['unsecured debt']), *olographe* (in the expression *testament olographe* ['holographic will', 'will written in testator's hand']), *synallagmatique* ['synallagmatic', 'imposing reciprocal obligations'], *police* ['police'; 'insurance policy', 'certificate'], *amnistie* ['amnesty'].

As with other legal languages, legal French has until our times used many archaic expressions. Examples include pronouns and certain petrified expressions such as: *icelui/icelle* ['this', 'the said'], *il appert* ['it appears', 'it is evident'], *il échet* ['it falls (to do)'].[54] Archaic words (of Germanic or Latin origin) include, e.g., *débouter (de sa demande)* ['to dismiss/reject (a) claim' which comes from the Frankish word *botan*], *ester en justice* ['to appear in court', 'to plead', Lat. *stare*] and *à huis clos* ['in camera', 'in private', 'behind closed doors', Lat. *ostium*].[55]

Of modern languages, Italian has been the main provider of loanwords to French (true, some of these borrowings go back to Latin in the final analysis), e.g.: *banqueroute* ['criminal bankruptcy'], *change* ['exchange']. Today, as can easily be imagined, the most important language source is English, e.g.: *dumping, leasing, franchising, factoring*. French language specialists, as is well known, take a dim view of these English borrowings. This is why neologisms have been created, obligatory in official contexts, to replace them: *leasing* = *crédit-bail, factoring* = *affacturage*.[56]

---

52 Cornu 2005: 146.
53 Cornu 2005: 170–171.
54 Krefeld 1985: 226 and Gémar 2005: 98.
55 Krefeld 1985: 207.
56 Troisfontaines 1981: 181.

2.4 Legal French Style

2.4.1 Text Construction French culture features the Cartesian spirit. One implication of this is that legal texts are contructed in a particularly logical and methodical way. This especially concerns the major laws. In France, legal rules are systematically assembled in highly voluminous laws called "codes".

> The Cartesian tradition is highly useful from the standpoint of foreign legal translators. With a code forming a logical whole, it is not usually difficult to locate the legal rules on a particular matter. In consequence, the relevant terminology is also found, which is important where the terminology is new and has not yet appeared in specialised dictionaries. Today, the French codes are quickly accessible on the Internet.

As for judgments of French courts, by contrast their construction was previously somewhat unclear. It is true that the different parts of a judgment and the specific grounds could be recognised by certain key words (e.g., *considérant que*), but the composition left much to be desired. Today, as we have seen,[57] the situation is clearly improved.

2.4.2 Textual Level At one time, French legal texts were somewhat difficult to understand. They contained long, complicated sentences, impersonal expressions, passive and negative forms (e.g., *il n'est pas exclu que* ['it is not impossible that']), repetitive phrases and formulas, inverted structures, pronouns called "legal pronouns" (e.g., *ledit* [the {afore}said]). These texts also featured a limited use of adjectives and an abundance of nouns. Stereotyped phrases, for example, *dont acte* [free translation: 'in witness / faith / testimony / verification'], littered these texts, which was also true of archaisms (e.g., old-fashioned prepositions, absence of articles). Some of these legal pronouns and petrified expressions typical of legal texts were: *ci-après* ['hereafter'], *ledit, susdit* ['aforesaid'], *précité* ['aforementioned'], *par ces présentes* ['by these presents'].[58] As for administrative language, a trait to mention was – and still is – the compliments presented in administrative letters to their addressees.[59]

As with other legal languages, these features often go back to the Latin of Medieval times. For example, the Latin *ablativus absolutus* has clearly been in evidence in the structures of legal French. In medieval legal documents, a Latin sentence might run to several pages. As for legal pronouns, the word *dictus* (*ledit*) was endlessly repeated.

Even today, hermetic legal texts are not uncommon. Here is a sentence that is quite difficult to follow: (...) *lorsque la loi le prévoit, en cas d'imprudence, de négligence ou de manquement de prudence ou de sécurité prévue par la loi ou les*

---

57 See pp. 85–86.

58 Eurrutia Cavero 1997: 111–115, Krefeld 1985: 216–230 and Sourioux & Lerat 1975: 48.

59 Catherine 1996: 24–25 and 132.

règlements, sauf si l'auteur des faits a accompli les diligences normales compte tenu le cas échéant, de la nature de ses missions ou de ses fonctions, de ses compétences ainsi que du pouvoir et des moyens dont il disposait.[60] ['(...) when the law foresees it, in case of recklessness, negligence, or lack of care or precaution foreseen by the law or regulations, except if the person concerned has taken normal precautions taking into consideration, should the occasion arise, of the nature of his tasks or duties, his competences as well the power and means at his disposal'. – Author's translation].

In legal French, repetitions are less frequent than in legal English. In spite of this, it is easy to find examples: *nous avons arrêté et arrêtons* ['we have decided and do decide'], *un seul et même jugement* ['one and the same judgment'], *les part et portion de chacun* ['the share and portion of each'], *la procédure de licenciement est nulle et de nul effet* ['the dismissal procedure is void and of no effect'], *le dépositaire doit rendre identiquement la chose même* ['the agent/trustee/depositary shall identically repay the same thing'], *dit inopérant ou mal fondé tous moyens, fins ou conclusions* ['declared invalid or ill-founded all pleas, grounds or arguments'].[61]

As to petrified phrases, among the clearest examples rank the traditional executory formulas for judicial decisions and expressions systematising the grounds of judgments: *attendu que* and *considérant que.*[62] These two judicial French expressions are very old, going back to the 15th century. Strict form requirements can also be seen in verbs: grounds should always be written in the indicative; using the conditional can lead to the judgment being quashed.[63]

The use of articles and prepositions in legal language also proves to differ from the norms of ordinary language. Lawyers have often dropped the article in cases where it is necessary under the rules of normal language. The explanation is simple: in Old French, the article was used less often than today. Since legal language is conservative, lawyers up to our times have said: *déposer copie* ['lodge (a) copy'], *obtenir paiement* ['obtain payment'], *toutes parties* ['all parties'], *suivant ordonnance* ['under (the) order / ruling / decree / ordinance / regulation'], *dont lecture faite* ['which has been read']. The use of prepositional syntax also differed from the norms of ordinary language, e.g.: *en la forme* ['in the form'], *près la Cour d'appel* ['with the Court of Appeal'], *près le Tribunal* ['with the Court'].[64]

As for legislative language, inversion should here be mentioned: *Seront exécutées, sous le titre de Code de la nationalité française, les dispositions dont la teneur suit...* [Author's translation: 'There shall come into effect, under the title of the French Nationality Code, the following provisions ...']. This not only involves a stylistic effect. Inversion fulfils a communicative function. Thanks to this, a complicated sentence becomes clearer. An example: *Attendu qu'aux termes de ce texte font partie de la communauté les biens mobiliers qui appartenaient aux époux avant leur union*

---

60 Gutman 1999: 83.
61 Eurrutia Cavero 1997: 107.
62 See pp. 84–85.
63 Krefeld 1985: 107–109.
64 Eurrutia Cavero 1997: 113–116.

ou qui leur sont advenus depuis et les revenus de ces biens, échus ou perçus pendant le mariage .... [Author's translation: 'Whereas, under the terms of the text, community (of property) shall include movable property belonging to the spouses before their union or subsequently acquired by them and the revenues of such property, falling due or received during the marriage…']. If the words *font partie de la communauté* ['form part of the community'] are transposed to the end of the sentence, it becomes far more dificult to understand.[65]

2.5 Improving the Quality of Legal Language

2.5.1 Measures of Modernization As everywhere in modern countries, recent decades have seen efforts made to simplify and modernise legal French. Illustrations include the *Association pour le bon usage du français dans l'administration* ['Association for Good Usage of French in Government'], the *Commission de modernisation du langage judiciaire* ['Commission for Modernisation of Judicial Language'], the *Centre d'enregistrement et de révision des formulaires administratifs* (CERFA) ['Centre for Recording and Revising Administrative Model Forms']. Terms felt to be discriminatory (e.g., *enfant adultère* ['child of adultery'], *enfant illégitime* ['illegitimate child']) have been replaced by new terms or circumlocutions. Notarial formulas have also been simplified and lawyers are required to avoid archaic expressions. The use of legal language by the courts has provided an object of particular attention on the part of the public authorities.[66]

In the 1970s, several ministerial circulars, based on the work of the Commission for Modernisation of Judicial Language, drew the attention of government and the courts to the quality of legal language.[67] As for the courts, the aim was to improve the composition of judgments and the drafting of summonses. At the same time, the recommendation was that courts should so far as possible avoid archaic terms and expressions, replacing these with modern ones. A good example is forms of address *le sieur X* ['Mr. X'], *la dame Y* ['Mrs Y'] and *la demoiselle Z* ['Miss Z'] as well as the expressions *es privé nom* ['in his own name'], *Oui M. X en son rapport* ['Having heard Mr. X's account'] and *en chambre du conseil* ['in camera', 'in private', 'in closed session'].[68]

A further proposal was that courts should eliminate useless repetitions that made texts more clumsy. For example, the expression *débouter X de toutes les demandes, fins et conclusions* ['dismiss all claims, pleas and arguments of X'] should be replaced by the expression *rejeter les demandes de M. X.* ['reject the claims by Mr. X']. This was again the case for the expressions *dit que le jugement sortira son plein et entier effet pour être exécuté selon ses forme et teneur* ['declare that the judgment shall come into full force and effect to be enforced according to its form

---

65 Krefeld 1985: 234–238.
66 Sourioux & Lerat 1998: 544–545.
67 Troisfontaines 1981: 167–168.
68 Troisfontaines 1981: 182–183.

and import'], more simply: *ordonne l'exécution du jugement* ['order enforcement of the judgment'], *droits, dus, actions et intérêts* ['rights, dues, shares and interests'], more simply: *droits* ['rights'] and *se déclare prêt et offrant de* ['declares (him)self ready and willing'], more simply: *offre de* ['offers to'].[69]

Some Latin maxims are the most hermetic expressions from the standpoint of the general public. For this reason, Latin terms are rare in French legislative texts. However, exceptions do exist. Examples include: *tuteur ad hoc* ['ad hoc guardian'], *provision ad litem* ['payment on account of costs incurred by a party to an action'], *compétence ratione materiae* ['material competence', competence (of a court) to judge a case by reason of the matter involved]. According to a circular from the Commission for Modernisation of Judicial Language, Latin maxims should also be avoided in court judgments, to be replaced with French expressions appearing in the appendix to the circular. Certain Latin words were, it is true, considered already to be established elements of the French language, e.g.: *pro forma, quorum, ratio*.[70]

Apart from judicial proceedings, an effort was made to ensure the clarity of legal language in other contexts, notably involving texts intended for general public use. A good example is insurance clauses. The former *souscripteur* ['underwriter'] is now written as *preneur d'assurance* ['insurance contractor / accepter']. In some cases, former terms have become easily intelligible circumlocutions: *valeur résiduelle* = *valeur du bien après sinistre* [lit. 'value of a good after a disaster', 'salvage value'] and *transaction* = *entente sur le montant de l'indemnisation* ['agreement on the amount of indemnity'].[71]

2.5.2 The Struggle against Anglicisms Some hundreds of years ago, French brought to an end the use in legal matters of the regional languages of France – also Latin at the international level.[72] It also exercised a great influence on other legal languages, notably as to vocabulary. Today, the situation is the other way around: French lawyers and language specialists are forced to defend themselves against the influence of English, which has risen to a dominant position, even in legal circles. For example, in 1992 the *Conseil d'État* deplored the poor quality of French in the European Communities, due – in the opinion of the *Conseil* – amongst other things to the ever-growing influence of the British in the frame of the Communities.[73] It therefore comes as no surprise that the Commission for Modernisation of Judicial Language also drew the attention of judges to loanwords of English origin. These had to be

---

69   Troisfontaines 1981: 182–185.

70   Troisfontaines 1981: 178–180.

71   Gutman 1999: 80 note 5.

72   See pp. 187–190 and pp. 191–192.

73   Gutman 1999: 86. However, some also underline that the French of the European Union is less formalistic and archaic than in France.

replaced by neologisms created to that end. Examples include *leasing* = *crédit-bail* and *royalty* = *redevance*.[74]

As for government and economic life, the never-ending strengthening of English has provoked particularly radical measures. In 1994, the French legislator promulgated a law called *loi Toubon*, baptised after Jacques Toubon, Minister of Justice at the time.[75] According to this law, the use of French is obligatory in certain public and private contexts, for example in advertising and consumer information. In relation to the legislation of the European Communities, this law has aroused disputes. Some see it as an obstacle to trade, while others as a completely legitimate measure justified by the needs of cultural policy.[76]

3 International Position Today

3.1 Continuing Importance of Legal French

Legal French became global due to colonialism. Apart from France, Belgium also contributed to this globalisation: in the Belgian Congo, the colonial administration and colonial courts used French. Despite the end of the colonial system, over a large part of the world French still possesses the status of official language, or language in use in legal circles. This is as true for Canada as it is for Northern, Western, and Central Africa. In Europe, apart from France, French is an official laguage in Belgium, Switzerland, and Luxembourg.

After the Second World War, the position of French as a global language of lawyers has weakened, while that of English has strengthened. However, establishment of the European Communities has to some extent meant a new flowering of French: it is one of the two main languages of Community institutions (recent enlargements of the European Union have, it is true, unsettled that position). On the other hand, French is still used in countries outside Europe and in the frame of global organisations.

3.2 Francophonia

3.2.1 Overview: Defining "Francophonia" French-speaking countries (as well as certain other countries attracted by the cultural radiation of France) established the international community called "Francophonia" (*la Francophonie*), promoting the interests of French culture. It should be noted, on the one hand, that some countries in which French possesses the status of an official language or in which in practice it is used by certain layers of the population (chiefly the elites), are not members of Francophonia. Two of these are Algeria and Switzerland. On the other hand, this

---

74 Troisfontaines 1981: 181.

75 Loi No 94-665, 4 août 1994 relative à l'emploi de la langue française, J.O. 5 août 1994 ['Law No 94–665, 4 August 1994 on the use of the French language, J.O. 5 August 1994'].

76 Bloch 1998: 400–402.

community includes countries where French is not an official language or even used in social life (except perhaps marginally). However, these countries are keen to support the use of French in the international arena.

Estimates of the number of people with a full or partial command of French vary considerably and are not always comparable. According to one source, at the end of the 1980s some 106 million people were using French as a daily language; an additional 55 million or thereabouts in countries where French has official status were using it as a language of occasional communication. The same source mentions that at the end of the 1980s the number of persons who had studied (or were studying) French outside French-speaking countries was around 100 million. For its part, the *Atlas de la langue française* ['French Language Atlas', 1995] gives a figure of 130 million. This figure covers everyone speaking French, whether regularly or occasionally. By contrast, Maurice Druon, former Permanent Secretary of the *Académie Française*, estimates that at least 400 or 500 million people understand French.[77] From the standpoint of use of the language in legal matters, the number of States where French is an (or the only) official language amounts to 33 (these, though, include several mini-States). Of these States, 18 are in sub-Saharan Africa.[78]

French influence also appears in legal science. This is ensured by the fact that a large section of African elite legal circles receive their training in France and use French in their publications. French publishing houses encourage African lawyers to publish in French. One example is the series *Bibliothèque africaine et malgache* ['African and Madagascan Library'].

3.2.2 North Africa The Maghreb (that is, Tunisia, Algeria, and Morocco) have always been a multilingual region. Two thousand years ago, Latin and Berber alternated in communication among the populations of the Western parts of North Africa. The Arabic language arrived in the Maghreb region with the Arab conquest and Islam. This language ousted the Romance languages in North Africa, although the process was a long one: Romance language islets still existed in the Maghreb in the 12th century. At the same time, former linguistic conditions exercised an influence on Arabic in the region.[79]

The Maghreb once again became partly Romance, in that it became Gallicised in the 19th and early 20th centuries, with colonisation. From the 1830s, the French began by conquering Algeria, where French was declared the official language of the country. It also obtained the position of highly placed language of local elites. Later, French troops marched on Tunisia, which became a protectorate, *de facto* in 1881 and *de jure* in 1883. At the Berlin Conference (1884–1885), the other colonial powers approved and ratified these conquests. After that, French was proclaimed the sole official language of the region. As we know, the French had to give up Algeria after a particularly bloody colonial war. In the case of Tunisia, separation

---

77 Barrat 1997: 15.

78 These States are presented, differently classified, in Turi 1996: 809-812.

79 Manzano 1995: 174–176.

from France was far easier, with Tunisia obtaining independence in 1956.[80] In the same way, Morocco's status as a protectorate was annulled in 1956 to become an independent country.

In today's Maghreb, only Arabic possesses the status of official language. In spite of that, French is doing well in the region at the start of the 21st century. It has become part of the identity of the people who live there: according to statistics, making all allowances, among natives of the Maghreb today are more people with a command of French than at the end of the colonial era. The position of French has therefore stabilised. The Maghreb media partly use French, and television programmes coming from France are followed in the region. Moreover, in Tunisia a good knowledge of French is a condition *sine qua non* for entry to universities, where French is the main language of instruction in the fields of technology and natural science. In the linguistic reality of the country, French and Arabic alternate.

Critics consider the use of French as a phenomenon underlying a dangerous relationship of dependency: the people of the Maghreb are not, even today, free from the manipulations of their former colonisers. However, for those who have been through the education system French is a door to the outside world. The French language symbolises the overture to Europe and modernisation. In Tunisia, one specialist concludes that French is an international passport to education and social improvement, whereas classical Arabic is the language of Muslim identity and Arabic-Islamic culture compared with local spoken Arabic, language of the genuine identity of the people of the Maghreb.[81]

3.2.3 Tunisia under the Microscope

The legal order. Tunisia is an example that well illustrates the influence of French legal culture in Africa. As mentioned, the country was a French protectorate from 1881 to 1956. During this period, the Tunisian legal order became strongly westernised. Following its independence in 1956, Tunisia carried out important legal reforms, e.g.: the Personal Status Code, the Civil Code, the Civil and Commercial Procedure Code, the Labour Code. As for legislative technique, legislative texts were prepared in imitation of French statutory drafting. On the other hand, much of the legislation promulgated during the Protectorate remained in force in independent Tunisia – indeed, many of these laws are still applied there (e.g., the Criminal Code of 9 July 1913).

Independent Tunisia's Islamic heritage appears partly in the fact that according to the Constitution, Islam is the Tunisian State religion and the President of the Republic must be a Muslim.[82] However, it should be noted that Islamic law is in evidence only in fragmentary form in several branches of the law, such as private law. In private law matters, it regulates only certain institutions of family law and inheritance law.[83]

---

80 Laroussi 1996: 706 and Manzano 1995: 177.
81 Laroussi 1996: 708–710 and Manzano 1995: 173, 181–182.
82 Mellouli 2000: 29–30.
83 Mellouli 2000: 31–32.

Of far more significance is that the foundations of the Tunisian legal order and the principles of legal interpretation are presented in Tunisian legal literature in exactly the same way as in Western legal literature, notably French. In legal interpretation, the application of Islamic law is the exception rather than the rule.

Linguistic conditions. During the Protectorate, French and Arabic enjoyed equal status as legislative languages. Laws and decrees were published in the official journal in both languages. In case of contradiction during the judicial process, preference for the French or Arabic version depended on the fact of knowing what type of court was competent in the particular matter. In 1955 – at which time Tunisia already enjoyed internal autonomy – a decree ordered that the Arabic text should be authentic. In spite of that, the French version remained important in interpreting former laws. A decision of the Tunisian Court of Cassation (1982) made the French version of an article of the Commercial Code prevail because that version was more logical and because the article had been inspired by the French Commercial Code. From 1993, "parliamentary acts, statutory orders, decrees and departmental orders are published in the official journal of the Tunisian Republic in Arabic". The French version is published in the journal "solely by way of information".[84]

Given that today's official language in Tunisia is Arabic, clearly that is the language of government and the courts. The situation differs as to legal science. It is true that basic legal education in the country's law faculties is provided in Arabic – but the language of postgraduate studies is largely French. About half of the doctoral theses of Tunisian lawyers are still written in French. The same is also evident as to other legal publications (e.g., treatises, textbooks, research reports). This is the case for all branches of the law (e.g., private law, administrative law, tax law). Legal compilations also exist in French, which is the language in which the journal *Actualités Juridiques Tunisiennes* is published. French is thus a fairly effective means of clarifying the content of Tunisian law. Further, French is an important tool for improving the country's legal order, since it enables comparison between national law and foreign laws.[85]

Tunisian law library collections well illustrate the state of languages in legal circles.[86] Taking the Tunis Faculty of Law and Political Science (Tunis III) as an example: according to the Student Guide (1999–2000: 14) and information given to me orally by the head librarian, in 2000 the faculty library held some 40,000 books in Arabic. Books in European languages were far more numerous: around 200,000 (of which about 130,000 were law-related). Of books on law and economics, about 70% were written in French, about 25% in English and about 5% in other languages. As for purely legal publications, the proportion of books in French was still higher: books in English were largely economics-related.

The same year, the library was also subscribing to some 800 publications and periodicals in law and economics. Of purely legal reviews, some 60% were

---

84   Mellouli 2000: 148–149.
85   Djerad 2000: 56, 63.
86   Djerad 2000: 70.

French-language, 30% English-language, and 10% came from other languages. The library was – and doubtless still is – further provided with the *Système francophone d'études et de documentation*. The system serves researchers, who can use it to contact dozens of databanks in the French-speaking world and obtain various documents that they need from abroad.[87]

To summarise, we can say that in Tunisia the language of practical legal matters is Arabic but that of legal science – and thus more generally of legal culture – is largely French. To explain this state of affairs, we have to recall the status of French during the Protectorate, the easy acquisition of independence, and later – notably thanks to Habib Bourguiba – close relations between Tunisia and France. Nor should we forget that legislation and legal techniques were strongly Gallicised during the Protectorate. For research and describing a system of French origin, the ideal tool is the French language. The terminology of legal French can easily be used to discuss Tunisian law. However, where this contains classical concepts from Islamic law, then French-language legal science and legislation published in French resort to Arabic quotations.

> An example is the title of Chapter VI of Book Nine of the Personal Status Code (*Code du statut personnel*): *De l'éviction en matière successorale "Hajb"* and Article 122 of the Code: *L'éviction en matière successorale "Hajb" consiste à évincer totalement ou partiellement un héritier de l'héritage* ['Ejection in inheritance cases "*Hajb*" consists of total or partial ejection of an heir from inheritance', Personal Status Code 2000: 38]. The French text uses the term *éviction* ['ejection'], which is not a concept in French inheritance law, to express the original character of *Hajb*. "Ejection" in inheritance cases differs from disinheritance by the fact that the first can be required by a co-heir.
>
> In the same way, in her guide on women's rights Alya Chérif-Chammari uses the quotation *nafaqa* to designate the obligation to maintain and support under Islamic law.[88]

3.2.4 Sub-Saharan Africa In many sub-Saharan African countries, French enjoys official status. Here, it is the language of government and the courts. French is the sole official language in, e.g., Benin, Burkina Faso, the Democratic Republic of Congo (Kinshasa), the Republic of Congo (Brazzaville), the Ivory Coast, Gabon, Guinea (Conakry), Mali, Senegal, Chad, and Togo. In these countries, government operates entirely in French, in which judgments of State courts are also delivered. Interpreters are used as needed. If an accused has no command of French, an interpreter will be called in on the spot. As for traditional justice, based on customary law and administered by village elders, this uses African languages.[89]

In some countries, French and the regional languages alternate in the various levels of government and the courts. In Rwanda and Burundi, government and local courts (including courts of first instance) use regional languages, whereas the central

---

87 Guide de l'étudiant ['Student Guide'] 1999–2000: 13–14.

88 Chérif-Chammari 1995: 59–62.

89 Diallo 1993: 234, Duponchel 1979: 397, Lafage 1996: 593, Moussirou-Mouyama & de Samie 1996: 608.

authorities (ministries) and higher courts make use of French.[90] In Djibouti, justice is administered in as many as four different languages. The higher courts only operate in French, while the Islamic courts (sharia courts) always use Arabic. In courts applying traditional customary law, the procedural language is Arabic, Somali, or Afar. However, in all cases judges have to draw up judgments in French so that they can be enforced.[91]

3.3 International Organisations

3.3.1 Overview: Extent of Use and Legislative Harmonization French occupies an important position in international organisations: statistically, half (49%) of these accord French the status of official language[92]

This is also the case for international organisations for legislative harmonisation. One of the most important illustrations is the Hague Conference on Private International Law, charged with drafting conventions in matters of private international law and international procedural law. Until 1960, the draft conventions of the Conference were only drawn up in French. Today, two languages (French and English) are used. However, the position of the French language remains strong in the frame of the Conference. A second example is Unidroit (*Institut international pour l'unification du droit privé* / International Institute for the Unification of Private Law), originally an organ attached to the League of Nations, today an international organisation aiming to unify national legislation on private law. As the acronym of the Institute (Unidroit) indicates, the Institute previously only operated in French. Currently, several languages possess the status of official language in the frame of the Institute but only English and French are used as working languages. The *Revue de droit uniforme* / Uniform Law Review, published by Unidroit, is also bilingual.

3.3.2 The European Union French occupies an important place in preparation of legal rules of the European Communities.[93] It is one of two working languages used in practice by the Commission. To protect the position of French in the frame of the European Union, the French Government gave its representatives instructions in terms that they should not in any circumstances give up their language rights.[94] The position of French within the European Union is strengthened by the fact that it is the internal language of the Court of Justice of the European Communities (and of the Court of First Instance). This means, in reality, that the original of a decision of

---

90 Shyirambere 1979: 477.

91 Maurer 1993: 194.

92 Crystal 1997: 79. – As to the position of French in the United Nations Organisation, see pp. 24–25.

93 See also pp. 25–27.

94 *Le français dans les institutions européennes* 1998: 4–5.

the Court is always drawn up in French, although only the version drawn up in the procedural language is authentic.

The prevalent position of the French language in the frame of the Court of Justice of the EC often causes problems of translation: French sentences, while long, are quite light, thanks to the means of expression that the language employs. By contrast, translations into some languages can be somewhat clumsy from the standpoint of their own means of expression. For example, in Finnish, the translation of a long French sentence entails using a large number of subordinate clauses. These interfere with the main proposition and make it more difficult to understand. To resolve this problem, one judge of the Court of Justice of the EC has proposed shortening the sentences in judgments of the the the Court and allowing cutting up sentences in judgments. Cutting up would be possible because the system of references relating to judgments is based not on indicating particular sentences but paragraphs.[95]

The special status of French at the Court of Justice of the EC means that the Court's French language translation division has more tasks, and more varied tasks, than the other translation divisions.[96] The French language division has, in particular, to translate into French all documents lodged by the parties in the frame of the proceedings in a procedural language other than French.[97] This allows the judges to familiarise themselves with the documents in the case in the language of deliberation, that is, in French. The special status of French is also evident in the opposite direction, as to the volume of source texts: texts drawn up in French alone amount to some 60% of texts for translation at the Court of Justice of the EC.[98] To ensure the quality of French-text judgments of the Court (and the Court of First Instance), they are always read by a judgment-reader whose job it is to ensure quality control.

The French language thus enjoys a very strong position in the European Union. The same can be seen in research on European law. Periodical publications dealing with this topic in French include: *Cahiers de droit européen, Journal des tribunaux: droit européen, Revue du marché commun et de l'Union européenne, Revue du droit de l'Union européenne* (previously: *Revue du marché unique européen*) and *Revue européenne de droit public* (bilingual periodical).

Two main reasons explain the strong position of the French language in the frame of the European Union. First of all, France was a political heavyweight in Europe during the founding of the European Communities. At the same time, thanks to this, the legal culture and legal techniques of the European Communities were received from the very outset from France. This guaranteed the position of French: it is always simple to describe a legal system by using the language by which the system was originally created.

---

95 Sevón 1998: 946.
96 Berteloot 1988.
97 Berteloot 2000: 522.
98 Gallo 1999: 78.

The influence of French law manifests itself in many Community institutions. One example is the institution of Advocate-General, created in the image of the *commissaire du Gouvernement* at the French *Conseil d'État* and lower administrative courts. Another example is the institution of judge rapporteur. It is symptomatic, from the standpoint of the originality of this institution, that the second word in the English version is a quotation from French: judge *rapporteur.* In addition, the method of bringing a case before the Court of Justice of the EC comes from French law (*recours pour excès de pouvoir* [lit. 'remedy based on *ultra vires* action / on abuse of power'; in the EU term bank TIS: 'remedy of illegality']). All this makes the French language a particularly appropriate tool for expressing European law.[99]

In recent years, the position of French in real terms has weakened in the frame of the European Union. Discussion has even taken place on the status of French as sole working language of the Court of Justice of the EC. According to some, a serious disadvantage exists: French-speaking judges are in a more favourable situation than other judges as to presenting convincing arguments in deliberative judgments. However, some others have presented several counter-arguments. First of all, adopting a single language as working language makes it possible to avoid resorting to interpreters, which always gives rise to the danger of mistakes and misunderstandings. Next, a common language strengthens the team spirit of the judges, also ensuring homogeneity of legal thinking. Finally, French is a language particularly well-suited to formulating precise expressions.[100]

3.4 Legal Science

Due to France's political and cultural supremacy, from the 17th century French rose to an important position as a language of publication of works of legal science. At the same time, lawyers used it in international communication, in universities too. As a heritage of that use, different legal languages of Europe still contain legal terms in the form of French quotations, e.g.: *pouvoir constituant, renvoi, ordre public.*

The high point of French as a language of science occurred around the 1920s. After that, the position of English clearly became stronger. However, it can be said that French remains well placed as a language of legal science. Every year, a considerable number of legal works appear in French, outside the French-speaking countries, while many internationally-recognised law reviews are published in French. This is the case for comparative law, public international law, private international law, and international economic law in particular. Further, French is often one of the working languages of international conferences with a legal flavour.

Surveys among lawyers from various countries on knowledge of foreign languages show that French is still in a position for use as a tool of international communication in legal circles. For example, at the beginning of the 1990s, 96% of German lawyers had at least some understanding of French; the percentage of

---

99 Berteloot 1998.
100 Mancini and Keeling 1995: 398.

German lawyers with a full understanding of French was somewhat less than 40%. About 25% of German lawyers used French in their publications. Among British researchers – without distinguishing lawyers – some 85% were capable of reading French scientific texts.[101]

101 Skudlik 1992: 397.

Chapter 8

Legal English

The conceptual system of English law was created under the operation of specific historical circumstances. At the same time, the development of legal English was strongly influenced by two languages: Latin and French (see below). All of this is still in evidence today: the characteristics of modern legal English are basically explained by the country's legal and linguistic history – a highly original history. On this basis, it is possible to understand why the modes of expression of legal English differ from those of the legal languages of continental Europe. This knowledge also enables avoidance of mistakes and misunderstandings: because of the peculiar history of English law, apparently identical terms can refer to totally divergent concepts in England and in continental Europe. On the other hand, English law contains many concepts that do not appear at all elsewhere and that are therefore incomprehensible for a foreigner.

We shall first concisely examine the birth of common law, then the history of English legal language. After these explanatory factors, we will deal with the characteristics of the language.[1] Finally, the position of English as a global legal language is brought into focus.

1 The Common Law System

The expression *common law* is used in three different senses.

Firstly, in a more general sense, common law refers to the systems of law of English origin as a whole, in particular the laws of England (and Wales), Ireland, the United States, Canada, Australia, and New Zealand, that is, to all that is characteristic of them. The common law is then considered as a major system of law, placed alongside the other major systems, notably the civil law system. At this level of language use, the expressions "*Anglo-Saxon law*" and "*Anglo-American law*" are often used as synonyms of common law. However, these two expressions are ambiguous: Anglo-Saxon law can also refer to the ancient (and archaic) law of England before the Norman conquest, while Anglo-American law can also denote simply North American laws, notably those of the United States (but also Canada).

---

1   The following paragraphs on the history and characteristics of legal English are mainly based on Mellinkoff 1963, Tiersma 1999 and, as to law of contracts, Beveridge 1998 and 2002 and Hill & King 2005. Reference is also made to Hiltunen 1990, Kurzon 1997, Solan 1993 and – in French – Wagner 2002. The background information given on the common law system is mainly founded on David & Brierley 1978.

Secondly, common law signifies law created by the courts of England and other countries that inherited English culture and language, set alongside written law (statute law, statutory law), in other words, legislation. In this sense, common law is the synonym of the expression *case law*. Thirdly, at a highly technical level of language use, the expression *common law* refers to one of the two main areas of English case law, set alongside the other, that is, *equity* (see below). Lawyers from common law countries are called *common-law lawyers* or – an expression less to be recommended – *common lawyers*.[2]

In the following paragraphs, we examine *common law* in the first sense indicated above, that is, as a major system of law.

1.1 Development of the English Legal System

1.1.1 Birth of Common Law   After the Norman conquest of England (1066), the country was divided into fiefs. The king reigned over the land but his position was somewhat insecure *vis-à-vis* powerful vassals. With a view to consolidating his dominance, the king sought to centralise the justice system of the realm by establishing the Royal Courts of Justice at Westminster. Needless to say, powerful vassals resisted the centralisation of justice. This is why at first the Royal Courts were only able to judge certain cases falling clearly within the king's competence. Progressively, as the king's position strengthened, ever-increasing categories of cases were transferred to these Courts.

A dispute could be brought before judges representing the central authority by an application addressed to the King's Chancellor (or the royal judges), where the author of the document petitioned for a specific order to remedy the legal situation that had been violated. If the Chancellor concluded that the king had competence to judge the case in question and that the claimant was right, then he issued, in the name of the King, a document on the matter, addressed to the local sheriff and entitled *writ* (Lat. *breve*). If the other party did not comply with the demand, the claimant could bring an action before the Courts of Westminster, so that the case could be examined in more detail. Later, this procedure was substantially developed.

To master this system of justice, which became increasingly complicated over time, lawyers began indexing and classifying the cases where a writ could be issued. Thus were born the divisions and concepts of English law, highly original in comparison with civil law. The common law system developed by the gradual consolidation of the forms of action that defined how the claimant should present an action in each case-type, and what kind of examination was necessary. A specific procedure, deriving from the suit in which a particular writ had first been applied for, corresponded to each of these forms of action. These differed as to trial procedure, permitted pleas or claims, rules of evidence, and so on. This led to the deep-rooted idea in English legal thinking, according to which the content of the legal order

---

2   Garner 1987: 178–179.

should be arranged according to legal remedies, that is, according to various actions and procedures.

Such a legal system, basing itself on case law, by its very nature presupposed that court judgments were of an importance that went beyond the particular cases in which they had been pronounced. To specify that importance, that is, the conditions and limits of the binding effect (obligatory force) of judgments, a refined rule of precedent was progressively created (see below). At the same time, a legal system built by case law strengthened the position of judges as a whole; their social status remains very high in England today.

1.1.2 Birth of Equity During the Middle Ages, the Royal Courts of England became transformed into archaic and formalistic judicial organs. Their activities were becoming routine; they judged cases blindly, without taking into consideration the requirements of particular circumstances. Under these conditions, it was necessary to find redress against the most scandalous judgments. The Chancellor, being the king's confessor besides other functions, thus began to rectify judgments of the Courts of Westminster, on the basis of natural justice. Thus was gradually born a new court, the *Court of Chancery*; the Chancellors became lawyers. Over time, this court created its own remedies at law and original legal concepts of a highly technical nature, maintaining only a distant link with the thinking of fairness and reasonableness.

In the 17th century, a fierce struggle for power broke out between the Courts of Westminster and the Court of Chancery. It ended in a compromise guaranteeing both courts their proper field of competence. In consequence, a fundamental technical division was formed within English case law – that between equity and common law. This division was maintained even after unification of the English justice system in the 19th century, when the Court of Chancery was abolished.

1.1.3 Continuity of the English Legal System After the Norman Conquest, the history of England did not undergo social upheavals leading to permanent reorganisation of the English justice system. Thus the country's old legal traditions became watertight. This is why the foundations of the English legal system remain unchanged to this day. Despite the welter of modern legislation, the English legal system remains case law at heart, with highly original structure. The social status and mentality of English judges therefore differ from those of continental judges. At the same time, it should be stressed that certain outmoded structures and solutions of common law have been reformed, notably in the 19th and 20th centuries, to respond to current needs.

1.2 The English Legal System Today

Traditionally, the English legal system is based on case law. Certainly, Parliament is sovereign: it can change any case-law rule whatever by the legislative route. Indeed, the amount of English legislation today is quite comparable with that of continental countries. In spite of that, case law remains the principal source of English law: it forms the framework of the law. Parliamentary laws are considered to be incomplete until the moment when they are "covered" by numerous precedents specifying the interpretation of their main provisions. It is also symptomatic that parliamentary laws are interpreted literally; they are held to be something exceptional in a legal system based on cases. Technically, the priority of cases as a source of law appears in the form of the doctrine of precedent (*stare decisis*). The significance of this lies in using judicial decisions as a basis for crystallising rules of law that have to be followed in later cases. The basic method of English lawyers lies not in interpreting laws but in the technique of distinctions – the art of distinguishing between the essential and secondary grounds of a judgment.

As emphasised above, common law differs considerably from civil law as to divisions of law and legal concepts. Even the fundamental common law–equity division is unknown in the legal systems of continental countries. In addition, many institutions, such as the *trust*, are foreign to civil-law Europe. As already concluded, these divisions and institutions were originally produced by the forms of action: the legal system was fashioned by the possibilities of a claimant to gain access to the legal remedies in each particular case-type.

The English legal system consists of an exceptionally large amount of detail. The explanation is simple: the system was originally developed by judicial organs. Unlike the legislator, the courts necessarily have to draw very fine distinctions, since they are obliged to decide highly varied individual cases (inevitably with certain diverging features). This is why the rules of law induced from these cases are remarkably concrete. These rules cannot easily be raised to a level of abstraction as high as rules formulated by scientific analysis in the frame of legal science. This fact is also evident in English legislation: since case law is composed of a network of rules with very fine threads, the laws have to be written in the same way, that is, highly detailed, to ensure coherence of the system and compatibility of the two types of rules. Indeed, English laws are often highly casuistic and therefore clumsy.

As mentioned, the courts of England have always had considerable authority, thanks to their great importance in forming the system. This authority is in part strengthened by the unity of the country's justice system: England does not have administrative courts. Further, quite the opposite to the countries of continental Europe, judges are appointed from among known advocates, while each judicial post has its attractions: for a judge of a lower court, it is not particularly important to move on to a position further up in the hierarchy. Given that judges should be experienced individuals, they are generally not appointed until they are fully mature. For that reason, an English judge is a high-class professional, although at the same time has a somewhat conservative approach to life.

2 Development of Legal English

2.1 The Anglo-Saxon Period

During the Anglo-Saxon period, the legal system of England was still barely developed at all. Nevertheless, some legal terminology emerged;[3] a few of these terms are still alive, as the following examples illustrate. The old Anglo-Saxons used documents adorned with seals, to certify the sale of real estate or some other act of transfer. These documents were called *gewrit* or *writ*. As described above, they were later – during the Norman era – to play an important role during creation of the common law system. Today, the word *writ* is still used in a sense whose roots go back to the Norman era: *writ of summons*. During the Viking occupation of the country, the Anglo-Saxons easily adopted Scandinavian words, thanks to linguistic kinship. A particularly important borrowing from this period is *law*. Old Norwegian also gave words such as *gift, loan, sale,* and *trust*.

Like all primitive communities, a mark of Anglo-Saxon society was verbal magic. For example, acts of transfer required complicated and precise language rituals. Here, a single mistake would nullify the act. At the same time, in the image of other Germanic tribes, the Anglo-Saxons' feel for language favoured the use of rhythmic expressions. For example, alliteration was common in maxims and binary (two-word) expressions. The Anglo-Saxons also used inversion to strengthen the impact of an expression, such as (orthography updated): *I with my eyes saw and with my ears heard.*[4] In old Anglo-Saxon laws, the language was gradually becoming more complex from the syntactic point of view but it still contained important elements of spoken language, notably abrupt turns and disconnected sequences.[5]

On the other hand, some words of Latin origin were taken into use. This is explained by royal legislation and the fairly rapid spread of Christianity throughout the country (from about 600 A.D.). Examples include the words *convict, admit, mediate,* and *legitimate*. At that time, Old English also adopted the word *clerk*, originally meaning priest (Lat. *clericus*). In the early Middle Ages, only the elites were literate, notably clerics. For this reason, priests often operated as scribes. Thus was born the modern meaning of the word in English:[6] office worker; secretary; recorder; clerk of the court; registrar.

2.2 The Latin and French Period

2.2.1 Dominance of Law Latin The Norman Conquest brought to England a French-speaking upper class. Many families belonging to the leisured classes arrived in the country from Normandy with William the Conqueror. Their language was

---

3   See for more detail: Mellinkoff 1963: 36–59 and Tiersma 1999: 10–17.
4   Tiersma 1999: 15 referring to Laurence Laughlin.
5   Hiltunen 1990: 45–46.
6   Tiersma 1999: 16–17.

French, which did not possess the status of legal language in England in the period immediately following the Norman Conquest – but this did not signify the use of Anglo-Saxon. At first, Latin was raised to a completely dominant position in legal matters. Anglo-Saxon, formerly used in these matters to some extent, fell into complete disuse because the Normans were accustomed to using Latin in important contexts. During the period immediately following the Norman Conquest (in the 11ᵗʰ and 12ᵗʰ centuries), Latin was the language of legal documents in England[7] – in line with practices across Europe. This is the period in which England's original legal system was created. That explains why many essential common law terms were originally formulated in Latin: *breve* ['writ'] is just one example.

Under these conditions, the vocabulary of Latin as used in English law acquired a particularly heightened local colour. This was notably the case for the meaning of terms: these had to express the original content of common law. At the same time, for grammatical reasons Latin words could take on a meaning that diverged from that of classical Latin. For example, the expression *indebitatus assumpsit* ['being indebted, he undertook'] meant, according to classical grammar, 'free from debts, he undertook'; the prefix *in* negates the meaning of the word in classical Latin. Further, the terminology of common law Latin was only partly developed on the basis of classical Latin vocabulary. Often, Norman French – even English – words were Latinised. For example, the Germanic word *morðer* was transferred into Latin under the form of *murdrum*.[8] Indeed, admirers of classical Latin have qualified primitive common law Latin as *dog Latin*. A final point to add: the orthography of Medieval Latin differed from that of classical Latin: *predictus / praedictus* ['the said'].

2.2.2 Rise of Law French Latin was later ousted by French in English legal circles. This occurred at the end of the 13ᵗʰ century. The first law was promulgated in French in 1275, over two centuries after the Norman Conquest. At the end of the 13ᵗʰ century, both Latin and French appeared as legislative languages but in the early 14ᵗʰ century French acquired the monopoly position as to drafting laws (except in Church matters). This was also the case for the courts. In the late 13ᵗʰ century, the Royal courts were – at least partly – using French during sessions. From this period, too, case reports were being prepared in French.[9]

In short, it can be said that French became the legal language in England from the late 13ᵗʰ century, both for legislation and the law courts. This state of affairs followed its course for 100–200 years, whether or not taking spoken language into account.[10] The use of French in English legal circles at the end of the Middle Ages is a strange phenomenon because in the 13ᵗʰ century French had already begun to disappear in England as a language of communication. Yet the rise of French as language of the law, later called *law French*, only started at that time.

---

7 See for more detail: Mellinkoff 1963: 71–82 and Tiersma 1999: 25–27.
8 Mellinkoff 1963: 74–75.
9 Tiersma 1999: 20–22.
10 See for more detail: Mellinkoff 1963: 94–111 and Tiersma 1999: 28–29.

This is explained by a number of reasons. First of all, it should be recalled that a section of the English aristocracy were still French-speaking at the end of the 13th century and that once again members of the French upper class had immigrated to Great Britain in connection with the marriage of Henry III, King of England, to Eleanor of Provence, in 1236. In the same era, the position of French, as a language of culture, generally began to strengthen. The centralisation of the justice system and the political coincidences of the times were apt to consolidate the status of French. Further, we should bear in mind the gradual secularisation of the English justice system in the 13th century: clerics no longer operated as judges in the courts of common law. Next, with its general disappearance from England, French had become the mark of the true elites. These were the elites who exercised judicial power in the higher courts of medieval England; the legal profession was the monopoly of these elites. Using French was a guarantee that the people would be unable to meddle in the justice system because they were unable to follow the course of the trial process due to the language barrier. Finally, a technical advantage existed: since law French was even then a dead language, its expressions had a clear legal meaning. These expressions were therefore particularly appropriate for use as legal terms.[11]

2.2.3 Decline of Law Latin and Law French The use of Latin and French in legal matters caused serious problems in England, beyond the legal elites (partly in favour of maintaining this state of affairs). The very first attempt to change the judicial language of the country took place in 1362 in the shape of the Statute of Pleading – drafted in French! The new law prescribed that judges were to use English but that court minutes could still be prepared in Latin.

In spite of this and later corresponding laws, English lawyers were to hold fast to using law French, for the reasons given above. Some formal justifications were paternalistic: according to Sir Edward Coke, it was better that the unlearned were not able to read legal materials because they would get it all wrong and harm themselves![12]

Law French long flourished in England, but over time its position was gradually to weaken.[13] Even by the end of the 14th century, parliamentarians were using spoken English. By the late 1480s, English had become the language of statute.[14] This last century also saw the first publication of legal works in English.[15] Nevertheless, it was still possible in the 17th century to hear law French in the Inns of Court and, occasionally, in the courts.[16] During the same century, a number of legal works had also been written in law French, despite the absolute dominance of English. The

---

11 Mellinkoff 1963: 99–101 and Tiersma 1999: 23–24.
12 Tiersma 1999: 28–29.
13 See for more detail Mellinkoff 1963: 111–135.
14 Tiersma 1999: 21 and 35.
15 Mellinkoff 1963: 113.
16 Mellinkoff 1963: 123 and 132.

status of French (and Latin) as a judicial language was only finally abolished in 1731. By then, nobody was using it any longer as a living language in the courts.

Correspondingly, the use of Latin also declined in the 16th and 17th centuries. Notwithstanding, it long remained as an important legal language: court records, writs and some other legal documents were written in Latin until the 18th century (Tiersma 1999: 25). The language was held in high esteem generally and offered a well-established terminology for legal purposes

The dominance of Latin, French, and English in English legal history can be illustrated as follows:

(year)	1000	1200	1500	2000
Latin	supremacy			
law French		supremacy		
English			supremacy	

2.2.4 Trilingualism of the Legal Profession The evidence we have already seen shows that for a long time the English legal profession was trilingual: it used Latin, French, and English – according to the context.[17] This suggests the term *legal trilingualism*.[18] Latin was for written pleadings and legal records, English was for hearing witnesses, while French was for oral pleadings. Sometimes, all three languages would appear in the same legal document. These languages also influenced one another reciprocally. For this reason, the law Latin of medieval England contains many anglicisms. Terms are often expressed in both languages, for greater certainty: *sorceri vocati wytches* ['sorcerers called *wytches*'].[19] A Latin term from the medieval period can also be a French word in changed form, e.g.: *attornatus*.[20] A good example is the case report on *Hawes v. Davye* (from the mid 16th century). The report begins in law French, then changes to English due to the language of the bond at issue forming the subject of the case (the text is also littered with Latin expressions) and ends up again in law French.[21] All of this largely explains the features of legal English today.

3 Characteristics of Legal English

An examination of the characteristics of legal English should take into account the fact of its many internal differences. The first point to bear in mind is that English is a global language: it is not exactly the same in all continents. Next, it varies according to different situations in which the language is used. Sometimes, legal English is stiff

---

17 Hiltunen 1990: 55–57.
18 Tiersma 1999: 33–34.
19 Tiersma 1999: 25–26.
20 Mellinkoff 1963: 80.
21 Tiersma 1999: 33–34.

and conservative, while at others it is innovative and creative. One especially major difference is evident between the spoken language of court sessions and written legal language. As pointed out by Peter Tiersma, this is because of the jury system. For oral addresses, an advocate uses informal and natural language to persuade the jury. On returning to chambers, the advocate reverts to heavy, hermetic language.[22] Seen against this background, it is paradoxical that jury instructions were earlier written in a formal and complicated way, causing serious problems of comprehension.[23]

3.1 Multiplicity of Linguistic Components

3.1.1 Influence of Other Languages Little by little, legal circles in England abandoned Latin and French. However, these languages left a deep imprint on legal English – an imprint that remains clearly visible. Lawyers' English teems with expressions from Latin and law French. Legal English is mixed in a particularly striking way as a language of interaction between Old English (Anglo-Saxon, with Scandinavian elements), Medieval Latin, and Old French. This especially applies to vocabulary but also to language structure. Often, Latin and French expressions form part of the most basic vocabulary of English law. Some of these express the very foundations of English legal thinking. On the other hand, account should be taken of the frequency of calques. The technical terms of English law are largely translations from Latin or French. They may also be alterations of Latin or French words: originally, *common law* was *comune ley*.

3.1.2 Latin Latin is in evidence everywhere in legal English.[24] The general principles of law illustrate this. Today, legal maxims are often still expressed in Latin: *ubi jus, ibi remedium* ['Where (there is) a right, there (is) a remedy']. As we have seen, the English legal system was essentially created by the courts. It is not by chance that Latin maxims are traditionally used to describe the intellectual process formulating legal rules on the basis of precedents, e.g.: *obiter dictum* [lit. 'mentioned in passing'; meaning: 'opinion given by a judge but not needed in support of the decision'], *stare decisis* [lit. 'to stand by things decided'; these words express the principle of the binding power of precedents]. Another shining example is the large number of Latin maxims in the field of law of defamation. This is simply explained: defamation cases were at one time judged by Church courts.[25]

Some Latin expressions in legal English can be at least roughly understood on the sole basis of ordinary Latin. To illustrate: the large number of expressions referring to the position of the parties in a case, e.g.: *versus* ['against'], *pro se* ['for (him/her)self', said of an individual representing themselves in court, i.e., without legal representation], *in propria persona* [lit. 'in one's own person' meaning the same as

---

22 Tiersma 1999: 5.
23 Charrow & al. 1982: 176–177.
24 See for more detail: Mellinkoff 1963:13–15 and Tiersma 1999: 25–27.
25 Tiersma 1999: 27.

pro se], *in forma pauperis* [lit. 'in the manner of a pauper'; meaning: 'exempt(ed) from filing fees and from paying court costs'], *in re* ['in the matter (of)'], *ex parte* ['on or from one party only'; 'done or made for the benefit of one party only']. Latin expressions are also many in cases where someone's mental state has to be defined: *mens rea* ['guilty mind / intent'], *scienter* ['knowingly'], *animus testandi* ['testamentary intention', 'intention to make a will'].

Often, ordinary Latin is of little or no help in understanding Latin expressions in legal documents. The meaning of an expression may be purely technical, in which case information can be had from a good common law dictionary. A good example is *amicus curiae*. Literally, these words mean 'friend of the court' and refer to someone who is not strictly speaking a party to a case but to whom the court grants leave to present an opinion in the matter. This expression is more common in the United States than in England. An *amicus curiae* (who may be a private individual but also a legal person, even the State) gives the court specific legal information (for example, on the content of foreign law in a case involving private international law) or – notably in the United States – draws the attention of the court to matters that fall within the interest of a party and at the same time in the public interest. For example, such may be the case in matters of civil rights.

As these examples show, a literal translation does not necessarily give the genuine sense of a Latin expression in legal English. Understanding such expressions is also often further hampered because a shortened version is involved, that is, it is only part of a longer expression or maxim. These may be totally incomprehensible as such. An illustration is *nisi prius*.[26] Further, Latin words in legal English are sometimes given a meaning where the original form or part of speech of words is changed. The word *affidavit* has already been mentioned.[27] Analogously, the word *posse* is used as a noun, in the sense of 'ability/capability'; originally, it was a verb.[28] Another good example is *habeas corpus*. Literally, these words mean 'you may have the body/that you have the body'. This involves a judge's order (a writ) to bring a prisoner before the court with the aim of clarifying the legality of detaining him.[29] A distinction is made between several types of *habeas corpus*, each with its own name in Latin.

On the other hand, it should also be noted that Latin has also influenced sentence structure in legal English. Structure is often exceptional in that it mimics a Latin sentence, where the word order is particularly free, thanks to noun declension. The typically Latin practice of using double negatives can also be seen in legal English. An example is jury instructions in California: *Innocent misrecollection is not uncommon*.[30]

---

26 See p. 151.
27 See p. 145.
28 Mellinkoff 1963: 74–75.
29 Mayrand 1994: 171.
30 Tiersma 1999: 66.

As with legal languages in general,[31] use of so-called "legal pronouns" – a heritage of Latin-speaking medieval lawyers – remains to an extent in evidence in legal English. These include, e.g., the words *aforesaid* and *said*.[32] Expressions of this kind are very common in texts dating from the Middle Ages and early modern times, e.g.: *the seid* (= *said*) *Viage, this his seid Realme*.[33] This involves direct translations of the words *predictus* and *dictus*. On this topic, a precise scheme was worked out in medieval England: when a person's name appeared for the first time, it was preceded by the word *quidam* ['a certain']; later, the words *predictus, dictus* or *idem* ['the same'] were used.[34]

3.1.3 Law French Law French is especially in evidence in the classic branches of English law.[35] The conclusion is easy to draw that some words do not belong to the vocabulary of ordinary English. The institution of *trust* is one of the most basic institutions of common law. The beneficiary is called *cestui que trust* (*cestui* ['he'; 'the one'] derives from *ecce iste*). The law of real property contains a large number of expressions that a French-speaker would easily recognise, e.g.: *pur autre vie* [legal meaning: 'for or during the lifetime of some third party'], *terre-tenant* [legal meaning: 'one who has the actual possession or occupation of land'; 'a person who has an interest in certain land'].

Nevertheless, the influence of Old French goes far deeper than might be thought on the basis of these examples.[36] Indeed, most of the technical vocabulary of legal English goes back to Old French (as to meaning, the [roughly] equivalent word in modern legal French often has another root, as seen in the translations below). A list of examples could go on almost endlessly (the translations only give the most important meanings), e.g.: agreement (Fr. *accord, convention, contrat*), arrest (Fr. *garde à vue*), assault (Fr. *assaut*), crime (Fr. *infraction*), damage (Fr. *dommage*), felony (Fr. *crime, infraction majeure*), heir (Fr. *héritier*), misdemeanor (Fr. *contravention, délit mineur*), trespass (Fr. *transgression, intrusion*). As for administration, examples include authority (Fr. *autorité*), chancellor (Fr. *chancelier*). In matters of the legal process, vocabulary of French origin is very strongly in evidence: action (Fr. *action*), appeal (Fr. *recours*), attorney (Fr. *avocat*), bailiff (Fr. *huissier*), bar (Fr. *barreau*), complaint (Fr. *plainte, réclamation, demande introductive d'instance*), counsel (Fr. *avocat, conseil, conseiller*), defendant (Fr. *défendeur*), judge (Fr. *juge*), jury (Fr. *jury*), party (Fr. *partie*), plaintiff (Fr. *demandeur*), process (Fr. *procès*), sentence (Fr. *jugement, condamnation, peine*), suit (Fr. *poursuite, action; affaire*), summons (Fr. *citation*), verdict (Fr. *verdict, décision du jury, jugement*), voir(e) dire ('judge's preliminary examination of a witness or examination of a member of the jury to

---

31 See pp. 148, 149 and 207.
32 Solan 1993: 128–130.
33 Rissanen 2000: 121.
34 Mellinkoff 1963: 340.
35 Mellinkoff 1963: 15–16.
36 Tiersma 1999: 30–33.

ascertain whether the individual concerned is qualified and suitable', Fr. *sélection des jurés*). Lastly, in general this vocabulary came from Latin, sometimes from other languages. An example is the word *franchising*. This goes back, through Old French, to Medieval Latin (*Francus*) but, at the end of the chain, we find a Germanic word denoting the tribe of the Franks.

On the other hand, law French strongly influenced the formation of English words.[37] The past participle in Old French was formed by adding to the word stem the letter -*e* or the letters -*ee* (corresponding to the letter -*é* in Modern French). Law French used this ending to denote, for example, the person obtaining something or forming the object of an action, e.g: *acquittee, arrestee, condemnee*. Correspondingly, a word denoting an active person (the doer) was given the ending -*or*. In this way, opposite positions were created: *employer/employee, trustor/trustee* ('person creating a trust', normally called *settlor* / 'person administrating property placed on trust'), *mortgagor/mortgagee, vendor/vendee*. Often, an Anglo-French verb (with the ending -*er* in the infinitive) was taken into use in English as a substantive (noun), e.g.: *interpleader* ('form of joinder open to one who does not know to which of several claimants he or she is liable, if liable at all'), *joinder* ('combining two or more lawsuits [claimants or defendants]'). Substantives were also formed by adding the ending –*al* or -*el* to a verb, e.g.: *acquittal, denial, proposal, rebuttal, trial, estoppel*. A feature typical of legal English, dating back to the time of law French, is that the adjective is often placed after the noun in petrified phrases, e.g.: *accounts payable, attorney general, court martial, fee simple* (a right equivalent to ownership of real property), *letters patent*.

3.2 Ritual and Formalism of Language

Continuity is a special feature of the history of English law. For this reason, English legal language contains some traits typical of the Middle Ages or early modern times. This concerns the ritual character of the language and the meticulous respect for legal forms.[38] These features largely stem from archaic verbal magic.[39]

3.2.1 The Tradition of Verbal Magic   The medieval law of England was marked by magical rites: the parties had to recite the words necessary for the course of the trial with absolute accuracy, under penalty of forfeiting their rights. This is clearly demonstrated by a mid 17th century trial: the claimant lost the case because the sheriff had written the word *praecipimus* ['we order'] in the incorrect form of *praecipipimus* in the writ.[40] This historical background, the fastidious approach of judges with regard to language – language as a fetish – is reflected in the common-law culture of today: English and American lawyers still scrupulously respect the

---

37 See for more detail Tiersma 1999: 30–33.
38 Mellinkoff 1963: 41–45.
39 See pp. 47–49.
40 Example given by Tiersma 1999: 40.

language forms in legal acts (at the same time, the ritual character of English legal language reflects common-law lawyers' concrete thinking).

This especially concerns the law of obligations. For greater certainty, today's common-law lawyers repeat all the phrases and expressions traditionally used in contracts and other documents that they draw up.[41] They are unwilling to move away from the phrases and expressions whose content has been fixed by the work of law courts over time. By way of precaution, American or English lawyers formulate their documents in exactly the same way as beforehand: why take risks? Their caution is well-founded. According to one author, the patent authorities in the United States require that a patent application be presented in the form of a single sentence. If not, the application is rejected.[42] However, mechanical copying sometimes appears in a document without proper basis. An expressive example is formed by the letters *ss*, forming a separate note in the document, that lawyers use in affidavits. Nobody now knows what these two letters once meant. Several theories exist. Some believe that the letters *ss* stem from the word *scilicet*; others consider that they are merely a medieval mark to signpost a new paragraph in the text. These two letters appeared in forms for American legal documents until recently – provided, it is true, with a note explaining that their omission is not fatal.[43]

Language rituals are also in evidence in the language of the courts: this often contains obsolete phrases and structures. This is notably the case in procedural matters. For example, the cry *Hear ye!* (*ye* is the old nominative plural form, and *you* is the oblique plural form) and the standard phrase in the minutes *Further affiant sayeth not = The affiant has nothing else to say*. The archaic character of legal language can also appear in word order: *Comes now plaintiff*.[44]

3.2.2 Repetition The ritual character of the language often manifests itself in the form of repetitions: this appears notably as use of binary expressions. During the Latin and French periods, the English language became enormously enriched in vocabulary. This facilitated the use of repetitions: in turn, this led to many more synonyms. Words with the same meaning (or almost) existed at the same time in the form of Latin-French variants and in the form of Anglo-Saxon variants. Simultaneously, repetitions ensured that legal messages were understandable in a multilingual society.

For these reasons, binary phrases are still in evidence in English legal language today.[45] One of the words in a binary phrase is usually of Latin-Romance origin and the other of Germanic origin: *acknowledge and confess, act and deed, devise and bequeath* ('give [immovable property] by will and leave [movable property] by will'), *fit and proper, goods and chattels, will and testament*. As a further example,

---

41 Tiersma 1999: 59–61.

42 Tiersma 1999: 56; originally pointed out by Margaret Churchill.

43 Mellinkoff 1963: 319–321.

44 Tiersma 1999: 100–101.

45 Mellinkoff 1963: 346–362, Gustafsson 1975: 9 and Hiltunen 1990: 54–55.

the ending of preambles to contracts simply means 'the parties agree to the following' = *Now; Therefore, for and in consideration of the premises and covenants herein contained, the parties hereto agree and contract as follows.*[46]

Repetition can even be triple: *null and void and of no effect*; *X is hereby authorized, empowered and entitled to...* . The solemnity value of repetition is often added to by the rhythmic nature of the phrase. For example, a witness promises to tell *the truth, the whole truth, and nothing but the truth.* Forms of will (testament) also offer a good example.[47]

Apart from ensuring the dignity of legal language, repetitions can also have another goal. English and American lawyers are determined in this way to ensure that the legal document in question should be faultless. Although the semantic field of a term used in a document later shows itself to be narrower than had been foreseen, synonyms and quasi-synonyms of the term, added in the same place, guarantee that the document covers all intended cases or eventualities. Here, common-law lawyers are often over-cautious. For example, a will may read as follows: *I give, devise and bequeath the rest, residue and remainder of my estate to Samantha.* The words *rest, residue and remainder* do not differ from the legal standpoint; nor do the words *give, devise and bequeath.* It could simply have been put like this: *I give the rest of my estate to Samantha.*[48]

> Legal English style, with its penchant for repetitions, often causes problems for legal translators. The Finnish language is a case in point. Given that it is fairly young as a legal language, it does not have the lexical layers dating from various historical eras as sources of synonyms. For this reason, Finnish translators may be unable to find appropriate legal words to translate English repetitions. However, even where they can find an equivalent for all words in a repetition, the solution may still prove difficult. Translating the whole repetition into Finnish may easily lead the Finnish lawyer to begin pondering the point of an apparently superfluous repetition, which in turn may lead to a wrong interpretation.

3.3 Wordiness of English Legal Language

3.3.1 Influence of the Case-law System Lawyers everywhere tend to be wordy. This is especially true of England. In 1596, in the case of *Mylward v. Weldon*, the plaintiff, represented by his son, produced a pleading running to 120 pages! The infuriated judge ordered the Warden of the Fleet to cut a hole in the bundle of papers containing the text of the pleadings, and to place it around the son's neck like a ruff or collar. The son was then led by the hand around the Court of Westminster, as an example not

---

46 Lehto 1998: 531.

47 See pp. 86–87.

48 Example given by Tiersma 1999: 64–65, referring to Jesse Dukeminier and Stanley Johanson; see also Charrow & *al.* 1982: 180 note 2.

to follow.[49] Despite this punishment, it is still common to find wordy common-law pleadings today. An American example given by J. Gordon Forester is illustrative:[50]

> *That at all pertinent times the defendant had the duty to operate his motor vehicle in a careful and prudent manner, to avoid endangering the plaintiff and any other persons lawfully operating motor vehicles upon said highway and it became and was the further duty of the defendant to keep said motor vehicle at such time under proper care and control, to give full time and attention to the operation of said motor vehicle, to be aware of other vehicles, to drive at a safe speed under the circumstances and to obey the traffic controlling devices; and to obey all rules and regulations of the District of Columbia.*

According to Forester, the same complaint could have been simply formulated by saying:

> *That at the time of the collision the defendant had a duty to operate his car in a careful manner and to obey the traffic regulations.*

The original tradition of English law has strongly contributed to the wordiness of legal English.[51] As noted already, English law largely consists of its own history: a symptom of this is that the older a legal rule, the more it is appreciated. Such an ideological climate is apt to preserve old and often wordy phrases in legal language. Another important point of note is that English law is essentially based on case law – as we have seen – so that distinctions between situations are exceptionally fine. This is why the concepts expressed by legal English terms are restricted and have to be narrowly interpreted. To ensure the harmony and internal coherence of a system based on case law, the statutes also have to take account as far as possible of the various combinations of situations that can appear in court decisions. A necessary consequence of this state of affairs is the wordiness and overall size of legal documents, including statutes. A good example is the law of 1731, finally confirming the status of English as official language of the courts of the land. A Continental legislator would have declared concisely that the law was to be observed in all court oral and written procedures. However, the English law of 1731 declares that it applies to:[52]

> *... all writs, process, and returns thereof, and proceedings thereon, and all pleadings, rules, orders, indictments, informations, inquisitions, presentments, verdicts, prohibitions, certificates, and all patents, charters, pardons, commissions, records, judgments, statutes, recognizances, bonds, rolls, entries, fines and recoveries, and all proceedings relating thereto, and all proceedings of courts leet, courts baron and customary courts, and all copies thereof, and all proceedings whatsoever in any courts of justice within that part*

---

49   Tiersma 1999: 199, referring to Monro's *Acta Cancellariae* (1847) and Spence's *The Equitable Jurisdiction of the Court of Chancery* (1846).

50   Forester 1998: 61.

51   Mellinkoff 1963: 24–25.

52   Mellinkoff 1963: 133.

of Great Britain called England, and in the court of exchequer in Scotland, and which concern the law and administration of justice ...

Correspondingly, the case-law system is also reflected in lawyers' pleadings and other procedural documents. A lawyer who requires all important documents in the possession of an opponent to be produced to the court can specify this request by writing:[53]

As used herein, the word "document" shall mean and include any and all letters, correspondence, memoranda, notes, working papers, bills, daily diaries, schedules, tape recordings, computer prints, any computer readable medium, reports, books, contracts, ledgers, logs, schedules, invoices, computations, projections, photographs, drawings, schematics, designs, tabulations, graphs, charts, drafts or revisions of any nature whatever, together with any attachments thereto or enclosures therewith, including the original, identical copies reproduced in any manner, and nonidentical copies thereof.

3.3.2 Law of Contract The features peculiar to legal English are clearly in evidence in the field of law of contracts. The language of this field of law is particularly wordy. Contracts prepared by English and American lawyers are normally sizeable. A continental lawyer (Ramón Mullerat) points out that he once received for signature a 130-page English loan contract.[54]

The lengthy mode of expression of English contractual language stands out against legal German, for example. Claire Hill and Christopher King state that Anglo-American contract forms are in substance at least twice as long as German forms. Sometimes, the difference is even greater: the American Bar Association's *Model Stock Purchase Agreement* is over ten times longer than the corresponding agreement in *Beck'sches Formularbuch zum Bürgelichen, Handels- und Wirtschaftsrecht*.

The divergence in legal cultures can be illustrated by a clause covering agency: *The [Agent] agrees that the [Principal] shall at its sole discretion be able to accept or reject any order obtained by the [Agent] for any reason including poor credit rating of the client, bad payment record, unavailability of materials or textiles, [and] conflict of interests with existing clients. The [Agent] shall not be entitled to receive any payment for any order so rejected.* In Germany, the analogous clause is conceived in the following terms: *Es steht dem Unternehmer frei, ein vom Handelsvertreter vermitteltes Geschäft anzuschließen oder abzulehnen.* ['It is open to the contractor (principal) to accept or reject business (transaction) introduced through the (commercial) agent'].

As for other Continental legal languages, a classic example told in literature on the subject concerns the course of US-Belgian negotiations in 1962. The American party began by submitting a 10,000-word draft contract. The Belgians, shocked by the length of the draft, proposed a contract of just 1,400 words for their part. The final contract was drawn up on the basis of the Belgian proposal.[55]

---

53 Example given by Tiersma 1999: 119.
54 Mullerat 1997: 11 note 44. – As to wordy wills, see pp. 86–87.
55 Hill & King 2005: 176, notes 11, 177 and 179.

The extraordinary verbosity of English law of contracts is caused by a number of factors (of which several have already been mentioned above). One of these is the perseverance of outdated ritualism, fought against by the Plain English Movement. Instead of saying: "We, Mary Smith and Fred Brown, agree that Mary Smith will sell to Fred Brown her cookery books for $20. The agreement will take effect 24 hours after this contract is signed", a much more complicated formula is normally to be found: "The vendor, Mary Smith, shall dispose of five books concerned with the art of cookery which are in the possession of the said vendor to the vendee, Fred Brown, for consideration of twenty US dollars which transaction shall take place twenty-four hours after the vendor and the vendee attach their signature hereto".[56]

On the other hand, in the common law system, the importance of written law (legislation) is more restricted than in the continental system. This is especially the case for law of contracts, where case law remains the very foundation of the legal system. No general legislation of any kind (peremptory or auxiliary) exists defining the legal situation of the parties to a contract. In consequence, the parties have to use the contract itself to address every possible situation that could take place in the future (without the opportunity to refer to written law). This is why a contract governed by common law may include whatever clause, provided that it does not contravene basic principles of law or legal rules determined by the legislator. If the parties omit something from the contract, they cannot rely on the courts to insert it later on their behalf by way of interpretation. Indeed, under common law the terms of a contract are always interpreted literally and narrowly. This rule of interpretation is called the *parol evidence rule*: if the meaning of a written contract is clear, then no other evidence is allowed as to its content. The contract should itself contain all that is needed on the matter.[57]

Therefore, as pointed out by Barbara Beveridge, the language of a contract governed by common law should be general enough to cover every situation, yet precise enough to ensure that the legal position of the parties is unambiguous. Put differently, the contract should show with certainty what it includes and what it does not. This involves a problem that is difficult to resolve. In practice, English and American contracts contain long lists that take into account every element that could come within their field of application, down to the last faint probability. Contract clauses are therefore wordy and clumsy. As an example, here is a clause from a publishing contract:

> *While this agreement is in effect, the Author shall not, without the prior written consent of the Publisher, write, edit, print, or publish, or cause to be written, edited, printed or published any other edition of the Work, whether revised, supplemented, corrected, enlarged, abridged, or otherwise ....*

A reservation is often added to foresee cases where someone who later interprets the contract considers that the document does not contain the words necessary

---

56 Example given by Kurzon 1997: 129.
57 Beveridge 2002: 65–69 and Hill & King 2005: 199–204.

to cover the situation then arising, in spite of all the lists included: *including, but without limiting the generality of the foregoing*, or an identical but shorter formula: *including without limitation* or *including but not limited to*. In this way, the author of the contract aims to emphasise the exemplary (i.e. not exhaustive) nature of the list, so that drawing conclusions *a contrario* is ruled out. For example: *All motorized vehicles, including without limiting the generality of foregoing, all cars, trucks, buses, tractors, motorcycles, and mopeds*.[58] This reservation is very popular in contract practice in the US.[59]

At the same time, the rule of precedent is applied in common law countries. When the Supreme Court, or a higher court, of these countries delivers an important judgment on the law of contracts, a precisely formulated sentence taking this judgment into consideration rapidly spreads into contracts concluded later. For example, the expression *signed, sealed and delivered* has such a background. For a contract to be valid, the courts once required that a copy of the contract be delivered to the two parties. Today, this requirement no longer need be fulfilled but the expression *signed, sealed and delivered* is still added to contracts by force of tradition.[60]

The common law is law evolved by the courts and which is still developed by way of decided cases. In the US in particular it is typical of this law that the threshold for filing a lawsuit is low and that people are inclined to look for grounds to litigate. This often means that lawyers battle over every word of a contract. If a contract contains a gap, it is certain that the lawyer for the party who benefits from the gap will reveal it. In consequence, English and American lawyers are reticent about giving up established expressions in contracts: these are left in for greater certainty.[61] This precaution also appears in another way: legal documents of common law countries are full of reservations, e.g.: *without admitting, without prejudice to...*

> Other factors, too, come importantly into play in the complexity of English contractual language. As pointed out by Claire Hill and Christopher King, one of these is the adversarial system in the common law trial process. The system includes a broad obligation to produce documents and disclose facts (*discovery*) and to present witness statements (*depositions*), at the request of the opponent in litigation. This allows manoeuvres by both sides to make litigation inconvenient and costly for opponents. These manoeuvres are not adequately controlled by costs penalties. Thus the great importance of trying to avoid future litigation in advance, by making the contractual text as exhaustive as possible, without gaps. In addition, business in America – unlike some countries – does not draw up standard clauses to which contracting parties can refer, without including these clauses in the contract itself.[62]

---

58 Beveridge 2002: 67.

59 Tiersma 1999: 81–85 and Hill & King 2005: 182 note 25, 192 note 49, and 210 note 100.

60 Beveridge 2002: 68.

61 Charrow & *al*. 1982: 187, Tiersma 1999: 59–61 and Hill & King 2005: 181–188.

62 Hill & King 2005: 188–192, 204 and 214.

3.4 Orthography and Pronunciation

Apart from other functions, legal language operates as a tool of group cohesion, or team spirit.[63] An original language is apt to strengthen links between members of the profession. In all countries, lawyers use specific expressions, notably Latin maxims. Further, belonging to the legal profession can be expressed through orthography: a common-law lawyer always writes *judgment*, even though *judgement* is also possible (notably in Great Britain).[64]

One interesting aspect, from the standpoint of team spirit, is common-law lawyers' original pronunciation of English. English lawyers traditionally pronounce certain words in a particular way. In recent times, a corresponding phenomenon is evident in the United States. For example, some American lawyers pronounce the vowel in the last syllable of the word *defendants* with great energy, so that what one hears is: "defend ants".[65]

Moreover, common-law lawyers normally pronounce phrases from law French and Latin in the same way as genuinely English words. For example, when the court begins its sessions the usher cries three times: *Oyez!* This word of French origin is pronounced: *oou-yès*, with the accent placed on the second syllable. Satirists have not been slow to comment on this pronunciation: according to one writer, *When the Crier cried "Oyez!", the people cried "O no!"*.[66] As for Latin, the expression *stare decisis*, for example, gives a good idea of the pronunciation of English-speaking lawyers. They say (according to Black's Law Dictionary): **stahr**-ee or **stair**-ee di-**sI**-sis.[67]

Nowadays, some younger American lawyers try to adopt a pronunciation of Latin that imitates that of the classical period (or, rather, that of the Italians), taught in schools and universities. As for law French, an equivalent trend is noted towards modern French. However, many lawyers also stand up against these changes: Anglo-Latin and Anglo-French pronunciation have an age-old tradition that should not be given up. In the case of modern French pronunciation, critics comment in particular that this involves the wrong time and the wrong place. Law French comes from the Normandy of the 11th century and was never pronounced in the same way as modern French. These critics do not understand young American lawyers, who – according to Peter Tiersma – "are increasingly pronouncing Law Latin in the style of Julius Caesar, and Law French in the style of Brigitte Bardot".[68]

This dispute remains unsettled. That is why confusion reigns amongst American lawyers over pronunciation of law French and Latin: there are some expressions

---

63 See pp. 52–53.
64 Tiersma 1999: 52.
65 Example given by Tiersma 1999: 51–52.
66 Tiersma 1999: 53, referring to The Oxford English Dictionary.
67 See for more detail: Kelly 1988: 195–207.
68 Tiersma 1999: 54.

with regard to which two or even three different pronunciations are in rivalry.[69] From the standpoint of continental lawyers, this means that it is even more difficult than before to understand Latin spoken by English-speaking lawyers.

4 Legal English as a Global Language

4.1 Expansion of Common Law and International Use of English

The common law became a global system with the growth of British colonial power. Today, it is the dominant legal system in (virtually) all countries where the population is English-speaking or in which English enjoys the status of an official language.

With its expansion, the common law has naturally changed. It is well known that the legal systems of the United States and England differ, despite the fact that classic common law as such is uniform. In the background to this difference lie several reasons. As we have seen, common law stems from a feudal society. In the United States, such a society was categorically rejected from the outset. In addition, the number of qualified lawyers was initially very weak in the United States. This is why the law there remained less technical for a long while. Other factors to bear in mind are the Americans' anti-British feeling after the War of Independence, along with civil law influences in territories that were previously possessions of Spain and France. Lawyers emigrating to the US from continental countries – such as Germany during the National Socialist era – also contributed to the originality of American law in comparison with that of England.

In some countries, such as Scotland, Quebec, and the Republic of South Africa, English law became mixed with the civil law system. At the same time, common law has also been received in many countries with a non-European culture. Examples include African countries where common law is mixed with the customary laws of various tribes. In Asia, account has to be taken of the continent's old cultures, such as that of India.

Common law is normally expressed with the help of the English language. The current importance of English is manifest by the fact that, according to one estimate, some 1,200–1,500 million people today have a fair command of the language; the number of individuals with a knowledge of the language comparable to a mother tongue stands at around 670 million. From the standpoint of language of the law, it is essential to know that English enjoys the status of official language, more or less completely, in 75 States (some of these, it is true, are mini-States) or administrative territories. This is the case for many African countries. However, it is the Indian sub-continent, with its enormous population, that offers the most important example of this state of affairs. Further, some 85% of international organisations use English as one of their languages or as their only language. As for international trade, the dominance of English is virtually absolute.[70]

---

69 Tiersma 1999: 54–55.
70 Crystal 1997: 61 and 79; Karlsson 1999: 64–68.

In the following paragraphs, we start by examining legal English in the United States. Then follows a brief presentation of legal English in India. Finally, problems related to using legal English in international trade deserve a short review.

4.2 Legal English in the United States

To understand the character of American legal English, we first have to look briefly at two background factors: American legal thinking, and the basic structure of the United States. The first factor signifies an important legal-cultural unity with England, whereas the second explains certain differences between the two countries.[71]

4.2.1 American Legal Culture
American legal thinking. The influence of English law in the territory that today constitutes the United States was practically terminated with the country's independence; today, it is decidedly weak. American judges only rarely cite British judgments; case-law rules developed in England are no longer received in the United States. Nevertheless, the approach to the legal order, fundamental principles and concepts of law, as well as essential legal terminology remain the same in England and the United States. It is symptomatic that British judgments from the days before the independence of the United States are still considered an important part of the American legal tradition.

In line with the English tradition, three fundamental ideas are deep-rooted in American legal culture: (1) the supremacy of the law, which means that even the public authorities are subject to legality checks by independent courts of law; (2) the rule of precedent, according to which judicial decisions are based on earlier decisions; and (3) the idea according to which the judicial process is thought of as a kind of combat in which the parties have to take the initiative as to the progress of the case; the chairman of the court and members of the jury are basically neutral arbiters in the combat.[72]

In the image of English law, the divisions of American law are not those of civil law. However, differences exist between English and American law. The division of law between equity and common law is also known, it is true, in the United States but the fields of application of these institutions are partly other than in England. Today, equity has merged with the common law system in the United States. This concerns all branches of the law: the law of property, the law of contracts, and so on. This is why American law faculties no longer offer separate courses in equity. Despite merger, the separation between the two institutions retains its importance in certain particular matters. This is notably the case when it comes to knowing whether trial of a case requires the presence of a jury. To resolve this question, one has to know whether the legal rules involved originate from common law or from equity.

---

71 See for more detail Farnsworth 1996 and Summers 1998: 1018–1033.
72 Farnsworth 1996: 12.

The distinction between these institutions is also evident at the level of terminology: rights going back to the system of equity are still called *equitable rights* today.

As in continental Europe, the separation between substantive and procedural law is important in the United States. If interpretation appears to involve a procedural rule, then the prohibition on retroactivity of laws is not applied. The separation between substantive and procedural law also provides a basis for resolving conflict-of-laws problems between the various states of the Federation: if a procedural rule is involved, then the Federal courts apply federal law, despite the possible application in the case of the substantive law of a particular state. The same applies at international level: American courts always apply the *lex fori* in procedural matters.

In line with the English tradition, the separation between public and private law is less important in the United States than in continental Europe. The United States has no administrative courts – that is, it does not have a system that imposes this separation, as in continental countries, with a view to defining the parameters of competence of the courts. American lawyers rarely speak of civil law as a branch of the law, although some Federal states may have put a civil code in force. These lawyers classify cases rather according to particular sectors of the branch, e.g.: contracts, torts, property. The explanation is straightforward. Like the British, American lawyers are chiefly interested in precedents, that is, in specific cases. This is why they avoid generalisations in their reasoning and think it strange to create abstractions far from practical legal matters.

Basic structure of the Federal State. The Constitution of the United States is characterised by certain important features, thanks to which it has served as a blueprint in different parts of the world. This notably applies to the separation of powers and the original federalism of the country.

According to the Constitution of the United States, the public authorities are divided into three. The distinction is between: (1) the executive organs (the president and the body of civil servants reporting to him), (2) the legislative organ (Congress, consisting of the House of Representatives and the Senate) and (3) the judicial system (the courts). However, the division of public powers is not absolute. In particular, the federal courts possess the power to declare that a law adopted by Congress (or state legislature) stands in violation of the Constitution. The application of that law can thus be prevented.

As for federalism, this means the sharing of public powers between the Federal State and the (individual) Federal states. It is essential in this sharing that the powers of the individual Federal states are not considered to be powers granted by the central Federal State. In consequence, the latter cannot reduce the powers of the Federal states. These powers are anchored in the Constitution of the Federal State. The Federal states have an independent competence in the fields that fall within their sphere of power. According to the Federal Constitution, the powers of the Federal states are general: they possess all the powers that are not expressly excluded from their competence by constitutional provisions. In line with this principle, each Federal state has its own separate legal order and independent justice system (see below). In recent decades, the Federal State's sphere of activity has widened, to some extent, because the Supreme Court has interpreted the Constitution extensively in favour of the Federal State. This is the case, for example, for regulation of trade between Federal states. In spite of this, the Federal states still enjoy great freedom of action in many legislative fields, such as criminal law.

4.2.2 Characteristics of American Legal English As we have just seen, the foundations of the legal order and legal thinking are the same in England and the United States. Thanks to that unity, earlier comments on the characteristics of English legal language are also valid for the United States. In effect, presentation of the language characteristics above is mainly based on two books published in the United States (Mellinkoff 1963 and Tiersma 1999). On the other hand, certain historical factors have partly shaped the American variant of the common law. This is reflected in the country's legal English: institutions whose structure differs from those in England usually have an original designation.

An example: names of courts. The United States has 51 hierarchies of courts: the Federal justice system and the justice systems of the individual Federal states. Usually, these hierarchies consist of three instances.

At first instance, the Federal justice system consists of U.S. district courts and certain specialised courts. The country is divided into judicial districts. Each Federal state contains at least one district (some larger states have several). Cases are usually heard by a single judge. The second instance comprises U.S. courts of appeals. The country is divided into twelve regional circuits; each circuit includes one or more Federal states. A Federal court of appeal hears appeal cases coming from district courts within its own circuit. Cases are heard by three judges. If a contradiction occurs in the jurisprudence of different chambers of a Federal court of appeal, then a case can be heard in plenary session. The U.S. Supreme Court is the only court whose establishment is foreseen by the Federal Constitution. Its tasks are threefold. Firstly, it maintains watch on observation of the provisions of the Constitution. Secondly, the Supreme Court ensures the uniform application of Federal legislation throughout the country as a whole. Thirdly, it hears disputes between Federal states and between the Federal State and individual states.

In most cases, the structure of the justice system of the states of the Federation resembles that of the Federal State itself. The states have their own courts of first instance, competent to hear civil and criminal matters within the state in question. These courts have general competence and cases are usually heard by a single judge. Sometimes, courts of first instance include a special chamber for criminal matters. In addition, some states have separate courts specialising in criminal cases, as for example for teenage offenders. Most states have courts of second instance. All states have established a supreme court. This last hears appeal cases coming from lower courts. Further, it determines disputes concerning interpretation of the Constitution of the state concerned.

As indicated, the Federal courts are called *district court, court of appeal* and *supreme court*. As for the first-instance courts of the individual states, these have names such as *district court, circuit court* or *court of common pleas*. In some states, the name is misleading: courts of first instance may be called *superior court* or even – in New York State – *supreme court*. The courts of second instance are usually designated by the name of *court of appeals* or *appellate court*. As for the supreme court, this is most often – but not necessarily – called the *Supreme Court*,

In England, by contrast, the tripartite division – court of first instance, court of appeal, supreme court – only very roughly describes the country's judicial system. At the same time, the names of English courts diverge radically from those of American courts.[73] In England can be found, at first instance, the *magistrates courts* (with orthographic alternatives: *magistrates' courts* or *magistrate's courts*) and the *county courts*. The second instance consists of a single court, the *Supreme Court of Judicature*, comprising three bodies: the *High Court of Justice, Crown Court*, and *Court of Appeal*. The first of these bodies (*High Court of Justice*) is composed of three divisions: *Queen's Bench Division, Chancery Division*, and *Family Division*. At final instance, judicial matters are heard in England by the *House of Lords*, or to be more precise, by the *Appellate Committee* of the House. Some appeal cases coming from the *Commonwealth* countries are heard by the *Judicial Committee of the Privy Council*.

Same concept – different term. It is also understandable that American legal terms sometimes differ from British terms in cases where the concepts behind the terms are the same. For example, in the United States, the appellate court *affirms* or *reverses* a lower court's judgment; in England, the synonyms of these verbs, *allow* and *dismiss*, are used. Correspondingly, the law of companies is called *corporate law* in the United States but *company law* in England.[74] In the field of family law, one example concerns the right of an absent parent in divorce cases to see the child or children of the family: in the United States this is called *visiting rights* and in England *right of access*. American terms are often more transparent (that is, their meaning is clearer) than British terms. This is due to two facts at least: on the one hand, American terms are less burdened by the dead weight of history, while on the other hand they have to be understood by lawyers in 50 states whose legislations sometimes differ considerably. Therefore, American terms cannot be linked to strictly defined legislative solutions – the reverse of British terms.

Ritualism and complexity of language. The ritual character of traditional legal English also appears in the United States. For example, the usher opens sessions of the U.S. Supreme Court, crying: *Oyez! Oyez! Oyez! All persons having business before the Honorable, the Supreme Court of the United States, are admonished to draw near and give their attention, for the Court is now sitting. God save the United States and this Honorable Court!*

As in England, American legal English is also otherwise complicated. Traditional expressions keep repeating themselves, e.g.: *hereafter, herein, hereof, herewith*. Even the language of jury instructions can be rather hermetic from the citizens' standpoint. These sometimes contain clumsy phrases including old-fashioned words: *failure of*

---

73 David & Jauffret-Spinosi 2002: 413–419 and Wagner 2002: 121–122.
74 Tiersma 1999: 134.

recollection is a common experience, even though this could be simply expressed as: *people often forget things*.[75]

For these reasons, it is unsurprising that a movement arose to simplify and modernise legal language: the *Plain English Movement* in the United States in the 1970s.[76] On the other hand, it can be pointed out that informal use of legal language often gives rise to hermetic abbreviations: *depo* (*deposition*), *in pro per* (*in propria persona*), *mal mish* (*malicious mischief*), *punies* (*punitive damages*), *pro tem* (*pro tempore*), *rogs* (*interrogatories*).[77]

American legal English from the translator's standpoint. Given the civil law influences in the United States, American legal concepts can be fairly similar to those of continental Europe; the concepts of English law are often more original. At the same time, American law has a great effect on the development of foreign laws throughout the world. Legal institutions created in the United States are taken into use in various countries. Examples include the fields of consumer protection, and air law. Further, as already pointed out, American legal terms are used in a country with a large number of different legislations, which makes them more elastic than British terms.

Thanks to all that, American legal terminology is in general easier than traditional British terminology to translate into continental languages (EU legislation is gradually changing the situation). This is also true in the opposite direction: American legal English is a particularly suitable tool when translating civil law texts into English. This is notably the case for translations intended for international use: American terms are often known everywhere, because of the global importance of American law.

4.3 Legal English in the Indian Sub-continent

4.3.1 The Indian Legal System
Anglo-Indian Law. In the colonial era, a system of law called *Anglo-Indian law* developed in India. The English legal tradition, notably common-law legal techniques, took root in the sub-continent, in spite of social conditions and original Indian institutions. At the same time, the traditional systems of law – Hindu law and Muslim law – remained in force in the colonial era and the rules from these systems are still applied there. However, it should be noted that their application is limited to traditional branches of law, notably those relating to the family and inheritance, in cases where all the parties in a case are members of the religious community in question.

---

75 Tiersma 1999: 194.

76 Hiltunen 1990: 103–110 and Solan 1993: 133–138; as to criticism: Phillips 2003: 37–44. See also: Presidential Documents, p. 31885. Memorandum of June 1, 1998: Plain Language in Government Writing; as to the United Kingdom, see The Woolf Report of 1999: www.open.gov.uk.

77 Tiersma 1999: 137 and 153.

The colonial power took over the higher justice system of India. A start was made towards codifying the law of the land, to create a modern territorial system of law. At the end of the 19th century, a large number of separate codes and laws came into force. This legislation was prepared by the British, often in London. Further, the Indian judicial organisation was reformed in the mid 19th century, and the judges then appointed were lawyers who had usually received common law training. The highest judicial organ in India, for hearing appeals, was the Judicial Committee of the Privy Council, based in London. Because of all this, legal techniques in India became essentially English – and continue to be so, despite great cultural differences with England. Clearly, not all English institutions were received in India. For example, the English distinction between common law and equity, without rational basis, is unknown there.

4.3.2 Expansion and Change of Legal English in India

General position of English. Generalising the application of common law in India would not have been possible without the effective linguistic tool that was the English language. The British colonial power made English the language of higher education and of the colonial administration on the Indian sub-continent, to assure British interests and an effective administration. The process was supported by the attitudes of the times. These are the words of Lord Macaulay, an enthusiastic partisan of the expansion of English culture and language: *A single shelf of a good European library is worth the whole native literature of India and Arabia.* In 1835, English became the language of Indian schools (taking the place of Sanskrit and Persian) and obtained the status of official language of India in 1837. From 1844, only those educated in an English-speaking school could be appointed civil servants in the colonial civil service.[78]

Today, the Indian sub-continent consists of several independent States. In the Republic of India, English remains the language of higher education and science. It is impossible to study medicine, the natural sciences or business without a command of English. Of the 800 million population of the Republic of India, the number using English regularly in their day-to-day communication amounts to only 3 to 4%. However, in absolute terms this number represents 20 million people. Further, this involves the country's elites, who control economic power and politics.[79] The situation is the same in Pakistan.[80]

As is usual in the case of former European colonies, feelings in India towards the English language were contradictory. According to the writer V. S. Naipaul, an Indian civil servant makes a fool of himself speaking English; his knowledge of the language is often lacking and is therefore of little use for citizens. To illustrate this complex attitude, here are the names of the central language institutes in India: *Central Institute of Indian Languages, Central Hindi Institute and Central Institute*

---

78   Gupta & Kapoor 1991: 35–36.
79   Gupta & Kapoor 1991: 21 and 190.
80   Ahmad 1997: 45–46 and Rahman 1993: 88.

of English and Foreign Languages. So, English is not considered as an Indian language, but nor is it strictly speaking a foreign language.

Indian English has certain characteristics of its own as to syntax and vocabulary (English neologisms are created in India) and its quality is sometimes poor from the standpoint of standard English. These features are chiefly visible in informal use of the language. Mixing is also typical of Indian English: Indian words are mixed with English, and *vice-versa*.

English in Indian legal circles. In the Republic of India, Hindi enjoys the status of National Official Language; certain other Indian languages are official at the level of individual states (State Official Languages). At the same time, English also possesses constitutional status: it is the Associate National Official Language. In reality, the position of English is stronger than implied by this status: it is the dominant language of government and the higher justice system in the Republic of India.[81] In Pakistan, the situation is similar; the position corresponding to that of Hindi is occupied by Urdu (a language very similar to Hindi). As for Bangladesh, which is more coherent from the ethnic standpoint, the only official language is Bangla, formerly called Bengali (Art. 3 Constitution).

The lower courts of the Republic of India use local languages or the languages of individual states. In the higher courts, apart from the languages of these states it is English that enjoys the status of procedural language, while the judgments of these courts are given in English. The Supreme Court of the Republic of India uses only English: hearing the parties is arranged in English, the advocates' pleadings are drafted in English, and the Court delivers its judgments in English. Analogically, the administrative organs of the Republic of India use English. This dominance has weakened somewhat in recent times. For example, knowledge of English is no longer required for some civil service posts.[82] In the same way, the higher courts of Pakistan use English. As for the lower courts, these use English and Urdu, but judgments are always drawn up in English.

Despite certain differences,[83] the variant of English used in India in judicial and administrative matters is essentially that of British common law. To understand this, it has to be recalled that much of the legislation prepared by the British during the colonial era remains in force in India. Further, Indian judges still refer to precedents from the colonial era – absolutely in line with common law tradition. Needless to say, this legislation and case law provide a language model for new laws and precedents. That explains why the legal terminology and style of India and Pakistan today are essentially British.

A typical example is legislation and legal writing concerning rules of evidence. This branch of the law is still regulated in India by the Indian Evidence Act (1872), prepared nearly a century and a half ago by Sir James Fitzjames Stephen. In legal literature, this law is covered, for example, in the work entitled *Principles and*

---

81 Gupta & Kapoor 1991: 16.
82 Gupta & Kapoor 1991: 16–18 and 192.
83 Bhatia 1987: 232 and Tiersma 1999: 134–135.

Digest of the Law of Evidence I–II, an enormous two thousand-page book, originally written by M. Monir in 1936. In independent India, several new editions of this work have appeared (the 6th edition in 1988). Almost every page of this work contains a large number of references to case law, often from the colonial era. At that time, the senior judges in India were British, and the most important cases were heard by the Judicial Committee of the Privy Council.

Islamic law and common law language. One branch of law exists where Indian legal terms diverge considerably from those of British legal English – but generally speaking even in this branch the language of law follows the English tradition. This involves Islamic law, applied in legal relationships between Indian Muslims in cases of family law, inheritance, and gifts.

During British rule in India, Sir Dinshah Fardunji Mulla, Law Member of the Council of the Governor General of India and Judge of the High Court of Bombay translated Islamic laws into English. His book *Principals of Islamic law* (1906) is considered to include the authentic content of statutory law on Islam. It is frequently quoted in Indian and Pakistani courtrooms.[84]

Another voluminous (one thousand-page) work on this topic, *Islamic Law-Personal being Commentaries on Mohammedan Law* (*in India, Pakistan and Bangladesh*), written by B. R. Verma, also dates back to the colonial era (1940). New editions of the work have appeared in India. Like all legal literature in India, *Islamic Law-Personal* shows clear signs of the common law tradition: the list of precedents (table of cases) covers 33 full pages, the authors having annexed a list of cases published pending publication of the work (*case law reported during publication*), and almost every page is provided with a large number of references to precedents.

The editors of the new editions of *Islamic Law-Personal,* M. H. Beg and S. K. Verma, profoundly admire the judges of the colonial era:

> ... In this regard the judicial committee of the Privy Council has done a great job bestowing their industrious learning and studied wisdom on the subject, taking tremendous pains in seeking guidance from the Holy Quran and the original commentaries of Islamic jurists. (...) ... the basic principles, so well laid down and after such studied research by the Privy Council as reported in Moore's Indian Appeals (M.I.A.) and Law Reports Indian Appeal (I.A.) have made a marvellous impact of vital importance in the exposition and formation of the law applicable to the Muslims. Without a thorough reference to these two law journals, no study, no research of Muslim Law can be considered complete. The analyses made by the Privy Council are so illuminating, so lucid and so informative, cut and dried, supported by extracts from the Holy Quran and from the commentaries of Islamic Jurists right after the death of the Prophet to the modern times. Most of the Privy Council decisions have found approval of the Supreme Courts both in India and Pakistan.[85]

In considering this admiration, it should be borne in mind that the Judicial Committee of the Privy Council is not an Islamic judicial organ, despite the fact

---

84 Ahmad 2005: 1–2.
85 Verma 1988: xii–xiii.

that in the colonial era it provided expertise in Islamic law in judging cases coming from India. However that may be, Verma's work clearly shows how common law English operated – and still operates – as a linguistic tool of Islamic law, a legal system connected with a non-Christian religion and originally created by using the Arabic language.

Under these conditions, original notions of Islamic law are expressed by quotations. Indeed, Verma's work is full of Arabic quotations, e.g.: *hiba, khula, mutwalli, nikah, quaraza-a Hasana, qiyas, sajjadanashin, shafi-i-jar, sunna, tajweez, talaq, taqlid, wakf, zihar*. Similar quotations can also be found in Indian statutory law on Islamic institutions. One example is the *Mussalman Wakf Act* (1923) and later legislation on the same theme. The term *wakf* refers to situations where a believer transfers – permanently and unconditionally – property in the name of God, with the aim that the revenue from this property be used for humanitarian purposes. This involves a kind of religious foundation regulated by Islamic law.

It should be emphasised that even where Indian legal English operates as a tool of Islamic law, it only differs from British legal English as to terms expressing original concepts of Islamic law. In other respects, legal English in India follows British usage of legal language. Most of the vocabulary, along with stylistics, is identical. As Naveed Ahmad, the Pakistani linguist specialising in legal English, puts it: "In Pakistan, the language of Islamic law is in fact legislative English".[86] This also holds true for the Federal Sharia Court, monitoring the application of Islamic law there. According to Ahmad, the decisions of the Court are written in the same way as are drafted judicial decisions on the application of common law. In his doctoral theses, submitted in December 2005, he states:

> Superior courts in India and Pakistan interpret this law [= Islamic law] as common law countries. Judges in India and Pakistan write their opinions in English keeping in view the British common law tradition in terms of style of writing a judicial opinion. (...) Also, Pakistan has a *Federal Shariah Court* (FSC) that monitors the application of Islamic law. The judges of the FSC like the judges of the other courts write their opinion in English. Stylistically, legal Englishes in India and Pakistan are identical to the British legal English: lexical syntactical and discourse features of these Englishes are identical to that of the British legal English. The only difference is in some Islamic terms expressing original concepts of Islam.[87]

More besides: documents coming from India are sometimes drawn up or put into proper order by an individual whose command of ordinary English is not perfect. One Spanish linguist points to cases where an Indian document in English is almost incomprehensible.[88]

---

86 Message by e-mail to the author, 2 December 2000.
87 Ahmad 2005: 1–2.
88 Mayoral 1999: 34.

4.4 Legal English in International Trade

4.4.1 Risk of Mistakes and Misunderstandings English is the most important language in international contracts. Non-native speakers of English also use it, whether in links with a native English speaker, or in cases where all parties only have an incomplete command of the language. Thousands of lawyers in non English-speaking countries are daily drawing up contracts in English. These documents often contain language similar to traditional common-law lawyers' contracts. This can give rise to serious problems.

> As for important commercial contracts, the parties are usually represented by experienced lawyers. In the case of consumer contracts, legal expertise is lacking. However, contracts of this kind, concluded over the Internet and thus crossing cultural and linguistic borders, are today very much on the increase. With such a contract, individuals with often modest knowledge of English commit themselves to complicated contractual conditions drawn up in English and expressed in traditional common law terms.

Sometimes, the usual conditions of a common law contract can provoke a cultural collision. A good example is the detailed affirmations (*representations and warranties*) as to the fact that legal ownership of goods forming the object of transfer genuinely belongs to the transferor – affirmations usually annexed as standard clauses in English and American contracts. These standard clauses often begin: *YXZ hereby represents and warrants to ABC as follows* [...]. In one case singled out in a legal linguistics article, a Spanish businessman had sold his company shares to a buyer in England. A contract in English containing the usual affirmations as above was sent to him for signature. Some days later, the businessman's lawyer announced to the English party that his client formally refused to sign "such an insulting contract". It is out of the question that a Spaniard, a man of honour, might intend to sell property not belonging to him![89]

There is another problem. A lawyer from a civil law country can copy, word for word, the text of a contract drawn up by a common-law lawyer, with a view to formulating a new contract. The reason is simple: the new contract has to be written in English. Sometimes, the continental lawyer who copies an English or American lawyer's contract has not the slightest idea of the real meaning of the expressions contained in the copied contract. It may be that the new contract becomes contradictory in itself, even quite incomprehensible from the legal standpoint; the parties risk understanding its content in different ways. The English of common-law lawyers can thus cause confusion, mistakes, and misunderstandings because continental lawyers and the translators of legal texts are not necessarily aware of the traps contained in the language.[90]

From the standpoint of a continental lawyer, understanding common law contracts is also hampered by the complicated character of legal English in this field.

---

89   Mullerat 1997: 11, note 44.
90   Beveridge 2002: 70.

For example, the fact that the entry into force of a contract requires certain approvals (according to some foreign legislation involved) can be expressed by writing: *This agreement is conditional upon the receipt by the parties hereto of the requisite approvals required to be obtained under the laws of Turkey...*[91]

Furthermore, some legal terms constitute a clear danger as to a proper understanding of contracts drawn up in English. A classic example, still current, is the word *equity*, originally expressing the idea of natural justice (this meaning may still appear in legal writing) but today mostly referring to the rules of a specific body of law developed over centuries by the English Court of Chancery. The expression *equitable remedies* does not signify 'fair and reasonable remedies' but 'legal redress under the system developed by the Court of Chancery', while the expression *equitable rights* does not signify 'fair and reasonable rights' but 'rights under the system developed by the Court of Chancery'. This is clearly evident in the following sentence (written by two Australian lawyers): *In such circumstances, a court may exercise its equitable jurisdiction to interfere with the rights that the parties would otherwise have at common law.*[92] A misleading interpretation would be: 'In such circumstances, a court may exercise its power of *moderation*, to interfere with the rights that the parties would otherwise have under common law'. In reality, the sentence means: 'In such circumstances, a court may exercise its power *under the rules developed by the Court of Chancery*, to interfere with the rights that the parties would otherwise have *under the rules developed by the Courts of Westminster*'.

Analogous mistakes and misunderstandings appear in the reverse direction, that is, in cases where a continental lawyer writes a contract in English. Barbara Beveridge, the Canadian lawyer-linguist, cites an English text drawn up by two continental lawyers: *Like other contracts, the agency contract is subject to the principles of equity*. A common-law lawyer risks understanding this sentence quite differently from the way the authors intended. The continental authors of the text intended to say that the principles of fairness and reasonableness apply to the contracts in question. However, an English or American lawyer could understand: 'The *rules developed by the Court of Chancery* (and *not* the rules *developed by the Courts of Westminster*) should apply [...]'. The authors should have used, instead of the word *equity*, a term such as, e.g., *reasonable commercial practice, natural justice*. According to Beveridge, "*This* (= reasonable commercial practice) *is certainly not the way a common lawyer would understand the phrase 'principles of equity'*".[93]

The word *equity* is not the only example of cases where the sense of an English word in the language of common-law lawyers differs from the sense of the word in everyday language; the legal meaning of an English word can also be strange in other ways to the uninitiated. A good example is *liquidated damages* ('amount contractually stipulated as a reasonable estimation of actual damages in case of contract breach'). The word *execution* can also cause serious misunderstandings. The

---

91 Example given by Beveridge 2002: 77.

92 Smith & Walton 1998: 394.

93 Beveridge 2002: 71.

Australian authors mentioned above write: *While it is open to the parties in dispute over a contract to adduce evidence as to the meaning of specific foreign words, it is not possible at common law to adduce evidence as to the actual intention of the parties when the contract was executed.*[94] A continental lawyer easily understands the word *executed* such that it involves the moment when the parties satisfy their obligations arising from the contract in question. Nevertheless, the word is polysemic (it has multiple meanings): it can also refer to the signing of the contract[95] and, in the above example, doubtless involves the second meaning. So, the end of the quotation means: '... to adduce evidence as to the actual intention of the parties at the moment the contract was signed'.

4.4.2 Contradictory Interpretations A contract in commercial law, with connecting factors with different States, is expressly submitted or may be submitted by way of interpretation, to a definite legal order. Legal disputes arising from the contract are heard either by an arbitration tribunal or the courts of some State.

Where litigation arising from a commercial contract has to be heard by a State's court, the interpretation of the contract may cause considerable surprise to one of the parties. A British or North American court tends to interpret the terms of a contract drawn up in English in line with traditional common law thinking. These terms can then acquire a meaning completely different from that imagined by the party from a continental country. Correspondingly, a common-law lawyer will doubtless feel that the terms and clauses that are so familiar in English are interpreted "bizarrely" by a court from a continental country. This can occur especially in cases where a contract drawn up in English is submitted – expressly or by way of interpretation – to a civil law legal order.[96] Indeed, the fact that a contract is drawn up in English does not automatically produce the application of common law to the contract.[97] To resolve problems of this kind, specialists in international commercial law are seeking to develop terminology that is not too closely linked to the legal orders of particular States.

4.5 An Example: Legal English in Finland

As we have seen, legal English is in course of conquering the world. Legal circles in various countries are using it increasingly. Finland is a good case in point. Here, legal English is a newcomer. However, in recent decades it has quickly risen to a dominant position in international communication for Finnish lawyers. The other major languages, previously used for such communication, have had to make way for English.

---

94 Smith & Walton 1998: 398.
95 Beveridge 1998: 390.
96 Beveridge 1998: 387–388.
97 Kurkela 1999: 169.

This tendency is clearly in evidence in the choice of languages of Finnish legal science. In the 20th century, Finnish lawyers usually wrote their doctoral theses in Finnish and – notably at the beginning of the century – in Swedish (the country's second official language). However, some Finnish theses were also prepared in the major languages. During the first half of the 20th century, four law theses were published in French and two in German. At that time, no theses were published in English. The situation began to change after the Second World War, though somewhat slowly it has to be said. In the 1960s and 1970s, two more theses were published in German, and one in French. After that, French no longer appears as a language of law in theses in Finland; in German, there is a single thesis. English has in practice replaced these two languages. The first law thesis in English in Finland dates from the 1950s, but this involves an isolated pioneer: in the 1960s, not a single Finnish lawyer undertook a thesis in English. The breakthrough for English as a language of Finnish law theses took place in the 1970s. In that decade, there were three. In the 1980s, there were already seven, that is, 12.5% of the global figure for Finnish law theses. During the same decade, the number of theses published in English for the first time overtook that of theses in Swedish.[98] In the last few years, this trend has strengthened still further: for the period from 1998 to 2003, the number of theses in English, undertaken in Finnish law faculties, represents 20% of the global figure for these theses; those published in Swedish were no more than about 3%.[99]

As for Finnish legal literature overall, the same tendency is noticeable, a little less accentuated than in the case of theses, it is true. Between 1993 and 2003, some 12,000 legal books and articles appeared in Finland. Amongst these, about 9,250 were in Finnish, about 1,300 in English, and about 1,250 in Swedish. The number of books and articles in other languages is no more than a few dozen.[100] Comparison with the figures for the preceding period shows that the number of publications in English presents the strongest relative increase.

Now, we examine translations of laws and decrees in Finland. For various reasons, translations are made of the laws and decrees of smaller countries into the major languages. In Finland, on this theme, English had already acquired a dominant position in the 1970s. The list of translations dating from this period enables the calculation that in total 150 Finnish laws and decrees were translated into English before the mid 1970s; the number of translations into German was 27 and into French 19.[101] Further, it should be noted that many translations into German and French are old: they date from the early 20th century. Today, the dominance of English in this field is still clearer. The databank of laws and decrees in Finland (Finlex) contains a list of their translations. Information concerning the last few years shows that the translations included in the bank are almost exclusively translations into English.

---

98 Kangas 1998: 416, 423, 429, 440, 450, 466, 483 and 498.
99 Author's calculation on the basis of databanks of Finnish legal literature.
100 Author's calculation on the basis of databanks of Finnish legal literature.
101 Wiitanen 1976: 37–45.

Translations into other major languages only occur in isolated cases (e.g., the new Constitution of 1999).

> However, a need continues in certain areas of legislation for translations into German, French, or Russian of laws and decrees in Finland. A commission report (1996/7) indicates that in some fields of specialism many translations of Finnish legislative texts have been prepared in German, French, or Russian and that requests for such translations are increasing.

PART 4
Conclusion

Chapter 9

Lexical Comprehension and Research Needs

1 Changes in Legal-linguistic Dominance in the International Arena

Bigger countries have always sought a position of dominance at the international level, and they continue to do so today. A traditional tool of importance in achieving this is the legal order. As we have seen throughout this book, each influential country has tried to make its law widespread, along with the language of that law. Let us once again summarise the essential features of the history of legal and linguistic dominance, examined in the preceding chapters.

1.1 Rivalry of Legal Systems

In Antiquity, Roman law became widespread over a very large area, by virtue of the extent of the Roman Empire; nor did that law die with the fall of Rome. In a highly developed form, it provided the basis of the legal order in Byzantium, despite the Hellenisation of legal dealings. In the territories that had belonged to the Western Roman Empire, Roman law was at first applied, in a more or less vulgar form, mixed with customary Germanic law. Later, after discovery of the *Corpus juris civilis* and the founding of Universities, Roman law once again attained a high technical level in the West. This law reborn, and called *jus commune*, exercised considerable influence throughout Catholic Europe, along with canon law. However, that influence did not come to an end in Protestant countries with the Reformation. It also made itself felt in Orthodox Europe, and even in England – despite the originality of common law.[1] Indeed, Roman law constitutes the foundation of all European law. However, on the basis of this law developed more or less original, often rival, legal cultures. At the close of the Middle Ages and the beginning of modern times, the commercial law of the Italian cities exercised a considerable influence abroad, while from the start of the 16th century Spanish and Portuguese law spread to the Americas. Later, it was notably France and Germany – not forgetting Russia (Imperial and Soviet) – whose laws exercised considerable influence throughout Europe as well as in other continents.

French law has enjoyed a high profile in various countries, notably at the beginning of the 19th century, through the coming into force of the *Code civil* or through its

---

1   See p. 126.

value as a model. In the wake of colonisation, French legal culture invaded many countries, notably the continent of Africa (some half of it). Also worthy of mention is the system of international law, to a large extent based on French legal thinking. In recent decades, the law of the European Communities – today's European Union – was largely built on French legal tradition.[2] Equally, German law has exercised an international influence since medieval times, notably in the territories of the Hanseatic League and also elsewhere in the Eastern parts of Central Europe. During the golden age of German legal science, in the 19th century, a second important wave occurred throughout Europe, including the Western side of the Continent.[3]

These laws of the Continent have been in a state of mutual rivalry. Today, the common law of English origin has been challenging them. The importance of this last law is particularly great: the legal systems of all the anglophone countries describe themselves as common law, along with those of many Asiatic and African countries, some of them highly populous. Moreover, the law of international commerce was developed on the basis of common law. In recent decades, the influence of this law has made itself felt ever more strongly in civil law countries. Various common law institutions have been received in these countries, under American cultural influence, notably in the modern branches of law. A recent example is the *class action* (in French designated *action de classe, action de groupe, action populaire* or *action collective*). As to the force of common law influence, it is also symptomatic that the institution of *trust*, peculiarly original to this law, has been received, in more or less adapted form, in some civil law countries.

1.2 Rivalry of Legal Languages

Along with Roman law, its language, Latin, also spread throughout Europe. And, just as Roman law itself, Latin survived the Roman Empire. In Byzantium, certainly, this language was preserved, in the long term, only in the form of Latin quotations or distortions of Latin words. However, in Western Europe it continued as the genuine language of the law – understood, it is true, only by the governing classes. Latin was needed notably in cross-border government and judicial matters. Indeed, Latin was the language of the Catholic Church and its legal order, canon law.[4] It is worth noting that Latin legal culture also flourished in England.[5]

Given the conservative character of legal dealings, it is understandable that the final transition from Latin to the new national languages has been particularly slow – as we have seen. Universities provide us with the clearest example. Throughout Europe, legal science employed Latin, at least in part, until the 19th century. As for international relations, Latin remained the language of negotiations and treaties until the 17th century – the era when French began to oust it. Furthermore, in the Middle

---

2   See p. 107.
3   See pp. 180–181.
4   See pp. 133–134.
5   See pp. 225–228.

Ages and up to the beginning of modern times, minutes and oral proceedings of the courts, the authorities, and notaries were often drawn up entirely or partly in Latin. The same also applied to legislation.

The dominance of Latin was not absolute, even in the Middle Ages. In regions bordering the Baltic, in practical lawyering its rival was Low German.[6] During modern times, the dominance of Latin has gradually broken down. From the 16th to the 20th centuries, Modern European languages first replaced Latin and then spread to other continents along with European colonisation.

As for languages of international relations, the outstanding phenomenon of recent centuries is the rivalry between French and English.[7] With France ever-stronger as a great power at the beginning of modern times, she imposed her language on the administration of international relations, that is, on diplomacy and inter-State treaties.[8] Following the displacement in the international arena of Latin, the language of the Holy Roman Emperor and the Pope, rivals of the King of France, French for a long time occupied a pre-eminent position in international relations. Its position has gradually weakened. However, it was only seriously called into question in the 20th century, notably during the second half of the century, with the lightning growth of the use of English in the international arena.

In fact, during the 20th century the international arena of legal dealings was characterised by an important language change: the dominance of French was first replaced by French-English bilingualism, and recently by the dominance of English. A good example is the Hague Conference on Private International Law. The same trend can also be seen as to the European Union. At the level of practical language use, the original dominance of French has been transformed into French-English bilingualism in the various organs of the Union (with the exception of the Court of Justice[9]). Within certain organs, English clearly dominates. At the beginning of the third millennium, it seems that the dominance of English is becoming ever stronger in international relations. Today, the other major languages are incapable of posing a threat to the position of English as the lawyers' *lingua franca*.

2 Terminological Interaction between Legal Languages

Linguistic dominance necessarily produces various forms of interaction between the dominant language and the subject language. This holds true as much for style as vocabulary. As for understanding and faultless translation of legal messages, it is particularly important to consider the phenomenon of terminological interaction.

---

6   See pp. 183–185.
7   See pp. 24–27.
8   See pp. 191–193.
9   See pp. 26–27.

2.1 Influence of Latin on Modern Languages

We saw, in the chapter on legal Latin, how in legal circles the gradual passage of Latin into modern languages brought about the large-scale adoption of Latin words in those languages.[10] In English and in the Romance languages, these words were borrowed in almost their original form. In other languages (e.g., German, the Nordic languages, the Slavic languages), many calques (loan translations) were incorporated, besides loanwords of Latin origin. Everywhere, words often obtained legal meanings derived from Latin. Likewise, certain Latin expressions and sayings remained in use as such, in the shape of quotations.

During the first centuries of modern times, these were considerable in number: legal languages were often a linguistic mix, where Latin words alternated with words from modern languages. This heritage can still be seen.[11] However, the volume and intensity of use of Latin quotations varies in different countries. Generally speaking, this use is far more frequent in legal science than in practical lawyering (e.g., legislation, case law, private documents). In certain countries (notably in the Nordic countries), legislative acts and judicial decisions hardly contain any Latin quotations. In other countries, such as Italy or the common law countries, it is easy enough to find such quotations in legal documents, public and private.

2.2 Borrowings between Modern Languages

Latin has never been the sole source of language borrowings. As we have seen earlier, in this respect legal French occupies an important place in the history of legal languages. From the 13th century to the end of the 14th century, partly to the 15th century (formally until the 18th century), it was one of the legal languages of England. In consequence, a vast volume of words passed, in a durable way, from French to legal English (deriving, it is true, from Latin in the final analysis[12]). Following the rise of France to the position of dominant great power in Europe, active in matters of diplomacy and international law, legal authors expressing themselves in various European languages employed a large number of French terms of public and private international law. These terms are often direct quotations: for example, *lettres de créance*, *renvoi*, *ordre public*. Today, a new wave of French legal vocabulary is making itself felt in Europe, in the wake of the founding of the European Communities (now the European Union), as much in the form of quotation words as in the form of adapted loanwords and borrowed meanings. A good example is the term *acquis communautaire*, which appears in all Community languages, whether as a direct quotation, or as a borrowing adapted to the system of word formation in the

---

10 See pp. 146–147.
11 See pp. 136–139.
12 See pp. 226–228 and pp. 231–232.

language in question, or as a word fashioned more freely on the basis of the French original.[13]

German legal science enjoyed its best years at the end of the 19th century, profoundly influencing lawyers throughout Europe, even in America. Thanks to this influence, legal German terms spread into international usage, notably those referring to the science of the celebrated schools of law: e.g., *Begriffsjurisprudenz, Pandektenrecht*. However, the number of German words in the shape of direct quotations in other languages is somewhat limited. Beneath the surface, the influence of German terminology has been far more important. The great German-speaking jurists created brand new legal categories and concepts, rapidly received in continental Europe, notably in the Northern and Eastern countries of the Continent.[14] In the legal languages of these countries, the terms necessary to express categories and concepts of German origin were formed, as calques, on the basis of German. A typical example is *Rechtsgeschäft*.

During the 19th and 20th centuries, English became the plainly dominant language of international commercial contracts. It is also used where both parties are not from English-speaking countries. This produced an important borrowing phenomenon: a large number of English commercial law terms were adopted in other languages. During recent decades, the same phenomenon can be seen in all branches of modern law, by reason of the global influence of American institutions. A case in point is the recent diffusion of common law Latin in continental Europe. In Finland, for example, some 10% of Latin quotations in use today come from common law Latin. Finland is not alone: terms such as *amicus curiae*, typical of Anglo-Saxon lawyers, appear in German dictionaries of legal Latin.[15]

3 Problems of Lexical Comprehension

As the above paragraphs show, dominant legal cultures have always influenced other legal cultures and their terminologies. On the other hand, however, every legal culture has developed to some extent autonomously. Common law and civil law are a clear example of this: the first was born in the royal courts of England, while the second was shaped in the European Universities. Even linked legal systems, such as those of Continental Europe, enjoy relative autonomy. Likewise, languages – ordinary as well as legal – always develop in a partly independent way.

All of that has produced highly complex combinations as to the similarity and dissimilarity of legal institutions and their designations. Sometimes, these institutions correspond legally, sometimes not. In the same way, at times their names are in accord with one another (as words of common origin or calques), at times they differ. Often, the designations of legal institutions and organs are meaningless if literally translated. In fact, a literal translation can even be clearly misleading. Likewise for

---

13 See pp. 120–121.
14 See p. 170 and p. 181.
15 See p. 153.

words of foreign origin understood on the basis of words outwardly similar in other languages. This problem manifests itself in different ways and in differing degrees.

3.1 Danger of Void Literal Translation

It can happen that the designation of a legal institution or organ is meaningless to a foreigner if literally translated: it is dictated by that country's original history. Examples of various denominations linked to the legal profession include the word *maître*, placed in front of the personal names of lawyers in French-speaking countries. Another example: *Queen's / King's Counsel*, an honorific title awarded to an elite, senior-level barrister or advocate in the United Kingdom (and Canada). A literal translation of these denominations is void from the outsider's standpoint.

A more serious problem, as to understanding legal messages, consists of the historical designations of courts. For example, in Greek judicial decisions the name *Áreios Págos* (Άρειος Πάγος) appears. This name goes back two and a half millenia: those familiar with the culture of Ancient Greece are also familiar with the *Areopagus* of Athens. However, this English variant of the original name is not to be recommended in legal translations. On the one hand, not all readers are specialists in the history of Antiquity and, on the other hand, the ancient *Areopagus* only judged Athenian matters. Today's reality is that this is the Supreme Court of Greece.[16] Given the specific nature of its decisions, the correct French translation is *Cour de cassation.*[17]

3.2 Danger of Misleading Literal Translation

A misleading translation is more dangerous than a meaningless one. Occasionally, the danger may be very serious: the position and functions of a legal institution or organ differ completely from what a literal translation in the reader's language leads to understand.

3.2.1 Manifestly Misleading Translations In cases where linguistic interaction between legal cultures has been more important than legal interaction, the designations of legal institutions or organs may be similar, in spite of a great divergence in content. A particularly striking example is the organ called *Consilium Status* in late Latin. The literal translation of this term is "Council of State."

Consilium Status appears as a literal translation in many countries. In France, there is *Conseil d'État;* in Italy, *Consiglio di Stato;* in Spain, *Consejo de Estado* and in Greece, *Symvoúlio tis Epikrateías* (Συμβούλιο της Επικρατείας). In the German Democratic Republic, there formerly existed the *Staatsrat* and in Poland *Rada Państwa*. The spectre of divergent concepts lurks behind these terms, whose literal

---

16 Kerameos & Kozyris 1988: 239.
17 Gadis p. 119.

translation is identical: the functions of the organ in question are absolutely not the same in the different countries.

In France, in Italy, and in Greece, the "Council of State" is an organ that, besides certain activities linked to preparation of laws and advising the Government, functions as a high judicial organ.[18] One part of this organ forms the supreme administrative court of the country; it is with that property that foreign lawyers usually come across it. In Spain, by contrast, the *Consejo de Estado* only fulfills tasks linked to preparation of laws and to advising the Government; judicial matters of an administrative character are dealt with, at the highest level, by a particular structure of the *Tribunal Supremo*.[19] As for the former German Democratic Republic and the former Polish People's Republic, the "Council of State" was a parliamentary organ that carried out certain functions belonging to the Head of State in Western Europe. In Finland, *valtioneuvosto* [lit. 'Council of State'] is the Government of the country (Cabinet), as also in Switzerland at the cantonal level: the terms *Staatsrat, Conseil d'État* and *Consiglio di Stato* are used to designate the Governments of the cantons.[20] Thus one can see how misleading it would be to translate these terms literally.

3.2.2 Translations Misleading Due to Polysemy Cases of polysemy are particularly difficult. This involves cases where an identical concept stands behind terms similar in two or more languages in certain contexts of usage but two or several divergent concepts in certain other contexts. Correct translation presupposes careful analysis of the contexts where the terms are used.

One example that well illustrates this problem is the term *jurisprudence*. In England and the United States, the original meaning of the term *jurisprudentia*, as used by the Ancient Romans, has *grosso modo* remained as such. In legal English, *jurisprudence* most often refers to legal theory. In France, by contrast, the meaning of the term began to change from the 17th century.[21] In modern legal French, it refers to the body of court decisions and to the law established on the basis of those decisions.[22] In the other Romance languages, the main meaning of the national variants of the term (*giurisprudenza / jurisprudencia / jurisprudência*) is the same as in France; however, they are occasionally used in the sense of 'legal science'.[23] On the other hand, the meaning of 'body of judicial decisions' is also known in the legal language of the United States and in English texts on public international law.[24] In sum, it can be said that the semantic emphasis of the term *jurisprudence* is differently placed in the Latin countries and the common law countries. In this first

---

18 Perrot 1998: 208–219, Favata 1999: 104, Kerameus & Kozyris 1988: 26 and *Nuovo dizionario giuridico* 2001: 352.

19 Ibán 1995: 30 and *Diccionario Trivium* 1998: 156.

20 *Brockhaus Enzyklopädie* 17/1973: 810.

21 Rey 1994: 1082.

22 Cornu 2004.

23 See, for example, Villa-Real Molina and Del Arco Torres 1999.

24 Garner 1987.

group, it normally refers to court decisions, while in the second it refers to legal science (theory). However, in both cases there are important exceptions to this rule that the translator should be aware of.

An analogous example, as to partial differences of meaning of legal English and French terms, is *jurisdictio*. The English term *jurisdiction* covers a semantic field distinctly wider than the French term *juridiction*.[25]

3.2.3 Misleading Legal Nuances These cases likewise form a very large number. Let us take two examples relating to essential terms of the judiciary system and procedural law.

Curia and tribunal. In the major legal languages of Western Europe, the designations of courts of law often come from the Latin words *curia, tribunal, judicium* and – a word of Greek origin – *dicasterium* (as well as *forum* in a specialised sense). These words are still very much alive in those languages. Variants coming from *dicasterium* and *judicium* only exist, it is true, in certain legal languages, and often in a highly specific sense. Thus, the word *dicastère* is used in legal French only in Canon law contexts. Normally, modern legal languages refer to various courts of law by using variants of the words *tribunal* and *curia* (mixed with the word *cohors*). But the field of usage of these words diverges in several details.

In France, the royal high-ranking courts, the *parlements*, long ago obtained the privilege of using the name of *curia*. This explains why, in legal French, the word *cour* is always connected with a higher or similarly important court of law: e.g., *cour d'appel, cour de cassation, cour d'assises*. Lower courts bear the name of *tribunal*, which is likewise a generic term, meaning a court of law in general.[26] This usage can also be seen in the frame of the European Union: in French, the Union's leading court of law is called the *Cour de justice des Communautés européennes* ['Court of Justice of the European Communities'] while the lower court bears the name of the *Tribunal de première instance des Communautés européennes* ['Court of First Instance of the European Communities'].

Nevertheless, these comments only concern the French-speaking world. In other modern legal languages, the fields of usage of words coming from *curia (cohors)* and *tribunal* differ. In the common law countries, both lower and higher courts of law bear the name of *court*. This word also has a generic meaning ('judicial organ in general'). Moreover, in these countries the word *tribunal* refers to specialised courts of law (for example, *military tribunal*) or to organs having competence in administrative matters. In the Spanish-speaking world, both *tribunal* and *corte* can appear in the designations of lower or higher courts of law. The highest court of law in Spain is called *Tribunal Supremo* but, in several Latin American countries, the corresponding organ bears the name of *Corte Suprema*.[27]

---

25 Beaudoin 2002: 120.

26 Cornu 2004.

27 Cabanellas 1981 II and VIII.

In France, the difference in meaning between the words *cour* and *tribunal* has also fluctuated in history. At the time of the French Revolution, lively discussion took place as to designating the highest court of law. Proposals included *Cour de cassation, Cour suprême* and *Cour plénière*. The final choice was *Tribunal de cassation*, in order to avoid the association with the word *cour* (court) in the sense of 'the royal circle'. However, it was not long before this position was reviewed, in adopting the designation *Cour de cassation* still in use.[28]

The term banca rotta. Another typical example concerns the consequences of insolvency. In Italian, in French, and in English, can be found the terms *bancarotta, banqueroute*, and *bankruptcy* (and the adjective *bankrupt*). These legal terms on failure stemming originally from the Italian (*banca rota,* 'smashed table') refer to the fact that the authorities symbolically broke the counter of an insolvent banker. In legal English, the term *bankruptcy* (which comes from the Latinized form, *banca rupta*, of the Italian term) generally designates failure. By contrast, in Italy and in France the terms *bancarotta* and *banqueroute* have obtained the meaning of 'criminal failure'. As in (earlier) French (*faillite;* today: *liquidation judiciaire*), an ordinary failure in Italian is called *fallimento*.[29] On that basis, it is not hard to understand the error of translating *bankruptcy* by the term *banqueroute*, and *vice-versa*.

4 The Need for Jurilinguistic Research on Legal Institutions and Concepts

The several examples above demonstrate the difficulties linked to correctly understanding legal institutions and concepts and translating them faultlessly. The content of these institutions and concepts and the terms expressing them always develop in a complex way: this involves a tangled web in which international legal-linguistic interaction is mixed with the autonomous development of legal cultures.

Despite clear gaps,[30] the general information given in this book on the history and usage of legal languages and their mutual links are, we would like to think, helpful to lawyers and translators in placing legal institutions and concepts, along with their designations, in the broadest of contexts. This makes it possible to avoid disastrous mistakes and misunderstandings. Nevertheless, this general background information is not enough. To eliminate all possibility of error, we need to have in our grasp detailed legal knowledge about these institutions and concepts themselves as well as linguistic information on the terms designating them. Moreover, such legal and linguistic information should be juxtaposed. This is particularly important as to branches of the law and areas of terminology that are essential from the standpoint of lawyers' international co-operation.

---

28 Brunot 1937: 1036, 1046.

29 Favata 1999 and Cornu 2004.

30 For example, as the introduction indicates, certain legal languages of global importance – notably Spanish, Portuguese, and Russian – are omitted from this work.

Combining institutional and linguistic analyses is not, as such, a novel idea in legal-linguistic research. This idea can be found behind every bilingual legal dictionary. In certain dictionaries, the results of these analyses are also presented, besides translations strictly speaking, as texts of an encyclopaedic character, notably in cases where a difference of content between the institutions or concepts in question only allows a direct translation with difficulty. Good examples of such dictionaries are available in various countries, often bilingual (like Canada) but also elsewhere. In Italy, for example, the dictionary of Francesco de Frachis comes to mind.[31]

However, these analyses – normally bilingual, occasionally trilingual – need to be completed by more extensive analysis: there is a need for systematic study and comparison of legal institutions and concepts and their designations, from the standpoint of many languages, in defined domains. In Europe, this particularly concerns branches of the law that are essential in European co-operation. Institutions and concepts of procedural law provide a good example of this viewpoint: an increasing number of judicial decisions have to be enforced outside the country where they are made. That produces a significant need for translating those decisions.

In this context, for example, the formulas stating the finality (and/or enforceability) of a judgment have caused many mistakes and misunderstandings in translation. Here, accurate translations are particularly important from the standpoint of legal protection of the parties to the case. In certain legal cultures, the final character of a judgment is expressed in terms that are unintelligible on the basis of ordinary language. This above all involves modern language variants of the Latin term *res judicata* ['a matter adjudged', 'a thing or matter settled by judgment'; 'final (non-appealable) judgment'; 'rule that final judgment constitutes an absolute bar to a subsequent action involving the same claim']. French legal authors, for example, employ a formula including direct translation of this term: *acquérir (passer en) force de chose jugée*. In certain countries, expressions coming from *res judicata* also appear in judgments. This is the case in Italy, for example. Italian judgments often contain the following expression: (...) *con attestazione di avvenuto passaggio in giudicato / in cosa giudicata*.

At the same time, a problem of principle also exists: theories of procedural law differ in common law from those of the civil law countries. For this reason, the French term *force de chose jugée* is often translated into English quite simply: *final (final and absolute)*. In order to achieve greater legal-technical accuracy, the quotation *res judicata* – the Latin term already mentioned – is sometimes used. However, neither is this quotation accepted unreservedly. This appears, for example, in documents relating to preparation of the Hague Convention on the Recognition and Enforcement of Foreign Judgments in Civil and Commercial Matters (1971). In the preliminary text of the Convention, the French expression *force de la chose jugée* was translated into English as *res judicata*. Due to criticisms of the Latin quotation, the two final texts, French and English, included a paraphrase in place of the term

---

31   de Franchis 1984.

strictly speaking: (...) *ne peut plus faire l'objet d'un recours ordinaire* / (...) *is no longer subject to ordinary forms of review.*[32]

So we see that the institution of *res judicata* would require a thorough legal-linguistic analysis from the standpoint of various languages. A study would be needed, in different legal systems, of the legal content of the institution (e.g., consequences of the finality of the decision: enforceability) and the ways of expressing this content at the language level, in legal literature and in legal documents (e.g., judgments, other decisions). It is true that comparative studies of procedural law analyse in detail the different aspects of the finality and enforceability of judicial decisions in different countries. Nevertheless, a jurilinguistic approach should be added to these analyses, by looking at the various ways of transmitting these concepts on the language plane (on this subject, differences often occur within one and the same country between the various judicial organs and notably between legal authors and the courts). In this way, one would have an overview of the translation problems in the matter.

Analyses of this type would complete the general information of a legal-cultural character set out in this work. These analyses could improve the chances of avoiding mistakes and misunderstandings in the comprehension and translation of legal texts. By the same token, they should have more general importance. The virtue of these analyses is that they would perfect the theory of legal translation, which is already abundant and highly useful.[33] This applies, for example, to strategies for choosing term equivalents in different situations (quoting the original term as such, a rough equivalent, explanation resembling a term, enumerative translation, neologism). In the same way, it is certainly possible to clarify the picture relating to the differences in meaning of words of Latin origin in the legal languages studied.[34]

32 Nadelman & Van Mehren 1966–67: 197–198.

33 See, especially, Arntz 1995, Gémar 1995 and Šarčević 1997.

34 Mattila 2002b: 50–69.

Alphabetic Bibliography

This English edition is partly abridged, in that it does not contain all chapters from the Finnish original. In particular, the main Nordic legal languages (Danish, Finnish, Norwegian, Swedish) are conspicuous by their absence. That said, the alphabetic and systematic bibliographies of the present edition retain the leading sources for these languages, out of concern for those readers with an interest in variety of legal languages.

In this edition, all Russian words, that is, titles in the bibliographies and quotations in the main text, are transliterated in accordance with the Library-of-Congress system (without diacritics), and all Greek words in accordance with the UN/ELOT system. In the names and other words of various languages given in the Latin alphabet, all the diacritic signs have been preserved.

AARNIO, A. (1984), 'On the Sources of Law. A Justificatory Point of View', *Rechtstheorie* (1984): 393–401.

_____ (1987), *The Rational as Reasonable: a Treatise on Legal Justification* (Dordrecht: Reidel, 1987).

_____ (1992), *Le rationnel comme raisonable: la justification en droit*. (Brussels & Paris: Éditions Story-Scientia, 1992).

_____ (1999), On the Semantic Ambiguity of Legal Interpretation, in *Dialectic of Law and Reality*. (Helsinki: Faculty of Law, 1999, Forum Iuris), pp. 17–24.

ABDEL HADI, M. (2001–2002), 'La juritraductologie et le problème des équivalences des notions juridiques en droit des pays arabes', in *Le facteur culturel dans la traduction des textes pragmatiques. Les Cahiers de l'ILCEA* 3 (2001–2002), pp. 71–78.

AHMAD, N. (1997), 'Analysis of linguistic competence of the ESP learners', in *Journal of Research – Humanities* (Bahauddin Zakariya University, Multan), 14 (1997).

_____ (2005), *Legal English: A Case for ESP* (Ph.D Thesis. Bahauddin Zakariya University, Department of English, Pakistan, December 2005).

AITCHISON, J. (1995), *Linguistics. An Introduction.* (London: Hodder & Stoughton, 1995).

ALONSO, A. (1998), 'Instrumentos de ayuda a la traducción', *Terminologie et traduction* 1 (1998): 7–11.

AMMON, U. (1992), 'On the Status and Changes in the Status of German as a Language of Diplomacy', in U. Ammon & M. Hellinger (eds), *Status Change of Languages* (Berlin & New York: Walter de Gruyter, 1992), pp. 421–438.

AMMON, U.(2002): 'Die Stellung der deutschen Sprache in Europa und Modelle der Mehrsprachigkeit', in P. Kelz (ed.), *Die sprachliche Zukunft Europas* (Baden-Baden: Nomos Verlagsgesellschaft, 2002), pp. 19–35.

AMMON, U. & HELLINGER, M. (eds), *Status Change of Languages* (Berlin & New York: Walter de Gruyter, 1992).

ANDERSEN, P. (1998), 'Translation Tools for the CEEC Candidates for EU Membership – an Overview', *Terminologie et traduction* 1 (1998): 140–163.

ANNERS, E. & ÖNNERFORS, A. (1972), *Latinsk juridisk terminologi*. 2nd ed., (Uppsala: Juridiska Föreningen i Uppsala, 1972).

ARNTZ, R. (1999), 'Rechtsvergleichung und Kontrastive Terminologiearbeit: Möglichkeiten und Grenzen interdisziplinären Arbeitens', in P. Sandrini (ed.), *Übersetzen von Rechtstexten* (Tübingen: Gunter Narr Verlag, 1999), pp. 185–201.

_____ (2001), *Fachbezogene Mehrsprachigkeit in Recht und Technik* (Hildesheim etc.: Georg Olms Verlag, 2001, Studien zu Sprache und Technik, Band 8).

_____ (2002), 'The Roman Heritage in German Legal Language', in H. Mattila (ed.), *The Development of Legal Language* (Helsinki: Talentum Media, 2002), pp. 33–54.

ARNTZ, R. (ed.) (1995), *La traduzione. Nuovi approcci tra teoria e pratica* (Bolzano: Accademia Europea Bolzano /CUEN, 1995).

AYMANS, W. & MÖRSDORF, K. (1991), *Kanonisches Recht* (Paderborn etc.: Ferdinand Schöningh, 1991).

BADER, K. (1963), 'Rechtssprache und Rechtskultur', *Zeitschrift für Schweizerisches Recht* (1963): 105–130.

BAGGIONI, D. (1996), 'Éléments pour une histoire de la Francophonie (idéologie, mouvements, institutions)', in D. Robillard & M. Beniamino (eds), *Le français dans l'espace francophone* (Paris: Honoré Champion Éditeur 1996), pp. 789–807.

BALLANSAT-AEBI, S. (2000): 'Attendu que – französische Gerichtsurteile als Herausforderung für den Übersetzer', in *La traduction juridique. Histoire, théorie(s) et pratique* (Berne & Geneva: ASTTI & ETI, 2000), pp. 713–736.

_____ (2002), 'Untersuchung der Kulturspezifik in französischen und englischen juristischen Lehrbüchern und ihrer Bedeutung für die Übersetzung ins Deutsche', in M. Koskela & al. (eds), *Porta Scientiae I. Lingua specialis* (Vaasa: Proceedings of the University of Vaasa, Reports 95, 2002), pp. 276–288.

BAR, S. (1999), 'La question des langues au sein des Nations Unies', in H. Guillorel & G. Koubi (eds), *Langues et droits. Langues du droit, droit des langues* (Brussels: Bruylant, 1999), pp. 291–316.

BARDACH, J., LEŚNODORSKI, B. & PIETRZAK, M. (1976), *Historia Państwa i prawa polskiego* (Warsaw: PWN, 1976).

BARRAINE, R. (1974), *Nouveau dictionnaire de droit de sciences économiques* (Paris: Librairie générale de droit et de jurisprudence, 1974).

BARRAT, J. (1997), *Géopolitique de la Francophonie* (Paris: Presses Universitaires de France, 1997).

BAUMANN, M. (1990), 'Recht und Rechtssprache', *Zeitschrift für Schweizerisches Recht* (1990): 79–96.

BEAUDOIN, L. (2002), 'Legal Translation in Canada', in H. Mattila (ed.), *The Development of Legal Language* (Helsinki: Talentum Media, 2002) pp. 115–130.

BEAVEN, J. (1998), 'Future MT Developments', *Terminologie et traduction* 1 (1998): 319–326.

BECKER, H.-J. (1991), 'Die Bedeutung der lateinischen Sprache für die Verfassung und das Recht der römischen Kirche', in J. Eckert (ed.), *Sprache – Recht – Geschichte* (Heidelberg: C. F. Müller Juristischer Verlag 1991).

BEHRENDS, O. (1991): Die Eindeutschung der römisch-rechtlichen Fachsprache, in J. Eckert (ed.), *Sprache – Recht – Geschichte* (Heidelberg: C. F. Müller Juristischer Verlag, 1991).

BELVEDERE, A. (1994), 'Il linguaggio del Codice civile: alcune osservazioni', in U. Scarpelli & P. Di Lucia (eds), *Il linguaggio del diritto* (Milan: LED, 1994), pp. 403–452.

BENEDETTI, G. (1999): 'Diritto e linguaggio. Variazioni sul "diritto muto"', in *Europa e diritto privato* 1 (1999), pp. 137–152.

BERGH, B. (2001): 'Översättarens förord', in S. Pufendorf, *Om de mänskliga och medborgerliga plikterna enligt naturrätten i två böcker* (Lund: City University Press, 2001), pp. 7–10.

BERGMANS, B. (1987), 'L'enseignement d'une terminologie juridique étrangère comme mode d'approche du droit comparé: l'exemple de l'allemand', *Revue internationale de droit comparé* 1 (1987): 90–110.

BERMAN, H. & REID, C. (1995), 'Römisches Recht in Europa und das ius commune', *Zeitschrift für europäisches Recht* (1995): 3–34.

BERTELOOT, P. (1988), *Babylone à Luxembourg: Jurilinguistique à la Cour de justice des Communautés européennes* (1988).

_____ (2000): 'La traduction juridique dans l'Union européenne, en particulier à la Cour de justice', in *La traduction juridique. Histoire, théorie(s) et pratique* (Berne & Geneva: ASTTI & ETI, 2000), pp. 521–535.

_____ (2002), 'Legal French in France and in the European Communities', in H. Mattila (ed.), *The Development of Legal Language* (Helsinki: Talentum Media, 2002), p. 81–99.

BERTZEL, K. (1993), 'Lex est quodcumque notamus. Zur Geschichte der Devise der Internationalen Union des Lateinischen Notariats und des Sonnenuhren-Emblems', *Deutsche Notar-Zeitschrift* (1993): 772–779.

BEVERIDGE, B. (1998), 'Introduction. Same Words, Different Meanings: English Legalese in Non-English Contracts', *International Business Lawyer* 9 (1998): 387–391.

_____ (2002), 'Legal English – How it Developed and Why it is not Appropriate for International Commercial Contracts', in H. Mattila, *The Development of Legal Language* (Helsinki: Talentum Media, 2002), pp. 55–79.

BHATIA, V. K. (1987), 'Language of the Law', *Language Teaching* 4 (1987): 227–234.

Black's Law Dictionary (2000). 7th ed. (St. Paul (Minn.): West Publishing, 2000).

BLATT, A. (1998), 'Translation Technology at the European Commission: Description of a Workflow', *Terminologie et traduction* 1 (1998): 38–43.

BLOCH, C. (1998), 'Language Protection and Free Trade: The Triumph of the Homo McDonaldus', *European Public Law* (1998): 379–402.

BOCQUET, C. (1994): *Pour une méthode de traduction juridique* (Prilly: Éditions CB, 1994).

_____ (1997), *Le discours juridique et le langage du droit en Allemagne et en France. Abord de la traduction*, 7th ed., (Geneva: École de traduction et d'interprétation, Université de Genève, 1997).

BOGDAN, M. (1994), *Comparative Law* (Deventer etc: Kluwer etc., 1994).

BONSDORFF, P. E. VON (1984), 'Om det svenska lagspråket i Finland', *Tidskrift utgiven av Juridiska Föreningen i Finland* (1984): 402–423.

BRAUN-CHEN, F. (1998), 'La traduction automatique à la Commission européenne: d'hier à aujourd'hui', *Terminologie et traduction* 1 (1998): 33–37.

BROMLEY, P. M. (1971), *Family Law*, 4th ed. (London: Butterworths, 1971).

BRUNET, J.-P. (1990), *Dictionnaire de la police et de la pègre americain–français, français–américain* (Paris: Maison du dictionnaire, 1990).

BRUNOT, F. (1917), *Histoire de la langue française des origines à 1900*. Tome V: *Le français en France et hors de France au XVIIe siècle* (Paris: Armand Colin, 1917).

_____ (1927), *Histoire de la langue française des origines à nos jours*. Tome V: *Le français en France et hors de France au XVIIe siècle* (Paris: Armand Colin, 1927).

_____ (1935), *Histoire de la langue française des origines à nos jours*. Tome VIII: *Le français hors de France au XVIIIe siècle* (Paris: Armand Colin, 1935).

_____ (1937), *Histoire de la langue française des origines à nos jours*. Tome IX: *La Révolution et l'Empire* (Paris: Armand Colin, 1937).

BRUUN, H. & PALMGREN, S. (eds.) (2004), *Svenskt lagspråk i Finland* (Helsingfors: Statsrådets svenska språknämnd & Schildts, 2004).

BRÆKHUS, S. (1956), *Sprogstrid og lovsprog* (Oslo: Universitetsforlaget, 1956).

BURR, I. & GALLAS, T. (2004), 'Zur Textproduktion im Gemeinschaftsrecht', in F. Müller & I. Burr (eds.), *Rechtssprache Europas. Reflexion der Praxis von Sprache und Mehrsprachigkeit im supranationalen Recht* (Berlin: Duncker & Humblot, 2004), pp. 195–242.

MÜLLER, F. & BURR, I. (eds), *Rechtssprache Europas. Reflexion der Praxis von Sprache und Mehrsprachigkeit im supranationalen Recht* (Berlin: Duncker & Humblot, 2004).

CABANELLAS, G. & ALCALÁ-ZAMORA Y CASTILLO, L. (1992), *Diccionario enciclopédico de derecho usual* I–VIII, 16a ed. (Buenos Aires: Editorial Heliasta, 1992).

CALONIUS, M. (1908), *Praelectiones in Jurisprudentiam Civilem* (Societas Heredum J. Simelii Typographica: Helsingforsiae, MCMVIII. Originally, the lectures were given at the beginning of the 19th century).

CALVET, L.-J. (2003), 'L'usage des langues dans les relations internationales', *Questions internationales* 1 (2003): 100–105.

CARBASSE, J.-M. (1998), *Introduction historique au droit* (Paris: Presses Universitaires de France, 1998).

CASTELLÓN ALCALÁ, H. (1998), 'Análisis normativo del lenguaje administrativo', *Revista de llengua i dret* (1998): 7–46.

CATHERINE, R. & JARRY, J.-M. (1996), *Le style administratif* (Paris: Albin Michel, 1996).

CEBALLOS GÓMEZ, D. L. (2001), *"Quyen tal haze que tal pague." Sociedad y prácticas mágicas en el Nuevo Reino de Granada*. Medellín (Colombia, 2001).

CHARROW, V., CRANDALL, J. & CHARROW, R. (1982), 'Characteristics and Functions of Legal Language', in R. Kittredge & J. Lehrberger, J. (eds), *Sublanguage: Studies of Language in Restricted Semantic Domains* (Berlin: de Gruyter, 1982), pp. 175–190.

CHÉRIF-CHAMMARI, A. (1995), *Le mariage. Guide des droits des femmes* (Tunis: Alif – Les Éditions de la Méditerranée, 1995).

CHILD, B. (1992), *Drafting Legal Documents* (St. Paul, Minn.): West Publishing, 1992).

CHIOTÁKIS (Χιωτάκης), M. (2000), *Ellino–angliko lexiko nomikis kai emporikis orologías* (Ελληνο–αγγλικό λεξικό νομικής και εμπορικής ορολογίας). (Athens: Sákkulas, 2000). – See also Hiotákis.

Code du statut personnel (Tunis: Éditions C.L.E., 2000).

Codex Iuris Canonici – Codex des kanonischen Rechtes (Kevelaer: Verlag Butzon & Bercker, 1983).

COHN, E. J. (1968 et 1971), *Manual of German Law*. I: *General Introduction. Civil Law*. II: *Commercial Law etc.*, 2nd edition (London: Ocena Publications, 1968 & 1971).

COLIN, J. & MORRIS, R. (1996), *Interpreters and the Legal Process* (Winchester: Waterside Press, 1996).

CONSTANTINESCO, L.-J. (1972), *Rechtsvergleichung. Band II. Die vergleichende Methode* (Cologne etc.: Carl Heymanns Verlag, 1972).

CORNU, G. (2005), *Linguistique juridique,* 3rd ed. (Paris: Montchrestien, 2005).

CORNU, G. (ed.) (2004), *Vocabulaire juridique*, 6th ed. (Paris: Presses Universitaires de France, 2004).

CRUZ, P. DE (1995), *Comparative Law in a Changing World* (London: Cavendish Publishing Ltd., 1995).

CRYSTAL, D. (1997), *English as a Global Language* (Cambridge: Cambridge University Press, 1997).

CUTTS, M. (2001), 'Clarifying Eurolaw. How European Community directives could be written more clearly so that Citizens of Member States, including lawyers, would understand them better'. European Law Conference. Stockholm, 2001. Published by the Plain Language Commission, on-line at: http://www. plain-language-commission.com/PDFS/EUROLAW.pdf

DAHM, G. (1963), *Deutsches Recht* (Stuttgart: Kohlhammer, 1963).

DAMIÃO, R. TOLEDO & HENRIQUES, A. (2000), *Curso de português jurídico*, 8ª ed. (São Paulo: Editora Atlas, 2000).

DAVID, R. & BRIERLEY, J. (1978), *Major Legal Systems in the World Today*, 2nd ed. (London: Steven, 1978).

DAVID, R. & JAUFFRET-SPINOSI, C. (2002), *Les grands systèmes de droit contemporains*. 11th ed. (Paris: Dalloz, 2002.

DE FRACHIS, F (1984), *Dizionario giuridico inglese-italiano – English-Italian Law Dictionary* (Milan: Giuffrè editore, 1984).

DIALLO, A. (1993), 'Le français en Guinée: une situation en plein changement', in D. Robillard & M. Beniamino (eds.), *Le français dans l'espace francophone*, Tome 1 (Paris: Honoré Champion Éditeur, 1993), pp. 228–242.

Diccionario Trivium de derecho y economía (Madrid: Editorial Trivium, 1998).

Dictionnaire juridique divorce (Paris: Dalloz, 1984).

DIDIER, E. (1990), *Langues et langages du droit* (Montreal: Wilson & Lafleur, 1990).

DJERAD, N. (2000), 'Langue française et champ juridique tunisien', in I. Lamberterie & D. Breillat (eds.), *Le français langue du droit* (Paris: PUF 2000), pp. 55–63 (discussion, pp. 69–71).

DUARTE I MONTSERRAT, C. (1993), 'L'evolució del vocabulari jurídic català medieval', in C. DUARTE I MONTSERRAT (ed.), *Llengua i administració* (Barcelona: Columna, 1993), pp. 123–129.

_____ (1998), 'Lenguaje administrativo y lenguaje jurídico', in J. Bayo Delgado (ed.), *Lenguaje judicial* (Madrid: Consejo general del poder judicial, 1998).

_____ ALSINA I KEITH, A. & SININA I CUNÍ, S. (1998), *Manual de llenguatge administratiu* (Barcelona: Generalitat de Catalunya, 1998).

_____ & MARTÍNEZ, A. (1995), *El lenguaje jurídico* (Buenos Aires: A–Z editora, 1995).

DUBOUCHET, P. (1990), *Sémiotique juridique. Introduction à une science du droit* (Paris: Presses Universitaires de France, 1990).

DU CANGE (1937–1938), *Glossarium mediae et infimae Latinitatis* (conditum a Carolo du Fresne, Domino Du Cange). Nouveau tirage (Paris: Librairie des sciences et des arts, 1937–1938).

DULLION, V. (1997), 'Lorsque traduire, c'est écrire une page d'histoire: la version française du Code civil suisse dans l'unification juridique de la Confédération', in *L'histoire et les théories de la traduction* (Berne & Geneva: ASTTI & ETI 1997), pp. 371–388.

DUNBAR, R. (2001), Language Rights under International Law. *International and Comparative Law Quaterly* 50 (2001): 90–120.

DUPONCHEL, L. (1979), 'Le français en Côte d'Ivoire, au Dahomey et au Togo', in A. Valdman (ed.), *Le français hors de France* (Paris: Éditions Honoré Champion, 1979), pp. 385–417.

EBEL, F. & SCHELLING, R. (2001), 'Die Bedeutung deutschen Stadtrechts im Norden und Osten des mittelalterlichen Europa. Lübisches und Magdeburger Recht als Gegenstand von Kulturtransfer und Träger der Moderne', in R. Schweitzer &

W. Bastman-Bühner (eds.), *Die Stadt im Europäischen Nordosten* (Helsinki und Lübeck: Veröffentlichungen der Aue Stiftung, 2001), pp. 35–46.

EBKE, W. & FINKIN, M. (eds) (1996), *Introduction to German Law* (The Hague etc.: Kluwer Law International, 1996).

ECKERT, J. (ed.), *Sprache – Recht – Geschichte* (Heidelberg: C. F. Müller Juristischer Verlag, 1991).

ENGBERG, J. (1997), *Konventionen von Fachtextsorten. Kontrastive analysen zu deutschen und dänischen Gerichtsurteilen* (Tübingen: Gunter Narr Verlag, 1997).

EURRUTIA CAVERO, M. (1997), 'Aspectos lingüísticos que caracterizan el discurso jurídico francés', in P. San Ginés Aguilar & E. Ortega Arjonilla (eds), *Introducción a la traducción jurídica y jurada (francés–español)* (Granada: Editorial Comares, 1997), pp. 81–127.

EYBEN, W. E. VON (1989): 'Juridisk stil og sprogbrug', in *Juridisk grundbog* 3 (Copenhagen: Jurist- og økonomforbundets forlag, 1989), pp. 11–62.

EYBEN, B., VON & EYBEN, W. E., VON (1999). *Juridisk ordbog*. (Copenhagen: Thomson Gadjura, 1999).

FARNSWORTH, E. A. (1996), *An Introduction to the Legal System of the United States*, 3th ed. (New York: Oceana Publications, 1996).

FAVATA, A. (1999), *Dizionario dei termini giuridici* (Piacenza: Casa editrice La Tribuna, 1999).

FERRERI, S. (2000), *Il giudice italiano e il contratto internazionale* (Padova: Cedam, 2000).

_____ (2003), 'The Interpretation of Contracts from a European Perspective', in R. Schulze & M. Ebers (eds), *Informationspflichten und Vertragsschluss im Acquis communautaire* (Tübingen: Siebeck, 2003), p. 117–139.

FILIP-FRÖSCHL, J. & MADER, P. (1999), *Latein in der Rechtssprache. Ein Studienbuch und Nachschlagewerk.* 3th ed. (Vienna: Braumüller, 1999).

FIORELLI, P. (1947), 'Vocabolari giuridici fatti e da fare, *Rivista Italiana per le Scienze Giuridiche* I (1947): 293–327.

_____ (1994), 'La lingua del diritto e dell'amministrazione', in L. Serianni & P. Trifone (eds), *Storia della lingua italiana* (Torino: Giulio Einaudi Editore, 1994), pp. 553–597.

FLUCK, H.-R. (1996), *Fachsprachen,* 5th ed. (Tübingen & Basel: Francke, 1996).

FOCSANEANU, L. (1970), 'Les langues comme moyen d'expression du droit international', *Annuaire français de droit international* (1970): 256–274.

FORESTER, J. G. (1998), 'The Language of the law', *Litigation* 41 (1998): 41–62.

FOSTER, N. (1996), *German Legal System & Laws*, 2nd ed. (London: Blackstone Press Limited, 1996).

FRANCESCHELLI, R. (1991), 'Sunt nomina rerum?', *Rivista delle società* (1991): 782–790.

FRANCHIS, F. de (1984), *Dizionario giuridico inglese–italiano. English–Italian Law Dictionary* (Milan: Giuffrè Editore, 1984).

FRICEK, A.: 'Die Bedeutung der lateinischen Sprache für die Rechtswissenschaft', *Österreichische Juristenzeitung* (1981): 260–267.

GADD, E. (1935), *Kihlakunnanoikeuden pöytäkirjat. Opastus ja mallikokoelma ynnä valikoima kiertokirjeitä, kirjeitä ja kirjelmiä* (Porvoo–Helsinki: WSOY 1935).

GADIS, V. D., *Dictionnaire français–grec et grec–français des termes juridiques* (Athens: Eptalofos, *sine anno*).

GALDIA, M. (2002), 'Juridisten tekstien kääntäminen erityisesti suomalais-saksalaisen vertailun näkökulmasta', *Lakimies* (2003): 3–22.

GALL, G. L. (1983), *The Canadian Legal System* (Toronto etc.: Carswell Legal Publications, 1983).

GALLEGOS ROSILLO, J. (1997), 'Lenguaje jurídico y lengua francesa', in P. San Ginés Aguilar & E. Ortega Arjonilla (eds), *Introducción a la traducción jurídica y jurada (francés–español)* (Granada: Editorial Comares, 1997), pp. 57–80.

GALLO, G. (1999), 'Les juristes linguistes de la Cour de justice des Communautés européennes. Quelques aspects de leurs activités', in R. Sacco & L. Castellani (eds), *Les multiples langues du droit européen uniforme* (Turin: Editrice L'Harmattan Italia, 1999), pp. 71–88.

GANDASEGUI, J. (1998), 'Historia del lenguaje judicial', in J. Bayo Delgado (ed.), *Lenguaje judicial* (Madrid: Consejo general del poder judicial, 1998).

GARAPON, A. (1997), *Bien juger. Essai sur le rituel judiciaire* (Paris: Éditions Odile Jacob, 1997).

GARNER, B. (1987), *A Dictionary of Modern Legal Usage* (New York & Oxford: Oxford University Press, 1987).

_____ (2002), *The Elements of Legal Style* (Oxford: Oxford University Press, 2002).

GAUTIER, P.-Y. (1994), 'Les nombres sacrés', in *Droit civil, procédure, linguistique juridique. Écrits en hommage à Gérard Cornu* (Paris: Presses universitaires de France, 1994), pp. 163–176.

GÉMAR, J.-C. (1995), *Traduire ou l'art d'interpréter. Langue, droit et société. Eléments de jurilinguistique.* Tome 2: *Application* (Sainte-Foy: Presses de l'Université du Québec, 1995).

_____ (1994): 'Les fondements du langage du droit comme langue de spécialité. Du sens et de la forme du texte juridique', *Revue générale de droit* (1990): 717–738.

GÉMAR, J.-C. & KASIRER, N. (eds) (2005), *Jurilinguistique: entre langues et droits – Jurilinguistics: Between Law and Language* (Brussels & Montreal: Bruylant & Les Éditions Thémis 2005).

GENDREL, M. (1980), *Dictionnaire des principaux sigles utilisés dans le monde juridique* (Paris: Montchrestien 1980).

GÉNY, F. (1921), *Science et technique en droit privé positif* III (Paris: Sirey 1921).

GIANNÓPOULOS (Γιαννόπουλος), K. (1982), 'I dimotikí sta nomiká. Istorikós kai vivliografikós odigós' (Η δημοτική στα νομικά. Ιστορικός και βιβλιογραφικός οδηγός), in *I dimotikí sti nomikí práxi* (Η δημοτική στη νομική πράξη). (Athens: Tekmíria syntagmatikoú dikaíou, tomos 2, 1982), pp. 31–58.

GODDARD, C. (2004), *English as an International Language of Legal Communication: Inter-cultural Aspects* (Riga: Riga Graduate School of Law, RGSL Working Papers no. 20, 2004).

_____ (2006), *Legal English: Making it Simple. Language Tools for Legal Writing* (to appear).

GOUTAL, J. L. (1976), 'Characteristics of Judicial Style in France, Britain and the U.S.A.', *The American Journal of Comparative Law* 24 (1976): 43–72.

Grande dizionario della lingua italiana (Torino: Unione Tipografico – Editrice Torinese 1961).

GRIDEL, J.-P. (1979), *Le signe et le droit. Les bornes. Les uniformes. La signalisation routière et autres* (Paris: Librairie Générale de Droit et de Jurisprudence, 1979).

GRODZISKI, S. (1971), *Historia ustroju społeczno-politycznego Galicji 1772–1848* (Wrocław *etc.*: Wydawnictwo Polskiej Akademii Nauk, 1971).

GROFFIER, E. & REED, D. (1990), *La lexicographie juridique. Principes et méthodes* (Cowansville: Les Éditions Yvon Blais 1990).

GROSSFELD, B. (1996), *Kernfragen der Rechtsvergleichung* (Tübingen: J.C.B. Mohr 1996).

Guide de l'étudiant 1999–2000. Faculté de droit et des sciences politiques de Tunis.

Guide pratique commun pour la rédaction des textes législatifs communautaires (2003). (Luxembourg: Office des publications officielles des Communautés européennes, 2003).

GUILLOREL, H. & KOUBI, G. (eds) (1999), *Langues et droits. Langues du droit, droit des langues* (Bruxelles: Bruylant, 1999).

GUPTA, R. S. & KAPOOR, K. (eds) (1991), *English in India. Issues and Problems* (Delhi: Academic Foundation, 1991).

GUSTAFSSON, M. (1975), *Some Syntactic Properties of English Law Language* (Turku: Dept. of English No 4, 1975).

GUTMAN, D. (1999): 'L'objectif de simplification du langage législatif', in N. Molfessis (ed.), *Les mots de la loi* (Paris: Economica, 1999), pp. 73–88.

HAAS, R. (1991): *Französische Sprachgesetzgebung und europäische Integration* (Berlin: Duncker & Humblot, 1991).

HALLBERG, P. (2001), 'Oikeuden aate ja todellisuus', in V. Harju (ed.), *Oikeuden symbolimaailmasta Suomessa* (Helsinki: Eduskunnan kirjasto ja Valtion taidemuseo, 2001), pp. 13–17.

HALVORSEN, E. (1983): 'Norsk språk', in B. Molde og A. Karker (eds), *Språkene i Norden* (Olso: Cappelen etc., Nordisk språksekretariat, 1983), pp. 21–42.

HAŁAS, B. (1995), *Terminologia języka prawnego* (Zielona Góra: Wydawnictwo Wyższej Skoły Pedagogicznej 1995).

HAMZAH, A. (1985), *Istilah dan peribahasa hukum bahasa Latin* (Bandung: Penerbit Alumni, 1985).

HARJU, V. (2000), 'Oikeuden kuvalliset kasvot', in V. Harju (ed.), *Oikeuden kuva* (Helsinki: Eduskunnan kirjaston tutkimuksia ja selvityksiä, 4/2000).

HARJU, V. (2001a): 'Oikeuden kuvat oikeudenmukaisuuden viestittäjinä', in V. Harju (ed.), *Oikeuden symbolimaailmasta Suomessa* (Helsinki: Eduskunnan kirjasto ja Valtion taidemuseo, 2001), pp. 19–30.

_____ (2001b): 'Suomen oikeuden symboleista', in V. Harju (ed.), *Oikeuden symbolimaailmasta Suomessa* (Helsinki: Eduskunnan kirjasto ja Valtion taidemuseo, 2001), pp. 31–45.

HARJU, V. (ed.) (2000), *Oikeuden kuva* (Helsinki: Eduskunnan kirjaston tutkimuksia ja selvityksiä 4, 2000).

HARTONO, S. (1991), *Dari hukum antar golongan ke hukum antar adapt* (Bandung: Penerbit Pt. Citra Aditya Bakti, 1991).

HATTENHAUER, H. (1987), *Zur Geschichte der deutschen Rechts- und Gesetzessprache* (Hambourg: Joachim Jungius-Gesellschaft der Wissenschaften, 1987).

HARJU, V. (2000): 'Zur Zukunft des Deutschen als Sprache der Rechtswissenschaft', *Juristenzeitung* (2000): 545–551.

HAUSEN, R. (ed.) (1890), *Registrum Ecclesiae Aboensis eller Åbo Domkyrkans Svartbok* (Helsingfors: J. Simelii Arfvingars Boktryckeri 1890, reed. 1996).

_____ (ed.) (1910–1933), *Finlands medeltidsurkunder I–VII. Samlade och i tryck utgifna af Finlands Statsarkiv genom R. Hausen* (Helsingfors: Kejserliga Senatens Tryckeri/Statsrådets Tryckeri, 1910–1933).

HÉBERT, M. (1997): 'Latin et vernaculaire: quelles langues écrit-on en Provence à la fin du Moyen Âge ?', in *Provence historique* 1997 (Fascicule 188), p. 281–299.

HEIKKINEN, V., HIIDENMAA, P. & TIILILÄ, U. (2000), *Teksti työnä, virka kielenä* (Helsinki: Gaudeamus, 2000).

HELIN, M. (1983), 'On the Semantics of the Interpretative Sentences in Legal Dogmatics', in *Essays in Legal Theory in Honor of Kaarle Makkonen. Oikeustiede – Jurisprudentia* (1983), pp. 65–88.

_____ (1999): 'Kieli oikeustodellisuuden rakentajana', in A. Jyränki (ed.), *Oikeuden kielet* (Turku: Turun yliopiston oikeustieteellisen tiedekunnan julkaisuja, B: 7, 1999), pp. 43–55.

HENNEMANN, K. (1999), 'Die Gerichtssprache ist Deutsch oder der Rotlauf der Justiz', *Neue Zeitschrift für Arbeitsrecht* (1999): 413.

HERDE, P. & JACOBS, H. (eds) (1999), *Papsturkunde und europäisches Urkundenwesen* (Cologne etc.: Böhlau Verlag, 1999).

HIESTAND, R. (1999), 'Die Leistungsfähigkeit der päpstlichen Kanzlei im 12. Jahrhundert mit einem Blick auf den lateinischen Osten', in P. Herde & H. Jacobs (eds), *Papsturkunde und europäisches Urkundenwesen* (Cologne etc.: Böhlau Verlag 1999).

HILL, C. & KING, C. (2005), 'How Do German Contracts Do As Much with Fewer Words?', in B. Pozzo (ed.), *Ordinary Language and Legal Language* (Milan 2005: Giuffrè Editore 2005), pp. 169–218.

HILTUNEN, R. (1990), *Chapters on Legal English. Aspects Past and Present of the Language of the Law* (Helsinki: Suomalaisen tiedeakatemian toimituksia B 251, 1990).

HILTUNEN, R.(2001): 'Some Syntactic Properties of English Law Language: Twenty-five Years after Gustafsson (1975)', in R. Hiltunen, K. Battarbee, M. Peikola & S.-K. Tanskanen (eds), *English in Zigs and Zags: A Festschrift for Marita Gustafsson* (Turku: University of Turku 2001, Anglicana Turkuensia No 23), pp. 53–66.

HIOTÁKIS (Χιωτάκης), M., *Dictionnaire français–grec/grec–français des termes juridiques, économiques, commerciaux et E.U.* (Athens: Sakkoulas, *sine anno*). – See also Chiotákis.

HOLM, G. (1970), *Epoker och prosastilar* (Lund: Studentlitteratur 1970).

HORN, N., KÖTZ, H. & LESER, H. (1982), *German Private and Commercial Law. An Introduction* (Oxford: Clarendon Press, 1982).

HUSA, J. (1998), *Johdatus oikeusvertailuun* (Helsinki: Kauppakaari 1998).

_____ (2001), 'Hallinnon ja oikeuden erottaminen Ranskassa. Conseil d'Etat'n ja KHO:n vertailua', in *Juhlakirja Esko Riepula* (2001), pp. 234–270.

IBÁN, I. (1995): *Introducción al derecho español* (Baden-Baden: Nomos 1995).

IISA, K. & PIEHL, A. (1992), *Virkakielestä kaikkien kieleen* (Helsinki: VAPK-kustannus, 1992).

_____ OITTINEN, H. & PIEHL, A. (2000), *Kielenhuollon käsikirja* (Helsinki: Yrityskirjat 2000).

IURTAEVA (ЮРТАЕВА), J. A. (2000): 'Zakonodatel'naia tekhnika i osnovy iazykovogo oformleniia zakonodatel'nykh aktov v Rossiiskoi imperii' (Законодательная техника и основы языкового оформления законодательных актов в Российской империи), *Zhurnal rossiiskogo prava* 8 (2000): 145–154.

JACKSON, B. (1997), *Semiotics and Legal Theory* (Liverpool: Deborah Charles 1997, orig. 1985)

JAYME, E. (1999a), 'Rapport général: Langue et droit', in E. Jayme (ed.), *Langue et droit. XVe Congrès International de droit comparé* (Brussels: Bruylant 1999), pp. 11–34.

JAYME, E. (ed.) (1999b), *Langue et droit. XVe Congrès International de droit comparé, Bristol 1998* (Bruxelles: Bruylant, 1999).

JENSEN, L. B. (1998): *Kancellistil eller Anders And-sprog?* 2. udg. (Roskilde: Roskilde Universitetsforlag, 1998).

JHERING, R. VON (1904), *Scherz und Ernst in der Jurisprudenz.* 9th ed. (Leipzig: Breit-kopf & Härtel 1904).

JOUTSEN, M. (1995), *Lakikielen sanakirja suomi–englanti* (Porvoo etc.: WSOY, 1995).

_____ (2000), *Lakikielen sanakirja englanti–suomi* (Helsinki: WSOY 2000).

JYRÄNKI, A. (ed.), *Oikeuden kielet* (Turku: Turun yliopiston oikeustieteellisen tiedekunnan julkaisuja B: 7, 1999).

JÄGERSKIÖLD, S. (1963), *Studier rörande receptionen av främmande rätt i Sverige under den yngre landslagens tid* (Stockholm &c.: Almqvist & Wiksell, 1963).

KAJANTO, I. (1991), Latin in Medieval Finland, *Ponto-Baltica* 4 (1991).

KALLIOINEN,0 M. (2001), 'Der deutsche Einfluss im mittelalterlichen Finnland', in R. Schweitzer & W. Bastman-Bühner (eds.), *Die Stadt im Europäischen Nordosten* (Helsinki und Lübeck: Veröffentlichungen der Aue Stiftung, 2001), pp. 75–81.

KALLIOKUUSI, V. (1999), 'Määrittelyn monet kasvot', in *Toimikunnista termitalkoihin*. *25 vuotta sanastotyön asiantuntemusta* (Helsinki: Tekniikan Sanastokeskus, 1999), pp. 43–57.

KANGAS, U. (ed.) (1998), *Oikeustiede Suomessa 1900–2000* (Helsinki: WSOY Lakitieto, 1998).

KANTOLA, M. (1987), 'Zur Sprache mittelniederdeutscher Urkunden aus Finnland', in K. E. Schöndorf & K.-E. Westergaard (eds), *Niederdeutsch in Skandinavien*. *Beihefte zur Zeitschrift für deutsche Philologie* 4 (1987), pp. 67–74.

KARKER, A. (1983): 'Det danske sprog', in Molde, B. og Karker, A. (eds), *Språkene i Norden* (Olso: Cappelen etc., Nordisk språksekretariat, 1983), pp. 7–20.

KARLSSON, F. (1994), *Yleinen kielitiede* (Helsinki: Yliopistopaino, 1994).

_____ (1999): 'Maailman kielitilanne, englannin kieli ja USA:n hegemonia', in A. Jyränki (ed.), *Oikeuden kielet* (Turku: Turun yliopiston oikeustieteellisen tiedekunnan julkaisuja B: 7, 1999), pp. 59–73.

KARVONEN, P. (1997), *Suomi eurooppalaisessa kieliyhteisössä* (Helsinki: Opetusministeriö, 1997).

KASER, M. (1989), *Römisches Privatrecht*. 15th ed. (Munich: Beck, 1989).

KAUFMANN, E. (1984), *Deutsches Recht. Die Grundlagen* (Berlin: Erich Schmidt Verlag, 1984).

KAVASSA, I. & PRINCE, M. (eds), *World Dictionary of Legal Abbreviations* (USA: Hein & Co., 1991).

KELLY, H. A. (1988), 'Lawyers' Latin: Loquenda ut vulgus?', *Journal of Legal Education* (1988): 195–207.

KEMPPINEN, K. (1999), 'Oikeudenkäyntirituaalit', in *Encyclopædia Iuridica Fennica* VII (1999), p. 658–661.

KERAMEUS, K. D. & KOZYRIS, P. J. (1988), *Introduction to Greek Law* (Athens: Sakkoulas, 1988).

KEVELSON, R. (ed.) (1987–1989), *Law and Semiotics* I–III (New York: Plenum Press, 1987–1989).

KHARITONOV (ХАРИТОНОВ), E. (1999), *Osnovy rimskogo chastnogo prava* (Основы римского частного права). (Rostov-na-Donu: Feniks, 1999).

KIRCHNER, H. (1993), *Abkürzungsverzeichnis der Rechtssprache*. 4th ed. (Berlin & New York: Walter de Gruyter, 1993).

KJÆR, A. L. (1997), 'Thi kendes for ret – om lemmata og eksemplar i juridisk fagleksikografi', *Hermes* 18 (1997): 157–175.

KLAMI, H. T. (1999a), 'Roomalainen oikeustiede', in *Encyclopædia Iuridica Fennica* VII (1999), p. 1014–1019.

_____ (1999b), 'Roomalainen yksityisoikeus', in *Encyclopædia Iuridica Fennica* VII (1999), p. 1025–1036.

KLEMPERER, V. (1969), *LTI (Lingua Tertii Imperii). Die unbewältigte Sprache*. 3th ed. (Deutscher Taschenbuch Verlag, 1969).

KNÜTEL, R. (1994), 'Rechtseinheit in Europa und römisches Recht', *Zeitschrift für Europäisches Privatrecht* (1994): 244–276.

Kofanov, L. L. (Кофанов, Л. Л.) (ed.) (2001–), *Digesta Iustiniani* I– / Digesty Iustiniana I– (Дигесты Юстиниана I–). Centrum iuris romani investigandi – Tsentr izucheniia rimskogo prava (Центр изучения римского права) (Moscow: Statut & Konsul'tant Plius / Москва: Статут & Консультант Плюс , 2001–).

Kramer, E. (1995), 'Lateinische Parömien zur Methode der Rechtsanwendung', in *Steuerrecht. Ausgewählte Probleme am Ende des 20. Jahrhunderts. Festschrift zum 65. Geburtstag von Ernst Höhn* (Bern etc.: Verlag Paul Haupt, 1995), pp. 141–158.

Krefeld, T. (1985), *Das französische Gerichtsurteil in linguistischer Sicht* (Frankfurt am Main: Verlag Peter Lang, 1985).

Kurkela, M. (1999), 'Kielen merkityksestä sovellettavan lain valintaan', in A. Jyränki (ed.), *Oikeuden kielet* (Turku: Turun yliopiston oikeustieteellisen tiedekunnan julkaisuja B: 7, 1999), pp. 167–180.

Kurzon, D. (1986), *It is hereby performed ... Explorations in Legal Speech Acts* (Amsterdam/Philadephia: John Benjamins Publishing Company, 1986).

_____ (1987), 'Latin for Lawyers: Degrees of Textual Integration, *Applied Linguistics* (1987): 233–240.

_____ (1997), 'Legal Language: Varieties, Genres, Registers, discourses', *International Journal of Applied Linguistics* 7 (1997): 119–139.

Künssberg, E. von (1926), *Rechtssprachgeographie* (Heidelberg: Winters Universitätsbuchhandlung, 1926).

Laakso, P. (1987), 'Kaakkois-Aasian kirjoitusjärjestelmät', in J. Seppänen (ed.), *Symboliikka 87: Kielet ja kirjoitusjärjestelmät* (Espoo: Teknillinen korkeakoulu, 1987).

Ladjili-Mouchette, J. (1990), *Histoire juridique de la Méditerranée. Droit romain, droit musulman* (Tunis: Publications scientifiques tunisiennes. Série histoire du droit N° 1, 1990).

Lafage, S. (1996), 'La Côte-d'Ivoire: une appropriation nationale du français', in D. Robillard & M. Beniamino (eds), *Le français dans l'espace francophone,* Tome 2 (Paris: Honoré Champion Éditeur, 1996), pp. 587–602.

Lainlaatijan opas. Helsinki: Oikeusministeriö & Edita 1996.

Lainlaatijan EU-opas. Helsinki: Oikeusministeriö & Edita 1997.

Lamberterie, I. & Breillat, D. (eds), *Le français langue du droit* (Paris: PUF, 2000).

Landqvist, H. (2000a), 'Finländska fingeravtryck i nutida författningar – finns det några sådana?', *Språkråd* 2 (2000): 1–4.

_____ (2000b), *Författningssvenska. Strukturer i nutida svensk lagtext i Sverige och Finland* (Gothenburg: Acta Unversitatis Gothoburgensis, 2000).

_____ (2001): 'Språklagstiftning ur ett språkvetenskapligt perspektiv', *Tidskrift utgiven af Juridiska Föreningen i Finland* 1 (2001): 63–89.

Laroussi, F. (1993), 'Le français en Tunisie aujourd'hui', in D. Robillard & M. Beniamino (eds), *Le français dans l'espace francophone*, Tome 1 et 2 (Paris: Honoré Champion Éditeur, 1993), pp. 705–721.

LASHÖFER, J. (1992), *Zum Stilwandel in richterlichen Entscheidungen. Über stilistische Veränderungen in englischen, französischen und deutschen zivilrechtlichen Urteilen und in Entscheidungen des Gerichtshofs der Europäischen Gemeinschaften* (Münster & New York: Waxmann, 1992).

LAURÉN, C. (1993), *Fackspråk. Form, innehåll, funktion* (Lund: Studentlitteratur, 1993).

Le français dans les institutions européennes (Premier ministre & al. République française, 1998).

LEHTO, L. (1998a), 'Lakienglanti', in *Encyclopædia Iuridica Fennica* VI (1998), pp. 528–535.

_____ (1998b), 'Lakikielen kääntäminen', in *Encyclopædia Iuridica Fennica* VI (1998), pp. 535–542.

LETTO-VANAMO, P. (1989), *Suomalaisen asianajajalaitoksen synty ja varhaiskehitys* (Helsinki: Suomalainen Lakimiesyhdistys, 1989).

_____ (1995), *Oikeuden Eurooppa. Luentoja oikeushistoriasta* (Helsinki: Helsingin yliopisto, Oikeushistorian julkaisuja 1, 1995).

_____ (1998), *Eurooppa oikeusyhteisönä* (Helsinki: Helsingin yliopiston Kansainvälisen talousoikeuden instituutin julkaisuja 36, 1998).

_____ (1999): 'Oikeus ja kieli: nykyajan käsitteet – menneisyyden oikeus', in A. Jyränki (ed.), *Oikeuden kielet* (Turku: Turun yliopiston oikeustieteellisen tiedekunnan julkaisuja B: 7, 1999), pp. 25–34.

LEVENEUR, L. (1999), 'Le choix des mots en droit des personnes et de la famille', in N. Molfessis (ed.), *Les mots de la loi* (Paris: Economica, 1999), pp. 11–29.

LIEBS, D. (1981), 'Rhytmische Rechtssätze', *Juristenzeitung* (1981): 160–164.

LIIRI, K. (1999), 'EY:n tuottamien oikeudellisten tekstien kääntämisestä', in A. Jyränki (ed.), *Oikeuden kielet* (Turku: Turun yliopiston oikeustieteellisen tiedekunnan julkaisuja B: 7, 1999), pp. 145–153.

LINDBERG, B. (1997), *Latina ja Eurooppa* (Jyväskylä: Atena, 1997).

LINKOMIES. E. (1974), *Latinan kielioppi* (1st ed. 1933). 20th ed. (Jyväskylä: Gummerus, 1974).

LIPSONEN, L. (1990), *Vankilaslangin sanakirja* (Helsinki: VAPK-kustannus, 1990).

LOHAUS, M. (2000), *Recht und Sprache in Österreich und Deutschland. Gemeinsamkeiten und Verschiedenheiten als Folge geschichtlicher Entwicklungen. Untersuchung zur juristischen Fachterminologie in Österreich und Deutschland* (Gießen: Köhler, 2000).

LOPES SABINO, A. (1999): 'Les langues dans l'Union européenne. Enjeux, pratiques et perspectives', *Revue trimestrielle de droit européen* 2/1999, pp. 159–169.

LÖFSTEDT, L. (1989), 'Une traduction médiévale française du Décret de Gratian', *Vox Romanica* 48 (1989): 108–141.

LÖFSTEDT, L. (ed.) (1992–2001), *Gratiani Decretum* I–V. Édition critique par Leena Löfstedt (Helsinki: Societas Scientiarum Fennica, 1992–2001).

MANCINI, G. & KEELING, D. (1995), 'Language, Culture and Politics in the Life of the European Court of Justice', *Columbia Journal of European Law* (1995): 397–413.

MANZANO, F. (1995), 'La Francophonie dans le paysage linguistique du Maghreb: contacts, ruptures et problématique de l'identité', in *Le français au Maghreb* (Aix-en-Provence: Publications de l'Université de Provence, 1995), pp. 173–186.

MARBURGER, P. (1984), 'Technische Begriffe und Rechtsbegriffe', in B. Rüthers & K. Stern (eds), *Freiheit und Verantwortung im Verfassungsstaat* (Munich: C. H. Beck 1984), pp. 275–293.

MARKESINIS, B. S., LORENZ, W. & DANNEMANN, G. (1997), *The German Law of Obligations*. I: *The Law of Contracts and Restitution. A Comparative Introduction* (Oxford: Clarendon Press, 1997).

MARQUÉS DE TAMARÓN (1995), 'El papel internacional del español', in Marqués de Tamarón (ed.), *El peso de la lengua española en el mundo* (Valladolid: Fundación Duques de Soria & INCIPE, 1995).

MARQUÉS DE TAMARÓN (ed.) (1995), *El peso de la lengua española en el mundo* (Valladolid: Fundación Duques de Soria & INCIPE, 1995).

MARQUÉZ, M. (2001), 'Paremie łacińskie w wystąpieniach Rzecznika Praw Obywatelskich', in W. Wołodkiewicz & J. Krzynówek (eds), *Łacińskie paremie w europejskiej kulturze prawnej i orzecznictwie sądów polskich* (Warsaw: Liber, 2001), pp. 227–244.

MARTÍN, J., RUIZ, R., SANTAELLA, J. & ESCÁNEZ, J. (1996), *Los lenguajes especiales. Lenguaje jurídico-administrativo. Lenguaje científico-técnico. Lenguaje humanístico. Lenguaje periodístico y publicitario. Lenguaje literario* (Granada: Editorial Comares, 1996).

MARTÍNES BARGUEÑO, M. (1992), 'Pasado y presente del lenguaje administrativo castellano', *Revista de llengua i dret* (1992): 7–23.

MARTÍNEZ, J. (1998), 'La buena salud de la traducción automática al español', *Terminologie et traduction* 1 (1998): 296–299.

MARTINY, D. (1998), 'Babylon in Brüssel. Das Recht und die europäische Sprachenvielfalt', *Zeitschrift für europäisches Privatrecht* (1998): 227–252.

MATTEI, U. (1994), 'Why the Wind Changed: Intellectual Leadership in Western Law', *The American Journal of Comparative Law* 42 (1994): 195–218.

MATTHÍAS (Ματθίας), S. (1983), 'Metaglóttisi ton kodíkon. O antílogos' (Μεταγλώττιση των κωδίκων. Ο αντίλογος), *Ellinikí Dikaiosýni* (Ελληνική Δικαιοσύνη) 24 (1983): 165–168.

MATTILA, H.(1979), *Les successions agricoles et la structure de la société. Une étude en droit comparé* (Helsinki: Juridica, 1979).

—— (2000), 'Latinet i den finländska juridiska litteraturen', *Tidskrift utgiven av Juridiska Föreningen i Finland* (2000): 269–322.

—— (2002a), 'De aequalitate Latinitatis jurisperitorum. Le latin juridique dans les grandes familles de droit contemporaines à la lumière des dictionnaires spécialisés', *Revue internationale de droit comparé* 3 (2002): 717–758.

—— (2002b): 'L'héritage latin dans les langages européens du droit', in M. Koskela & al. (eds), *Porta scientiae I. Lingua specialis* (ediderunt) (Vaasa: Proceedings of the University of Vaasa n:o 95, 2002), pp. 50–66.

MATTILA, H. (2002c), 'Les matériaux non finnois dans l'interprétation juridique en Finlande', in R. Sacco (ed.), *L'interprétation des textes juridiques rédigés dans plus d'une langue* (Turin: L'Harmattan Italia 2002), pp. 151–182.

_____ (2005a), 'The History of Legal Language', in *The Elsevier Encyclopedia of Language and Linguistics*, 2005.

_____ (2005b), 'Jurilinguistique et latin juridique', in J.-C. Gémar & N. Kasirer (eds), *Jurilinguistique: entre langues et droits – Jurilinguistics: Between Law and Language* (Brussels & Montreal: Bruylant & Les Éditions Thémis, 2005), pp. 71–89.

_____ (2006), 'Comparative Jurilinguistics: a Discipline *in statu nascendi*', in B. Pozzo (ed.), *The Language Policies of EU Institutions After the Enlargement* (Milan: Giuffrè, in press).

_____ (ed.) (2002), *The Development of Legal Language* (Helsinki: Talentum Media, 2002).

MATZNER, E. (ed.), *Droit et langues étrangères: concepts, problèmes d'application, perspectives* (Perpignan: Presses Universitaires de Perpignan, 2000).

MAURER, B. (1993), 'Le français en République de Djibouti: une importance croissante, une fonction identitaire marquée', in D. Robillard & M. Beniamino (eds), *Le français dans l'espace francophone*, Tome 1 (Paris: Honoré Champion Éditeur, 1993), pp. 191–204.

MAYER, F. (2001), 'Die deutsche Rechtssprache in Südtirol: Stand und Perspectiven', in F. Mayer (ed.), *Language for Special Purposes: Perspectives for the New Millennium*, Vol. 2 (Tübingen: Gunter Narr Verlag, 2001), pp. 667–678.

MAYER, F. (ed.) (1998), *Terminologisches Wörterbuch zur Südtiroler Rechts-und Verwaltungssprache – Dizionario terminologico del linguaggio giuridico-amministrativo in Alto Adige* (Bozen/Bolzano: Europäische Akademie/Accademia Europea, 1998).

MAYORAL, R. (1999), 'Las fidelidades del traductor jurado: una batalla indecisa', in M. Feria García (ed.), *Traducir para la Justicia* (Granada: Editorial Comares, 1999), pp. 17–57.

MAYRAND, A. (1994), *Dictionnaire de maximes et locutions latines utilisées en droit*, 3ᵗʰ ed. (Cowansville: Les éditionsYvon Blais, 1994).

MELLINKOFF, D. (1963), *The Language of the Law* (Boston & Toronto: Little, Brown and Co., 1963).

MELLOULI, S. (2000), *Droit civil. Introduction à l'étude du droit* (Tunis: Publications de l'Imprimerie Officielle de la République Tunisienne, 2000).

MEYER, R. (1994), *Bona fides und lex mercatoria in der europäischen Rechtstradition* (Göttingen: Wallstein Verlag, 1994).

MICHALSEN, D. (1998), 'Juridisk sakprosa og rettsutviklingen i samfunnet', in E. Johnsen & T. Eriksen (eds), *Norsk litteraturhistorie. Sakprosa fra 1750 til 1995*. Bind I (Oslo: Universitetsforlaget, 1998), pp. 255–265.

MIKKOLA, T. (1999), *Oikeudellisen tiedon yhtenevyys ja sen esteet* (Helsinki: Suomalaisen Lakimiesyhdistyksen julkaisuja A: 233, 1999).

MIMIN P. (1970), *Le style des jugement*. 4ᵗʰ ed. (Paris: Librairies techniques, 1970).

MINCKE, W. (1987), 'Vertalen binnen een tweetalig rechtssysteem (Finland)', in J. P. Balkema & G. R. de Groot (eds), *Recht en vertalen* (Deventer: Kluwer, 1987), pp. 103–111.

MODÉER, K. Å. (2000), 'Det heliga rummet. Domstolsbyggnadernas roll i det civila samhället', *Lakimies* (2000): 1060–1072.

MOLFESSIS, N. (1999), 'Le renvoi d'un texte à un autre', in N. Molfessis (ed.), *Les mots de la loi* (Paris: Economica, 1999).

MOLFESSIS, N. (ed.) (1999), *Les mots de la loi* (Paris: Economica, 1999).

MONIR, M. (1988), *Principles and Digest of the Law of Evidence* I–II. 6th ed. by Deoki Nandan Agarwala (Allahabad: The University Book Agency, 1988).

MORENO FERNÁNDEZ, F. (1995), 'La enseñanza del español como lengua extranjera', in Marqués de Tamarón (ed.), *El peso de la lengua española en el mundo* (Valladolid: Fundación Duques de Soria & INCIPE, 1995).

MORI, E. (1999), *Dizionario dei termini giuridici e dei brocardi latini* (Piacenza: Casa editrice La Tribuna 1999).

MOROZOVA (МОРОЗОВА), L. A. (2000), 'Iuridicheskaia tekhnika. Obzor materialov nauchno-metodicheskogo seminara' (Юридическая техника. Обзор материалов научно-методического семинара), *Gosudarstvo i pravo* 11 (2000): 108–120.

MOUSSIROU-MOUYAMA, A. & DE SAMIE, T. (1996), 'La situation sociolinguistique du Gabon', in D. Robillard & M. Beniamino (eds), *Le français dans l'espace francophone*, Tome 2 (Paris: Honoré Champion Éditeur, 1996), pp. 603–613.

MULLERAT, R. (1997), 'Communication in Cross-cultural Legal Agreements', in *Language and Law – the Clash of Legal Cultures in Central and Eastern Europe*. International Bar Association. 7th Eastern European Regional Conference. Bratislava, 7–10 September 1997 (unpublished).

MYKLEBUST, H. (1996), *Nynorsk som lovspråk. Historisk og språgleg utvikling* (Bergen: Hovudfagsoppgåve ved Nordisk institutt. Universitetet i Bergen, 1996).

MÜLLER, F. (ed.) (1989), *Untersuchungen zur Rechtslinguistik* (Berlin: Duncker & Humblot, 1989).

MÜLLER, F. & BURR, I. (eds.) (2004), *Rechtssprache Europas. Reflexion der Praxis von Sprache und Mehrsprachigkeit im supranationalen Recht* (Berlin: Duncker & Humblot, 2004).

MÜLLER-DIETZ, H. (1997), 'Rechtssprache. Die Macht der Sprache, die Sprache der Macht', in S. Fritsch-Oppermann (ed.), *Loccumer Protokolle* 15 (1997), pp. 19–44.

MÖRSDORF, K. (1967), *Die Rechtssprache des Codex Juris Canonici* (Paderborn: Verlag Ferdinand Schöningh, 1967).

NADELMAN, K. & VAN MEHREN, A. (1966–67), 'Equivalences in Treaties in the Conflicts Field', *The American Journal of Comparative Law* (1966–67): 195–203.

NASUTION, B. J. & WARJIYATI, S. (1998), *Bahasa Indonesia Hukum* (Bandung: Benerbit Pt. Citra Aditya Bakti, 1998).

NIEMIVUO, M. (1998), *Kansallinen lainvalmistelu* (Helsinki: Kauppakaari, 1998).

NORDMAN, M. (1984), 'Om juridisk svenska', *Svensk Juristtidning* (1984): 955–968.

Nuovo dizionario giuridico. 4ᵗʰ ed. (Naples: Esselibri Simone, 2001).

NUSSBAUMER, M. (1997), *Sprache und Recht* (Heidelberg: Groos 1997).

_____ (2002): 'Grenzgänger – Gesetzestexte zwischen Recht und Politik', in U. Haß-Zumkehr (ed.), *Sprache und Recht* (Berlin & New York: de Gruyter, 2002), pp. 181–209.

NYKÄNEN, O. (1999), 'TSK – 25 vuotta sanastotyön asiantuntemusta', in *Toimikunnista termitalkoisiin* (Helsinki: Tekniikan Sanastokeskus, 1999).

ODELMAN, E. (1997), 'Latinet i Norden. Grannar emellan', in *Årsbok för Riksarkivet och Landsarkiven* (1997).

OKSAAR, E. (1989), 'Alltagssprache. Fachsprachen. Rechtssprache', *Zeitschrift für Gesetzgebung* (1989): 210–237.

Ordbok över svenska språket (1945). Utgiven af Svenska Akademien. Band VII (Lund: Lindstedts Univ.-Bokhandel, 1945).

ORLOV, V. (1996), *Yritystoiminta Venäjällä* (Helsinki: Suomen Lakimiesliiton Kustannus, 1996).

_____ (2001), *Venäjän sopimusoikeus* (Helsinki: Kauppakaari, 2001).

OTERO, J. (1995): 'Una nueva mirada al índice de importancia internacional de las lenguas', in Marqués de Tamarón (ed.), *El peso de la lengua española en el mundo* (Valladolid: Fundación Duques de Soria & INCIPE, 1995).

PAASIVIRTA, E. (1997), 'The European Union: from an Aggregate of States to a Legal Person', in *International Legal Personality*. The Hofstra Law & Policy Symposium. Vol. 2 (Hofstra University. School of Law, 1997), pp. 37–59.

PAJULA, P. (1960), *Suomalaisen oikeuskielen historia pääpiirteittäin* (Porvoo & Helsinki: WSOY, 1960).

PALMGREN, S. (1998), Review on: H. Landqvist, Författningssvenska, *Tidskrift utgiven av Juridiska Föreningen i Finland* (2000): 678–680.

_____ (2000b), 'Utvecklingsmöjligheterna för det nordiska lagstiftningssamarbetet', in *Utvecklingen av det nordiska lagstiftningssamarbetet under inverkan av EU och EES. TemaNord* (2000: 614), pp. 80–85.

PAPACHRÍSTOS (Παπαχρίστος), A. K. (1982), 'Dimotikí glóssa kai nomikí sképsi' (Δημοτική γλώσσα και νομική σκέψη), in *I dimotikí sti nomikí práxi* (Η δημοτική στη νομική πράξη). (Athens: Tekmíria syntagmatikoú dikaíou, tomos 2, 1982), pp. 195–198.

PERROT, R. (1998), *Institutions judiciaires*. 8ᵗʰ ed. (Paris: Montchrestien, 1998).

PESCATORE, P. (2004), 'Zu Rechtssprache und Rechtsstil im europäischen Recht', in F. Müller & I. Burr (eds), *Rechtssprache Europas. Reflexion der Praxis von Sprache und Mehrsprachigkeit im supranationalen Recht* (Berlin: Duncker & Humblot 2004), pp. 243–259.

PETER, H. (1997), *Texte zum römischen Obligationenrecht mit Verweisen auf das schweizerische Recht. Textes de droit romain des obligations avec références au droit suisse* (Zurich: Schulthess Polygraphischer Verlag, 1997).

PETERSEN, TH. & SOUKKA, P. (1965), *Englannin oikeuslaitos* (Helsinki. Suomen Lakimiesliiton Kustannus, 1965).

PEYRÓ, F. (1999), 'Le "qui-dit-quoi" de l'acquis communautaire', *Terminologie et traduction* 2 (1999): 52–69.

PHILLIPS, A. (2003), *Lawyers' Language* (London & New York: Routledge, 2003).

PICOCHE, J. & MARCHELLO-NIZIA, C. (1994), *Histoire de la langue française*. 3th ed. (Paris: Nathan, 1994).

PIEŃKOS, J. (1993), *Przekład i tłumacz we współczesnym świecie* (Warsaw: Wydawnictwo Naukowe PWN 1993).

_____ (1999), *Podstawy juryslingwistyki. Język w prawie – Prawo w języku* (Warsaw: Muza 1999).

PIGOLKIN (Пиголкин), A. S. (ed.) (1990), *Iazyk zakona* (Язык закона) (Moscow: Iuridicheskaia literatura, 1990).

PIHLAJAMÄKI, H. (1997), 'Den rättsliga formalismen och kritiken av den', *Retfærd* 78 (1997): 51–67.

_____ (2002), 'Eurooppa meren takana: oikeus Espanjan amerikkalaisissa siirtomaissa', *Historiallinen aikakauskirja* 1 (2002).

_____ (2002), 'Lo europeo en derecho: ius politiae y el derecho indiano', in *Derecho y administración pública en las Indias Hispánicas. Actas del XII Congreso Internacional de Historia del Derecho Indiano* (1998), pp. 1363–1375.

PITKÄRANTA, R. & VILKKONEN, E. (1986), 'Lakimieslatinaa', *Lakimies* (1986): 183–188.

POLENZ, P. VON (1991, 1994 & 1999), *Deutsche Sprachgeschichte vom Spätmittelalter bis zur Gegenwart* I, II & III (Berlin: Walter de Gruyter, 1991, 1994 & 1999).

POLITIS, L. (1973), *A History of Modern Greek Literature* (Oxford: Clarendon Press, 1973).

POZZO, B. (ed.) (2005), *Ordinary Language and Legal Language* (Milan: Giuffrè Editore, 2005).

_____ (ed.) (2006), *The Language Policies of EU Institutions After the Enlargement* (Milan: Giuffrè, in press).

PRIETO DE PEDRO, J. (1991), *Lenguas, lenguaje y derecho* (Madrid: Editorial Civitas, 1991).

PUUMALAINEN, M. (1999), 'Tosiasialliset kielisuhteet Euroopan unionissa', in A. Jyränki (ed.), *Oikeuden kielet* (Turku: Turun yliopiston oikeustieteellisen tiedekunnan julkaisuja B: 7, 1999), pp. 155–163.

RABELAIS, F. (1533): *Pantagruel* (Paris: Éditions Gallimard et Librairie Générale Française, 1964, orig. 1533).

RAHMAN, T. (1993), 'The Urdu-English Controversy', in *Journal of English Language Teaching and Studies* (Department of English Language and Literature, University of the Punjab), 1/1 (1997).

RASEHORN, TH. (1984): 'Über den Wandel in der juristischen Publikationskultur', *Zeitschrift für Rechtspolitik* 1 (1984): 267–273.

RAUTALA, H. (1999), 'Sopeutuuko Suomi', *Terminologie et traduction* 3 (1999): 59–64.

REICHLING, A. (1998), 'Gestion centrale de la terminologie, EURODICAUTOM et ses outils satellites', *Terminologie et traduction* 1 (1998): 172–201.

REMY, D. (1994), *Légistique. L'art de faire les lois* (Paris: Éditions Romillat, 1994).

REY, A. (ed.) (1994), *Dictionnaire historique de la langue française* (sous la direction de). 9th ed. (Paris: Dictionnaires Le Robert, 1994).

RÍGOS (Ρήγος), G. (1982), 'Katharévousa kai dimotikí sto dikastikó chóro apó to 1901 sta 1976' (Καθαρεύουσα και δημοτική στο δικαστικό χώρο από το 1901 στα 1976), in *I dimotikí sti nomikí práxi* (Η δημοτική στη νομική πράξη). (Athens: Tekmíria syntagmatikoú dikaíou, tomos 2,1982), pp. 209–214.

RIIHO, T. & EERIKÄINEN, L. J. (1993), *Crestomatía iberorrománica. Textos paralelos de los siglos XIII–XVI* (Helsinki: Suomalainen Tiedeakatemia 1993, B 268).

RINTALA, P. (2001), 'Käräjäarkusta tuomarinviittaan', in V. Harju (ed.), *Oikeuden symbolimaailmasta Suomessa* (Helsinki: Eduskunnan kirjasto ja Valtion taidemuseo, 2001), pp. 46–53.

RISSANEN, M. (2000), 'Standardisation and the Language of Early Statutes', in *The Development of Standard English: Theories, Descriptions, Conflicts* (Cambridge: C.U.P., 2000), pp. 117–130.

RISTIKIVI, M. (2003), 'Ladina keel ajakirjas Juridica 1993–2002', *Juridica* X (2003): 727–732.

ROBBERS, G. (1994), *Einführung in das deutsche Recht* (Baden-Baden: Nomos Verlagsgesellschaft, 1994).

ROBILLARD, D. & BENIAMINO, M. (eds.) (1993), *Le français dans l'espace francophone*, Tome 1 et 2 (Paris: Honoré Champion Éditeur, 1993).

ROLAND, H. & BOYER, L. (1998), *Locutions latines du droit français* (Paris: Litec, 1998).

RONTU, H. (1974), *Ymmärrettävää virastokieltä* (Helsinki: Oikeusministeriön lain-säädäntöosasto, 1974).

ROSSI, K. (1999), 'Sanastotyö Euroopan unionissa', in *Toimikunnista termitalkoihin. 25 vuotta sanastotyön asiantuntemusta* (Helsinki: Tekniikan Sanastokeskus, 1999), pp. 106–110.

ROUHETTE, G. (1999), 'L'article premier des lois', in N. Molfessis (ed.), *Les mots de la loi* (Paris: Economica 1999).

RUDOKVAS, A. (2001), 'The Roman Law in the Legal Education of Russia' (unpublished paper, 2001)

RUUTH, J. W. (1916), *Åbo stads historia under medeltiden och 1500-talet. Tredje häftet* (Helsingfors: Helsingfors Central-Tryckeri, 1916).

SAARENPÄÄ, A. (1999a), 'Oikeusinformatiikka', in *Encyclopædia Iuridica Fennica* VII (1999), p. 713–726.

_____ (1999b), 'Oikeusviestintä', in *Encyclopædia Iuridica Fennica* VII (1999), pp. 938–940.

SACCO, R. (1994), 'La traduzione giuridica', in U. Scarpelli & P. Di Lucia (eds), *Il linguaggio del diritto* (Milan: LED, 1994), pp. 475–490.

_____ (1995): 'La circolazione del modello giuridico francese', *Rivista di diritto civile* (1995): 515–523.

SACCO, R. (1999), 'Langue et droit', in R. Sacco & L. Castellani (eds), *Les multiples langues du droit européen uniforme* (Turin: Editrice L'Harmattan Italia, 1999), pp. 71–88.

SACCO, R. (ed.) (2002), *L'interprétation des textes juridiques rédigés dans plus d'une langue* (Torino & Paris: L'Harmattan, 2002).

SACCO, R. & CASTELLANI, L. (eds) (1999), *Les multiples langues du droit européen uniforme* (Turin: Editrice L'Harmattan Italia, 1999).

SAJAVAARA, A. (1999), 'Oikeuskielet Euroopan unionin toimielimissä', in A. Jyränki (ed.), *Oikeuden kielet* (Turku: Turun yliopiston oikeustieteellisen tiedekunnan julkaisuja B: 7, 1999), pp. 131–144.

SALMI-TOLONEN, T. (1994), *English Legislative Language in National and Supranational Context. European Community Law English from the Syntactic, Discursive and Pragmatic Perspective* (Tampere: Tampereen yliopisto, 1994).

SALOGUBOVA (САЛОГУБОВА), J. B. (1997), 'Vliianie rimskogo prava na rossiiskoe grazhdanskoe protsessual'noe zakonodatel'stvo' (Влияние римского права на российское гражданское процессуальное законодательство), *Vestnik Moskovskogo Universiteta*, Ser. 11, pravo 2 (1997): 29–37.

Sanastotyön käsikirja. Soveltavan terminologian periaatteet ja työmenetelmät (Helsinki: Suomen standardoimisliitto, 1989).

SANDRINI, P. (1996), *Terminologiearbeit im Recht. Deskriptiver begriffsorientierter Ansatz vom Standpunkt des Übersetzers* (Vienna: TermNet, 1996).

SAUER-STIPPERGER, R. (1998), 'Probleme der automatischen Sprachverarbeitung', *Terminologie et traduction* 1 (1998): 257–280.

SCHMIDT, C. (1997), *Introduction à la langue juridique française. Kompendien zu Recht und Terminologie 1* (Baden-Baden: Nomos Verlagsgesellschaft, 1997).

SCHMIDT, F. (1965), 'The German Abstract Approach to Law. Comments on the System of the Bürgerliches Gesetzbuch', *Scandinavian Studies in Law* (1965): 131–158.

SCHMIDT, H.-G. (1999), 'Der Einfluss der päpstlichen Justizbriefe auf die Justizbriefe der französischen Königskanzlei um 1300', in P. Herde & H. Jacobs (eds), *Papsturkunde und europäisches Urkundenwesen* (Cologne etc.: Böhlau Verlag, 1999).

SCHMIDT-WIEGAND, R. (1990), 'Rechtssprache', in A. Erler & E. Kaufmann (eds), *Handwörterbuch zur deutschen Rechtsgeschichte* 4 (Berlin: Erich Schmidt Verlag, 1990), pp. 344–360.

SCHOEK, R. (1973), 'Neo-Latin Legal Literature', in *Acta conventus Neo-Latini Lovaniensis* (Munich: Wilhelm Fink Verlag, 1973), pp. 577–588.

SCHWAB, W. & PAGÉ, R. (1981), *Les locutions latines et le droit positif québécois. Nomenclature des usages de la jurisprudence.* Dossiers du Conseil de la langue française. Études juridiques 7 (Quebec: Éditeur officiel du Québec, 1981).

Selvitys käännöstoiminnasta Euroopan yhteisöjen tuomioistuimessa (Luxemburg 1999).

SENEZ, D. (1998), 'The Machine Translation Help Desk and the Post-Editing Service', *Terminologie et traduction* 1 (1998): 289–295.

SEOK, J. (1991), *Die Rezeption des deutschen Verwaltungsrechts in Korea* (Berlin: Ducker & Humblot, 1991).

SÉRIAUX, A. (1996), *Droit canonique* (Paris: PUF, 1996).

SEVÓN, L. (1998), 'Languages in the Court of Justice of the European Communities', in *Scritti in onore di Giuseppe Federico Mancini* (1998), pp. 933–950.

SHYIRAMBERE, S. (1979), 'Le français au Rwanda et au Burundi', in A. Valdman (ed.), *Le français hors de France* (Paris: Éditions Honoré Champion, 1979), pp. 473–492.

SIÁMKOURIS (Σιάμκουρης), G. (1983), 'I metaglóttisis ton kodíkon. O antílogos' (Η μεταγλώττισις των κωδίκων. Ο αντίλογος), *Ellinikí Dikaiosýni* (Ελληνική Δικαιοσύνη) 24 (1983): 168–171.

SILNIZKI, M. (1997), *Geschichte des gelehrten Rechts in Rußland. Jurisprudencija an den Universitäten des Russischen Reiches 1700–1835* (Frankfurt am Main: Vittorio Klostermann, 1997).

SKUDLIK, S. (1992), 'The Status of German as a Language of Science and the Importance of the English Language for German-Speaking Scientists', in U. Ammon & M. Hellinger (eds), *Status Change of Languages* (Berlin & New York: Walter de Gruyter, 1992), pp. 421–438.

SMITH, A. & WALTON, S. (1998), 'Australia. Same Words, Different Meanings: English Legalese in Non-English Contracts', *International Business Lawyer* 9 (1998): 393–399.

SNOW, G. (1999), 'Techniques de transfert du droit dans un contexte multilingue', in R. Sacco & L. Castellani (eds), *Les multiples langues du droit européen uniforme* (Turin: Editrice L'Harmattan Italia 1999), pp. 187–192.

SOLAN, L. M. (1993), *The Language of Judges* (Chicago & London: The University of Chicago Press, 1993)

SOLAN, L. M. & TIERMA, P. M. (2005), *Speaking of Crime. The Language of Criminal Justice* (Chicago et London: The University of Chicago Press, 2005).

SOURIOUX, J.-L. & LERAT, P. (1975), *Le langage du droit* (Paris: Presses Universitaires de France, 1975).

STÂNGU, M. L. (2000): 'Quelques réflexions sur le Code civil français, en tant que source d'inspiration pour le langage du Code civil roumain', in I. Lamberterie & D. Breillat (eds), *Le français langue du droit* (Paris: Presses Universitaires de France, 2000), pp. 73–82.

STAVRÁKIS (Σταυράκης), A. (1995), *Neoellinikí nomikí glóssa kai orología* (Νεοελληνική νομική γλώσσα και ορολογία). (Athens: Nomikí Vivliothíki, 1995).

STEFANI, G., LEVASSEUR, G. & BOULOC, B. (1996), *Procédure pénale* (Paris: Dalloz, 1996).

STENVALL, E. (1999), 'Vierassanoilla sijansa', in *Toimikunnista termitalkoihin. 25 vuotta sanastotyön asiantuntemusta* (Helsinki: Tekniikan Sanastokeskus, 1999), pp. 58–61.

STĘPKOWSKI, A. (2001), 'Maksymy prawne na wyspach brytyjskich', in W. Wołodkiewicz & J. Krzynówek (eds.), *Łacińskie paremie w europejskiej kulturze prawnej i orzecznictwie sądów polskich* (Warsaw: Liber, 2001), pp. 71–107.

STOWASSER (1998). *Lateinisch–deutsches Schulwörterbuch* (von Stowasser, J. M., Petschenig, M. und Skutsch, F.). (Vienna & Munich: HTP-Medien-AG etc., 1998).

STROUHAL, E. (1986), 'Rechtssprache und Bürokratismus', in T. Öhlinger (ed.), *Recht und Sprache* (Vienna: Manz, 1986).

STURM, F. (2002), 'Lingua Latina fundamentum et salus Europae', *The European Legal Forum – Forum iuris communis Europae* 6 (2002): 313–320.

SUKHANOV (Суханов), E. A. (2001): 'Predislovie ('Предисловие', Foreword), in L. L. Kofanov (Л. Л. Кофанов) (ed.), *Digesta Iustiniani* I / Digesty Iustiniana (Дигесты Юстиниана) I. Centrum iuris romani investigandi – Tsentr izucheniia rimskogo prava (Центр изучения римского права) (Moscow: Statut & Konsul'tant Plius / Москва: Статут & Консультант Плюс, 2001).

SUMMERS, R. S. (1998), 'Yhdysvaltain oikeus' in *Encyclopædia Iuridica Fennica* VI (1998), pp. 1018–1033.

SUNDSTRÖM, M.-P. (1997), 'Svenskan inom Europaparlamentet – några ögonblicksbilder', *Språksbruk* 2 (1997): 3–7.

SUONUUTI, H. (1999), 'Käsiteanalyysi työmenetelmänä', in *Toimikunnista termitalkoihin. 25 vuotta sanastotyön asiantuntemusta* (Helsinki: Tekniikan Sanastokeskus 1999), pp. 29–42.

Säädöskäännöstyöryhmän mietintö (Helsinki: Valtioneuvoston kanslian julkaisusarja 7, 1996).

ŠARČEVIĆ, S. (1997), *New Approach to Legal Translation* (The Hague etc.: Kluwer Law International, 1997).

TALLON, D. (1999), 'Le choix des mots au regard des contraintes de traduction', in N. Molfessis (ed.), *Les mots de la loi* (Paris: Economica 1999), pp. 31–36.

TAMM, D. (1991), 'Latein oder Dänisch. Zur Entwicklung einer dänischen Gesetzessprache im 13. Jahrhundert', in J. Eckert (ed.), *Sprache – Recht – Geschichte* (Heidelberg: C. F. Müller Juristischer Verlag, 1991), pp. 37–48.

TENGSTRÖM, E. (1973), *Latinet i Sverige* (Lund: Bonniers, 1973).

TERCIER, P. (1999), *La recherche et la rédaction juridiques*. 3th ed. (Fribourg: Éditions Universitaires, 1999).

TIERSMA, P. (1999), *Legal Language* (Chicago & London: The University of Chicago Press, 1999).

TOMÁS Y VALIENTE, F. (1983), *Manual de historia del derecho español* (Madrid: Tecnos, 1983).

TROISFONTAINES, P. (1981), 'Le langage judiciaire', *Annales de la Faculté de droit, d'économie et de sciences sociales de Liège* (1981): 153–169.

Tuomioistuinsanasto. Domstolsordlista. Glossary of Court Terms. Glossar der Gerichtsterminologie. Vocabulaire de la Justice (Helsinki: Oikeusministeriö, Valtioneuvoston kanslia & Edita, 2001).

TURI, J. G. (1996), 'L'emploi du français dans la Francophonie du point de vue juridico-constitutionnel', in D. Robillard & M. Beniamino (eds), *Le français dans l'espace francophone*, Tome 2 (Paris: Honoré Champion Éditeur 1996), pp. 807–813.

TYYNILÄ, M. (1984), *Lainvalmistelukunta 1884–1964* (Helsinki: Suomalainen Lakimiesyhdistys 1984, A: 166).

ULRICH, H. (1998), 'La mise en place du Translator's Workbench (TWB): Concurrence avec SYSTRAN et élément humain', *Terminologie et traduction* 1 (1998): 102–116.

Uusi kielilaki (Helsinki: Kielilakikomitean mietintö, 2001: 3).

Valtioneuvostosanasto (Helsinki: Edita – Valtioneuvoston kanslia, 1998).

VERMA, B. R. (1988), *Islamic Law-Personal being Commentaries on Mohammedan Law (in India, Pakistan and Bangladesh)*. 6ᵗʰ ed. by Beg, M. H. & Verma, S. K. (Allahabad: Law Publishers (India) Private Limited, 1988).

VERONESI, D. (2000), 'La metafora negli articoli scientifici giuridici: linguaggio, testo, discorso', in D. Veronesi (ed.), *Linguistica giuridica italiana e tedesca* (Padova: Unipress, 2000), pp. 363–380.

VERRYCKEN, M. (1995), 'Le français juridique en Belgique', in G. Snow & J. Vanderlinden (eds.), *Français juridique et science du droit* (Brussels: Bruylant, 1995), pp. 363–375.

VIHONEN, I. (1998), 'Eurokääntäjät termintekijöinä', *Terminfo* 4 (1998): 16–20.

VILLA-REAL MOLINA, R. & DEL ARCO TORRES, M. A. (1999), *Diccionario de términos jurídicos* (Granada: Comares, 1999).

VINCENT, J. & GUINCHARD, S. (1996), *Procédure civile* (Paris: Dalloz, 1996).

VINJE, F.-E. (1990), 'Moderne norsk lovspråk og annen juristprosa', in *Språket i lover og annet regelverk* (Oslo: Tano, 1990), pp. 9–76.

VLASENKO (ВЛАСЕНКО), N. A. (1997), *Iazyk prava* (Язык права). (Irkutsk: Vostochno-Sibirskoe knizhnoe izdatel'stvo, 1997).

VOGEL, H.-H. (1998), *Juridiska översättningar* (Lund: Jurisförlaget i Lund, 1988).

VOSSEN, C. (1980), *Latein – Muttersprache Europas*. 4ᵗʰ ed. (Düsseldorf: Druckerei und Verlag Hoch, 1980).

WACKE, A. (1990), 'Lateinisch und Deutsch als Rechtssprachen in Mitteleuropa', *Neue Juristische Wochenschrift* (1990): 877–886.

WAGNER, A. (2002), *La langue de la common law*. (Paris: L'Harmattan, 2002).

WAQUET, F. (1998), *Le latin ou l'empire d'un signe. XVIᵉ–XXᵉ siècle* (Paris: Albin Michel, 1998).

WELLANDER, E. (1974), *Kommittésvenska* (Stockholm: Esselte Studium, 1974).

WIIO, O. A. (1989), *Viestinnän perusteet*. 5ᵗʰ ed. (Espoo: Weilin + Göös, 1989).

_____ (2000), *Johdatus viestintään*. 9ᵗʰ ed. (Espoo: Weilin + Göös, 2000).

WIITANEN, K. (1976), *Luettelo Suomen säädöksistä tehdyistä käännöksistä* (Helsinki: Oikeusministeriön lainsäädäntöosasto 10, 1976).

WILHELMSSON, T. (2001), 'Europeiseringen av privaträtten: för ett fragmenterat utbyte av erfarenheter', *Tidsskrift for Rettsvitenskap* 1–2 (2001): 1–32.

WOŁODKIEWICZ, W. (2001a), 'Lex retro non agit', in W. Wołodkiewicz & J. Krzynówek (eds.), *Łacińskie paremie w europejskiej kulturze prawnej i orzecznictwie sądów polskich* (Warsaw: Liber, 2001), pp. 153–192.

WOŁODKIEWICZ, W.(2001b), 'Łacińskie paremie prawne w orzecznictwie sądów polskich', in W. Wołodkiewicz & J. Krzynówek (eds.), *Łacińskie paremie w europejskiej kulturze prawnej i orzecznictwie sądów polskich* (Warsaw: Liber, 2001), pp. 7–30.

_____ (ed.) (2001c), *Regulae Iuris. Łacińskie inskrypcje na kolumnach Sądu Najwyższego Rzeczypospolitej Polskiej* (Warsaw: Wydawnictwo C. H. Beck, 2001).

_____ & J. KRZYNÓWEK (eds) (2001), *Łacińskie paremie w europejskiej kulturze prawnej i orzecznictwie sądów polskich* (Warsaw: Liber, 2001).

WOODLAND, P. (1991), 'Spécificité et ambiguïtés du langage du droit communautaire', in L. Ingber & P. Vassart (eds), *Le langage du droit* (Brussels: Editions Nemesis,1991), pp. 87–105.

WURM, C., WAGNER, H. & ZARTMANN, H. (1989), *Das Rechtsformularbuch*. 16th ed. (Cologne: Verlag Otto Schmidt, 1989).

XAVIER, R. CALDEIRA (2000), *Latim no direito*. 5th ed. (Rio de Janeiro: Editora Forense, 2000).

_____ (2001), *Português no direito (Linguagem forense)*. 15th ed. (Rio de Janeiro: Editora Forense, 2001).

XIRINACHS, M. (2002), 'Promoting Legal Catalan', in H. Mattila (ed.), *The Development of Legal Language* (Helsinki: Talentum Media, 2002).

YBÁÑEZ BUENO, E. (1995), 'El idioma español en las Organizaciones Internacionales', in Marqués de Tamarón (ed.), *El peso de la lengua española en el mundo* (Valladolid: Fundación Duques de Soria & INCIPE, 1995).

YLIKANGAS, H. (1983), *Miksi oikeus muuttuu* (Porvoo etc.: WSOY, 1983).

ZAMORA MANZANO, J. L. (2000), 'Algunas consideraciones sobre la recepción del derecho romano en el Common Law', *Revista de Ciencias Jurídicas* (Universidad de Las Palmas de Gran Canaria) 5 (2000): 417–430.

ZILLIACUS, H. (1935), *Zum Kampf der Weltsprachen im oströmischen Reich* (Helsingfors, 1935).

ZIMMERMANN, R. (1997), 'Südafrikanische Übersetzungen gemeinrechtlicher Literatur', *Zeitschrift für europäisches Privatrecht* (1997): 536–549.

ZWEIGERT, K. & KÖTZ, H. (1996), *Einführung in die Rechtsvergleichung auf dem Gebiete des Privatrechts*. 3th ed. (Tübingen: Mohr, 1996).

_____ (1998), *An Introduction to Comparative Law*. 2nd ed. Volume I (Oxford: Clarendon Press, 1998.)

ŻMIGRODZKA, B. (1997), *Testament jako gatunek tekstu* (Katowice: Wydawnictwo Uniwersytetu Śląskiego 1977. Prace naukowe Uniwersytetu Śląskiego w Katowicach nr 1698).

Systematic Bibliography

A selection of literature arranged according to the structure of the book.

A General

AITCHISON, J. (1995), *Linguistics. An Introduction* (London: Hodder & Stoughton, 1995).

BENEDETTI, G. (1999), 'Diritto e linguaggio. Variazioni sul "diritto muto"', in *Europa e diritto privato* 1 (1999): 137–152.

BHATIA, J., CANDLIN, C.N. & GOTTI, M. (eds) (2003), *Legal discourse in multilingual and multicultural contexts: arbitration texts in Europe* (Bern: P. Lang, 2003).

COLIN, J. & MORRIS, R. (1996), *Interpreters and the Legal Process* (Winchester: Waterside Press, 1996).

CORNU, G. (2005), *Linguistique juridique*, 3th ed. (Paris: Montchrestien, 2005).

DUBOUCHET, P. (1990), *Sémiotique juridique. Introduction à une science du droit* (Paris: Presses Universitaires de France, 1990).

GARAPON, A. (1997), *Bien juger. Essai sur le rituel judiciaire* (Paris: Éditions Odile Jacob, 1997).

GÉMAR, J.-C. & KASIRER, N. (eds) (2005), *Jurilinguistique: entre langues et droits – Jurilinguistics: Between Law and Language* (Brussels & Montreal: Bruylant & Les Éditions Thémis 2005).

HAFT, F. (1999), *Juristische Rhetorik*. 6th ed. (Munich: Verlag Karl Alber Freiberg, 1999).

HARJU, V. (ed.) (2001), *Oikeuden symbolimaailmasta Suomessa* (Helsinki: Eduskunnan kirjasto ja Valtion taidemuseo, 2001).

JACKSON, B. (1997), *Semiotics and Legal Theory* (Liverpool: Deborah Charles, 1997; orig. 1985).

JAYME, E. (ed.) (1999), *Langue et droit. XVe Congrès International de droit comparé, Bristol 1998* (Brussels: Bruylant, 1999).

JYRÄNKI, A. (ed.) (1999), *Oikeuden kielet* (Turku: Turun yliopiston oikeustieteellisen tiedekunnan julkaisuja B: 7, 1999).

GUILLOREL, H. & KOUBI, G. (eds) (1999), *Langues et droits. Langues du droit, droit des langues* (Brussels: Bruylant, 1999).

KEVELSON, R. (ed.) (1987–1989), *Law and Semiotics* I–III (New York: Plenum Press, 1987–1989).

MATTILA, H. (ed.) (2002), *The Development of Legal Language* (Helsinki: Talentum Media, 2002).

_____ (2005), 'The History of Legal Language', in *The Elsevier Encyclopedia of Language and Linguistics* (2005).

MOLFESSIS, N. (ed.) (1999), *Les mots de la loi* (Paris: Economica, 1999).

MÜLLER, F. (ed.) (1989), *Untersuchungen zur Rechtslinguistik* (Berlin: Duncker & Humblot, 1989).

MÜLLER, F. & BURR, I. (eds) (2004), *Rechtssprache Europas. Reflexion der Praxis von Sprache und Mehrsprachigkeit im supranationalen Recht* (Berlin: Duncker & Humblot, 2004).

ÖHLINGER, T. (ed.) (1986), *Recht und Sprache* (Vienna: Manz, 1986).

POZZO, B. (ed.) (2005), *Ordinary Language and Legal Language* (Milan 2005: Giuffrè Editore, 2005).

———— (ed.) (2006), *The Language Policies of EU Institutions After the Enlargement* (Milan: Giuffrè Editore, in press).

SAARENPÄÄ, A. (1999), 'Oikeusinformatiikka', in *Encyclopædia Iuridica Fennica* VII (1999), pp. 713–726.

SACCO, R. (ed.) (2002), *L'interprétation des textes juridiques rédigés dans plus d'une langue* (Turin & Paris: L'Harmattan, 2002).

B Legal language as a language for special purposes

ARNTZ, R. (2001), *Fachbezogene Mehrsprachigkeit in Recht und Technik* (Hildesheim etc.: Georg Olms Verlag, 2001. Studien zu Sprache und Technik, Band 8).

GÉMAR, J.-C. (1994), 'Les fondements du langage du droit comme langue de spécialité. Du sens et de la forme du texte juridique', *Revue générale de droit* (1990): 717–738.

GUILLOREL, H. & KOUBI, G. (eds) (1999), *Langues et droits. Langues du droit, droit des langues* (Brussels: Bruylant, 1999).

GRIDEL, J.-P. (1979), *Le signe et le droit. Les bornes. Les uniformes. La signalisation routière et autres* (Paris: Librairie Générale de Droit et de Jurisprudence, 1979).

GROFFIER, E. & REED, D. (1990), *La lexicographie juridique. Principes et méthodes* (Cowansville: Les Éditions Yvon Blais, 1990).

JAYME, E. (ed.) (1999), *Langue et droit. XVe Congrès International de droit comparé, Bristol 1998* (Brussels: Bruylant, 1999).

LASHÖFER, J. (1992), *Zum Stilwandel in richterlichen Entscheidungen. Über stilistische Veränderungen in englischen, französischen und deutschen zivilrechtlichen Urteilen und in Entscheidungen des Gerichtshofs der Europäischen Gemeinschaften* (Münster & New York: Waxmann, 1992).

LAURÉN, C. (1993), *Fackspråk. Form, innehåll, funktion* (Lund: Studentlitteratur, 1993).

MARTÍN, J., RUIZ, R., SANTAELLA, J. & ESCÁNEZ, J. (1996), *Los lenguajes especiales. Lenguaje jurídico-administrativo. Lenguaje científico-técnico. Lenguaje humanístico. Lenguaje periodístico y publicitario. Lenguaje literario* (Granada: Editorial Comares, 1996).

MATTILA, H. (ed.) (2002), *The Development of Legal Language* (Helsinki: Talentum Media, 2002).

MOLFESSIS, N. (ed.) (1999), *Les mots de la loi* (Paris: Economica, 1999).

MÜLLER-DIETZ, H. (1997), 'Rechtssprache. Die Macht der Sprache, die Sprache der Macht', in S. Fritsch-Oppermann (ed.), *Loccumer Protokolle* 15, 1997), pp. 19–44.

ÖHLINGER, T. (ed.) (1986), *Recht und Sprache* (Vienna: Manz, 1986).

OKSAAR, E. (1989): Alltagssprache. Fachsprachen. Rechtssprache. *Zeitschrift für Gesetzgebung* 1989, pp. 210–237.

PRIETO DE PEDRO, J. (1991), *Lenguas, lenguaje y derecho* (Madrid: Editorial Civitas, 1991).

SACCO, R. & CASTELLANI, L. (eds) (1999), *Les multiples langues du droit européen uniforme* (Turin: Editrice L'Harmattan Italia, 1999).

SANDRINI, P. (1996), *Terminologiearbeit im Recht. Deskriptiver begriffsorientierter Ansatz vom Standpunkt des Übersetzers* (Vienna: TermNet, 1996).

SOURIOUX, J.-L. & LERAT, P. (1975), *Le langage du droit* (Paris: Presses Universitaires de France, 1975).

TIERSMA, P. (1999), *Legal Language* (Chicago & London: The University of Chicago Press, 1999).

Toimikunnista termitalkoihin. 25 vuotta sanastotyön asiantuntemusta. (Helsinki: Tekniikan Sanastokeskus 1999, pp. 43–57).

C The major legal languages

I The heritage of legal Latin

ANNERS, E. & ÖNNERFORS, A. (1972), *Latinsk juridisk terminologi.* 2nd ed. (Uppsala: Juridiska Föreningen i Uppsala, 1972).

CALONIUS, M. (1908), *Praelectiones in Jurisprudentiam Civilem* (Helsingforsiae: Societas Heredum J. Simelii Typografica, MCMVIII).

Codex Iuris Canonici – Codex des kanonischen Rechtes (1983) (Kevelaer: Verlag Butzon & Bercker, 1983).

DU CANGE (1937–1938), *Glossarium mediae et infimae Latinitatis* (conditum a Carolo du Fresne, Domino Du Cange). Nouveau tirage (Paris: Librairie des sciences et des arts, 1937–1938).

ECKERT, J. (ed.) (1991), *Sprache – Recht – Geschichte* (Heidelberg: C. F. Müller Juristischer Verlag, 1991).

FILIP-FRÖSCHL, J. & MADER, P. (1999), *Latein in der Rechtssprache. Ein Studienbuch und Nachschlagewerk.* 3rd ed. (Vienna: Braumüller, 1999).

HAUSEN, R. (ed.) (1890), *Registrum Ecclesiae Aboensis eller Åbo Domkyrkans Svartbok* (Helsingfors: J. Simelii Arfvingars Boktryckeri 1890, reed. 1996).

———— (ed.) (1910–1933), *Finlands medeltidsurkunder I–VII. Samlade och i tryck utgifna af Finlands Statsarkiv genom R. Hausen* (Helsingfors: Kejserliga Senatens Tryckeri / Statsrådets Tryckeri, 1910–1933).

HERDE, P. & JACOBS, H. (eds) (1999), *Papsturkunde und europäisches Urkundenwesen* (Cologne etc.: Böhlau Verlag, 1999).

KURZON, D. (1987), 'Latin for Lawyers: Degrees of Textual Integration', *Applied Linguistics* (1987): 233–240.

MATTILA, H. (2000a), 'Latinet i den finländska juridiska litteraturen', *Tidskrift utgiven av Juridiska Föreningen i Finland* (2000): 269–322.

_____ (2002), 'De aequalitate Latinitatis jurisperitorum. Le latin juridique dans les grandes familles de droit contemporaines à la lumière des dictionnaires spécialisés', *Revue internationale de droit comparé* 3 (2002).

_____ (2005b), 'Jurilinguistique et latin juridique', in J.-C. Gémar & N. Kasirer (eds), *Jurilinguistique: entre langues et droits – Jurilinguistics: Between Law and Language* (Brussels & Montreal: Bruylant & Les Éditions Thémis, 2005), pp. 71–89.

MÖRSDORF, K. (1967), *Die Rechtssprache des Codex Juris Canonici* (Paderborn: Verlag Ferdinand Schöningh, 1967).

PITKÄRANTA, R. & VILKKONEN, E. (1986), 'Lakimieslatinaa', *Lakimies* (1986): 183–188.

SCHOEK, R. (1973), 'Neo-Latin Legal Literature', in *Acta conventus Neo-Latini Lovaniensis* (Munich: Wilhelm Fink Verlag, 1973), pp. 577–588.

WAQUET, F. (1998), *Le latin ou l'empire d'un signe. XVIᵉ–XXᵉ siècle* (Paris: Albin Michel, 1998).

WOŁODKIEWICZ, W. (ed.) (2001c), *Regulae Iuris. Łacińskie inskrypcje na kolumnach Sądu Najwyższego Rzeczypospolitej Polskiej* (Warsaw: Wydawnictwo C. H. Beck, 2001).

_____ & J. KRZYNÓWEK (eds) (2001), *Łacińskie paremie w europejskiej kulturze prawnej i orzecznictwie sądów polskich* (Warsaw: Liber, 2001).

XAVIER, R. CALDEIRA (2000), *Latim no direito.* 5ᵗʰ ed. (Rio de Janeiro: Editora Forense, 2000).

ZILLIACUS, H. (1935), *Zum Kampf der Weltsprachen im oströmischen Reich* (Helsingfors, 1935).

II Modern legal languages

1. The international position of the major languages

AMMON, U. & HELLINGER, M. (eds), *Status Change of Languages* (Berlin & New York: Walter de Gruyter, 1992).

BAR, S. (1999), 'La question des langues au sein des Nations Unies', in H. Guillorel & G. Koubi (eds), *Langues et droits. Langues du droit, droit des langues* (Brussels: Bruylant, 1999), pp. 291–316.

BERTELOOT, P. (1988), *Babylone à Luxembourg: Jurilinguistique à la Cour de justice des Communautés européennes* (1988).

CALVET, L.-J. (2003), 'L'usage des langues dans les relations internationales', *Questions internationales* 1 (2003): 100–105.

LOPES SABINO, A. (1999), 'Les langues dans l'Union européenne. Enjeux, pratiques et perspectives', *Revue trimestrielle de droit européen* 2 (1999): 159–169.

MANCINI, G. & KEELING, D. (1995), 'Language, Culture and Politics in the Life of the European Court of Justice', *Columbia Journal of European Law* (1995): 397–413.

MARQUÉS DE TAMARÓN (ed.) (1995), *El peso de la lengua española en el mundo* (Valladolid: Fundación Duques de Soria & INCIPE, 1995).

MARTINY, D. (1998), 'Babylon in Brüssel. Das Recht und die europäische Sprachenvielfalt', *Zeitschrift für europäisches Privatrecht* (1998): 227–252.

POZZO, B. (ed.) (2006), *The Language Policies of EU Institutions After the Enlargement* (Milan: Giuffrè, in press).

SACCO, R. & CASTELLANI, L. (eds) (1999), *Les multiples langues du droit européen uniforme* (Turin: Editrice L'Harmattan Italia, 1999).

SEVÓN, L. (1998), 'Languages in the Court of Justice of the European Communities', in *Scritti in onore di Giuseppe Federico Mancini* (1998), pp. 933–950.

WOODLAND, P. (1991), 'Spécificité et ambiguïtés du langage du droit communautaire', in L. Ingber & P. Vassart (eds), *Le langage du droit* (Brussels: Editions Nemesis,1991), pp. 87–105.

2. Legal German

AMMON, U. (1992), 'On the Status and Changes in the Status of German as a Language of Diplomacy', in U. Ammon & M. Hellinger (eds), *Status Change of Languages* (Berlin & New York: Walter de Gruyter, 1992), pp. 421–438.

ARNTZ, R. (2002), 'The Roman Heritage in German Legal Language', in H. Mattila (ed.), *The Development of Legal Language* (Helsinki: Talentum Media, 2002), pp. 33–54.

BEHRENDS, O. (1991): Die Eindeutschung der römisch-rechtlichen Fachsprache, in J. Eckert (ed.), *Sprache – Recht – Geschichte* (Heidelberg: C. F. Müller Juristischer Verlag, 1991).

BERGMANS, B. (1987), 'L'enseignement d'une terminologie juridique étrangère comme mode d'approche du droit comparé: l'exemple de l'allemand', *Revue internationale de droit comparé* 1 (1987): 90–110.

ECKERT, J. (ed.), *Sprache – Recht – Geschichte* (Heidelberg: C. F. Müller Juristischer Verlag, 1991).

HATTENHAUER, H. (1987), *Zur Geschichte der deutschen Rechts- und Gesetzessprache* (Hamburg: Joachim Jungius-Gesellschaft der Wissenschaften, 1987).

POLENZ, P. VON (1991, 1994 & 1999), *Deutsche Sprachgeschichte vom Spätmittelalter bis zur Gegenwart* I, II & III (Berlin: Walter de Gruyter, 1991, 1994 & 1999).

SCHMIDT-WIEGAND, R. (1990), 'Rechtssprache', in A. Erler & E. Kaufmann (eds), *Handwörterbuch zur deutschen Rechtsgeschichte* 4 (Berlin: Erich Schmidt Verlag, 1990), pp. 344–360.

SKUDLIK, S. (1992), 'The Status of German as a Language of Science and the Importance of the English Language for German-Speaking Scientists', in U.

Ammon & M. Hellinger (eds), *Status Change of Languages* (Berlin & New York: Walter de Gruyter, 1992), pp. 421–438.

WACKE, A. (1990), 'Lateinisch und Deutsch als Rechtssprachen in Mitteleuropa', *Neue Juristische Wochenschrift* (1990): 877–886.

3. Legal French

BEAUDOIN, L. (2000a), *Expressions juridiques en un clin d'oeil.* 2ⁿᵈ ed. (Cowansville: Les Éditions Yvon Blais, 2000).

_____ (2000b), *Les mots du droit. Lexique analogique juridique* (Cowansville: Les Éditions Yvon Blais, 2000).

BERTELOOT, P. (2002), 'Legal French in France and in the European Communities', in H. Mattila (ed.), *The Development of Legal Language* (Helsinki: Talentum Media, 2002), p. 81–99.

BRUNOT, F. (1917), *Histoire de la langue française des origines à 1900.* Tome V: *Le français en France et hors de France au XVIIᵉ siècle* (Paris: Armand Collin, 1917).

_____ (1935), *Histoire de la langue française des origines à nos jours.* Tome VIII: *Le français hors de France au XVIIIᵉ siècle* (Paris: Armand Collin, 1935).

_____ (1937), *Histoire de la langue française des origines à nos jours.* Tome IX: *La Révolution et l'Empire* (Paris: Armand Collin, 1937).

CATHERINE, R. & JARRY, J.-M. (1996), *Le style administratif* (Paris: Albin Michel, 1996).

CORNU, G. (2005), *Linguistique juridique*, 3ᵗʰ ed. (Paris: Montchrestien, 2005).

_____ (ed.) (2004), *Vocabulaire juridique*, 6ᵗʰ ed. (Paris: Presses Universitaires de France, 2004).

DIDIER, E. (1990), *Langues et langages du droit* (Montréal: Wilson & Lafleur, 1990).

EURRUTIA CAVERO, M. (1997), 'Aspectos lingüísticos que caracterizan el discurso jurídico francés', in P. San Ginés Aguilar & E. Ortega Arjonilla (eds), *Introducción a la traducción jurídica y jurada (francés–español)* (Granada: Editorial Comares, 1997), pp. 81–127.

GALLEGOS ROSILLO, J. (1997), 'Lenguaje jurídico y lengua francesa', in P. San Ginés Aguilar & E. Ortega Arjonilla (eds), *Introducción a la traducción jurídica y jurada (francés–español)* (Granada: Editorial Comares, 1997), pp. 57–80.

GÉMAR, J.-C. (1995), *Traduire ou l'art d'interpréter. Langue, droit et société. Eléments de jurilinguistique.* Tome 2: *Application* (Sainte-Foy: Presses de l'Université du Québec, 1995).

GUILLOREL, H. & KOUBI, G. (eds) (1999), *Langues et droits. Langues du droit, droit des langues* (Bruxelles: Bruylant, 1999).

KREFELD, T. (1985), *Das französische Gerichtsurteil in linguistischer Sicht* (Frankfurt am Main: Verlag Peter Lang, 1985).

LAMBERTERIE, I. & BREILLAT, D. (eds), *Le français langue du droit* (Paris: PUF, 2000).

MATZNER, E. (ed.), *Droit et langues étrangères: concepts, problèmes d'application, perspectives* (Perpignan: Presses Universitaires de Perpignan, 2000).

MOLFESSIS, N. (ed.) (1999), *Les mots de la loi* (Paris: Economica, 1999).

SCHMIDT, C. (1997), *Introduction à la langue juridique française. Kompendien zu Recht und Terminologie* 1 (Baden-Baden: Nomos Verlagsgesellschaft, 1997).

SNOW, G. & VANDERLINDEN, J. (eds), *Français juridique et science du droit* (Brussels: Bruylant, 1995), pp. 363–375.

SOURIOUX, J.-L. & LERAT, P. (1975), *Le langage du droit* (Paris: Presses Universitaires de France, 1975).

TROISFONTAINES, P. (1981), 'Le langage judiciaire', *Annales de la Faculté de droit, d'économie et de sciences sociales de Liège* (1981): 153–169.

4. Other Romance legal languages

CABANELLAS, G. & ALCALÁ-ZAMORA Y CASTILLO, L. (1992), *Diccionario enciclopédico de derecho usual* I–VIII. 16ᵗʰ ed. (Buenos Aires: Editorial Heliasta, 1992).

DAMIÃO, R. TOLEDO & HENRIQUES, A. (2000), *Curso de português jurídico*. 8ᵗʰ ed. (São Paulo: Editora Atlas, 2000).

DUARTE I MONTSERRAT, C. (1998), 'Lenguaje administrativo y lenguaje jurídico', in J. Bayo Delgado (ed.), *Lenguaje judicial* (Madrid: Consejo general del poder judicial, 1998).

_____ ALSINA I KEITH, A. & SININA I CUNÍ, S. (1998), *Manual de llenguatge administratiu* (Barcelona: Generalitat de Catalunya, 1998).

_____ & MARTÍNEZ, A. (1995), *El lenguaje jurídico* (Buenos Aires: A–Z editora, 1995).

FIORELLI, P. (1994), 'La lingua del diritto e dell'amministrazione', in L. Serianni & P. Trifone (eds), *Storia della lingua italiana* (Torino: Giulio Einaudi Editore, 1994), pp. 553–597.

GANDASEGUI, J. (1998), 'Historia del lenguaje judicial', in J. Bayo Delgado (ed.), *Lenguaje judicial* (Madrid: Consejo general del poder judicial, 1998).

MARQUÉS DE TAMARÓN (ed.) (1995), *El peso de la lengua española en el mundo* (Valladolid: Fundación Duques de Soria & INCIPE, 1995).

SCARPELLI, U. & DI LUCIA, P. (eds), *Il linguaggio del diritto* (Milan: LED, 1994).

VILLA-REAL MOLINA, R. & DEL ARCO TORRES, M. A. (1999), *Diccionario de términos jurídicos* (Granada: Comares, 1999).

XAVIER, R. CALDEIRA (2001), *Português no direito (Linguagem forense)*. 15ᵗʰ ed. (Rio de Janeiro: Editora Forense, 2001).

XIRINACHS, M. (2002), 'Promoting Legal Catalan', in H. Mattila (ed.), *The Development of Legal Language* (Helsinki: Talentum Media, 2002).

5. Legal English

BEVERIDGE, B. (1998), 'Introduction. Same Words, Different Meanings: English Legalese in Non-English Contracts', *International Business Lawyer* 9 (1998): 387–391.

_____ (2002), 'Legal English – How it Developed and Why it is not Appropriate for International Commercial Contracts', in H. Mattila, *The Development of Legal Language* (Helsinki: Talentum Media, 2002), pp. 55–79.

BHATIA, V. K. (1987), 'Language of the Law', *Language Teaching* 4 (1987): 227–234.

Black's Law Dictionary (2000). 7th ed. (St. Paul: West Publishing, 2000).

CHARROW, V., CRANDALL, J. & CHARROW, R. (1982), 'Characteristics and Functions of Legal Language', in R. Kittredge & J. Lehrberger, J. (eds), *Sublanguage: Studies of Language in Restricted Semantic Domains* (Berlin: de Gruyter, 1982), pp. 175–190.

CHILD, B. (1992), *Drafting Legal Documents* (St. Paul: West Publishing, 1992).

CRYSTAL, D. (1997), *English as a Global Language* (Cambridge: Cambridge University Press, 1997).

GARNER, B. (1987), *A Dictionary of Modern Legal Usage* (New York & Oxford: Oxford University Press, 1987).

GODDARD, C. (2004), *English as an International Language of Legal Communication: Inter-cultural Aspects* (Riga: Riga Graduate School of Law, RGSL Working Papers no. 20, 2004).

_____ (2006), *Legal English: Making it Simple. Language Tools for Legal Writing* (to appear).

GUPTA, R. S. & KAPOOR, K. (eds) (1991), *English in India. Issues and Problems* (Delhi: Academic Foundation, 1991).

HILL, C. & KING, C. (2005), 'How Do German Contracts Do As Much with Fewer Words?', in B. Pozzo (ed.), *Ordinary Language and Legal Language* (Milan 2005: Giuffrè Editore 2005), pp. 169–218.

HILTUNEN, R. (1990), *Chapters on Legal English. Aspects Past and Present of the Language of the Law* (Helsinki: Suomalaisen tiedeakatemian toimituksia B 251, 1990).

KURZON, D. (1997), 'Legal Language: Varieties, Genres, Registers, discourses', *International Journal of Applied Linguistics* 7 (1997): 119–139.

MELLINKOFF, D. (1963), *The Language of the Law* (Boston & Toronto: Little, Brown and Co., 1963).

PHILLIPS, A. (2003), *Lawyers' Language* (London & New York: Routledge, 2003).

SALMI-TOLONEN, T. (1994), *English Legislative Language in National and Supranational Context. European Community Law English from the Syntactic, Discursive and Pragmatic Perspective* (Tampere: Tampereen yliopisto, 1994).

SOLAN, L. M. (1993), *The Language of Judges* (Chicago & London: The University of Chicago Press, 1993).

SOLAN, L. M. & TIERSMA, P. M. (2005), *Speaking of Crime. The Language of Criminal Justice* (Chicago & London: The University of Chicago Press, 2005).

SMITH, A. & WALTON, S. (1998), 'Australia. Same Words, Different Meanings: English Legalese in Non-English Contracts', *International Business Lawyer* 9 (1998): 393–399.

TIERSMA, P. (1999), *Legal Language* (Chicago & London: The University of Chicago Press, 1999).

WAGNER, A. (2002): *La langue de la common law* (Paris: L'Harmattan, 2002).

6. Slavic legal languages; modern legal Greek

HAŁAS, B. (1995), *Terminologia języka prawnego* (Zielona Góra: Wydawnictwo Wyższej Szkoły Pedagogicznej 1995).

HUSA, J. (2006), *Kreikan oikeus ja oikeuskieli. Johdatus Kreikan oikeusjärjestykseen ja oikeuskieleen & kreikka–suomi-oikeussanasto* (Helsinki: Suomalaisen Lakimiesyhdistyksen julkaisuja, E 14, in press).

PIEŃKOS, J. (1999), *Podstawy juryslingwistyki. Język w prawie – Prawo w języku* (Warsaw: Muza, 1999).

PIGOLKIN (Пиголкин), A. S. (ed.) (1990), *Iazyk zakona* (Язык закона) (Moscow: Iuridicheskaia literatura, 1990).

STAVRÁKIS (Σταυράκης), A. (1995), *Neoellinikí nomikí glóssa kai orología* (Νεοελληνική νομική γλώσσα και ορολογία). (Athens: Nomikí Vivliothíki, 1995).

VLASENKO (Власенко), N. A. (1997), *Iazyk prava* (Язык права). (Irkutsk: Vostochno-Sibirskoe knizhnoe izdatel'stvo, 1997).

7. The Nordic legal languages

BRUUN, H. & PALMGREN, S. (eds.) (2004), *Svenskt lagspråk i Finland* (Helsingfors: Statsrådets svenska språknämnd & Schildts, 2004).

EYBEN, W. E. VON (1989): 'Juridisk stil og sprogbrug', in *Juridisk grundbog* 3 (Copenhagen: Jurist- og økonomforbundets forlag, 1989), pp. 11–62.

HEIKKINEN, V., HIIDENMAA, P. & TIILILÄ, U. (2000), *Teksti työnä, virka kielenä* (Helsinki: Gaudeamus, 2000).

IISA, K. & PIEHL, A. (1992), *Virkakielestä kaikkien kieleen* (Helsinki: VAPK-kustannus, 1992).

_____ (1999), *Kielenhuollon käsikirja*. 4ᵗʰ ed. (Helsinki: Yrityskirjat, 1999).

LANDQVIST, H. (2000b), *Författningssvenska. Strukturer i nutida svensk lagtext i Sverige och Finland* (Gothenburg: Acta Unversitatis Gothoburgensis, 2000).

LAURÉN, C. (1993), *Fackspråk. Form, innehåll, funktion* (Lund: Studentlitteratur, 1993).

MYKLEBUST, H. (1996), *Nynorsk som lovspråk. Historisk og språgleg utvikling* (Bergen: Hovudfagsoppgåve ved Nordisk institutt. Universitetet i Bergen, 1996).

NORDMAN, M. (1984), 'Om juridisk svenska', *Svensk Juristtidning* (1984): 955–968.

PAJULA, P. (1960), *Suomalaisen oikeuskielen historia pääpiirteittäin* (Porvoo & Helsinki: WSOY, 1960).

Språket i lover og annet regelverk (Oslo: Tano, 1990).

TAMM, D. (1991), 'Latein oder Dänisch. Zur Entwicklung einer dänischen Gesetzessprache im 13. Jahrhundert', in J. Eckert (ed.), *Sprache – Recht – Geschichte* (Heidelberg: C. F. Müller Juristischer Verlag, 1991), pp. 37–48.

Foreign Terms and Expressions

This table contains the various foreign language terms and other expressions appearing in the main text, including Latin expressions and maxims. Laws and institutions in foreign languages are also included by name.

Terms and other expressions in English appear in the index (pp. 317–347).

Entries in the table come from many linguistic zones. They appear in alphabetical order, irrespective of language. However, the arrangement of the entries takes into account where each word that includes special letters, such as ü, ö, ź, å and æ, would appear according to the alphabet of the language in question. For example, „źródło" after „Zuweisung", „gældende fællesskapsret" after „guter Glaube", and „på grunn av" after „pur autre vie". Further, terms and expressions in Cyrillic and Greek script appear under separate headings (2 and 3). Use of upper case (block capitals) follows established convention, especially as to German substantives, Latin maxims (first letter of the first word), and names of certain laws and institutions.

1 Terms and expressions in Roman script

a contrario 103
a die 155
a fortiori 141
a priori 141
ablativus absolutus 207
ablativus instrumentalis 149
Abogado General 120
Abschrift 169
abuso de poder 153
Académie française 190
acceptare 200
acervo comunitario 121
acervo comunitário 121
acquérir (passer en) force de chose jugée 266
acquis communautaire 118, 120, 260
acquis comunitario 120
acte 194
action collective 258
action de classe 258
action de groupe 258
action populaire 258
ad formam recentiorum codicum 135
ad hoc 141
ad rem 143

adat 116
advocaat-generaal 120
advogado-geral 120
aequitas mercatoria 144
affacturage 206
affidavit 145, 230
Aktenversendung 162
aktsionernaia kompaniia 95
Alimentation 355
alínea 81
Allgemeines Bürgerliches Gesetzbuch 130, 144, 168
Allgemeines Landrecht für die preußischen Staaten 96, 168, 172
Ambiguitas contra stipulatorem 145–146
amicus curiae 153, 230, 261
amodiation 197
Amtsgericht 178
anfechten 161
angazhement 112
angloamerikanischen Recht (im) 153
animus testandi 230
Anschluß 177
antichrèse 206
apostoł 5
appert (il) 206
approbata 134

2. Terms and expressions in Cyrillic script

3. Terms and expressions in Greek script

Index

This index points the way to those pages of the book dealing with items of interest to the reader. Key-words include terms and expressions in English as well as the names of institutions and individuals appearing in the main text

Expressions in languages other than English appear in a separate Table of Foreign Terms and Expressions (pp. 305–315).

All references in the index are supplied with descriptive labels showing the textual context, so that the reader will know at once if the reference is of interest or not.

The alphabetical order is based on the most distinctive word in each expression made up of two or more words (except in case of names or petrified expressions). This explains why words such as « legal » are placed after the descriptive label. When necessary, the index contains an internal reference. For example: « organisations (international -) see international organisations ». The sign « - » represents the key word in question. As the example shows, brackets are used if the words do not apper in normal word order. Furthermore, synonyms in common use have been added as internal references.

The following fragment illustrates the index system of the book:

This example shows that the book treats problems involving binary expressions from the standpoint of several legal languages : canonic language, i.e. Latin (p. 133), legal English (pp. 233–234), and legal German (pp. 165–167). The magical character of binary expressions is also discussed (pp. 47–48), as well as reasons for their use (p. 82 and – as for English – 233–234). The descriptive labels "canon", "English", "German", "magical" and "reasons" enable immediate contextual recognition of each reference. The alphabetical order is based on the word "binary" as more distinctive than the word "expression" on the topic (the latter word could well have been replaced by the word "terms", for example). In addition, and finally, for those unfamiliar with the word « binary », the simplified alternative « two-word » is given as an internal refence under the letter "t".